GOVERNING MARKETS AS KNOWLEDGE COMMONS

This volume develops a theoretical framework for the analysis of the production, reproduction, and transformation of intellectual and legal infrastructures that enable market interactions using the Governing Knowledge Commons (GKC) framework. A distinctive contribution of this volume is the conceptualization of market-supporting knowledge structures as shared goods (established through cooperation) and contribution goods (established through competition). There are four building blocks around which the edited volume revolves. First, the chapters show that markets are cultural; they depend on various kinds of knowledge, some of which are governed as commons. Second, unlike physical commons, the market-supporting knowledge commons are produced and reproduced by contributions and sharing. Third, these knowledge commons serve as economic inputs in private production processes. Finally, the volume highlights the social and cultural effects of entrepreneurship. Through innovation and slight evasions of existing rules, entrepreneurs change not merely market goods but also social conventions and cultural meanings. Building on the GKC framework, the book highlights the entanglement of markets with society and the broader culture of which markets are part.

Erwin Dekker is Senior Research Fellow at the Mercatus Center at George Mason University. He has previously published *Jan Tinbergen (1903–1994) and the Rise of Economic Expertise* (2021) and *The Viennese Students of Civilization* (2016), both with Cambridge University Press. He has also published numerous journal articles in the fields of history of economic thought, cultural economics, and economic sociology. He is currently working on a history of the intellectual descendants of the German Historical School.

Pavel Kuchař is a lecturer at the Department of Political Economy, King's College London. He is a member of the History of Economic Thought Society (THETS) and the World Interdisciplinary Network for Institutional Research (WINIR). His work has been published in the *Journal of Evolutionary Economics*, *Econ Journal Watch*, and the *Research in the History of Economic Thought and Methodology*, among others.

CAMBRIDGE STUDIES ON GOVERNING KNOWLEDGE COMMONS

The mission of the series is to provide an authoritative space for high quality scholarship on the governance of knowledge commons. Following the path pioneered by Elinor Ostrom, recipient of the Nobel Prize in Economics for her work on institutional analysis of commons regimes in the natural environment, and the editors' work in *Governing Knowledge Commons*, this series uses a similar framework to systematically study knowledge commons in various sectors. Readers seeking more information on knowledge commons and this series can visit http://knowledge-commons.net, a repository for scholarship produced by an international, interdisciplinary group of knowledge commons researchers.

Series Editors

Katherine J. Strandburg
Brett M. Frischmann
Michael J. Madison

Governing Markets as Knowledge Commons

Edited by

ERWIN DEKKER

Mercatus Center at George Mason University

PAVEL KUCHAŘ

King's College London

CAMBRIDGE
UNIVERSITY PRESS

CAMBRIDGE
UNIVERSITY PRESS

University Printing House, Cambridge CB2 8BS, United Kingdom

One Liberty Plaza, 20th Floor, New York, NY 10006, USA

477 Williamstown Road, Port Melbourne, VIC 3207, Australia

314–321, 3rd Floor, Plot 3, Splendor Forum, Jasola District Centre, New Delhi – 110025, India

103 Penang Road, #05–06/07, Visioncrest Commercial, Singapore 238467

Cambridge University Press is part of the University of Cambridge.

It furthers the University's mission by disseminating knowledge in the pursuit of education, learning, and research at the highest international levels of excellence.

www.cambridge.org
Information on this title: www.cambridge.org/9781108483599
DOI: 10.1017/9781108692915

First published 2022

A catalogue record for this publication is available from the British Library.

Library of Congress Cataloging-in-Publication Data
NAMES: Dekker, Erwin, 1984– editor. | Kuchař, Pavel, 1985– editor.
TITLE: Governing markets as knowledge commons / edited by Erwin Dekker, Mercatus; Pavel Kuchar, Kings College, London.
DESCRIPTION: Cambridge, United Kingdom ; New York, NY : Cambridge University Press, 2021. | Series: Cambridge studies on governing knowledge commons | Includes bibliographical references.
IDENTIFIERS: LCCN 2021045745 (print) | LCCN 2021045746 (ebook) | ISBN 9781108483599 (hardback) | ISBN 9781108728959 (paperback) | ISBN 9781108692915 (epub)
SUBJECTS: LCSH: Knowledge economy. | Information commons. | Intellectual capital. | Intellectual property.
CLASSIFICATION: LCC HC79.155 G68 2021 (print) | LCC HC79.155 (ebook) | DDC 303.48/33–dc23
LC record available at https://lccn.loc.gov/2021045745
LC ebook record available at https://lccn.loc.gov/2021045746

ISBN 978-1-108-48359-9 Hardback

Contents

Contributors

Darcy W. E. Allen is a Senior Research Fellow at the RMIT Blockchain Innovation Hub, the world's first dedicated social science research center studying blockchain technology, based at RMIT University, Melbourne, Australia. His recent books include *The New Technologies of Freedom* (coauthored with Chris Berg and Sinclair Davidson, American Institute for Economic Research, 2020) and *Cryptodemocracy* (coauthored with Chris Berg and Aaron Lane, Lexington, 2019). He has published articles in journals such as *Research Policy* and the *Harvard Negotiation Law Review* on a wide range of topics including the economics of technology, entrepreneurship, and regulation. He holds an award-winning PhD in economics.

Chris Berg is an Associate Professor and Codirector of the RMIT Blockchain Innovation Hub. He is the author of eleven books, including most recently *The New Technologies of Freedom* (coauthored with Darcy Allen and Sinclair Davidson, American Institute for Economic Research, 2020). He is a member of the Steering Committee of the Australian government's National Blockchain Roadmap.

Young Back Choi is Professor of Economics at St. John's University in New York. He has published in the areas of entrepreneurship, institutional economics, economic development, income distribution and mobility, and the history of economic thought. He is best known for his book *Paradigms and Conventions: Uncertainty, Decision Making and Entrepreneurship* (1993). His recent research interests include reexamination of Adam Smith, and he has a long-standing research interest in various issues of institutional reform for economic and social development.

Carolina Dalla Chiesa is a PhD candidate in Cultural Economics at Erasmus University Rotterdam. Her research interests include digitalization in the cultural sectors, sociology of markets, and funding models for the arts. She holds an MA in Cultural Anthropology and an MA in Organization Studies, both from the Federal

University of Rio Grande do Sul (UFRGS), Brazil, where she studied entrepreneurship and digital culture.

Sinclair Davidson is Professor of Institutional Economics at the RMIT Blockchain Innovation Hub at RMIT University, an Adjunct Fellow at the Institute of Public Affairs, an Academic Fellow at the Australian Taxpayers' Alliance, an Adjunct Economics Fellow at the Consumer Choice Center, and a research associate at the University College London Centre for Blockchain Technologies. He is a member of the Centre for Independent Studies Council of Academic Advisers. Davidson has published in academic journals such as the *European Journal of Political Economy*, *Journal of Economic Behavior and Organization*, *Economic Affairs*, and *The Cato Journal*. He is a regular contributor to public debate. His opinion pieces have been published in *The Age*, *The Australian*, *Australian Financial Review*, *The Conversation*, *Daily Telegraph*, *Sydney Morning Herald*, and *Wall Street Journal Asia*.

Brett Frischmann is the Charles Widger Endowed University Professor in Law, Business, and Economics at Villanova University; an affiliated scholar of the Center for Internet and Society at Stanford Law School; an affiliated faculty member of the Vincent and Elinor Ostrom Workshop in Political Theory and Policy Analysis at Indiana University; and a trustee for the Nexa Center for Internet & Society, Polytechnic University of Turin [Politecnico di Torino]. Frischmann also recently served as the Microsoft Visiting Professor of Information and Technology Policy at Princeton University's Center for Information and Technology Policy. Frischmann's interdisciplinary work includes widely acclaimed books, such as *Re-Engineering Humanity* (coauthored with philosopher Evan Selinger, Cambridge University Press, 2018); *Infrastructure: The Social Value of Shared Resources* (Oxford University Press, 2012); and *Governing Knowledge Commons* (coauthored with Michael Madison and Katherine Strandburg, Oxford University Press, 2014). His work also appears in leading scholarly publications, including *Columbia Law Review*, *Journal of Institutional Economics*, *Journal of Economic Perspectives*, *University of Chicago Law Review*, and *Science* among others. In addition, he writes popular articles on the intersection of technology and humanity for *Scientific American*, the *Guardian*, and other publications. Frischmann received his BA in Astrophysics from Columbia University, an MS in Earth Resources Engineering from Columbia University, and a JD from the Georgetown University Law Center.

Yugank Goyal teaches at FLAME University in Pune (India) where he leads an initiative to compile regional data on cultures of India. He is also a Governing Council member of the Indian School of Public Policy in New Delhi. Goyal holds a bachelor's degree in technology, and master's and PhD in law and economics (Erasmus University Rotterdam, University of Hamburg, and University of Bologna). His research interests and publications broadly lie at the intersection of regulation, institutional economics, informality, and law and development. As of recently, he has been helping establish a community school in rural India through crowdfunding, hoping it can be governed as a commons.

Julien Gradoz is a PhD candidate at the University of Lille. In his research, Gradoz focuses on how the notion of quality has been conceptualized and quantified by economists from a methodological and historical perspective. He has also studied the impact of moderation and reputation systems on the quality of content shared on online platforms.

Terence Kealey trained in medicine at Barts Hospital Medical College of the University of London, and in biochemistry at Oxford University. He lectured in clinical biochemistry for many years at Cambridge University before moving to the University of Buckingham as vice chancellor. There he met Martin Ricketts, and from their joint interest in the economics of science they published an article "Modelling Science as a Contribution Good" (2014). Terence Kealey is currently an adjunct scholar with the Cato Institute, Washington DC.

Arjo Klamer is Professor Emeritus of Cultural Economics at Erasmus University. His work on the relationship between culture and economy culminated in the value-based approach. *Doing the Right Thing: A Value Based Economy* (2017) lays the groundwork. A project that emanates from this is the Humane Economy, which may result in a bachelor program at the Free University in Amsterdam.

Edward J. López is Professor of Economics and director of the Center for the Study of Free Enterprise at Western Carolina University, where he teaches microeconomics, public finance, and the ethics of capitalism. His research interests include public choice, law and economics, and institutional change. He has published over fifty scholarly articles and two books, and is executive director and past president of the Public Choice Society.

Jason Potts is a Distinguished Professor of Economics at RMIT University and Codirector of the RMIT Blockchain Innovation Hub, a world leading research center on blockchain economics. His work focuses on economics of innovation and institutions. Potts is a fellow of the Academy of Social Sciences of Australia, vice-president of the International Joseph A. Schumpeter Society, and editor of the *Journal of Institutional Economics*. His latest book is *Innovation Commons: The Origin of Economic Growth* (2019).

Renée Prendergast is Reader in Economics in the Management School at Queen's University Belfast, Northern Ireland. Her main research interests are in technology and development and in the history of economic thought. Publications include: *Choice of Technique in Iron Founding* (with B. A. Bhat); *Machine Tools in Developing Countries* (with M. M. Huq); *Development Perspectives for the 1990s* (with H. W. Singer); *Market Forces and World Development* (with F. Stewart);

Contributions to the History of Economic Thought (with A. Murphy); and *A History of Irish Economic Thought* (with T. Boylan and J. D. Turner).

Raphaël Raux is a PhD student in economics at Harvard University. Through his interest in public and political economics, he came to think about the structures allowing the exploitation of common resources on online platforms.

Martin Ricketts studied economics at the University of Newcastle and public finance at the University of York. He worked with Alan Peacock and Jack Wiseman at the Institute of Social and Economic Research (York) before lecturing at the newly established University College at Buckingham, where he later became successively Dean of Business and Dean of Humanities. His interest in the economics of science and innovation was initially stimulated by working for John Jewkes in the early 1970s, and later during a stint as Economic Director of the National Economic Development Office (NEDO). He is the author of *The Economics of Business Enterprise* (2019, 4th ed.) – an introduction to the New Institutional Economics.

Kyle Vachris is an economist in the Producer Price Index program at the U.S. Bureau of Labor Statistics. He holds a BA in Economics from the College of William and Mary and is a graduate student at George Mason University, pursuing an MA in Economics.

Michelle Albert Vachris is Professor of Management, Business, and Economics at Virginia Wesleyan University and Professor Emerita at Christopher Newport University. She holds a BA in Economics from the College of William and Mary and an MA and a PhD in Economics from George Mason University. Dr. Vachris began her career with the Bureau of Labor Statistics and has served as a consultant to the International Monetary Fund. Her research areas include public choice economics, teaching pedagogy, and economics in literature. She is coauthor of *Pride and Profit: The Intersection of Jane Austen and Adam Smith* (2015).

Youn Sun Won has conducted programs on the value-based approach on behalf of Society of Culture and Economy and Institute of Public Collaboration, since she finished her PhD. Her research areas include quality assessment of urban development and regeneration, based on the value-based approach, by bringing a different way of thinking within an institutional framework and practical applications for urban creative transition.

Preface

New concepts have the power to open new ways of thinking, new ways of seeing the world, and new ways of inspiring us. That is precisely what the *commons* did. When Garret Hardin examined the tragedy of the commons, he argued that overuse and overpopulation would exhaust the resources of the world. But with the revolutionary work of Elinor Ostrom, and many others in her wake, the story of the commons became a story of promise. The governance mode known as the commons, in which communities succeed in finding solutions to collective action problems through self-governance, has become an essential part of thinking about economic development. Wikipedia and other crowdsourced resources demonstrated that the commons were a thing of not only the past but also the future. By now the commons are inspiring thinkers of the right and the left to think beyond the market and state dichotomy.

We believe that the potential of the commons have not been exhausted; far from it. What the commons, as a concept, has allowed us to realize is how ubiquitous cooperation is in the modern economy. For a long time, we have thought of the economy as primarily a domain of competition. So blind were economists to the idea of cooperation that when competitive markets were opposed to cooperation within firms, it was done under the banner, courtesy of Oliver Williamson's *Markets and Hierarchies*. Since then we have come to realize that firms are often quite different from hierarchies, and that between firms there is often a great deal of knowledge-sharing and other forms of cooperation. And no, we are not (merely) referring to cartel-like practices.

The study of the commons as a mode of governance has also allowed for the realization that individuals pursue a great many of their goals collectively. Within clubs, associations, churches, online communities, artistic scenes, unions, social networks, and the modern sharing economy, individuals join forces to pursue shared goals. Most of the time this does not require the public (government) provision of shared infrastructures. Instead, shared infrastructures and the rules that manage them tend to be jointly produced and organized by these groups themselves. Sometimes access to the shared goods produced by these groups has been restricted to members; at other times they have been made available to others. The commons have enriched our view of the richness and variety of organizational forms in contemporary society.

These insights are even more pertinent in the modern knowledge economy. Knowledge has always been a difficult "thing" to theorize; its intangible and non-additive nature has made it hard to say definite things about it. This has been no different for economists who have struggled to conceptualize knowledge. On the one hand, there were those who suggested that unless subsidized by the government, there would be no reason to expect that sufficient knowledge would be produced by market actors. On the other hand, the idea of human capital suggested that the knowledge was stored up in individuals, who could employ it for personal gain.

Recent work on the knowledge commons has rightly suggested that much knowledge is shared and produced with communities and is one of the most important resources for these communities. The knowledge shared within different communities is often only partially compatible. The knowledge of one community is not simply qualitatively different from that of another community; the bodies of knowledge can also be incompatible with or contradictory to each other. These differences are directly reflected in cultural differences but are also one of the key resources on which members of these communities can draw. From the common sense instilled in them by their parents and friends, through the cultural habits that unconsciously guide their behavior, to the cultural knowledge reflected in stories and other cultural artifacts, and the social norms reflected in conventions to the more systematized knowledge acquired at school, they are all crucial elements for human action, including commercial and market initiatives.

The goal of this book is simple. We want to investigate the importance of knowledge commons for the functioning of markets. We want to understand how they facilitate trust. How market participants learn that someone is creditworthy. How they create shared frameworks of understanding that allow, for example, for the distinction between product categories, such as (single malt) scotch and other types of whisky. How they function as resources for the development of new products, or the development of new identities. How do knowledge commons help govern online platforms or meeting places for fashion designers? Or how can knowledge commons function to establish relationships between otherwise unconnected individuals through blockchain technology or crowdfunding platforms?

We have long understood that markets are places of individual action. But the commons allow us to see that they are just as much places of collective action. Markets are places where shared knowledge is produced, or indeed where conflict may sometimes prevent that from happening. When shared knowledge does get produced, it fosters cooperation as well as competition. We believe that these knowledge commons are a precondition for the emergence and continued existence of markets.

Acknowledgments

This volume has been several years in the making and we are grateful for having met many inspiring people along the way and for the help we have received. We would like to thank the editors of the Governing Knowledge Commons series for inviting us to contribute to the project and, in particular, appreciate Brett Frischmann's continued encouragement. We thank Matt Gallaway at the Cambridge University Press for his support and we appreciate the detailed comments from the three referees. We are delighted to be a part of the Governing Knowledge Commons Research Coordination Network, a community of scholars that carries forward institutional analysis in spirit of Elinor and Vincent Ostrom. In 2018, this volume received a kickstart from the workshop in Arlington, VA generously supported by the Mercatus Center at George Mason University, and with the invaluable support from Stefanie Haeffele, Malia Dalesandry, Alice Calder, Haley Larsen, and Connor Currie. Thanks to the generous support of the Mercatus Center we were able to meet with the contributors and spend a couple of days discussing the contents of this volume together. Later that year a smaller number of contributors gathered for a workshop on Markets as Knowledge Commons in Rotterdam, generously supported by the Erasmus School of History, Culture, and Communication. Finally, Kuchař would like to appreciate the opportunity to discuss the outlines of this volume at the 2019 Workshop on Growth in the Modern World that took place at the University of Buckingham. We especially appreciate the thoughts and observations that David Gindis, Matthias Klaes, and Deirdre McCloskey shared with us.

Introduction

Governing Markets as Knowledge Commons

Erwin Dekker and Pavel Kuchař

INTRODUCTION

Ceaseless acts of bargaining, haggling, buying, and selling happen around us all the time. Places where people gather to buy and sell goods and services emerge all around the world. in parts that are poor, in parts that are rich, at the old fashioned market square, and in the modern digital world. We call these gatherings markets. Market forms vary from highly personalized services to commodities that are sold to millions of people at a time, from illicit goods to some of the most revered works of art. Originally, markets were meeting places that emerged at the frontier between villages as grounds where strangers could meet to trade. Trade generally did not emerge within a family or a tribe.[1] Today buyers no longer have to be physically present, although personal connections remain a crucial part of many markets. What small-scale and global markets have in common is the requirement of communication. Buyers and sellers must communicate and they must share some kind of a common understanding.[2] When they trade, buyers and sellers must share a system of signs and interpretations, an enforceable set of rules, customs, and laws governing contracts and an established system of property rights.

We tend to take for granted that people in markets can buy low and sell high without much trouble in understanding or trusting one another. Markets appear so natural, that Adam Smith (1776/1981) considered that the propensity to 'truck, barter, and exchange' to be an innate part of human nature. It was the original sin of modern economics to proceed as if markets were natural phenomena. As if their

[1] Henri Pirenne (1937: 140), wrote that although it might seem strange "medieval commerce developed from the beginning not of local but of export trade" . . . Karl Polanyi (1945: 274) agreed: "Trade does not arise within a community; it is an external affair involving different communities." The problem that arises from an exchange between strangers, then, is how to define, recognize and enforce transfers or property.

[2] See Frank Fetter's chapter on "Money and markets" (1915: 50–60).

emergence and continued existence itself did not have to be explained. As if self-interest alone was sufficient to explain why people would engage in exchanges of various kinds with each other.

Behind these seemingly natural interactions there is an intricate web of mostly invisible relationships that specify the peculiar conventions of different markets. Who can buy and sell? What are legitimate objects of exchange, and which things are off-limits? Is money an acceptable means of exchange, or should one pay in kind? What is a just price? And what is the appropriate way of valuing a particular good? Should customers tip, or sellers reward the buyer for their loyalty? Should one haggle? We take for granted that entrepreneurs can retain their profits; that at times, they might even enjoy a monopoly position after their invention is patented. All these assumptions require formal rules and informal norms to be in place. This book is about the routines, conventions, and shared pools of knowledge that underpin market exchange generally and specific markets in particular.

The legal framework is probably the most studied of these market-enabling social infrastructures. Within law and economics, the legal infrastructure has received ample attention, albeit with a strong emphasis on formal rights of property and contract. The rules of property and contract are the most basic defining characteristics of markets. But there is nothing natural about these rules. In fact, the rules of property and contract come in a great variety extending beyond formal rights; they include informal norms and enforcement mechanisms, which together make up the legal infrastructures on which markets rely (Hodgson 2001; Ostrom 2005). Our work extends beyond formal legal infrastructures and takes into account social infrastructures that may facilitate or hamper markets. We suggest that these infrastructures are of crucial importance in legitimizing markets; they create shared understandings, facilitate trust and, more generally, transform transaction costs to facilitate exchanges (van Waarden 2012).[3]

[3] Our project closely parallels the work of John Searle (1995, 2005) in seeking to understand the social processes that lead to shared understandings, and the consequences of human coordination (or conflict) in the presence of institutional facts that sustain market interactions. The emergence of markets is in part a problem of critical mass, and as such it is captured in the difference that economists make between thick and thin markets (Roth 2015). But it is also a problem of coherence (Lachmann 1971). What allows us to call a market "thin" is that we, by whatever criteria, judge there to be few similar (enough) transactions that make up this market. What allows us to call a market "thick" similarly is a judgment call about finding a great number of similar transactions that cohere enough with each other. What makes a market cohere, we argue, is the social infrastructure, the framework, a set of intersubjective beliefs and expectations, formal rules and shared knowledge about classifications and categories. This framework, according to Douglass North, evolves in all societies "to structure human interaction. This framework is the basic 'capital stock' that defines the culture of a society. Culture, then, provides a language-based conceptual framework for encoding and interpreting the information that the senses are presenting to the brain. As a consequence, culture not only plays a role in shaping the formal rules, but also underlies the informal constraints that are a part of the makeup of institutions" (North 2005).

Elinor Ostrom argued that the social infrastructure that sustains a "competitive market – the epitome of private institutions – is itself a public good," this, as Ostrom points out, is because once the market is there, "individuals can enter and exit freely whether or not they contribute to the cost of providing and maintaining the market" (Ostrom 1990: 15). This volume shows, following the late work of Elinor Ostrom, that the social infrastructures that sustain markets are not public goods but rather a form of knowledge commons. Social infrastructures are key resources required for the emergence and continued existence of markets and their production and maintenance is not costless.

Increasingly, scholars across disciplines have realized the importance of social infrastructures made up of institutionalized classificatory systems within which voluntary private interactions take place. Development economists have come to argue that historically determined social infrastructures captured in part by language are central in explaining long-run economic performance (Hall and Jones 1999). More recent work in economic sociology has explored the moral nature of markets. Marion Fourcade and Kieran Healy (2007), for instance, talk about the moralized-markets approach, in which scholars are concerned with 'social sources of moral ideas'; Jens Beckert (2009) discusses the problem of valuation emphasizing the moral orders that support markets. In law and economics, Brett Frischmann (2012; see also Kornberger et al. 2019) highlights the importance of shared intellectual infrastructures in sustaining market orders. Gillian Hadfield (2016) has extended the analysis of normative frameworks to legal infrastructures while Kaushik Basu (2018) emphasized the coordinative role of shared beliefs about the rules of the game.

We are critical of naturalistic accounts of markets that assume that private interests and opportunities for exchange alone are sufficient for the emergence and continued existence of markets. But we are equally critical of the standard assumption that infrastructural resources should be publicly provided. Two recent volumes entitled *Manufacturing Markets* (Brousseau and Glachant 2014) and *Marketcraft* (Vogel 2018) argue that states are crucial in the design and governance of markets. While we do acknowledge that states have a role in limiting violence (North, Wallis, and Weingast 2009), we also suggest that key infrastructural resources for the emergence and continued existence of markets are developed by market participants and related communities. Markets require organization (Eucken 1940). But governance structures are often organized communally, not purely privately or publicly (although entanglements abound). The key analytical question is how and why such resources are developed and maintained.

FOUNDATIONS AND THE THEORETICAL FRAMEWORK

How do markets emerge? Who bears the costs and efforts of producing the market-sustaining knowledge commons? How are knowledge commons, such as the intellectual and legal infrastructures maintained? Charlotte Hess and Elinor Ostrom, in their book on Governing Knowledge Commons, highlighted the concept of a contribution to a shared resource (Hess and Ostrom 2006: 52). They defined it as a right to change (contribute to) a content of a common resource. The concept of a contribution is key to understanding the creation and maintenance of knowledge commons.

Along with access, extraction, management, exclusion, and alienation, the right to contribute is, according to Hess and Ostrom, a kind of a property right. The right to contribute to a common resource is a kind of a right that is particularly important when we zero in on knowledge commons. We have every reason to think that, rather than being a public good, a market is made up by rules that are closer to a particular form of a knowledge commons that is produced and reproduced by way of contributions and that might be adjusted by removals. Who has the power and the right to contribute, and who can be excluded from contributing and removing the shared aspects of the infrastructure that sustains markets become key issues in the analysis of market governance. Who has access to markets, how goods are supposed to be produced, bought, and consumed, how is exchange supposed to take place? These questions are directly related to how the market at hand is understood.[4] The wide variety in rules means that it makes little sense to talk of markets in the abstract, instead markets should be studied as specific institutional settings. And the meaning attributed to the institutions of exchange will depend on the place of markets in social life (Hodgson 2001).

These questions can be better understood when considered in context of the Institutional Analysis and Development (IAD) framework developed by Elinor Ostrom and her collaborators. This framework was first developed to study the governance of commons in the natural environment (Ostrom 1990) and later modified for use in the study of *Governing Knowledge Commons* (GKC) series by Brett Frischmann, Michael Madison, and Katherine Strandburg (2014; Strandburg, Frischmann, and Madison 2017). In this theoretical framework, *commons* refers to

> a form of community management or governance. It applies to resources and involves a group or community of people, but it does not denote the resources, the community, a place, or a thing. Commons is the institutional arrangement of these elements.
>
> (Strandburg, Frischmann, and Madison 2017: 10)

Importantly, what distinguishes commons from other kinds of governance (such as individual private property rights) "is institutionalized sharing of resources among members of a community" (Frischmann, Madison, and Strandburg 2014: 2). The intellectual infrastructure that enables and regulates market is a kind of a resource.

[4] Such shared understandings might also prevent markets from emerging because they are considered undesirable, corrupting, or repugnant (Satz 2010).

But the infrastructure, besides being a resource, is in the first place a kind of knowledge.

In general, we say that *knowledge* "refers to a broad set of intellectual and cultural resources" (Strandburg, Frischmann, and Madison 2017: 10). Intellectual and legal infrastructures are a part of our knowledge. Mental models and shared classification schemes are knowledge too. Institutional aspects such as formal rules, informal norms, and instruments of interpretation; classification schemes, and enforcement mechanisms are forms of social infrastructures that all constitute knowledge as we understand it. That perspective is in line with the knowledge perspective developed in markets, in which the price system and firms both play a key role in the coordination of the expectations and hence the actions of different individuals (Coase 1934; Hayek 1945). The meaning of prices and the way we interpret and understand price movements are important aspects of that shared knowledge (Velthuis 2005).

Knowledge commons, then, is a

> shorthand for the institutionalized community governance of the sharing and, in many cases, creation of ... intellectual and cultural resources. Demand for governance institutions arises from a community's need to overcome various social dilemmas associated with producing, preserving, sharing, and using [these resources].
>
> (Strandburg, Frischmann, and Madison 2017: 10)

While the demand side for governance institutions has received a good deal of attention in the new institutionalist literature, the supply side of many institutions in general and those governing knowledge commons in particular still seems to be somewhat of a mystery. The chapters in this book contribute to the GKC research program by asking how the intellectual and legal infrastructures, on which markets depend, are produced and reproduced; how they grant coherence to our actions and interactions in markets while at the same time permitting change.

FOUR BUILDING BLOCKS

This volume presents a couple of basic ideas that run through the following chapters. First, markets are cultural; they rely on a form of knowledge that is governed as a knowledge commons. A corollary of this idea is that the growth of markets depends as much on relevant knowledge commons as it does on changes in technology or geography.

Second, the market-supporting forms of knowledge are produced and reproduced by contributions and sharing. They are thus neither privately nor publicly provided. Rather, the mode of governance for the production and maintenance of market-supporting forms of knowledge is the commons. While markets are not natural, they are in many instances self-supporting.

Third, knowledge commons include intellectual and legal infrastructures that serve as economic inputs to new production processes. The knowledge infrastructures we discuss in the book do not merely legitimate and structure economic exchange in markets, they also function as jointly produced resources on which market participants can draw for private initiatives. They are quite literally a pool of knowledge from which market participants can draw.

Fourth, our volume conceptualizes the social and cultural effects of entrepreneurship. Entrepreneurs draw on the knowledge infrastructures to make new combinations, to engage in slight evasions of existing rules, and to provide new justifications (or condemnations) of particular acts. In doing so they bring new products on the market, alter existing practices, or try to prevent existing ones. This has not merely economic effects, but also impacts the knowledge commons that sustain markets. As such entrepreneurial acts feed back into the cultural framework of markets. Let us situate each of these building blocks in the wider academic conversation on markets.

Markets Are Cultural and Rely on Knowledge Commons

Anthropologists and sociologists have long argued that markets are part of social systems (K. Polanyi 1945; Appadurai 1986; Granovetter and Swedberg 1992; Gudeman 2001). In economics there has been less attention to this fact. But, as one of us has demonstrated, in the crucial interwar period a large group of Central-European intellectuals rediscovered the importance of institutional frameworks that constitute the social infrastructure of market societies (Dekker 2016). In more stable times that framework is easily taken for granted, but during the major upheavals of the 1930s it became acutely visible how important these frameworks were. Neoliberal thinkers of various political and national backgrounds rediscovered the importance of the legal, social, and cultural preconditions for flourishing markets (Foucault 2008).

In economic sociology these ideas became known as the embeddedness thesis associated with the work of Karl Polanyi (Dale 2010). The debate made Friedrich Hayek realize the importance of the rules and institutions that have supported liberal civilization (Hayek 1960; Boettke 2018). It made Joseph Schumpeter argue that capitalism could not survive in an unrestrained democratic state (Schumpeter 1976; Allen 1994). It made Norbert Elias inquire into the process by which the West became civilized, and how this process was reversed (Elias 2000). It made the Ordoliberal thinkers in Germany inquire into the framework that allows for peaceful competition on markets (Eucken 1940; Röpke 1950; Peacock and Willgerodt 1989). And it made Michael Polanyi and Karl Popper inquire, in different ways, into the ways in which free scientific inquiry is embedded and part of an open society, and a set of shared attitudes (Popper 1945; M. Polanyi 1958).

Many of these writers used the term 'civilization' to refer to this set of frameworks.[5] Sigmund Freud, who reflected on the same set of development suggested that the term civilization "describes the sum of achievements that serve two types of purposes: to protect men against nature, and to adjust their mutual relations" (Freud 1930/1961: 36). What protects man against nature is primarily a set of technologies, but what interests us is the sum of achievements that allow humans to adjust their mutual relations. What this perspective allows us to realize is that this shared set of achievements, which differs between societies and over time, consists of shared knowledge. This consists of common sense knowledge, social conventions, classification schemes, and a wide variety of institutional forms that allow for peaceful human interaction. Markets are an integral part of these, and directly related to the wider set of knowledge. They therefore depend on these shared social infrastructure and feed back into them.

As the ordoliberal writers argued persuasively, society consists of different orders (Luhmann 1995; Goldschmidt and Wohlgemuth 2008). These different orders, social, legal, political, and economic, overlap in complex ways; we have elsewhere compared these orders to plate tectonics, due to having stable internal structures, but also being partly incommensurable with other orders (Dekker and Kuchař 2017). Between these orders potentially serious friction may emerge, along with a great possibility for conflict (Boltanski and Thévenot 2006; Stark 2009). It is precisely at the borders of the orders that we expect opportunities for entrepreneurial action, consisting in part of arbitrage between different normative orders (whether legal, social or both), to emerge.

Knowledge Commons Are Produced and Reproduced by Contributions and Sharing

To conceptualize the production side of shared infrastructures we rely on the notion of contribution, and in particular on two types of goods that are discussed in this book: contribution goods and shared goods. Contribution goods are conceptualized by Kealey and Ricketts as "goods whose benefits are non-rival over contributors but that cannot be accessed by non-contributors" (Kealey and Ricketts 2014: 1015). For instance, in order to access scientific knowledge one has to become a scientist since important parts of the knowledge is simply inaccessible to outsiders, and other important parts are tacit. It is only through contributions to science that one gains

5 When we talk about civilization, we refer to those societies with developed and open state bureaucracies, codified legal systems and legally sanctioned rules of property and exchange. As Geoffrey Hodgson writes, property and contract are key for markets to exist "there must be a system of law that recognises 'legal persons' making transactions – individuals or groups that are deemed to have collective discretion and choice, and may enter into contracts with others. Once again, such conditions are associated with the rise of civilisation and the existence of a state with a relatively developed legal apparatus" (Hodgson 2001: 331).

meaningful access to science. The production of scientific knowledge depends on the contributions of many different scientists, who should feel sufficiently motivated to contribute to science. Such contributions are more worthwhile for the individual when other individuals are also making contributions. Science is a noncooperative coordination game (see also Kealey and Ricketts, Chapter 1).

Shared goods, on the other hand, are defined by Arjo Klamer as coproduced non-divisible goods. Klamer emphasizes their non-rival nature and suggests that exclusion is nearly automatic for shared goods (Klamer 2016: 72–76). His favorite example is that of a friendship between two people from which non-friends, or non-contributors, are excluded. Ownership of such goods, including scientific knowledge, is not clearly defined, but that is not necessary for its production. Unlike Kealey and Ricketts, Klamer thinks of the production of such goods as requiring cooperation: the production of a good friendship is a cooperative game (see also Potts 2019). What Klamer adds to his discussion of shared goods is that they are typically practices, which derive value from an active engagement (see also Won and Klamer, Chapter 11). In that sense one becomes a scientist by doing science, and a friend by practicing friendship.[6]

Knowledge Commons Serve As Economic Inputs to New Production Processes

A major step toward understanding the function of social infrastructures has been the work of Brett Frischmann. Infrastructural resources run in the background of any kind of social and economic interaction. More specifically, we can say that these resources are "consumed non-rivalrously for some appreciable range of demand," that a "demand for the [infrastructural] resource is driven primarily by downstream productive activity," and finally, that the infrastructural resources tend to "be used as an input into a wide range of goods and services" (Frischmann 2012: xiv). Typically, things like roads and highways, railways, bridges, lighthouses, water systems, power grids, optical fibers, etc., come to mind. Very often, we tend to think about these kinds of infrastructure as public goods in the sense that their consumption is non-rival and non-excludable. A standard textbook scenario demonstrates that private initiative will fall short of providing these kinds of infrastructures in a satisfactory quality and quantity and that, therefore, these goods should be provided by a political authority.

Frischmann extends the analysis of physical infrastructures to include intellectual infrastructures. We might think of language as a central example of intellectual infrastructure. But apart from language, intellectual infrastructures "include a broad

6 Elsewhere we have suggested that a subset of institutions we called 'instruments of interpretation' arise out of individual market exchanges, so that market participants help the knowledge infrastructure evolve (Dekker and Kuchař 2019; see also Cornes and Sandler 1996). What all concepts have in common is that they provide a rationale for continued contribution to the goods that sustain it.

set of resources that create benefits for society primarily through the facilitation of downstream productive activities, many of which generate spillovers" (Frischmann 2012: 275). Intellectual infrastructures are simply non-rival inputs into a wide variety of outputs; think basic research, general purpose technologies, or infrastructural ideas.

The importance of infrastructures seems to be most conspicuous in the case of malfunction. That is especially true when we talk about "legal infrastructures," as Gillian Hadfield does in her book titled *Rules for a Flat World* (Hadfield 2016). We recognize the importance of uncongested highways or high-speed railways during our daily commutes, we are well aware of the enabling power of language and such realizations become much more vivid when the road becomes congested, when the railway workers go on a strike, or when we cannot simply "plug in," as Hadfield puts it, into a framework of people who share our language or adhere to a common legal code. With legal infrastructure, which may be considered a subset of Frischmann's intellectual infrastructure, things are different to the extent that the enabling function of legal and institutional rules is almost always hidden, it mostly runs in the background, and what we typically notice about law is that it tells us what not to do. Law, however, also has a constructive enabling role which facilitates interaction and coordination.

Hadfield (2016: 89) – as Buchanan (1975) had also similarly suggested – makes the case that legal infrastructure is a form of capital that is, because of its widespread availability, a shared good. Just like with other kinds of infrastructure, we do not typically have the legal infrastructure tailored and constructed just for our purposes. The legal infrastructure must be general enough to allow entrepreneurs with different kinds of plans to plug into it and make use of it. As such, the legal infrastructure seems to be a part of the environment, "it was there before you got here" (Hadfield 2016: 87). But what can flourish in a given (legal) environment is a question of the complementarity between the environment and the activities employed by individuals and groups.

The importance of the complementarity between different types of capital goods has been emphasized in economics by Ludwig Lachmann (1978) who argued that in order for individual plans to succeed they must be compatible with each other (Endres and Harper 2013). That is the same type of interdependence that is also stressed by game theorists on the micro level.[7] This interdependence can cause

[7] Interdependence is at the very heart of economic theory, Adam Smith's theory of division of labor is fundamentally a theory of interdependence. Not only do individuals become dependent on each other's skills, goods, and services, but the associated regime of free trade also makes regions and countries dependent on one another. Alfred Marshall, developing political economy along Smithian lines, realized that the interdependence of transacting individuals may generate increasing returns. This idea becomes apparent when we look into Marshall's interaction between organization and the growth of knowledge. First, Marshall considers knowledge and organization to be a part of the capital structure: "By Capital is meant all stored-up provision for the production of material goods … Capital consists in a great part of

individuals' plans to fail, since others don't act as expected. But the interdependence can also give rise to positive reinforcing effects and lead to increasing returns of being part of the same community or culture. It is now well established that this is the case at least for knowledge of the R&D type (B. Hall, Mairesse, and Mohnen 2010; see also Kealey and Ricketts, Chapter 1).

Entrepreneurship Has Social and Cultural Effects

A recent volume has argued for a regime of permissionless innovation (Thierer 2016). We suggest that even if governments would remove all barriers to innovation and new technologies, entrepreneurial action would still be anything but completely free. Entrepreneurs must draw on the existing knowledge resources for their innovations, and the extent to which novel innovations might be accepted is in large part determined by their compatibility with existing social norms.

Entrepreneurs do more than buy low and sell high. In fact, entrepreneurs are important agents of change who tend to change social norms and classification schemes in general (Elert and Henrekson 2017). Besides direct efforts to shape and mold our existing knowledge, entrepreneurs contribute to the joint production of new product categories (Navis and Glynn 2010), new ways of valuing goods (De Marchi 2008), and new legitimations for exchanges previously believed to be illegitimate or repugnant (Kuchař 2016). More broadly they change the existing set of conventions (Choi, Chapter 5). Entrepreneurship thus has effects beyond the economic realm. It also jointly impacts social and cultural norms and beliefs.

Wadwhani and Lubinski (2017) have suggested the term 'New Entrepreneurial History' for a field of study that explicitly recognizes the importance of legitimizing novelty. The focus on legitimation of economic actions has long been left by economists to sociologists and organizational scholars (Swedberg 2005). We believe

knowledge and organization ... and of this some part is private property and other part is not" (Marshall 192: 138). Might the part of knowledge and organization that is not private property be a kind of a knowledge commons? The mode of governance, or in Marshall's terms "organization" was clearly important: "Knowledge is our most powerful engine of production; it enables us to subdue Nature and force her to satisfy our wants. Organization aids knowledge; it has many forms, e.g. that of a single business, that of various businesses in the same trade, that of various trades relatively to one another, and that of the State providing security for all and help for many" (Marshall 1920: 139). If organization aids the knowledge – our most powerful engine of production – Marshall thought therefore "it seems best sometimes to reckon Organization apart as a distinct agent of production" (Marshall 1920: 139). We agree. Secondly, Marshall intuited the shared nature of knowledge by discussing cases in which "the law of diminishing return does not apply to the total capital and labour" (Marshall 1920: 165). This happens because under some circumstances "the pressure of population on the means of subsistence may be restrained for a long time to come by the opening up of new fields of supply ... by the growth of organization and knowledge" (Marshall 1920: 166). Marshall thus suggests that "an increase of labour and capital leads generally to improved organization, which increases the efficiency of the work of labour and capital" (Marshall 1920: 318).

that in order to understand the importance of knowledge commons in enabling market exchange, the study of legitimation of existing practices as well as the justification for new practices will prove to be crucial (Jensen 2010). Legitimation might not always be direct and can initially take the form of evasive entrepreneurship (Elert and Henrekson 2016) in which attempts are made to sidestep existing rules. The rise of the new sharing economy with firms like AirBnB and Uber are good examples (Munger 2018). At other times new practices are explored in gray zones or through active boundary work (Liu 2015; Fernandez and Figueiredo 2018). In one of the chapters in this volume, the boundary work between single malt scotch and other types of whisky is explored (Vachris and Vachris, Chapter 8). At other times entrepreneurs might build on social changes elsewhere in society. The struggle to legitimize the Queer Museum in Brazil (Dalla Chiesa, Chapter 10) might pave the way for entrepreneurial actions in related markets, which could potentially build on the newly recognized identities and social groups.

Entrepreneurship is therefore important for two reasons. First, disputes over novelty and the active justification process that entrepreneurs engage in highlight the interdependence between markets and the related knowledge commons. Secondly, entrepreneurial action, through active contributions, feeds back into the knowledge commons and therefore completes the circle of our framework. Markets depend for their existence on the social infrastructure of the knowledge commons. Interaction in markets leads to new contributions to these knowledge commons, and therefore to broader social and cultural processes in society. Markets are in important ways self-sustaining social processes.

ORGANIZATION OF THE BOOK

The chapters in this volume can be divided in two groups. There are five primarily conceptual chapters, followed by six primarily applied chapters. The conceptual chapters develop aspects of the theoretical framework while focusing on certain elements of the market-supporting knowledge commons. The applied chapters utilize the framework to analyze specific cases of market governance.

The first chapter lays out an ambitious argument for the importance of the knowledge commons. Terence Kealey and Martin Ricketts show how institutional changes within the British organization of science before the Industrial Revolution relied on contribution goods. The resulting rapidly expanding knowledge commons, to which the entrepreneurs of the age had access and made active contributions, was the basis for the Industrial Revolution. The theoretical addition of their chapter is the model of the contribution good they develop. When the scientific enterprise attracts a sufficient number of contributors, the argument goes, it gives rise to a knowledge commons to which access is almost naturally restricted, because only active contributors have sufficient tacit knowledge to draw on the knowledge commons.

In the second chapter Renée Prendergast argues that while knowledge in general tends to be built cumulatively over time, present knowledge is an input into future knowledge. Highlighting the cumulative nature of knowledge production, Prendergast develops a historical account going back to the ideas of Francis Bacon, Bernard Mandeville, Adam Ferguson, Charles Babbage, and Karl Marx suggesting that the state of present knowledge results from a wide collective process of learning derived to a large extent from everyday involvement in the ordinary business of life. People act without awareness of the full consequences of their actions. This way, actors jointly produce outputs that result from their actions but which these actors didn't, and often even couldn't, possibly anticipate. Prendergast relates her discussion to modern innovation theory and the concept of industrial commons.

In Chapter 3, Ed López, picks up on the cumulative character of knowledge arguing that knowledge commons are, on the one hand, coproduced in provision and, on the other hand, shared in consumption. His chapter drives home an important distinction – also highlighted in Chapter 4 by Brett Frischmann – that knowledge commons is a mode of governance that involves knowledge goods that are characterized by their non-subtractable nature. López suggests, along the lines of Prendergast, that agents often contribute to the production of knowledge commons as a result of their ordinary economic activity. Entrepreneurship within the rules of the game and rule-altering entrepreneurship are thus not distinct actions. By way of economic exchanges, people also exchange knowledge, and in exchanging knowledge they contribute to the collective processes of forming the very knowledge commons on which market exchange relies.

Brett Frischmann, in Chapter 4, examines what it means to think of knowledge as a commons through the study of common sense. He analyzes common sense as a social infrastructure for everyday market transactions and social interactions consisting of classifications, common understandings, and beliefs. Frischmann highlights that common sense understanding of the world forms part of a knowledge commons understood here as a mode of knowledge governance of, by, and for the community. Using the GKC framework, Frischmann explains that the governance of knowledge commons is nested. From the mundane knowledge commons of common sense, to the more specialized knowledge commons that support particular markets.

The market-supporting shared cognitive infrastructures are further discussed in the fifth chapter by Young Back Choi who argues that conventions are a necessary consequence of the human predicament of decision-making in the face of uncertainty. Following Frischmann, this chapter examines the role of everyday knowledge in resolving uncertainty so that actors get to "know what to do" in unfamiliar situations. The role of imagination, resemblance, and classification is brought forward in Choi's discussion of entrepreneurship, a disruptive force that feeds into a perpetual tension between stability and change in knowledge systems, and consequently the foundation of market interactions. Entrepreneurship in relation to knowledge commons entails the alteration of existing understandings and expectations and can thus play a vital role in the emergence, flourishing, or limitation of particular markets.

In the first applied chapter, Darcy Allen, Chris Berg, Jason Potts, and Sinclair Davidson analyze the new blockchain technology as one possible way of governing the knowledge commons. They suggest that one of the most fundamental knowledge commons that facilitates market is the shared knowledge about who owns what, along with the relevant rules of exchanging property. By analyzing blockchain in the context of the GKC framework, the team of authors suggest that knowledge about property rights is a shared resource that needs to be produced, and that there is a risk of this knowledge being underproduced. The chapter contends that Blockchains are a technology for the distribution, maintenance, and verification of social facts such as "who owns what?" and "who can trade?" that may, without a central authority, contribute to a more robust governance of market-supporting knowledge commons.

While the chapter on blockchain demonstrates how new technologies are useful in the governance of markets, Yugank Goyal analyzes a market in which crucial knowledge for the functioning of the market is part of dense local social networks. Goyal analyzes the shoe market in Agra, India and suggests that the knowledge of creditworthiness is one of the key elements of the market-supporting knowledge commons and a key resource that determines the individual costs of production for any shoemaker in the market. Illustrating what it means to say that exchanges are speech acts in this specific setting, Goyal illustrates the role of rumors in determining the rates at which credit can be obtained in the market. The local nature of the knowledge commons, "being in the market," facilitates an incredible richness in the shared knowledge infrastructure but also acts as a high barrier of entry for outsiders. Goyal demonstrates this through the analysis of specific barriers such as the role of caste in stratifying the division of tasks within the production process. This chapter also illustrates Prendergast's point about the cumulative nature of knowledge production by suggesting that incremental elements of knowledge will be worthless for someone who is not already "in the market."

The next group of chapters illustrates the importance of speech and language in both enabling and limiting the actions and interactions within markets *and* non-market settings. These chapters also highlight the role of entrepreneurs in managing the tension between stability and change. In this sense, they pick up on some of the themes brought up in the conceptual chapters by Frischmann, Choi, Prendergast, and López.

In their chapter Michelle Albert Vachris and Kyle Vachris present an analysis of the ways and means through which producers of whisky avoid the dilution of the category of Scotch. The very category of Scotch involves a knowledge of the do's and don'ts in production and consumption of whisky. The chapter suggests that the category of Scotch is a jointly produced resource that is maintained by the community of stakeholders who invest in upholding the quality of the knowledge commons that separates Scotch whisky from other whisky-like products. They suggest, however, that the protection of Scotch has become the dominant force and has led to stagnation. New producers, particularly outside of Scotland, were denied access and have in turn developed alternatives that not only compete for the term, but have also led to the development of new product categories and quality conventions that threaten to end the dominance of single malt Scotch.

Raphaël Raux and Julien Gradoz examine the theme of repugnance in speech in their chapter on online transgression spaces. Their chapter looks at the role of internet trolls in creating pockets of free speech on a French online forum. Their analysis demonstrates that through a combination of a rapidly evolving shared language and hermeticism, access to the commons is restricted, and the transgressive space as knowledge commons is maintained. Language in this case is the very resource that is modified and transformed by transgressions on the margin by internet trolls who find ways to express themselves freely but also safely. In this case study the transgressive space is financed through related commercial activities by the platform provider. Markets thus emerge as almost a corollary of shared communities, perhaps not too differently from the way gatherings around music has led to a thriving festival market.

The chapter by Carolina Dalla Chiesa is similar in that it deals with issues of identity in particular of the LGBTQ-community. But rather than seeking to develop a relatively closed space, this community seeks acceptance and recognition in Brazilian society. Her case study of the Queer Museum, which encountered extensive social and political opposition, demonstrates the importance of alternative institutional frameworks. When denied by major funders and official venues, the entrepreneurs behind the museum drew on crowdfunding and alternative space to continue their practice. Dalla Chiesa, drawing on Ostrom's notion of polycentricity, argues that museums manage an important knowledge commons of social and national identities. She investigates how these can be managed as a commons. Unique about the case examined in this chapter is that the shared framework of the crowdfunding platform, a knowledge commons, ends up supporting the Queer Museums, another initiative managed as a commons.

Rosa Won and Arjo Klamer contribute to the discussion of shared goods by suggesting that to acquire a shared good, one must contribute to its production and maintenance. Willingness to contribute is thus a key to consuming shared goods in online forums, in communities of Scotch aficionados, or in the context of a queer museum. Their own case is that of independent creative producers in urban contexts. They demonstrate, through the analysis of social media data, the qualities present in the knowledge commons on which these creatives draw. They argue that taking account of the qualitative nature of the knowledge commons in different cities is crucial to understand why some cities are able to attract 'the creative class' and others are not. Their chapter addresses the challenges of urban planning and suggests that much of its success is dependent on how well specific types of knowledge commons are fostered through urban policies.

REFERENCES

Allen, Robert L. 1994. *Opening Doors the Life and Work of Joseph Schumpeter, Volume 1: Europe*. Opening Doors the Life and Work of Joseph Schumpeter. Piscataway, NJ: Transaction Publishers.

Appadurai, Arju. 1986. *The Social Life of Things: Commodities in Cultural Perspective*. Cambridge, MA: Cambridge University Press.

Basu, Kaushik. 2018. *The Republic of Beliefs: A New Approach to Law and Economics*. Princeton, NJ: Princeton University Press.

Beckert, Jens. 2009. "The Social Order of Markets." *Theory and Society* 38 (3): 245–269. https://doi.org/10.1007/s11186–008-9082-0.

Boettke, Peter J. 2018. *F.A. Hayek: Economics, Political Economy and Social Philosophy*. London: Palgrave Macmillan.

Boltanski, Luc, and Laurent Thévenot. 2006. *On Justification: Economies of Worth*. Princeton, NJ: Princeton University Press.

Brousseau, Eric, and Jean-Michel Glachant. 2014. *The Manufacturing of Markets: Legal, Political and Economic Dynamics*. Cambridge, MA: Cambridge University Press.

Buchanan, James M. 1975. *The Limits of Liberty: Between Anarchy and Leviathan*. Chicago: University of Chicago Press.

Coase, Ronald H. 1934. "The Nature of the Firm." *Economica* 4 (16): 386–405.

Cornes, Richard, and Todd Sandler. 1996. *The Theory of Externalities, Public Goods, and Club Goods*. Cambridge: Cambridge University Press.

Dale, Gareth. 2010. *Karl Polanyi: Limits of the Market*. London: John Wiley & Sons.

De Marchi, Neil. 2008. "Confluences of Value." In *Beyond Price*, edited by Michael Hutter and David Throsby, 200–219. Cambridge: Cambridge University Press.

Dekker, Erwin. 2016. *The Viennese Students of Civilization: The Meaning and Context of Austrian Economics Reconsidered*.

Dekker, Erwin, and Pavel Kuchař. 2017. "Heterarchy." In *Encyclopedia of Law and Economics*, edited by Alain Marciano and G. Ramello. New York: Springer.

2019. "Lachmann and Shackle: On the Joint Production of Interpretation Instruments." *Research in the History and Methodology of Economic Thought* 37B: 25–42. https://doi.org/10.1108/s0743–41542019000037b005.

Elert, Niklas, and Magnus Henrekson. 2016. "Evasive Entrepreneurship." *Small Business Economics* 47 (1): 95–113. https://doi.org/10.1007/s11187–016-9725-x.

2017. "Entrepreneurship and Institutions: A Bidirectional Relationship." *Foundations and Trends in Entrepreneurship* 13 (3): 191–263. https://doi.org/10.1561/0300000073.

Elias, Norbert. 2000. *The Civilizing Process: Sociogenetic and Psychogenetic Investigations (Revised Edition)*. Malden: Blackwell.

Endres, Anthony M., and David A. Harper. 2013. "'Wresting Meaning from the Market': A Reassessment of Ludwig Lachmann's Entrepreneur." *Journal of Institutional Economics* 9 (03): 303–328. https://doi.org/10.1017/S174413741300009X.

Eucken, Walter. 1940. *Die Grundlagen der Nationalökonomie*. Jena: Verlag von Gustav Fischer.

Fernandez, Karen V., and Bernardo Figueiredo. 2018. "Bridging Boundaries in Consumption, Markets, and Culture." *Consumption Markets & Culture* 21 (4): 295–300. https://doi.org/10.1080/10253866.2018.1460906.

Fetter, Frank. 1915. *Economics. Vol. 1: Economic Principles*. New York: The Century Company.

Foucault, Michel. 2008. *The Birth of Biopolitics*. New York: Palgrave Macmillan.

Fourcade, Marion, and Kieran Healy. 2007. "Moral Views of Market Society." *Annual Review of Sociology* 33: 285–311. https://doi.org/10.1146/annurev.soc.33.040406.131642.

Freud, Sigmund. 1930. *Civilization and Its Discontents*. W. W. Norton & Company.

Frischmann, Brett M. 2012. *Infrastructure: The Social Value of Shared Resources*. Oxford: Oxford University Press.

Frischmann, Brett M., Michael J. Madison, and Katherine J. Strandburg. 2014. *Governing Knowledge Commons*. Oxford: Oxford University Press.

Goldschmidt, Nils, and Michael Wohlgemuth. 2008. "Social Market Economy: Origins, Meanings and Interpretations." *Constitutional Political Economy* 19 (3): 261–276. https://doi.org/10.1007/s10602-008-9047-3.

Granovetter, Mark, and Richard Swedberg. 1992. *The Sociology of Economic Life*. Boulder, CO: Westview Press.

Gudeman, Stephen. 2001. *The Anthropology of Economy*. Malden, MA: Blackwell.

Hadfield, Gillian. 2016. *Rules for a Flat World*. Oxford: Oxford University Press.

Hall, Bronwyn, Jacques Mairesse, and Pierre Mohnen. 2010. "Measuring the Returns to R&D." In *Handbook of the Economics of Innovation*, edited by Bronwyn Hall and Nathan Rosenberg, 1033–1082. Dordrecht: North Holland.

Hall, Robert E., and Charles I. Jones. 1999. "Why Do Some Countries Produce So Much More Output per Worker than Others?" *The Quarterly Journal of Economics* 114: 83–116.

Hayek, Friedrich A. 1945. "The Use of Knowledge in Society." *The American Economic Review* 35 (4): 519–530.

1960. *The Constitution of Liberty*. Chicago: The University of Chicago Press.

Hess, Charlotte, and Elinor Ostrom. 2006. *Understanding Knowledge as a Commons from Theory to Practice*. Cambridge, MA: MIT Press.

Hodgson, Geoffrey M. 2001. *How Economics Forgot History: The Problem of Historical Specificity in Social Science*. London: Routledge.

Jensen, Michael. 2010. "Legitimizing Illegitimacy: How Creating Market Identity Legitimizes Illegitimate Products." *Research in the Sociology of Organizations* 31: 39–80. Elsevier. https://doi.org/10.1108/S0733-558X(2010)0000031004.

Kealey, Terence, and Martin Ricketts. 2014. "Modelling Science as a Contribution Good." *Research Policy* 43: 1014–1024. https://doi.org/10.1016/j.respol.2014.01.009.

Klamer, Arjo. 2016. *Doing the Right Thing: A Value Based Economy*. London: Ubiquity Press.

Kornberger, Martin, Geoffrey Bowker, Julia Elyachar et al. 2019. *Thinking Infrastructures*. Vol. 62. Research in the Sociology of Organizations. New York: Emerald.

Kuchař, Pavel. 2016. "Entrepreneurship and Institutional Change: The Case of Surrogate Motherhood." *Journal of Evolutionary Economics* 26 (2): 349–379.

Lachmann, Ludwig M. 1971. *The Legacy of Max Weber*. Berkeley, CA: The Glendessary Press.

1978. *Capital and Its Structure*. Kansas City: Sheed Andrews and McNeel.

Liu, Sida. 2015. "Boundary Work and Exchange: The Formation of a Professional Service Market: Boundary Work and Exchange." *Symbolic Interaction* 38 (1): 1–21. https://doi.org/10.1002/symb.137.

Luhmann, Niklas. 1995. *Social Systems*. Stanford: Stanford University Press.

Marshall, Alfred. 1920. *Principles of Economics*. 8th ed. London: Macmillan.

Munger, Michael C. 2018. *Tomorrow 3.0: Transaction Costs and the Sharing Economy*. Cambridge: Cambridge University Press.

Navis, Chad, and Mary Ann Glynn. 2010. "How New Market Categories Emerge: Temporal Dynamics of Legitimacy, Identity, and Entrepreneurship in Satellite Radio 1990–2005." *Administrative Science Quarterly* 55 (3): 439–471.

North, Douglass C. 2005. "The Contribution of the New Institutional Economics to an Understanding of the Transition Problem." In *Wider Perspectives on Global Development*, edited by UNU-WIDER, 1–15. London: Palgrave Macmillan UK.

North, Douglass C., John J. Wallis, and Barry R. Weingast. 2009. *Violence and Social Orders: A Conceptual Framework for Interpreting Recorded Human History*. Cambridge: Cambridge University Press.

Ostrom, Elinor. 1990. *Governing the Commons: The Evolution of Institutions for Collective Action*. Cambridge: Cambridge University Press.

2005. *Understanding Institutional Diversity*. Princeton, NJ: Princeton University Press.

Peacock, Alan T., and Hans Willgerodt. 1989. *German Neo-Liberals and the Social Market Economy*. New York: Palgrave Macmillan.

Pirenne, Henri. 1937. *Economic and Social History of Medieval Europe*. New York: Harcourt Brace.

Polanyi, Karl. 1945. *Origins of Our Time: The Great Transformation*. London: Victor Gollancz.

Polanyi, Michael. 1958. *Personal Knowledge: Towards a Post-Critical Philosophy*. London: Routledge & Kegan Paul.

Popper, Karl R. 1945. *The Open Society and Its Enemies, Volume 1: The Spell of Plato*. London: Routledge.

Potts, Jason. 2019. *Innovation Commons: The Origin of Economic Growth*. Oxford: Oxford University Press.

Röpke, Wilhelm. 1950. *The Social Crisis of Our Time*. Chicago: The University of Chicago Press.

Roth, Alvin E. 2015. *Who Gets What – and Why*. Boston: Houghton Mifflin Harcourt.

Satz, Debra. 2010. *Why Some Things Should Not Be for Sale: The Moral Limits of Markets*. Oxford: Oxford University Press.

Schumpeter, Joseph A. 1976. *Capitalism, Socialism, and Democracy*. London: George Allen & Unwin.

Searle, John R. 1995. *The Construction of Social Reality*. New York: Free Press.

2005. "What Is an Institution?" *Journal of Institutional Economics* 1: 1–22. https://doi.org/10.1017/S1744137405000020.

Smith, Adam. 1981. *An Inquiry into the Nature and Causes of The Wealth of Nations*. Indianapolis, IN: Liberty Fund.

Stark, David. 2009. *The Sense of Dissonance: Accounts of Worth in Economic Life*. Princeton, NJ: Princeton University Press.

Strandburg, Katherine, Brett M. Frischmann, and Michael J. Madison. 2017. *Governing Medical Knowledge Commons*. Cambridge, MA: Cambridge University Press.

Swedberg, Richard. 2005. "Economic versus Sociological Approaches to Organization Theory." In *Oxford Handbook of Organization Theory*, edited by Christian Knudsen and Haridimos Tsoukas, 373–391. Oxford: Oxford University Press.

Thierer, Adam. 2016. *Permissionless Innovation: The Continuing Case for Comprehensive Technological Freedom*. Arlington, VA: Mercatus Center.

Velthuis, Olav. 2005. *Talking Prices: Symbolic Meanings of Prices on the Market for Contemporary Art*. Princeton, NJ: Princeton University Press.

Vogel, Steven Kent. 2018. *Marketcraft: How Governments Make Markets Work*. Oxford: Oxford University Press.

Waarden, Frans van. 2012. "The Governance of Markets: On Generating Trust in Transactions." In *The Oxford Handbook of Governance*, edited by David Levi-Faur, 355–371. Oxford: Oxford University Press.

Wadhwani, R. Daniel, and Christina Lubinski. 2017. "Reinventing Entrepreneurial History." *Business History Review* 91 (4): 767–799. https://doi.org/10.1017/S0007680517001374.

1

The Contribution Good as the Foundation of the Industrial Revolution

*Terence Kealey and Martin Ricketts**

The Industrial Revolution emerged when research became collective, which is a transition that can be modelled using a contribution good model of technical change. The Industrial Revolution cannot readily be modelled if research is treated as a public, private or club good. Recent work on the knowledge commons and on 'network' and 'anti-rival' goods has offered more promising perspectives, but we have proposed that research is most suitably considered as a novel good, namely a 'contribution good.' A contribution good is a non-depletable good jointly available only to those who have contributed to its creation. Here we show that the Industrial Revolution, and some of the institutional developments that accompanied it, conform well with a contribution good model of technical change.

When individuals require access to the contributions of others before the costs of their own research activity can be recovered, a critical number of participants is necessary to establish a self-sustaining group. Before the number of contributors reaches that threshold, technical development and therefore economic growth are low; but after the number of contributors crosses that threshold, technical development and therefore economic growth rise dramatically. The Industrial Revolution represented a 50-fold acceleration in the long-term rates of economic growth, and the threshold characteristic of a contribution good model will account for that acceleration of long-term rates of economic growth.

A contribution good gives rise to a collective action problem that can be characterised as one of 'pure coordination.' The combined contributions of a sufficient

* We thank Professors Meir Kohn and John Scott of Dartmouth College for consistently invaluable advice; we thank Professor Emeritus Eric Jones for deep conversations; we thank Drs. Benjamin Powell, Robert Murphy and Vincent Geloso of Texas Technical University and Dr. Maria Pia Paganelli of Trinity University, TX, for key insights; we thank Dr. Patrick Michaels and Messrs. Andrew Forrester and Joseph Verruni of the Cato Institute for many helpful discussions; and we thank Professor David Edgerton and Dr. Thomas Kelsey of Kings College London for their shrewd and generous observations.

number will produce a result that no individual participant will regret. But confidence that others will take part is required to induce participation. Here we describe the institutions that, fuelling the Industrial Revolution, emerged to provide that pure coordination. Such institutions represented the voluntary association of researchers in contributing knowledge to each other and into a common pool.

The emergence of research institutions does not in itself confirm that the Industrial Revolution can be modelled using a contribution good model of technical change. Scholars of research have previously modelled research as fully non-excludable, and such scholars have posited the emergence of research institutions to foster knowledge commons as solutions to the collective action problems that consequently arise.

But if research institutions arose to address the problem of non-excludability, they would have institutionalised exclusion and punishment. If, on the other hand, research institutions had emerged to address the problem of a threshold or 'critical mass,' they would have institutionalised inclusion and pure coordination. Here we show that the research institutions of the Industrial Revolution indeed institutionalised inclusion and pure coordination, which reinforces the idea that the Industrial Revolution can be modelled using a contribution good model of technical change.

1.1 DEFINING THE INDUSTRIAL REVOLUTION

The Industrial Revolution represented the acceleration of economic growth, and to fully characterise that acceleration would require measuring GDP, and GDP per capita, over the millennia, which cannot easily be achieved. Yet it is generally understood that, before the demographic transition that followed on the Industrial Revolution, humanity inhabited a Malthusian world, where advances in GDP were largely translated into increases in population, which suggests we might use total population to proxy total GDP (Kirk 1996). In Gregory Clark's (2007: 32) words, "In the preindustrial world, sporadic technological advance produced people, not wealth."

Figure 1.1 summarises the total human population data since 10000 BCE as estimated from the archaeological and anthropological evidence by McEvedy and Jones (1978), and it shows that, between circa 5000–4000 BCE and circa 1500 CE, annual rates of global population growth averaged circa 0.04 per cent. At a first approximation, therefore, we can conclude that annual rates of GDP *in toto* growth were circa 0.04 per cent.

To look more closely at the British example, between 1250 and 1700 the population grew from circa 4.23 million to circa 5.20 million (Broadberry et al. 2015), which was an annual growth rate of 0.05 per cent, and though the growth was not smooth (Black Death 1349) that rate was comparable to that of previous centuries. The data in Figure 1.2 show, moreover, that between 1270 and 1650, with the exception of the

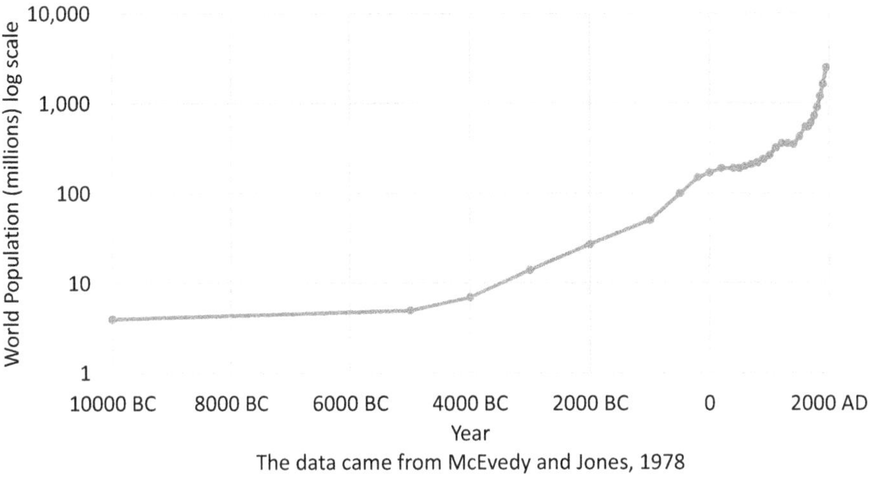

FIGURE 1.1. World population 10000 BC (BCE) to 1950 AD (CE) log scale

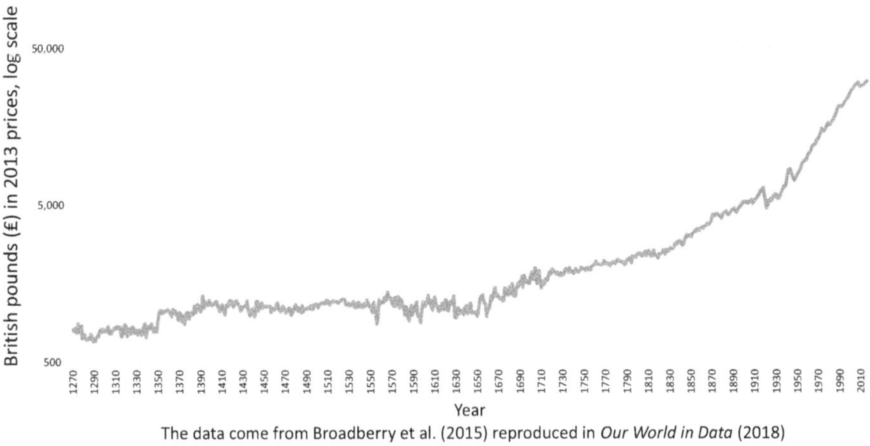

FIGURE 1.2. GDP per capita in England 1270–2016 log scale

Black Death years, GDP *per capita* growth rates in Britain were nugatory, which is also comparable with that of previous centuries.

After circa 1650, however, and coinciding with the increase in agricultural productivity per worker (Apostolides et al. 2008), the British growth rate in GDP *per capita* accelerated, eventually to achieve, around 1920, a long-term, sustained rate of circa 1.8 per cent PA. This is characteristic of the long-term growth rates of many lead countries, though by 1830 the USA had already attained its modern rates of GDP *per capita* growth of circa 2 per cent. GDP *per capita* is not, of course, synonymous with GDP *in toto* but, following a demographic transition, population growth is dwarfed by GDP growth, which allows here to define the Industrial Revolution as the process that started in the seventeenth century in England but which has since been transmitted to a number of other now-lead countries, whereby rates of economic growth increased circa 50-fold, from a rate of circa 0.04 per cent annually to a rate of circa 2 per cent annually.

1.2 MODELLING THE INDUSTRIAL REVOLUTION

1.2.1 *The Legacy of Nelson and Arrow*

The technical change that characterised the Industrial Revolution has not been modelled satisfactorily. Four of the great historians of the Industrial Revolution are Joel Mokyr, Deirdre McCloskey, Robert Allen and Eric Jones, and

- in Mokyr's words (2016: 6), scholars "know remarkably little about the kind of institutions that foster and stimulate technological progress and, more widely, intellectual innovation";
- in words from the subtitle of one of McCloskey's books (2010), "*Economics Cannot Explain the Modern World*";
- in Allen's words (2009: 3), "explaining the Industrial Revolution has been a long-standing problem in social science";
- and in Jones's words (2000: xx), explaining technological change is "something that is very hard to solve within the usual parameters of economics."

Two earlier significant scholars who studied the Industrial Revolution were Angus Maddison and David Landes, and

- in Maddison's words (1982: 56), "technical progress is the most essential characteristic of modern growth and the one that is the most difficult to quantify or explain";
- while in Landes's words (1969: 359), "it is impossible in the present state of our knowledge to evaluate the parameters of economic development."

These six scholars were articulating the lack of an economic model to account for the technical change that drove the Industrial Revolution. All six followed Solow (1957), as do we, in supposing that economic growth emerges by advances in knowledge, but all six were also aware of the conventional model for economic growth that was offered in their classic papers by Nelson (1959) and Arrow (1962), in which those two authors argued that research is a public good that would be underfunded privately and thus requires public subsidies. Yet the Industrial Revolution arose in Britain, and was relayed to the USA, both of which were largely *laissez faire* in research. In the words of Phyllis Deane (1979: 2): "The first industrial revolution occurred in Great Britain and is of particular interest in that it occurred spontaneously, without the government assistance that has been characteristic of most succeeding industrial revolutions."

As was also true of the USA. We have chronicled elsewhere the empirical evidence for research not needing government support (Kealey 2013) and we have also chronicled the failure of the conventional theoretical argument of knowledge being non-excludable (Kealey and Ricketts 2020).

1.2.1.1 Tacitness

Knowledge is of course non-rivalrous, but Nelson and Arrow had argued that knowledge is also non-excludable. But when their assertion that research is freely copied was tested in real life, it failed. When Mansfield et al. (1981) examined 48 products that had been copied within the major industries of New England during the 1970s, they reported the direct costs of copying were on average 65 per cent of the costs of innovation. A survey by Levin et al. (1987) of 650 Research and Development (R&D) managers provided similar results for the direct costs of industrial copying; and Mansfield et al. and Levin et al. reported that the marginal costs of copying were so high because the copiers had to rediscover for themselves the tacit knowledge embedded in the original innovation.

Mansfield et al. and Levin et al., however, had reported only the marginal costs of the actual copying; and Rosenberg (1980) and Cohen and Levinthal (1989) showed that companies seeking success in the market need first to sustain the fixed costs of a research staff whose activities are directed towards maintaining their own tacit expertise, which requires them to pursue active, and therefore expensive, research programmes, as fixed costs. Stigler (1961), moreover, has shown that companies also need to bear the costs of information, as well as the costs of failed imitation attempts. We may, therefore, not know for certain what the average costs of copying in industry are, but they appear to be so high that research, in industrial practice, is excludable in the sense that it is not available to free-riders. Any economic model for research must, therefore, accommodate the tacit nature of knowledge.

The fact that knowledge, including scientific and research knowledge, is tacit, was recognised from the outset of the enterprise of research: thus in 1543, in the two opening texts of the Scientific Revolution, Nicolaus Copernicus wrote in his *De revolutionibus* (1543) that he was writing only for those qualified to read it: "mathematics is written for mathematicians" (quoted in Shapin 1996: 122), while Vesalius dedicated the introduction to his *De humani corporis fabrica* to reiterating that only by working with their hands could physicians acquire useful knowledge. The following year, in a letter to Duke Albrecht of Prussia describing his discovery of the inclination of the compass, Georg Hartmann wrote, "I would right gladly explain to your Grace, as far as it can be done by writing, for such things are more easily shown by handling than by letter" (Hartmann 1943 [1544]).

Technological tacitness, too, has been long recognised, and in 1180, Gervase, on describing a vault in Canterbury Cathedral in his *Chronicle*, wrote that its rebuilding "will be better understood by inspection than by any description" (Erlande-Brandenburg 1995: 152). Similar statements continued to be made: Diderot wrote in the *Encyclopédie* (1751–1766) that "in all techniques, there are specific circumstances relating to the material, instruments and their manipulation that only experience teaches" (Mokyr 2002: 28); while in 1820, Richard Edgeworth (see also below) reiterated the role of tacitness in knowledge transfer when he recounted how, after he had been shown around the Soho and other Birmingham workshops, he had become: "intimately acquainted with many parts of practical mechanicks, which I could not otherwise have learned in many months" (Edgeworth 1844: 73).

It was Michael Polanyi, moreover, who noted in his *Personal Knowledge* that because of the tacitness of knowledge "we can know more than we can tell" (1958: 4), and who described "the ultimately tacit nature of all our knowledge" (1958: 95). For these reasons, therefore, we have generated a model for economic growth that recognises knowledge as tacit. That tacit character, in turn, provides a private incentive to do research, because only with that tacit knowledge will individuals be able to access, and thus exploit, the discoveries of others.

Being tacit, knowledge is therefore not a public good. But nor is it a private good in the sense of being rivalrous and conventionally excludable. Rather, it can be generated by voluntary institutions of coordination.

1.2.2 *A Contribution Good Model of Technical Change*

Suppose that the flow of results and ideas that make up 'research progress' at any point in time is related to the number of researchers (n) who are active. The private benefit net of costs (c) to each of these researchers might be written H(n) – c, where H(n) is assumed to increase with the number of active researchers. We call new scientific and technical knowledge emerging under these conditions a 'contribution good,' because its benefits are available only to those who have contributed by incurring the cost c and who have thus acquired the tacit knowledge by which to access the research of others.

As H(n) increases with the increase in the number of contributing researchers, so do the private benefits of using the collectively accessible knowledge created. We can envisage that, at low levels of n, this private pay-off is negative – the costs of participating in research outweigh the achievable private benefits. At some sufficiently large and 'critical' value of n (say n^*), however, the net pay-off becomes positive, and new researchers will have a private incentive to both contribute to, and exploit, the collective flow of new knowledge.

Thus the Industrial Revolution can be modelled as a quantitative phenomenon, dependent on the numbers of researchers crossing a threshold. When the numbers of potential contributors fall below that threshold it is privately unprofitable to share knowledge ($c > H(n)$ for $0 < n < n^*$), but when the number of potential contributors exceeds a threshold, researchers will find it profitable to contribute ($c < H(n)$ for $n > n^*$), and thereafter the numbers of contributors will explode in size because, with each additional contributor, the value to all, including to pre-existing contributors, increases. Consequently, the growth in the community of researchers becomes self-sustaining – there is a 'take-off' – which will be sustained by new researchers contributing to and exploiting the collective flow of new knowledge.

It is this ability to provide a conceptual underpinning for a relatively abrupt historical transition from very low rates of productivity growth to higher and sustained levels that leads us to propose that a mechanism of this type lay behind the Industrial Revolution. And we are encouraged in the suggestion that the Industrial Revolution was primarily a quantitative rather than qualitative phenomenon by the conclusions of other scholars. Thus, Robert Allen (2009: 257) wrote:

> Eighteenth-century experimentalism was, therefore, not novel. It had precedents running back centuries. The difference between the eighteenth century and earlier periods was quantitative – an increase in the volume of experimenting – rather than qualitative.

If we follow Arthur (2009) in modelling growth as the consequence of a rearrangement of ideas, we can see how propitious the sharing of ideas can be. If 10 individuals, for example, each produce one idea, and if those 10 individuals each share their idea, then – for the cost of generating only one idea – each individual gets access to many potential combinations of new ideas. For example there will be $10!/(10 - 3)!3!$ or 120 possible combinations of 3 out of the 10 contributions, and 252 ways of combining 5 together. In total, 1,023 combinations of different sizes will be potentially available. Koppl et al. (2018) use this concept in their 'combinatorial model of world economic history' to show how the generation of successive ideas increases the value of the pre-existing ones in a process that generates exponential growth. Koppl et al. did not, however, describe human agency, and in this chapter we describe the institutional changes that accelerated the rate of exponential growth 50-fold in the process known as the Industrial Revolution.

It might seem that the joint use by researchers of the flow of new research developments means that our approach must have affinities with the Nelson/Arrow 'public goods' view of research. What distinguishes the two models is the assumed nature of the spillovers. In the public goods framework, the benefits from new knowledge are 'freely' available to all, while in the contribution good model they are available only to those who have made a contribution and have paid the cost c. Only by participation in the collective endeavour, and only by contributing new knowledge, can an individual gain the tacit knowledge by which to transfer the knowledge from the collective pool into their own profitable opportunities. Remodelling research as a contribution good, rather than as a public good, thus changes the game from a 'prisoner's dilemma' to one of 'pure coordination.'

There is no longer a free-rider problem but a 'critical mass' problem. The main fear on the part of participants is not that their ideas will be picked up and used by others, but that other potential contributors will not have the confidence to engage and will underestimate the private advantages that access to the collective resource will bring. This fear was articulated by Michael Polanyi (1962: 54):

> [C]onsider the effect which a complete isolation would have on the progress of science. Each scientist would go on for a while ... but in the absence of further information about the results achieved by others, new problems of any value would cease to arise and scientific progress would come to a standstill.

So, researchers do research to acquire the tacit knowledge by which to access the research of others; and it's the hope of copying that *incentivises* research; it doesn't disincentivise it. Here we show – by quoting from a succession of observers who explained why they created such institutions – how the Industrial Revolution was characterised by the formation of institutions which, by implicitly recognising the special character of research as a 'contribution good,' were uniquely suitable for assembling a 'critical mass' of new knowledge. Such institutions were necessary because, as Michael Polanyi, noted in his *Personal Knowledge*, the tacitness of knowledge "restricts the range of diffusion to personal contacts" (1958: 55). As Thomas Spence asked during the 1770s, who is most likely to attain

> a distinct knowledge of any intricate subject, he who searches it by contemplation and the help of books only, or he who attends a well-regulated society, where the subject is freely debated as a question on both sides or demonstrated by the joint endeavours of the members?
>
> (Jackson 2019: 77)

Pure coordination is the solution to the collective action problem posed by the contribution good, namely achieving critical mass, and this chapter describes the emergence of the institutions that provided that pure coordination and thus facilitated the Industrial Revolution.

1.2.3 *Some Related Perspectives*

The contribution good framework shares some features of other approaches but differs from each in important respects.

Research as a Club Good. Problems of joint consumption can be addressed by private action through the establishment of clubs. Clubs form when exclusion mechanisms can be introduced at some economic cost and the 'club resource' – whether a golf course, swimming pool or local fishing ground – can be protected from 'free-riders.'

The evolution of club-like arrangements clearly plays a part in the history of the Industrial Revolution, but though a contribution good shares similarities with club goods, 'club like' resources are subject to potential crowding and 'over-use,' which is not the case for new knowledge and information: new club members in the contribution good framework automatically add to the joint pool of knowledge.

Research as a Network Good. Recent innovations have drawn attention to the role of network effects in raising productivity. A modern social media platform, for example, is more valuable to each user as the total number of users increases. The 'critical mass' idea that we use to explain the 'take-off' phase of the Industrial Revolution clearly has affinities with network externalities. Yet, though a contribution good shares similarities with network goods, Metcalfe's Law proposes in the case of telecommunications networks that the value of new knowledge rises exponentially with the number of contributors, while in Kealey and Ricketts (2014) existing researchers always benefit from newcomers but these additional researchers may make contributions of declining value.

Goods subject to strong network effects have been labelled 'anti-rival' (Weber 2004) on the grounds that additional users are welcome and do not harm incumbents. Clearly our 'contribution good' approach to science and research makes it 'anti-rival.' However, we dispute the widely accepted view that all anti-rival goods are non-excludable as well as non-rival, and that they are therefore types of public good. Because of the tacit nature of much new knowledge, spillovers of knowledge are in reality mainly confined to contributors, which therefore produces a different game theoretic structure from the usual prisoners' dilemma. In reality, non-contributors to knowledge will not benefit, and to that extent they are excluded – even if the incentives are such that contributions are eagerly sought and willingly supplied.

Research as an Outcome of Iterative Games. Solutions to free-rider problems have been proposed that rely on continued repetition of a game to induce cooperation. Where defection in a round (e.g. departing from the norms of 'openness' in pursuit of private gain) can be punished by future exclusion or loss of 'reputation,' it is possible to argue that institutions can evolve which embody the values of 'the republic of science.' This possibility is explored by Dasgupta and David (1994) – research results are shared amongst those who are deemed trustworthy and abide by the rules establishing recognition and priority – in the context of the development of pure science.

But whereas the evolution of institutions that secure the social benefits of openness in science is a common thread running between the repeated game approach and the contribution good framework, the former is focused on methods of exclusion as a response to the free-rider problem, while the latter is focused on securing coordinated engagement and the critical mass problem (see also below for a discussion on innovation commons).

Research in Endogenous Growth Theory. The difficulty of incorporating technical change into a model of growth without departing from the assumption of perfectly competitive 'price-taking' behaviour led to the explicit incorporation of market power into the analysis – for example, Paul Romer (1986, 1990). In Romer

(1990: 84–85), patent rights in producer goods incorporating design improvements are secure and permit the receipt of streams of quasi rents. New knowledge is thus rendered partially excludable.

To the extent that Romer's model renders new knowledge partially excludable, it has similarities to the contribution good. But in Romer's model, knowledge is innately non-excludable and is rendered partially excludable only by virtue of government-supplied temporary legal monopolies; while under the contribution good model, new knowledge is innately tacit. Consequently, Romer's model seeks to resolve the collective action problem of non-excludability by positing the promotion of excludability, while under the contribution good model, the collective action problem of excludability is resolved by the creation of institutions of coordination. As we show here, the empirical history of the Industrial Revolution is of the creation of institutions of coordination, not of promoting excludability: indeed, a key characteristic of the Industrial Revolution was the move from secrecy to openness, in industrial as well as academic research. Moreover, there is no empirical evidence (outside of pharmaceuticals, which are a special case by virtue of the weight of government safety regulation) that patents do promote technical innovation (for a review of the literature, see van Gompel 2019: 878).

Research as an Innovation Commons. Innovation commons theorists subscribe to the Nelson/Arrow public good model of knowledge: "new information, being nonrivalrous and nonexcludable, has properties of a public good. Markets do not efficiently supply public goods" (Potts 2019: 7). But since empirical evidence shows that investments in research are undertaken privately, innovation commons theorists argue that researchers have solved the collective action problem by collaborating in ways similar to the ways players collaborate in the cooperative games that Ostrom and her colleagues described for the management of common pool resources (1990). Consequently, innovation commons theorists posit the institutionalisation of cooperative games within research societies. For example, Allen and Potts (2016: 1040) write: "As a collective action problem, the innovation problem can be re-diagnosed as one in which a community of interest – nominally the enthusiasts for the new technology – need to develop institutional rules of governance to enable them to effectively pool and contribute innovation resources."

1.3 GOVERNING SCIENCE AS CONTRIBUTION GOOD

The societies that arise to resolve (i) the collective action problem of an Ostromian common pool resource (which is rivalrous but non-excludable), (ii) an innovation commons problem (in which knowledge is modelled as non-rivalrous and non-excludable), and (iii) a contribution good problem (where knowledge is modelled as non-rivalrous but, by virtue of its tacitness, excludable) will share many features in common, but the first two will be characterised by the punishment, by exclusion, of rule-breakers, and this is not a prominent feature of science.

Research societies certainly have codes of conduct. The oldest surviving research society is the Royal Society of London (founded 1660) whose leading spirit was Robert Boyle, and in his *Sceptical Chymist* of 1661, Boyle required researchers to be "sober and modest men … diligent and judicious … drudges of industry" who would "avoid contumelious language" and who would criticise only a man's "observation, not his want of sincerity" (Shapin and Schaffer 1985).

Codes of conduct might be helpful in any institution which is looking to overcome some social dilemma – be it the encouragement of engagement and openness within the group (as in modelling research as a contribution good) or the restriction of information flows to those outside (as in modelling research as an innovation commons), so we cannot use standards of conduct to distinguish between societies that are responses to free-riding (as postulated in the case of innovation commons) versus those that are building networks to address critical mass (as postulated in the case of the contribution good).

Nor can we use friendship to distinguish between research institutions that arose to address (i) the common action problem of research as non-excludable and (ii) institutions that arose to coordinate the solution to research knowledge being tacit. Research societies can certainly be rooted in friendship, as was illustrated by the Lunar Society, created in 1765. The Society met regularly around Birmingham in the English midlands (the meetings were held when the moon was full, to allow the attendees to get home by its light) and amongst its regular attendees were its convener and early proselytiser of evolution Erasmus Darwin, the steam engine pioneers Matthew Boulton and James Watt, the chemists Joseph Priestley and James Keir, the pottery industrialist Josiah Wedgwood, and William Withering the research doctor (to say nothing of Benjamin Franklin when he was passing through).

Also amongst its regular attendees was the inventor Richard Edgeworth, who in his *Memoirs* of 1820 wrote how the "mutual intimacy" of its members, even as they competed as well as collaborated with each other, "has never been broken but by death" (Edgeworth 1844: 81). But friendship would surely be a useful feature of any society, whatever the reasons for its creation. Punishment, though, would not. Punishment is a feature of the cooperative games that characterise an innovation commons, yet the innovation commons theorists themselves acknowledge that "innovation commons tend to be rather poor at endogenously dealing with punishment and conflict" (Potts 2019: 126).

Exclusion as punishment is indeed rare in research. In 1785, for example, Erasmus Darwin falsely claimed the discovery of digitalis as a treatment for heart failure that had actually been made by a fellow Lunatic, William Withering. Withering rarely spoke socially to Darwin again, but the Society understood that punishment by exclusion was self-defeating, so it localised the rupture to the social interactions of the two principals to the argument. Darwin was not punished by exclusion from the Society.

The early Royal Society apparently excluded. Skinner (1969) has chronicled a long list of distinguished researchers who were apparently excluded from the early Royal Society,[1] but he explains that the very length of the list shows that those people were not excluded as punishments for behaving badly but simply because the Society was then run as a social club; and those 15 or so distinguished researchers were simply members of different research circles – only after Newton became president did the Society seek to become an all-inclusive professional body. Thereafter, the Society excluded only those who had nothing to contribute (i.e. persons who were not distinguished scientists), which was a pattern of exclusion not of exclusion-as-punishment (as prescribed by cooperative games) but, rather, of 'pre-exclusion' for having nothing to contribute – such persons were simply not elected to membership; as is compatible with the Royal Society being the institutionalisation of a contribution game.

We can, therefore, use the pattern of exclusion to confirm that research societies were indeed created to encourage participation rather than to control free-riding, as is revealed by the allocation of kudos, for the institutions of research do not punish those who extract maximum benefit from accessing the research of others – rather the contrary, for some of the most celebrated episodes in research emerged when individuals such as Newton, Darwin, Wallace, Einstein, Crick and Watson, while working as theorists, reinterpreted and built on the findings of others. Newton is admired, not deprecated, for having acknowledged that, "If I have seen further, it is because I have stood on the shoulders of giants."[2]

To conclude this section, therefore, the pattern of exclusion from research societies suggests they did not emerge to reinforce the governance of common pool resources nor the management of innovation commons but, rather, to facilitate the production of contribution good resources.

1.4 THE BRITISH INDUSTRIAL REVOLUTION IN RELATION TO THE COMMERCIAL AND SCIENTIFIC REVOLUTIONS

There seem to have been at least two, earlier, aborted proto-Industrial Revolutions. During the high medieval period, the Italians invented or adopted double-entry bookkeeping, premium insurance, cheques, bills of exchange, deposit banking, and patents, amongst other technological innovations (which included the optical lens), and those developments were, in aggregate, revolutionary (as has been recognised in the term 'Commercial Revolution'), for by 1450 Italian GDP per capita was double

[1] Amongst the early excluded persons were (notoriously) Thomas Hobbes, Josiah Pullen, Edmund Dickinson, Sir Robert Sibbald, Leonard Plukenet, Robert Morison, Thomas Sydenham, Sir Thomas Browne, Samuel Collins, Peter Barwick, Nathanial Hodges, Arthur Dacres, Richard Wiseman, Sir John Hinton and William Whiston. Women were also excluded, not being admitted as fellows until 1945.

[2] Even it was said ironically, as an attack on his frenemy the very short Robert Hooke.

that of England's; indeed, between 1350 and 1420 Italian GDP per capita grew at 0.8 per cent PA (Fouquet and Broadberry 2015). The Dutch, too, were to enjoy a Golden Age (GDP per capita growth rates of 1.3 per cent between 1505 and 1595; Fouquet and Broadberry 2015).

Those two proto-revolutionary periods were, however, not sustained; not because they proved to be innately unsustainable but because, as Kohn (2005) has shown, they were aborted by predation and violence. Yet these two earlier revolutionary periods illustrate that the iconic British Industrial Revolution should not be characterised as a happy coincidence of natural resources such as coal and iron ore but, rather, as the product of a British culture that seized on those natural resources as the most propitious routes to private and public enrichment.[3] The evolution of that culture, which was nascent in Italy 1350–1420, the Netherlands 1505–1595 and the UK 1650–, was to be described by Deirdre McCloskey in her trilogy as 'bourgeois,' and by Kohn as 'commercial,' and the purpose of this chapter is to illuminate the institutions by which that bourgeois, commercial culture effected the revolutionary creation of new technology and thus wealth.

In characterising the early institutions of the Scientific and Industrial Revolutions, we shall make little distinction between them. It is now usual to distinguish between pure and applied science, but it not clear that that distinction would have been very apparent to contemporaries. Thus, Pastorino (2017) has shown how Francis Bacon's elaboration of the scientific method was informed by his experience when, first as Solicitor General (1607–1613) and then as Attorney General (1613–1618), he acted as a patent examiner when England already enjoyed a culture of commercial invention and innovation, and which seems therefore to have coincided with – and perhaps have anticipated – the inauguration of more disinterested scientific enquiry. Moreover, England's earliest formal research institution, the Royal Society, was founded in 1660 to "improve the knowledge of natural things and all useful arts, Manufactures, Mechanic practices, Engynes and Inventions by Experiment," while the Society of Arts, to name another London research body, was founded in 1754 "to embolden enterprise, to enlarge science, to refine art, to improve manufacture and to extend our commerce." The early institutions of the British research, in short, seemed to make little distinction between pure and applied research, and Robert Allen (2009: 257) has noted how autonomous from basic science much Industrial Revolutionary technology was: "invention in metals and textiles was largely independent [of pure science]."

Nor do we make much distinction between scientific and commercial entrepreneurialism and innovation, for in the story Aristotle told of Thales, the iconic

[3] Thus Allen (2009) argues that the steam engine emerged in Britain only because coal was abundant, but Greener (2015) showed that Thomas Newcomen's early steam engines were fuelled by peat and turf, and that Newcomen moved to coal fuelling only opportunistically, not obligatorily.

'first scientist' of the sixth century BCE, we can see that the entrepreneurial method of the market is indistinguishable from the entrepreneurial method of the scientist. In Book 1 of his *Politics*, section 1259a, Aristotle reported of Thales that

> from his knowledge of astronomy he had observed while it was still winter that there was going to be a large crop of olives, so he raised a small sum of money and paid round deposits for the whole of the olive presses on Miletus and Chios . . . when the season arrived, there was a sudden demand for a number of the presses [so] he realised a large sum of money, so proving that it was easy for philosophers to be rich if they chose.
>
> (Aristotle, Politics, Book 1, section 1259a)

A commercial culture, therefore, will facilitate the emergence of research. Yet in itself it will not foster an industrial revolution, and the contribution good framework suggests that, for most of human history, the 'critical mass' of research activity required for spontaneous commercially driven growth was not achieved; and our initial task is to investigate those institutional developments that ultimately permitted it to be approached and eventually surpassed.

Here we consider the many early research societies that were formed, often with aristocratic patronage, which made use of incentives that were not necessarily entirely commercial in nature but which would have enabled the wider dispersion of scientific and technical knowledge than had generally prevailed before. Take-off, however, required that McCloskey's bourgeois attitudes and Kohn's commercial attitudes had become sufficiently established for the profit opportunities latent in the growing pool of scientific knowledge to become the main motivating force. At a certain point the profit motive, combined with a large enough research community, gave rise to a spontaneous and cumulative increase in the rate of technical advance as more participants were attracted. After this 'take-off,' the competitive pursuit of innovation rents would itself create incentives to gain access to the ever-growing pool of knowledge and, within the 'contribution good' framework, would imply incentives actively to share knowledge. This 'post take-off' world, we argue, is characterised by a significant degree of 'collective invention' within and across industries. Moreover, we argue that the world today can still be described as a 'post take-off' world: the current Industrial Age is the seamless continuation of the Industrial Revolution.

Although we do not attempt precisely to identify the point at which the profit motive, combined with a large enough research community, gave rise to a spontaneous and cumulative increase in the rate of technical advance as more participants were attracted into research, we note that Derek de Solla Price (1963: 9) showed that the increase in scientific knowledge globally, as judged by the numbers of journals and by other quantitative measures, entered into its current rate of exponential growth, with a half-life of about 12.5 years, around 1750.

Carol Shiue and Wolfgang Keller (2007), moreover, have shown that by 1750 Britain's economy was quantitatively unique: by 1750, Britain's markets – as judged by the co-movement of prices – not only performed stronger and were more integrated than hitherto, but they were also stronger and more integrated than anyone else's. David Landes (1998: 246) has described another unique aspect of the British (then English) economy: "[L]ocal tolls had largely disappeared by the fifteenth century; as a result they had the largest internal market in Europe." The British economy in 1750, in short, was stronger, more integrated, and larger than any the Western world had seen. It could thus support the quantitative phenomenon of a threshold that the contribution good demonstrates.[4]

It can be hard to disentangle the simultaneous actions of social from quantitative factors. Alan Macfarlane (1978: 268) for example noted:

> England was as "capitalist" in 1250 as it was in 1550 or 1750. That is to say, there was already a developed market, mobility of labour, land was treated as a commodity, and full private ownership as established, there was very considerable social and geographical mobility, a complete distinction between farm and family existed, and rational accounting and the profit motive were widespread.

Gregory Clark (2007) has asked, therefore, if England was as capitalist in 1250 as it was in 1750, why did the Industrial Revolution not happen then? The same question was posed, in a different form, by Bennet Woodcroft FRS, who between 1864 and 1876 had been the clerk to the commissioners of patents in Britain. Woodcroft had been puzzled by John Kay's invention, in 1733, of the flying shuttle, which though a technically trivial advance, was nonetheless of vast commercial significance. Why was it, Woodcraft asked, that weaving had been "performed for upwards of five thousand years, by millions of skilled workmen, without any improvement being made to expedite the operation, until the year 1733?" (Howes 2017a: 6)

The answer to these questions is at least in part social. Thus a clue is provided by John Kay's own life story: as a young man he was apprenticed to a reed-maker (reeds were loom combs), and he is said to have returned home only after a month,

4 The dependence of research take-off on market size might help explain the sequential appearance of the different sciences. Thus (simplistically), reliable mathematics emerged in ancient Greece, physics in seventeenth-century Europe, chemistry and experimental industrial technology during the eighteenth century, and biology during the nineteenth century with the publication of Darwin's *The Origin of Species*. This progression seems not to track the innate difficulties of the different sciences (Newton's *Principia* is surely a harder read than Darwin's *The Origin of Species*) but, rather, their increasing complexity. The problems of complexity can be addressed, at least in part, by increasing the size of researchers' networks, which will expand their sources of information – witness Charles Darwin's dependence, when developing his idea of evolution by natural selection, on Lyell's *Principles of Geology*, Malthus's *Essay on the Principle of Population* and John Gould's taxonomy of the finches of the Galapagos Islands. It may, therefore, not be a coincidence that the emergence of the more complex sciences tracked with the increasing size of markets; and to the extent that industrial development depended on the more complex sciences, so the two phenomena may have fuelled each other.

claiming to have already mastered the business (Lord 1903: 91). Whether the story was true or only apocryphal, that it could have been propagated speaks to the weakening of the guilds for, in earlier eras of monopoly capitalism, apprenticeships were enforced, and breaking them precluded any further involvement in the trade. But, dating from around 1500, in England and the Netherlands uniquely in Europe, monopoly capitalism gradually succumbed to competitive capitalism (Ogilvie 2014). In the words of the scholar who popularised the term 'Industrial Revolution,' Arnold Toynbee (1884): "The essence of the Industrial Revolution was the substitution of competition for the medieval regulations that had previously controlled the production and distribution of wealth."

Ogilvie (2014: 171) has noted that by 1733 the textile guilds had been so weakened in England that entry into weaving had been freed. Moreover, Ogilvie also noted that guilds had always arisen where markets had arisen, regardless of geography or culture; so, because English guilds were only emblematic of the way markets had been regulated for 5,000 years, we can see why the invention of the flying shuttle had to wait until 1733 in Britain.

But if the substitution of competition for medieval regulations is the essence of the Industrial Revolution, this chapter largely limits itself to the downstream event, namely the development of institutions implicitly aimed at solving the collective action problem of critical mass.

1.5 CHRONOLOGY OF THE BRITISH INDUSTRIAL REVOLUTION

England's first impactful contribution to research was William Gilbert's (1600) *De magnete* (Robert Norman's *Newe Attractive* of 1581 made less impact). It was from *De magnete* that we acquired the terms 'electric' and 'electricity,' and Gilbert advanced the science of navigation in important ways. And in his paper 'The origins of William Gilbert's scientific method,' Zilsel (1941) showed how Gilbert did it: for Gilbert, who was famously social, was embedded within a network of scientific friends with whom he exchanged information. So Gilbert learned that the compass worked at latitudes up to the 80th degree because "This our most famous Neptunus Francis Drake, and the other circumnavigator of the globe, Thomas Cavendish, have told and confirmed to me" (Zilsel 1941: 18). Zilsel showed, moreover, either directly or by inference, that the other English compass pioneers of the time were all Gilbert's friends.[5] Many of those pioneers were sailors, or they were gentlemen who, unusually for the era, were friendly with sailors; and Zilsel concluded that English research was facilitated by the breakdown of social barriers – as markets accelerated,

[5] The English compass pioneers included Edward Wright, Thomas Harriot, Robert Hues, Abraham Kendall, Thomas Blundeville and William Barlowe. William Gilbert's papers were lost in the Great Fire of London, so Zilsel could not prove directly that all the pioneers were friends with Gilbert: in some cases he inferred the friendship from circumstantial evidence.

so gentlemen like Gilbert exchanged information with artisans, to enlarge the mass of researchers contributing into the common pool of knowledge.[6]

Gilbert's was only one of at least five distinct mathematical/geographical/navigational research circles in England: three were centred on Thomas Allen, Henry Briggs and John Dee, respectively (Cormack 1997: 127), while another was centred on Henry Percy (1564–1632), the ninth or 'Wizard' Earl of Northumberland.[7]

The best-known research circle may have been yet another, Mary Herbert's at Wilton House. Here, from Aubrey's *Brief Lives* (1669–1696), is a record of Wilton House in the final decades of the sixteenth century:

> In her time Wilton house was like a College, there were so many learned and ingeniose persons. She was the greatest patronesse of witt and learning of any lady in her time. She was a great chymist and spent yearly a great deale in that study. She kept for her laborator in the house Adrian Gilbert (vulgarly called Dr. Gilbert)[8] halfe brother to Sir Walter Ralegh, who was a great chymist ... She also gave an honourable yearly pension to Dr. Thomas Mouffett, who hath writt a booke *De insectis*. Also one ... Boston, a good chymist ... At Wilton is a good library

Latham (2010: 14) moreover has shown that Mary Herbert was embedded in yet another research network, one of aristocratic ladies including Lady Margaret Hoby and Margaret Clifford, Countess of Cumberland.

These research circles may seem unexceptional to us today, but it was not then unusual for researchers to seek seclusion and excludability. Thus Francis Bacon wrote in 1603 in *Valerius Terminus*:

> The discretion anciently observed ... of publishing part, and reserving part to a private succession, and of publishing in a manner whereby it shall not be to the capacity nor taste of all, but shall as it were single and adopt his reader, is not to be laid aside, both for the avoiding of abuse in the excluded, and the strengthening of affection in the admitted.
>
> (quoted in Howard 2004: 477)

And later, Bacon (1626: 215) was still writing that: "we have consultations, which of the inventions and experiences we have discovered shall be published, and which not; and take an oath of secrecy."

6 Zilsel's thesis is supported by the observation that, after having eschewed breakfast for a millennium on the grounds it was a meal fit only for manual labourers, during the later sixteenth century the English upper classes started to eat breakfast again; thus was one barrier between the classes broken down (Terence Kealey 2013: 13–15).

7 Percy's coterie included Nathanial Torporley and Nicholas Hill, but also Thomas Harriot, Robert Hues and Walter Warner, who were the "three Magi" whom Percy supported financially (Gordon Batho 2000: 31–32). Researchers like Harriot and Hues could move from one circle to another as the patterns of patronage shifted, thus diffusing information beyond individual circles in ways not dissimilar from those described by Mark Granovetter (1973).

8 No relation to William Gilbert.

Thus too, in 1610, did Galileo publish his discovery of the rings of Saturn as *omaiomrmilmepetaleumibunenugttauiras*, which he only later revealed transcribed into *Alitissimum planetam tergeminum obervavi*, "I have observed the most distant planet to have a triple form" (Reeves 1999). In 1656, to quote another example of secrecy, the Dutch scientist Christiaan Huygens published his discovery of the ring-like nature of Saturn's satellites as the anagram *aaaaaaccccdeeeee-hiiiiiiillllmmnnnnnnnnnooooppqrrstttttuuuuu*, "Saturn is encircled by a thin, flat ring, nowhere touching, inclined to the ecliptic" (Howard 2004: 485). While in 1660, in a further example of exclusion, Robert Hooke published his law of elasticity as *ceiiinosssttuv* (for *ut tension sic vis*; stress is proportional to strain) (Brown and Slawinski 2017: 110). Other researchers might lodge their findings with a lawyer or university, to reveal them and thus claim priority only when a later competitive publication arose.

Yet the same Robert Hooke who in 1660 had published his Law as an anagram, was one of the founders in that same year of the Royal Society in London, and in 1666 Hooke explained why research needed institutions like the Royal Society: it was to shift researchers away from the very culture of secrecy, atomisation and Intellectual Property rights (IPR) he had himself so recently embodied:

> There hath not been wanting in all ages and places great numbers of men whose genius and constitution hath inclined them to delight in the inquiry into the nature and causes of things ... But their Indeavours having been only single ... have ended only in some small inconsiderable product.
>
> (quoted in Mokyr 2002: vii)

Hooke was saying, in short, that when researchers' "Indeavours" were "only single," they "ended only in some small inconsiderable product," which, in the model of research as a contribution good sketched briefly above, can be represented as $c > H(1)$, where c is the private cost to a player of doing research, and where $H(1)$ is the private value of only one researcher's research (which, when researchers' "Indeavours" were "only single," was their own).

Hooke argued that collectivisation was the research way forward, and reinforcing that collaborative message Thomas Sprat, in his official *History of the Royal Society* published in 1667, condemned individual "pride, and the lofty conceit of men's own wisdom." Truth, he said, could advance only through the collective and "unanimous advancement of the same works" (Sprat 1667: 428). That is, research advanced best when organised collectively, which can be modelled as $c < H(n)$, where c remains the private cost to a researcher of doing research, and where $H(n)$ is the private value to a researcher of accessing the research of all researchers including their own.

And the transition from discreet to open knowledge was also seen in for-profit sphere; to quote Anton Howes (2017b: 12):

> Ralph Rabbards, in a 1574 list of inventions sent to Queen Elizabeth I, promised to reveal the details only in exchange for a "small chardge." Hugh Plat, writing in 1592, would do exactly the same, offering inventions that "the author proposed to disclose upon reasonable considerations." From the late sixteenth century, however, this reticence to share gave way to a culture of openness, sharing and even active evangelism.

We can represent the Royal Society as the institutionalisation of the informal circles (including the "invisible college" of which Robert Boyle wrote in 1646–1647; Purver 1967: 64) that had characterised English research since the latter decades of the sixteenth century. Amongst later societies was the Lunar Society (created in 1765 as noted earlier), which the inventor Richard Edgeworth had described in his *Memoirs* of 1820. He also described how a similar collection of researchers met regularly, first at Jack's and then at Young Slaughter's Coffee House in London.[9] Edgeworth described how such luminaries could be persuaded to share their advances with each other. It wasn't just to enjoy the excitement of "the first hints of discoveries, the current observations, and the mutual collision of ideas." It was also because "the knowledge of each member of such a society becomes in time disseminated through the whole body, and (…) combines the talents of numbers to forward the ideas of a single person" (Edgeworth 1844: 82–83).

Edgeworth was saying, therefore, that even competitors – especially competitors – benefitted from sharing their advances with each other, because such sharing "combines the talents of numbers to forward the ideas of a single person," thus echoing Hooke's lament that when researchers' "Indeavours" were "only single," they "ended only in some small inconsiderable product," and thus anticipating Kealey and Ricketts's (2014) model of a contribution good by which researchers, on contributing into a common pool of knowledge, increase the return on c from H(1) to H(n).

A later industrialist whose words echoed Hooke's and Edgeworth's was Gerard Muntz, the British steel maker, who in 1909 explained that his industry had created the Institute of Metals because:

> Each individual has some cherished bit of knowledge, some trade secret which he hoards carefully. Perhaps by sharing it with others he *might* impart useful information; but by an open discussion and interchange he would, almost for certain, learn a dozen things in exchange for the one given away. General increase of knowledge would give general improved practice.[10]

[9] This latter group included John Hunter the surgeon; Sir Joseph Banks, the President of the Royal Society; Daniel Solander, the follower of Linnaeus; Sir Charles Blagden, the Secretary of the Royal Society; Dr. George Fordyce FRS, the colleague of John Hunter; Nevil Maskelyne, the Astronomer Royal; Captain Cook; Sir George Shuckburgh the polymath; John Smeaton, the engineer; and Jesse Ramsden the instrument maker.

[10] "Institute of Metals Annual General Meeting in London." *Page's Weekly* 14: 160–162, 22 January 1909.

Muntz was saying that once researchers pool their knowledge, an individual – on disclosing a first-mover discovery – would receive, in return, information on many others' first-mover discoveries, one or more of which he or she might then exploit as a second-mover advantage. And in his phrase "learn a dozen things in exchange for the one given away," Muntz was echoing Edgeworth's "combines the talents of numbers to forward the ideas of a single person," and Hooke's lament about single 'indeavours' ending "only in some small inconsiderable product." The incentives for researchers to share knowledge have thus characterised the Scientific and Industrial Revolutions since their inaugurations.

The contribution good, moreover, explains why researchers are incentivised to do their own first-mover research, because without it they cannot obtain the second-mover advantage of accessing the first-mover research of the other members of the research society. In his review of the British Agricultural Revolution of the eighteenth century, Eric Jones (1981) wrote that "the central puzzle is the emergence of the British taste for … agricultural improvements." The contribution good solves that puzzle, because without their own involvement in agricultural R&D ("improvements"), British farmers would not be able to access the advances of others.

On studying the development of steel in Britain during the nineteenth century, when that country dominated the industry and when men like Muntz were influential, Robert Allen (1983) systematised such chains of second-mover advantages into a model by which trade-offs from disclosing first-mover discoveries for second-mover opportunities were so mutually beneficial that collective invention became, to a remarkable degree, the dominant form of invention: "if a firm constructed a new plant of novel design and that plant proved to have lower costs than other plants, these facts were made available to other firms." The extent of research cooperation between Industrial Revolutionary firms was dramatic, and firms would even research their competitors' factories: thus one British steel master, Bell, reported that another, Vaughan, "let him measure the thermal characteristics of his [Vaughan's] 75 feet furnaces built in 1862."

Allen, moreover, found that collective invention still underpins the modern economy:

> [R]ecent engineering literature indicates such behaviour [collective invention] is rampant today. To the degree that economists have considered this behaviour at all, it has been regarded as an undesired 'leakage' that reduces the incentives to invent. That firms desire such behaviour and that it increases the rate of invention by allowing cumulative advance are possibilities not yet explored. They should be.
>
> (Allen 1983: 21)

Indeed. So Thomas Allen (1983) found in an international survey of 102 firms that no fewer than 23 per cent of their important innovations came from swapping information with their rivals: "managers approached apparently competing firms in other countries directly and were provided with surprisingly free access to their technology." While von Hippel (1998), in a survey of 11 steel companies in the USA, showed that 10 of them regularly swapped proprietary information.

John Scott (1996) has reported, moreover, in a study on cooperative research to reduce toxic air emissions, that:

> the cooperative R&D ventures do not appear to be a way for companies to avoid Schumpeterian competitive pressures that stimulate R&D investment. New, primary data at the disaggregated level of a particular type of R&D for particular companies support the belief that cooperative R&D ventures among manufacturing companies may well promote economic efficiency.

And Albert Link and Laura Bauer (1989), in their survey of cooperative research in US manufacturing, have confirmed it continues to drive economic growth and corporate profits. The patent data, moreover, confirms the importance of connectivity to innovation: thus Jaffe et al. (1993) showed that US patent citations were three to four times more likely to come from the same state as the originating patents, while Agrawal et al. (2008) not only confirmed that co-location promoted knowledge flow between inventors (by 24 per cent, correcting for ethnicity), but so too did co-ethnicity (by 14 per cent, correcting for proximity). Bailey et al. (2018) found that social connectiveness between US counties, as judged by the frequency of Facebook ties between counties, and after correcting for technology class and geographic distance, predicts the probability of cross-county patent citations. Mansfield (1995: 59), moreover, on looking at 66 examples of industrial–university links in the USA, found that "holding faculty quality constant, the probability of a firm supporting research at a college or university less than 100 miles away tends to be several times as great as the probability that it will support this research at a college or university 1,000 or more miles away."

Emphasising the role of connectivity in innovation, Dudley (2016) has argued that the clustering of important innovations between 1700 and 1850 in England, New England, and France, speaks to the UK and France preceding, by a century, other countries' adoptions of standardised national languages. Meanwhile, reporting on a natural experiment in connectivity, Burchardi and Hassan (2011) found that West German households and West German regions that had personal links to East Germany before the fall of the Berlin Wall in 1989 enjoyed, after the fall of the Wall, greater rates of economic growth than did West German families and regions that had fewer of those personal links; Burchardi and Hassan argued that that difference was attributable to West German entities converting their links into cooperative entrepreneurial opportunities.

The Industrial Revolution represented, we suggest, the outcome of a more collaborative and open approach to the development of new ideas of potential commercial value, as was exemplified in England by the evolution of the terms "chemistry" and "alchemy."

References to alchemists can be found as early as the fourteenth century in English literature (Linden 1974), and the early scientific giants respected the alchemists for being experimenters. Thus in 1623 Bacon wrote that: "I should call in some alchemist to help me; one of those who advise the studious to sell their books and build furnaces [i.e., laboratories]" (quoted in Linden 1974: 552), while in his *Sceptical Chymist* of 1661, Boyle also praised the experiments of the "alchemists" (West 1961: 106). Newton also admired the alchemists' experiments for, as Maynard Keynes reported, Newton was as much an alchemist as a physicist:

> Newton was not the first of the age of reason. He was the last of the magicians, the last of the Babylonians and Sumerians, the last great mind which looked upon the visible and intellectual world with the same eyes as those who began to build our intellectual inheritance rather less than 10,000 years ago.
>
> (Fanning 2009: xiv)

But the reverse of the alchemists' experimental coin was that they were secretive.

Newman and Principe (1998) have shown that the terms 'chemistry' and 'alchemy' were synonymous until the late seventeenth century, but that thereafter the discipline was to divide into two parts: the term "chemistry" was to be bestowed on that part that became open, whereas "alchemy" was to be bestowed on that part that remained, in the 1675 words of Nicholas Lemery, "in shadows" (Newman and Principe 1998: 61.) And in reflection of the shift of culture towards openness during the seventeenth century, the term 'alchemy' became derogatory. Thus William Gilbert in 1600 criticised alchemists for "veiling things in darkness and obscurity by means of silly words" (Zilsel 1941: 25), Bacon in 1605 condemned those who "sought to veil over and conceal by enigmatic writings" (quoted in Linden 1974: 552), and in 1661 Boyle denounced the alchemists for their "aenigmatical ... cloudy expressions," their "intolerable ambiguity," and their "abuse [of] words" to keep their research secretive (West 1961: 108).

It was in further reflection of the shift towards openness during the seventeenth century that Bacon defended grants of patents, not because he approved of monopolies, but because they enforced disclosure: "No discovery should be sanctioned save that it be put in writing. Only when that becomes standard practice, with experience at last becoming literate, should we hope for better things" (Pastorino 2017: 765).

1.6 HOW WIDESPREAD WAS COLLECTIVE INVENTION?

In a 1755 publication, *Histoire et secret de la peinture en cire*, Diderot reported that the mechanical invention of his day was collective (Hilaire-Pérez 2002). Mokyr (2009: 81), however, denies that collective research was an important feature of the Industrial Revolution, writing that it seems to have been limited only to three examples, namely the case of the Cleveland steel industry described by Allen (above), the case of the English clock and instrument manufacturers (below), and the case of the early high-pressure steam engine in Cornwall after 1800 (below).

MacLeod has described the case of the English clock and instrument makers:

> The Clockmakers and Spectacle Makers Companies retained an active control into at least the second quarter of the eighteenth century that included an inveterate opposition to patents. The members, meanwhile, were consistently improving the standards of their wares though the steady accretion of skills and ingenuity, and in cooperation with scientific investigators who were also their most exacting customers. New types of microscope were invented, new standards of accuracy achieved in astronomical and surveying instruments, and a variety of scientific instruments developed, notably the thermometer and barometer. English clocks and watches were justly famous. This was one area where Campbell had to acknowledge no Continental superiority or contribution (. . .)
>
> The Clockmakers . . . spent over £500 to defeat 3 patents and 2 Acts between 1688 and 1718 (. . .)
>
> . . . with the argument that they [patents and Acts] restricted the free exercise of a skill whose development had always depended on small improvements, freely exchanged among craftsmen.
>
> (MacLeod 1998: 112, 113, 188)

With the consequence, in Adam Smith's words (1910: 224–225), that a watch that "about the middle of the last century could have been bought for twenty pounds, may now perhaps be had for twenty shillings [i.e., a twentieth of the price]."

Nuvolari (2004) has described the development by collective invention of high-pressure steam engines in Cornwall. Watt's patent had aroused such frustration that, after its expiry in 1800, the engineering community in Cornwall (then a major centre of mining) adopted a collective ethos of cooperative research. This was coordinated by Joel Lean, who launched a monthly newsletter *Lean's Engine Reporter* that, between 1810 and 1904, circulated individual engineers' advances, which helped raise the so-called duty or efficiency of the engines from 20 to 90 million pounds between 1810 and 1840. The engineers' cooperation was supported by the investors, one of the most prominent of whom, John Taylor, explained in 1830 why most investors supported a number of different engineers: "We [investors] are not the partisans of any individual engineer or engine maker; we avail ourselves of the assistance of many" (quoted in Nuvolari 2004).

Despite suggesting collective invention was rare, Mokyr (2009: 82) nonetheless concedes there was "a great deal of cooperation in the generation of technological progress," and we would argue that such cooperation is synonymous with technological progress being modellable as a contribution good. Bessen and Nuvolari

(2016), who have catalogued a large number of advances made by mutual contribution, make no substantial distinction between collective invention and research collaboration.[11]

Initially, the acceleration of exponential industrial revolutionary research was incubated within individual industries, but the novel technologies then fructified other industries (the textile industry was revolutionised by watchmakers, who supplied gears and precision in part-making; while watchmaking itself had earlier been revolutionised by its meeting the needs of navigation; Allen 2009: 204), and as successive industries embarked on their accelerated exponential research expansions, so the whole economy was modernised not just by skilled craftsmen but also by entrepreneurial researchers expanding into fresh industries in a new *modus operandi*. Indeed, in his review of 1,452 innovators in Britain between 1547 and

[11] Amongst the examples of successful advances by mutual contribution cited by Bessen and Nuvolari (2016) were (1) the development of the *fluyt* (the favourite cargo ship of the Dutch East India company during the seventeenth century); (2) the eclipse during the eighteenth century of the London silk industry (which was characterised by secrecy and patents), by the Lyonnaise silk industry (where innovation was collective); (3) the introduction of wind power on a massive scale for the first time during the seventeenth century by the Zankstreet millwrights in the Netherlands; (4) the development of coal-burning houses in London during the seventeenth century; (5) the adoption of clover, sainfoin and turnips in crop rotations by open field farmers (which was against a long background in the UK of the sharing of agricultural knowledge, as embodied in such institutions as the Highland and Agricultural Society of Scotland (1785) or the Royal Agricultural Society of England (1830), and facilitated by such proselytisers as Arthur Young (1741–1820) whose *Farmer's Kalendar* went into its 215th edition in 1862) and which mirrored the culture of knowledge sharing amongst American farmers during the nineteenth and the early twentieth centuries, as evidenced by the fostering by the American Rose Society of the successful sharing of knowledge amongst breeders, and as evidenced by Faber's (1931) book *Cooperation in Danish Agriculture* reporting how Danish farmers formalised the sharing of knowledge by establishing 'control societies'; (6) the improvements in James Hargreaves's spinning jenny; (7) the development of high-pressure steam engines for western steamboats in the USA, which led to the greatest rate of transport productivity growth of the period; (8) the development of the early cotton industry in the USA as led by William Gilmour; (9) the development of 'Viennese chairs' during the nineteenth century; (10) the sharing of knowledge amongst the successful paper makers in Berkshire, Massachusetts, and amongst the early cotton manufacturers in Industrial Revolutionary Rockdale, Pennsylvania; (11) the Sewing Machine Combination or patent pool, which was created in 1856 when the four leading manufacturers, Singer, Wheeler & Wilson, Grover and Baker agreed to pool their patents but not to enforce them, so they shared their advances with each other – a similar example of such sharing was the semi-automatic cross-licensing and knowledge sharing in American railways during the nineteenth century; (12) the Bessemer Association or patent pool, which promoted collective invention in American steel production, with consequent dramatic increases in production; the sharing of knowledge was led by Alexander Holley, who was also the president of the American Institute of Mining Engineers, the vice president of the American Society of Civil Engineers and a founder of the American Society of Mechanical Engineers; and to promote the sharing of commercially important knowledge, the institutes with which Holley was associated published journals such as the *Transactions of the American Institute of Mining Engineers* or the *Transactions of the American Society of Mechanical Engineers* or the *Journal of the United States Association of Charcoal Iron Workers*.

1851, Anton Howes (2017a) showed that most of them improved more than one industry, and that 34 per cent of them improved industries for which they lacked relevant training, thus suggesting that entrepreneurs had learned to exploit the operation of contribution goods in themselves, regardless of the industry in which they were rooted.

Howes has also shown how the Industrial Revolutionary innovators acquired, by personal contact with each other, the very propensity to innovate: Charles Darwin may have shown in his *Descent of Man, and Selection in Relation to Sex* (1871) how human creativity had evolved by sexual selection, and Baumol (1990) may have shown how such creativity can be channelled into entrepreneurial activity, but Howes showed how that latent creativity could be honed by the institutions and societies to which individuals were exposed. The universities of Edinburgh and Leiden, for example, were much more innovatory in their cultures and produced many more innovatory graduates than did otherwise comparable universities. Similar observations can be made today, and Bell et al. (2019: 648) have shown how individual Americans' propensity to invent depends on "role-model or network effects" rather than on general levels of education.

During the Industrial Revolution, engineers across different industries proved very collaborative in their R&D, as was witnessed in Britain by the proliferation of engineering institutes, which included the Institute of Civil Engineers (1818), the Institute of Mechanical Engineers (1847), the Federated Institute of Mining Engineers (1850), the North of England Institute of Mining and Mechanical Engineers (1851), the Society of Engineers (1854), the Scottish Institution of Shipbuilders and Engineers (1860), the Institution of Naval Architects (1860), the Surveyors Institution (1868), the Iron and Steel Institute (1869), the Institute of Electrical Engineers (1871), the Institute of Municipal Engineers (1873), the Institute of Marine Engineers (1889), the Institute of Mining and Metallurgy (1892), the Institute of Sanitary Engineers (1895), the Institute of Water Engineers (1896), the Institute of Heating and Ventilating Engineers (1897), the Institute of Refrigeration (1900), the Institute of Metals (1908), the Institute of Concrete Engineers (1908) and the Institute of Foundry Engineers (1912) (Inkster 1991: 108). These institutes, like the American ones, organised meetings and published journals and newsletters.

In addition to the societies and institutions mentioned above, Britain witnessed the founding of a further cohort of industrial research societies including the Dublin Philosophical Society (founded in 1683), the Gentlemen's Society of Spalding in south Lincolnshire (1710; Isaac Newton was a member), the Dublin Society for Improving Husbandry, Manufactures and other Useful Arts (1731), the Royal Society of Edinburgh (1737), the Edinburgh Society for Encouraging Arts, Sciences, Manufactures and Agriculture in Scotland (1755), the Society of Civil Engineers (founded by Smeaton in 1771), the Derby Philosophical Society (founded in 1784 and immortalised by Wright's paintings), the Royal Irish Academy

(1785; focused primarily on the sciences), the Newcastle Literary and Philosophical Society (1793, initially for mining research), Anderson's Institution in Glasgow (1796), the Pneumatic Institution in Bristol (1799), the Royal Institution in London (1799), the Geological Society of London (1808, "for public improvement and utility," i.e. mining), and the Institution of Royal Engineers (1818, despite the name a civil body).

The Scottish enlightenment, where scholars, engineers and doctors came together to share knowledge (Adam Smith's executors were a chemist, Joseph Black, and a geologist, James Hutton), was particularly characterised by the creation of clubs. These included the Rankenian Club, the Literary Society of Glasgow, the Aberdeen Philosophical Society, the Oyster Club, the Philosophical Society of Edinburgh (to become the Royal Society of Edinburgh as noted above), the Wise Club of Aberdeen, and the Poker Club. The culture of the Scottish enlightenment was captured by its historian, Alexander Broadie, when he wrote, "thinking was regarded as essentially a social activity. People thought with each other, that is, they *shared* their thoughts" (Broadie quoted in Paganelli 2015: 3; italics in the original).

By 1828, an observer could therefore note of Britain that "in every town, nay almost every village, there are learned persons running to and fro with electrical machines, galvanic troughs, retorts, crucibles, and geologist hammers" (Inkster 1991: 73). By the middle of the nineteenth century, indeed, no fewer than 1,020 institutions of technical and scientific knowledge existed in Britain, with a membership of about 200,000 (Inkster 1991: 78–79). James Dowey (2017) concluded in his survey of those institutions that they comprised "the world's first infrastructure for commercial R&D," which thus facilitated "the acceleration in technological innovation that lay behind the transition to modern economic growth." And on studying the origins of 117 major innovations between 1700 and 1850, Dudley (2012) showed they emerged out of the social networks of which those organisations were the nodes. Those organisations, in short, were the incubators of the Industrial Revolution.

Not all those institutions prioritised research; many were mechanics' institutes, which concentrated on tuition, but those were just as important to technical progress because many of the advances of the Industrial Revolution were micro-advances made by artisans. On 19 October 1826 (p. 459), Dr. Olinthus Gregory told the Deptford Mechanics' Institution that Britain's advances in "agriculture, manufactures, commerce, navigation, the arts and sciences" could be attributed to "[n]ew societies for improvement (among which such societies as this must necessarily be classed)."

Gregory, who taught mathematics at the Royal Military Academy at Woolwich, further praised the Mathematical Society in Spitalfields (founded in 1717) and the Literary and Philosophical Societies of Newcastle upon Tyne, Manchester, Liverpool, Norwich, Sheffield and other industrial and commercial cities, for their promotion of research. Smaller towns were not excepted from these developments, and in the North East, to consider one region, "There were equivalent 'Lit & Phils' at North Shields and Seaham and at Sunderland" (Jackson 2019: 78). These societies, moreover, did not necessarily exclude women: in 1820 the Literary Society of Alnwick (population approximately 5,000) invited Annabel Carr of Newcastle-upon-Tyne, the author of the 1807 book *Conversations on Chemistry*, to lecture on 'mechanics and hydrostatics' (Jackson 2019: 71).

Such societies were particularly associated with eighteenth- and nineteenth-century Britain, not because other countries did not have them – other countries did have them – but because, as Ian Inkster (1991: 78–79) has shown, the British had more than anyone else. We can thus model the take-off of the Industrial Revolution not only as a qualitative matter but as a quantitative one: British industrial research had, in aggregate, crossed the threshold required by the contribution good model.

Meyer (2015) has further shown how the airplane – perhaps the twentieth century's iconic advance – was a product of collective invention. In Meyer's words, "contributors routinely shared inventions and discoveries without explicit exchanges or payoffs ... the invention of the first airplanes – a macro-invention – was based largely on open-source information and networks of colleagues." Before the Wright brothers flew in 1903, there were already nearly 50 aeronautical societies and clubs in existence across the globe (mainly in France, Germany, the USA and Britain) sharing information through meetings, newsletter and publications; and Brockett had listed more than 13,000 relevant research publications, and many hundreds of patents, that had appeared by the time he published his *Bibliography of Aeronautics* in 1910 (Meyer 2015).

Meyer has also chronicled how Octave Chanute played the role of information networker amongst the early airplane pioneers, and amongst his many correspondents were the Wright brothers, who sent him no fewer than 177 letters and to whom, in turn, he sent at least 230 letters (Short 2011). The emergence of a person like Chanute is characteristic of the contribution good, for Kealey and Ricketts (2014) have shown that while a public good model of research presents a 'prisoner's dilemma' problem, a contribution good model presents a 'pure coordination' problem, requiring leadership to help resolve it, and the history of the Scientific and Industrial Revolutions (aka the Research Revolution) confirms the importance of such leadership. Thus, coinciding with the advent of those revolutions, a new vocation appeared, that of 'intelligencer.'

One of the first intelligencers was Samuel Hartlib (1600–1662) who, though originally German, settled in London to dedicate himself to receiving and sending letters to fellow researchers, and who by 1630 had forged a network of around 400 correspondents, from all over Europe. Other early intelligencers included Nicolas-Claude de Peiresc (1580–1637), Marin Mersenne (1588–1648) and Ismaël Boulliau (1605–1694), all of whom lived in France, yet the most consequential was to be Henry Oldenberg, the Royal Society's first Secretary and eventual founding editor of the first scientific journal, *Philosophical Transactions*, whose surviving correspondence for the years 1641–1677 exceeds

3,100 letters from all over Europe.[12,13] Other scientific leaders were to include Mary Herbert of Wilton House, Robert Boyle of the Royal Society and Erasmus Darwin of the Lunar Society.

Industrial research was to demonstrate the same phenomenon. So, the Clockmakers Company presented an example of collective leadership, while Joel Lean (*Lean's Engine Reporter*) performed that role for the Cornish mining industry, and as noted above, Alexander Holley performed that role within the Bessemer Association or patent pool, while Arthur Young and Gerard Muntz performed that role within agriculture and steel, respectively. Meyer (2015) has noted, moreover, that the Homebrew Computer Club, from which Apple and many other Silicon Valley start-ups spun out during the 1970s (which, like the free software movement, speaks to the continued vigour of collective invention today) was facilitated by Lee Felsenstein as a latter-day intelligencer; and Meyer (2003) has further noted that such latter-day information networkers are characteristically "charismatic founders who encouraged openness and did not seize chances to keep the technology secret and extract maximum profit."

Eventually, though, profit will be sought. Meyer (2015) and John Scott and Troy Scott (2017) have noted that researchers' incentives shift during the development of a new field of technology: during the early or 'open technology' phase of development, when 'technological uncertainty' dominates, researchers are motivated primarily by psychic reward, and in Meyer's words, "contributors routinely share(d) inventions and discoveries openly without explicit exchanges or payoff." Or, as the Australian aeronautical pioneer Lawrence Hargrave wrote in 1893 of early airplane research, "workers must root out the idea [that] by keeping the results of their labours to themselves, a fortune will be assured to them" (quoted in Meyer 2012). But when data approach close to commercial exploitation, researchers will default

[12] John Chamberlain (1553–1628) anticipated the scientific intelligencers by being a political, diplomatic and social intelligencer who met with a wide range of similar intelligencers every day at St Paul's Cathedral between the hours of 11.00 a.m. and 12.00 a.m., and 3.00 p.m. and 6.00 p.m., before writing to his political, diplomatic and domestic contacts with the latest news (Osborne 1689: 449–451). Chamberlain was a good friend of William Gilbert, England's first great scientist, with whom he sometimes lodged, thus showing how Gilbert's style of research, being based on a network of scientific contacts, emerged out of, and overlapped with, similar political, diplomatic and social networks (Thomson 1966: x).

[13] The need for scientific intelligencers is perhaps illustrated by Georg Hartmann's discovery of the inclination of the compass, which in 1543 he demonstrated to Charles V and which in 1544 he described in a letter to Duke Albrecht of Prussia. But because the Emperor did not disseminate the information, and because the Duke did not forward the letter to anyone, and because Hartmann apparently did not write to anyone else about the observation (perhaps because he was discouraged by failure of either the Emperor or the Duke to be interested in an observation they all found puzzling), it was lost until inclination was independently rediscovered by Robert Norman, a London instrument maker, who published it in his *Newe Attractive* of 1581. In his pioneering 1269 *Epistola de magnete* or *Letter on the Magnet* (where, like Hartmann and Norman after him, he advocated the experimental method of science), Petrus Peregrinus was luckier than Hartmann, for 39 manuscript copies survive.

in the process Meyer called 'entrepreneurial exit,' to commercialise their discovery: thus the Wright brothers, who were long extremely open in their research, suddenly became secretive in 1903 when they realised they had developed an airplane that worked (Short 2011).

That caesura between pre-competitive and competitive research still operates today. The *Financial Times* described recently how research into Alzheimer's Disease is still at the pre-competitive stage, so the different drug companies have congregated in research roundtables to share their findings. The *Financial Times* reported (cited in Green 2019) of Dr. Mintun, a vice president for R&D at Eli Lilly:

> Lilly's Dr Mintun is encouraged: "It is hard to find an example of such a major disease in which pharmaceutical companies and academic scientists collaborate more than we do in Alzheimer's."
>
> Research roundtables, such as those organised by the Alzheimer's Association, have created "places where we can talk in a pre-competitive way and ask: 'Are there are ideas that haven't had enough hearing? Are there new diagnostic techniques that could affect the way we do trials?'"
>
> Disappointing trials involving BACE inhibitors,[14] which impeded the enzymes that led to the creation of amyloid, started to fit together once companies shared their findings.
>
> "Companies had clinical data that individually they might struggle to make sense of, but when they shared this, we could quickly understand what it meant and make sure we rapidly gained understanding." He challenges the popular narrative that pits large pharma companies against each other in a race to discover a blockbuster cure. "This is genuinely an area where, if any company announced good results, we would all be happy," he says.

Academic scientists, too, will exit when their data come close to publication. Doudna and Sternberg (2017: 242) wrote in their account of the discovery of CRISPR that the "twin poles of science [are] competition and collaboration," which Philip Marsden (2020: 35) echoed when he wrote of the "camaraderie and competitiveness" of research, and which is how the model of innovation as a contribution good remains economically benign, because contribution goods continue, even amongst commercial competitors, to promote the sharing of knowledge: thus Mansfield (1985) has shown that, thanks in part to the mutual contribution of knowledge, industrial secrecy is a myth, and competitors know of each other's advances within 12–18 months of their having made them. Thus we also see that the contribution good is, amongst other things, a mechanism for dispersing second-mover advantage across the research and therefore the industrial communities. James Schmitz (1989) has modelled second-mover advantage as the basis of both

[14] β-site amyloid precursor protein cleaving enzyme inhibitors.

economic growth and of private profit, and the operation of the contribution good is compatible with that model.

To conclude this section, it can be seen that ever since Allen wrote his 1983 paper on collective invention in the Cleveland steel industry during the nineteenth century, further examples have multiplied, and it is probable that many more examples will emerge once the conventions in the discipline change: some economic historians see industries as being either patent-driven or collectively driven (so they look for collective invention only if an industry seems not to be patent-driven) but this may be a false dichotomy, because in the process of entrepreneurial exit many industries may foster patents against a background of collective invention. Thus, Meyer (2015) describes how researchers "may optimally work together, even anticipating that one of them will want to break away when he or she suddenly sees an outside option to (perhaps) get rich."

That an industry is characterised by patents, therefore, does not preclude the possibility that collective invention nonetheless underpins the growth of that industry.

1.7 INTERNATIONAL COMPARISONS

Recognising research as emerging out of institutions of mutual contribution highlights an intriguing historical lacuna. We've already noted two proto-industrial revolutions in Italy and the Netherlands respectively, and each was associated with the inauguration of collective institutions of knowledge exchange; the Western world's first university, Bologna, was founded in 1088, while the Dutch agricultural revolution, which emerged from a cooperative or 'polder' culture, was associated with the creation of universities such as the University of Leuven (1425; Vesalius and Mercator were graduates). Yet, though it has long been recognised that Chinese science and technology were, in many respects, long in advance of Europe's, China nonetheless had no Industrial Revolution. And China appears never to have created associations for the pursuit of knowledge. Universities, for example, represent such associations, but as Macfarlane (2002) wrote: "Another kind of association, for the pursuit of knowledge, is the university, an archetype in the west of fellowship and equality ... yet it never developed in China and Japan."

The university is only one type of institution that nurtures the contribution good, but the absence of universities in China reflects the fact that China seems not to have produced societies such as the Royal Society or the Lunar Society for the mutual advance of science and technology. Its advances were therefore limited only to those of individuals, which under a model of the contribution good would preclude the development of an Industrial Revolution.[15]

[15] Kelly argues that China's markets were sufficient to maintain only Smithian as opposed to Schumpeterian growth (Morgan Kelly 1997: 939–964). Needham argued that China failed to

It was Japan that was to realise "the first completely successful instance of Asian assimilation of modern Western manufacturing technology," which Japan achieved during the nineteenth century in cotton-spinning Saxonhouse (1974: 150). And Saxonhouse showed this was achieved by the different firms, though being highly competitive, nonetheless sharing knowledge with each other with marked openness in the Dai Nihon Bōseki Rengōkai (All Japan Cotton Spinners Association).

Saxonhouse also showed that the Japanese success in cotton-spinning occurred only after the government had ceased to involve itself in the industry, which illustrates a recurring theme; thus, Lux and Cook (1998) have advanced an observation that further illustrates British *laissez faire* advantage during the seventeenth century over France's research under absolutism and *dirigisme*. Complementing its role as a collective research laboratory, the Royal Society also operated as a node in a long-distance information network; when, for example, in July 1665 Henry Oldenburg, the Secretary of the Royal Society, received a letter from a researcher in Lyons, France, describing a novel spherical mirror; he wrote to at least ten other researchers (probably more, but not all the correspondence has survived) with the news. And he received at least 11 letters of commentary (five from abroad) in response.

But Oldenburg's information network was disrupted after 1666 when the French King created the *Academie des Sciences*. The *Academie* crowded out the pre-existing, private, Thevenot Academy in Paris, but whereas Thevenot Academy had promoted the open disclosure of knowledge, the *Academie* opened under an official policy of secrecy. Whereupon Oldenburg's most important French correspondents simply stopped corresponding usefully. So in December 1666 Adrien Auzout, who had been writing to Oldenberg on a monthly basis, wrote to apologise for his silence over the previous six months with: "Although I had the honour to be appointed by the King as a mathematician and physicist, I can't give you more details than are known to everybody," while by December 1667 Henri Justel, another of Oldenburg's most assiduous correspondents but not an academician, is writing, "I cannot tell you what our academicians are to work at, as they keep it secret." In the words of Lux and Cook, the founding of "the Paris Academy and the closing of the Thevenot seriously broke the chain of communications." Only with the reforms of 1699, a third of a century later, did the *Academie* embrace openness; thus had the government funding of science in France held back the advance of knowledge.

Further, the *Academie* excluded entrepreneurs. So Francis Vernon, the secretary to the English ambassador, reported in May 1669 that: "[T]he Royal Academie are not as ours in Engld – a great assembly of Gentlemen, Butt only a few Persons wch are eminent [in science], & not in number above 13. or 14." No-one was recognised

create a Scientific or Industrial Revolution because it failed to generate "a mercantile culture" (Joseph Needham 2003: xiii). Here we need note only the absence in China of associations for the pursuit of knowledge.

by the *Academie* unless he was already an academician in receipt of a state salary of 1500 Livres per annum, whereas – in contradistinction – the Charter of the Royal Society conferred upon it the freedom "to enjoy mutual intelligence and knowledge with all and all manner of strangers and foreigners, whether private or collegiate, corporate or politic, without any molestation, interruption, or disturbance whatsoever."

The Royal Society's Charter thus incarnated a similar culture to that of the Greek city states of the first Scientific Revolution, as was articulated by Pericles in his funeral oration of circa 430 BCE, as quoted by Thucydides in his *History of the Peloponnesian War*: "We throw open our city to the world, and never by alien acts exclude foreigners from any opportunity of learning or observing" (Thucydides 2000). Thus the linkage that private societies such as the Royal Society achieved in England, when they brought together holders of financial capital and creators of human capital, and which the private Thevenot Academy had fostered, was destroyed in France when the state started to fund science. And governments can still seek to supress the free creation and sharing of knowledge. As revealed by the title of his book *Crypto: How the Code Rebels Beat the Government – Saving Privacy in the Digital Age* (2001), Steven Levy reported how the US and UK governments sought to suppress not only their own research into public-key technologies but also that of private sector businesses. The federal government in the USA, moreover, has systematically obstructed research into psychoactive agents (Burrus 2019) despite their therapeutic potential (Carhart-Harris et al. 2016).

Vernon's report of how the Royal Society attracted to its meetings "a great assembly of Gentlemen" further supports the suggestion that academic science and commercial research advanced together from the seventeenth century. Thus Francis Bacon, during his years as a senior law officer, 1607–1621, handled about 20 of the 40 patents Parliament then awarded (patents were then awarded by Act of Parliament) and he personally oversaw patents for the "making of copper by dissolution," "water pumps," "tillage of seeds," "conversion of iron into steel," "making of salt," and the "making of glass by sea coal and pit coal." His patentees included Sir David Murray, Lord Edmund Sheffield, Sir John Bourchier, Lord Philip Herbert, Sir Thomas Howard, Sir Robert Mansell, Sir Edward Zouch and Lord Edward Somerset (Pastorino 2017), which illustrates how the social and financial elite in England was then committed to innovation – which was why its members were to attend the meetings of the Royal Society, and which was how the French were to damage themselves when, on their government funding science, they excluded the private sector from the meetings of the *Academie*.

That markets fostered innovation better than did governments was well-understood by British Industrial Revolutionaries. Friedrich Koenig was the German inventor of the high-speed steam-powered printing press, which inaugurated mass-circulation newspapers (*The Times* converted to Koenig presses on 29 November 1814), and Koenig spoke of:

> *The well-known fact* that almost every invention seeks, as it were, refuge in England, and is there brought to perfection, seems to indicate that the continent has yet to learn from her the best manner of encouraging the mechanical arts. I had my full share in the ordinary disappointments of continental projectors, and after having spent, in Germany and Russia, upwards of two years in fruitless applications, I proceeded to England. [italics in the original]
>
> (Gregory 1826: 459–460)

Or, in Dr. Olinthus Gregory's words to the Deptford Mechanics' Institution (1826: 460): "What could not be accomplished by the encouragement of *princes* on the continent, was effected by the aid of private individuals in London" [italics in the original].

1.8 CONCLUSION

We do not suggest that commercially motivated research is the only agent of growth in a modern economy: since the sixteenth century there have been philanthropic, geopolitical and swagger research, which might have stimulated growth. There may be, moreover, some marginal uncompensated spillovers of knowledge, which are emphasised by standard analysis of the economics of science and which are used to make a case for greater levels of research effort. And there will always be secret research, which will produce sub-optimal levels of aggregate growth. The research landscape is therefore complex, yet we nonetheless suggest that the contribution good model of scientific knowledge best explains modern rates of economic growth. In particular, the explosive rate of growth it generates once a threshold has been passed will also account for the explosion of economic growth from circa 0.04 per cent PA to circa 1.8–2.0 per cent PA that characterises the lead industrialised countries today.

The spontaneous 'take-off' that occurs when a sufficient 'critical mass' of scientists and entrepreneurs has been achieved clearly implies that McCloskey's 'bourgeois virtues' have evolved and taken over from aristocratic norms. Without the 'bourgeois deal' and the attraction of talented people to the pursuit of commercial gain, the system would lose its motive force. Our point, however, is that recognising the nature of knowledge as a 'contribution good' rather than a 'public good' is crucial to explaining the historical record. If scientific knowledge is a pure 'public good,' then bourgeois values in themselves will not produce an industrial revolution. Indeed it is possible to argue that the evolution of the 'bourgeois deal' itself would have been much more difficult if scientific advance had, in the nature of things, to be derived from courtly, centralised and elite efforts to raise productivity rather than being the outcome of decentralised commercial activity and the pursuit of 'trade tested betterment' to use McCloskey's phrase.

REFERENCES

Agrawal, Ajay, Devesh Kapur and John McHale. 2008. "How Do Spatial and Social Proximity Influence Knowledge Flows? Evidence from Patent Data." *Journal of Urban Economics* 64: 258–269.

Allen, Darcy and Jason Potts. 2016. "How Innovation Commons Contribute to Discovering and Developing New Technologies." *International Journal of the Commons* 10: 1035–1054.

Allen, Robert. 1983. "Collective Invention." *Journal of Economic Behaviour and Organization* 4: 1–24.

2009. *The British Industrial Revolution in Global Perspective*. Cambridge: Cambridge University Press.

Allen, Thomas, Diane B. Hyman and David L. Pinckney. 1983. "Transferring Technology to the Small Manufacturing Firm." *Research Policy* 12: 199–211.

Apostolides, Alexander, Stephen Broadberry, Bruce Campbell, Mark Overton and Bas van Leeuwen. 2008. *English Agricultural Output and Labour Productivity, 1250–1850, Some Preliminary Estimates*. www.basvanleeuwen.net/bestanden/agriclongrun1250to1850.pdf

Arrow, Kenneth. 1962. "Economic Welfare and the Allocation of Resources for Invention." In *The Rate and Direction of Inventive Activity: Economic and Social Factors*, edited by Richard R. Nelson, pp. 609–625. Princeton, NJ: Princeton University Press.

Arthur, Brian. 2009. *The Nature of Technology: What It Is and How It Evolves*. New York: Free Press.

Aubrey, John. 1982. *Brief Lives*, edited by Richard Barber. Woodbridge: The Boydell Press.

Bacon, Francis. 1626. *New Atlantis*, Reproduced in *The Works of Lord Bacon* (1838). London: William Ball.

Bailey, Michael, Rachel Cao, Thersea Kuchler, Johannes Stroebel and Arlene Wong. 2018. "Social Connectedness: Measurement, Determinants, and Effects." *Journal of Economic Perspectives* 32: 259–280.

Batho, Gordon. 2000. "Thomas Harriot and the Northumberland Household." In *Thomas Harriot: An Elizabethan Man of Science*, edited by Robert Fox, pp. 31–32. London and New York: Routledge.

Baumol, William. 1990. "Entrepreneurship: Productive, Unproductive, and Destructive." *Journal of Political Economy* 8: 893–921.

Bell, Alex, Raj Chetty, Xavier Jaravel, Neviana Petkova and John van Reenen. 2019. "Who Becomes an Inventor in America? The Importance of Exposure to Innovation." *Quarterly Journal of Economics* 134: 647–713.

Bessen, James and Alessandro Nuvolari. 2016. "Knowledge Sharing among Inventors: Some Historical Perspectives." In *Revolutionizing Innovation: Users, Communities, and Open Innovation*, edited by Dietmar Harhoff and Karim R. Lakhani, pp. 135–157. Cambridge, MA: MIT Press.

Broadberry, Stephen, Bruce M. S. Campbell, Alexander Klein, Mark Overton and Bas van Leeuwen. 2015. *British Economic Growth, 1270–1870*. Cambridge: Cambridge University Press.

Brown, James and Michael Slawinski. 2017. *On the Foundations of Seismology: Bringing Idealizations Down to Earth*. Singapore: World Scientific.

Burchardi, Konrad and Tarek Hassan. 2011. *The Economic Impact of Social Ties: Evidence from German Reunification*. NBER Working Paper No. 17186.

Burrus, Trevor. 2019. "The Systematic Prohibition of U.S. Drug Science." In *Scientocracy*, edited by Patrick Michaels and Terence Kealey, pp. 139–160. Washington, DC: The Cato Institute.

Carhart-Harris, Robin, Mark Bolstridge, James Rucker et al. 2016. "Psilocybin with Psychological Support for Treatment-resistant Depression." *Lancet Psychiatry* 3: 619–627.

Clark, Gregory. 2007. *A Farewell to Alms: A Brief Economic History of the World*. Princeton, NJ: Princeton University Press.

Cohen, Wesley and Daniel Levinthal. 1989. "Innovation and Learning: The Two Faces of R&D." *Economics Journal* 99: 569–596.

Cormack, Lesley. 1997. *Charting an Empire: Geography at the English Universities 1580–1620*. Chicago: University of Chicago Press.

Darwin, Charles. 1871. *The Descent of Man, and Selection in Relation to Sex*. London: John Murray.

Dasgupta, Partha and Paul David. 1994. "Toward a New Economics of Science." *Research Policy*. 23: 487–521.

Deane, Phyllis. 1979. *The First Industrial Revolution*. Cambridge: Cambridge University Press.

Doudna, Jennifer and Samuel Sternberg. 2017. *A Crack in Creation*. Boston: Houghton, Mifflin, Harcourt.

Dowey, James. 2017. *Mind over Matter: Access to Knowledge and the British Industrial Revolution*. PhD thesis, University of London.

Dudley, Leonard. 2012. *Mothers of Innovation: How Expanding Social Networks Gave Birth to the Industrial Revolution*. Newcastle upon Tyne: Cambridge Scholars.

2016. "Language Standardization and the Industrial Revolution." *Oxford Economic Papers* 69: 1138–1161.

Edgeworth, Richard. 1844 [1820]. *Memoirs*. London: Richard Bentley.

Erlande-Brandenburg, Alain. 1995. *The Cathedral Builders of the Middle Ages*. London: Thames and Hudson.

Faber, Harald. 1931. *Cooperation in Danish Agriculture*. London: Longmans.

Fanning, Philip. 2009. *Isaac Newton and the Transmutation of Alchemy*. Berkeley, CA: North Atlantic Books.

Fouquet, Roger and Stephen Broadberry. 2015. "Seven Centuries of European Economic Growth and Decline." *Journal of Economic Perspectives* 29: 227–244.

Gilbert, William. 1900 [1600]. *On the Magnet*. Translated by Silvanus Thompson. London: The Chiswick Press, 1900, London.

Granovetter, Mark. 1973. "The Strength of Weak Ties." *American Journal of Sociology* 78: 1360–1380.

Gompel, Stef van. 2019. "Patent Abolition: A Real-Life Historical Study." *Amsterdam University International Law Review* 34: 877–922.

Greener, James. 2015. "Thomas Newcomen and His Great Work." *Journal of the Trevithick Society* 42: 64–127.

Gregory, Olinthus. 1826. "Speech Delivered at the First Anniversary of the Deptford Mechanics' Institution." *Mechanics' Magazine* 6: 458–462.

Green, Adam. 2019. "Failed Trials Spark New Approaches and Ideas." *The Financial Times. FT Health Business & Dementia*, 18 September 2019, 4.

Hartmann, Georg. 1943 [1544]. "The Letter of Georg Hartmann to Duke Albrecht of Prussia," translated by Sydney Chapman. *Journal of Geophysical Research* 48: 128–130.

Hilaire-Pérez, Liliane. 2002. "Diderot's Views on Artists' and Inventors' Rights: Invention, Imitation and Reputation." *The British Journal for the History of Science* 35: 129–150.

Hippel, Eric von. 1998. "The Economics of Product Development by Users." *Management Science* 44: 629–644.

Howard, Nicole. 2004. "Rings and Anagrams: Huygens's System of Saturn." *The Papers of the Bibliographic Society of America* 98: 477–510.

Howes, Anton. 2017a. *The Spread of Improvement: Why Innovation Accelerated in Britain 1547–1851*. Working Paper. www.antonhowes.com/uploads/2/1/0/821082490/spread_of_improvement_working_paper.pdf

2017b. *The Relevance of Skills to Innovation during the British Industrial Revolution, 1547 1851*. Working Paper. https://antonhowes.weebly.com/uploads/2/1/0/8/21082490/howes_innovator_skills_working_paper_may_2017.pdf

Inkster, Ian. 1991. *Science and Technology in History: An Approach to Industrial Development*. Camden, NJ: Rutgers University Press.

Jackson, Dan. 2019. *The Northumbrians: North-East England and Its People*. London: Hurst.

Jaffe, Adam, Manual Trajtenberg and Rebecca Henserson. 1993. "Geographical Location of Knowledge Spillovers as Evidenced by Patent Citations." *Quarterly Journal of Economics* 108: 577–598.

Jones, Eric. 1981. "Agriculture 1700–1780." In *The Economic History of Britain 1700–1900*, edited by Rodney Floud and Deirdre McCloskey, pp. 66–86. Cambridge, MA: Cambridge University Press.

2000. *Growth Recurring: Economic Change in World History*. Ann Arbor: University of Michigan Press.

Kealey, Terence. 2013. *The Case against Public Science*. Washington, DC: The Cato Institute.

Kealey, Terence and Martin Ricketts. 2014. "Modelling Science as a Contribution Good." *Research Policy* 43: 1014–1024.

2020. *Innovative Economic Growth: Seven Stages of Understanding*. Washington, DC: The Cato Institute. www.cato.org/publications/economic-policy-brief/innovative-economic-growth-seven-stages-understanding

Kelly, Morgan. 1997. "The Dynamics of Smithian Growth." *The Quarterly Journal of Economics* 112: 939–964.

Kirk, Dudley. 1996. "Demographic Transition Theory." *Population Studies* 50: 361–387.

Kohn, Meir. 2005. *Origins of Western Economic Success*. https://sites.dartmouth.edu/mkohn/origins/

Koppl, Roger, Abigail Deveraux, Jim Herriott and Stuart Kauffman. 2018. "A Simple Combinatorial Model of World Economic History." *arXiv*. https://arxiv.org/pdf/1811.04502.pdf

Landes, David. 1969. *The Unbound Prometheus: Technical Change and Industrial Development in Western Europe from 1750 to the Present*. New York. Cambridge University Press.

1998. *The Wealth and Poverty of Nations*. New York: Norton.

Latham, Sienna. 2010. *"Lady Alcumy": Elizabethan Gentlewomen and the Practice of Chymistry*. MA thesis, Victoria University of Wellington. https://researcharchive.vuw.ac.nz/xmlui/bitstream/handle/10063/1546/thesis.pdf?sequence=6

Levin, Richard, Alvin K. Klevorick, Richard R. Nelson and Sidney G. Winter. 1987. "Appropriating the Returns from Industrial Research and Development." *Brookings Papers on Economic Activity* 3: 783–820.

Levy, Stephen. 2001. *Crypto: How the Code Rebels Beat the Government – Saving Privacy in the Digital Age*. New York: Penguin Books.
Linden, Stanton. 1974. *Alchemy and the English Literary Imagination, 1385–1633*. Minneapolis: University of Minnesota Press.
Link, Albert and Laura Bauer. 1989. *Cooperative Research in US Manufacturing*. Lexington: Lexington Books.
Lord, John. 1903. *Memoir of John Kay of Bury, Inventor of the Flying Shuttle*. Rochdale: James Clegg.
Lux, David and Harold Cook. 1998. "Closed Circles or Open Networks?: Communications at a Distance during the Scientific Revolution." *History of Science* 36: 179–211.
MacFarlane, Alan. 1978. "The Origins of English Individualism: Some Surprises." *Theory and Society* 6: 255–277.
2002. *The Making of the Modern World: Visions from the West and East*. Basingstoke: Palgrave.
MacLeod, Christine. 1988. *Inventing the Industrial Revolution: The English Patent System, 1660–1800*. Cambridge: Cambridge University Press.
Maddison, Angus. 1982. *Phases of Capitalist Development*. Oxford: Oxford University Press.
2001. *The World Economy: A Millennial Perspective*. Paris: OECD.
Mansfield, Edwin, Mark Schwartz and Samuel Wagner. 1981. "Imitation Costs and Patents: An Empirical Study." *The Economic Journal* 91: 907–918.
Mansfield, Edwin. 1985. "How Rapidly Does New Technology Leak Out?" *Journal of Industrial Economics* 34: 217–223.
1995. "Academic Research Underlying Industrial Innovations: Sources, Characteristics and Funding." *The Review of Economics and Statistics* 77: 55–65.
Marsden, Philip. 2020. "Silent Witnesses." *The Spectator*, 13 June, 34–35.
McCloskey, Deirdre. 2010. *Bourgeois Dignity: Why Economics Cannot Explain the Modern World*. Chicago: University of Chicago Press.
McEvedy, Colin and Richard Jones. 1978. *Atlas of World Population History*. London: Penguin.
Meyer, Peter. 2003. *Episodes of Collective Invention*. Washington, DC: Bureau of Labor Statistics Working Papers No. 368.
2012. *Open Technology and the Early Airplane Industry*. eh.net/eha/wp-content/uploads/2013/11/Meyer.pdf
2015. "The Catapult of Riches: The Invention of the Airplane and Its Industry." In *Institutions, Innovation and Industrialization: Essays in Economic History and Development*, edited by Avner Greif, Lynne Kiesling and John Nye, pp. 201–224. Princeton, NJ: Princeton University Press.
Mokyr, Joel. 2002. *The Gifts of Athena: Historical Origins of the Knowledge Economy*. Princeton, NJ: Princeton University Press.
2009. "The Institutional Origins of the Industrial Revolution." In *Institutions and Economic Performance*, edited by Elhanan Helpman, pp. 64–116. Cambridge, MA: Harvard University Press.
2016. *A Culture of Growth: The Origins of the Modern Economy*. Princeton, NJ: Princeton University Press.
Needham, Joseph. 2003. *Science and Civilisation in China, Vol. 7: Science and Chinese Society*. Cambridge: Cambridge University Press.
Nelson, Richard R. 1959. "The Simple Economics of Basic Scientific Research." *Journal of Political Economy* 67: 297–306.

Newman, William and Lawrence Principe. 1998. "Alchemy vs. Chemistry: The Etymological Origins of a Historiographic Mistake." *Early Science and Medicine* 3: 32–65.
Nuvolari, Alessandro. 2004. "Collective Invention during the British Industrial Revolution: The Case of the Cornish Pumping Engine." *Cambridge Journal of Economics* 28: 347–363.
Ogilvie, Sheilagh. 2014. "The Economics of Guilds." *Journal of Economic Perspectives* 28: 169–192.
Osborne, Francis. 1689. *Works*, 9th ed., pp. 449–451, quoted in Thomson, Elizabeth. 1966. *The Chamberlain Letters*. New York: Capricorn, p. 1.
Ostrom, Elinor. 1990. *Governing the Commons: The Evolution of Institutions for Collective Action*. Cambridge: Cambridge University Press.
Paganelli, Maria Pia. 2015. "Recent Engagements with Adam Smith and the Scottish Enlightenment." *History of Political Economy* 47: 363–394.
Pastorino, Cesare. 2017. "The Philosopher and the Craftsman: Francis Bacon's Notion of Experiment and Its Debt to Early Stuart Inventors." *Isis* 108: 749–768.
Polanyi, Michael. 1958. *Personal Knowledge: Towards a Post-Critical Philosophy*. Chicago: University of Chicago Press.
1962. "The Republic of Science: Its Political and Economic Theory." *Minerva* 1: 54–74.
Potts, Jason. 2019. *Innovation Commons*. Oxford: Oxford University Press.
Price, Derek de Solla. 1963. *Little Science, Big Science*. New York: Columbia University Press.
Purver, Margery. 1967. *The Royal Society: Concept and Creation*. Cambridge, MA: MIT Press.
Reeves, Eileen. 1999. *Painting the Heavens: Art and Science in the Age of Galileo*. Princeton, NJ: Princeton University Press.
Romer, Paul. 1986. "Increasing Returns and Long-Run Growth." *Journal of Political Economy* 94: 1002–1037.
1990. "Endogenous Technical Change." *Journal of Political Economy* 98: S71–S102.
Rosenberg, Nathan. 1980. "Why Do Firms Do Basic Research (with Their Own Money)?" *Research Policy* 19: 165–174.
Saxonhouse, Gary. 1974. "A Tale of Japanese Technological Diffusion in the Meiji Period." *Journal of Economic History* 34: 149–165.
Schmitz, James. 1989. "Imitation, Entrepreneurship and Long-Run Growth." *Journal of Political Economy* 97: 721–739.
Scott, John. 1996. "Environmental Research Joint Ventures among Manufacturers." *Review of Industrial Organization* 11: 655–679.
Scott, John and Troy Scott. 2017. *Intellectual Property, Competition and Science versus Technology*. https://papers.ssrn.com/sol3/papers.cfm?abstract_id=3077524
Shapin, Steven and Simon Schaffer. 1985. *Leviathan and the Air-Pump: Hobbes, Boyle and the Experimental Life*. Princeton, NJ: Princeton University Press.
Shapin, Steven. 1996. *The Scientific Revolution*. Chicago: Chicago University Press.
Shiue, Carol and Wolfgang Keller. 2007. "Markets in China and Europe on the Eve of the Industrial Revolution." *American Economic Review* 97: 1189–1216.
Short, Simine. 2011. *Locomotive to Aeromotive: Octave Chanute and the Transportation Revolution*. Chicago: University of Illinois Press.
Skinner, Quentin. 1969. "Thomas Hobbes and the Nature of the Early Royal Society." *The Historical Journal* 22: 217–239.
Smith, Adam. 1910 [1776]. *Wealth of Nations*. London: Dent.
Solow, Robert. 1957. "Technical Change and the Aggregate Production Function." *Review of Economics and Statistics* 39: 312–320.

Sprat, Thomas. 1667. *The History of the Royal Society of London, for the Improving of Natural Knowledge*. London: The Royal Society.
Stigler, George. 1961. "The Economics of Information." *The Journal of Political Economy* 69: 213–225.
Thucydides. 2000 [ca 431 BCE]. "The History of the Peloponnesian War." *Ancient History Sourcebook*. http://classics.mit.edu/Thucydides/pelopwar.html
Toynbee, Arnold. 1884. *Lectures on the Industrial Revolution in England*. London: Rivington.
Weber, Steven. 2004. *The Success of Open Source*. Harvard, MA: Harvard University Press.
West, Muriel. 1961. "Notes on the Importance of Alchemy to Modern Science in the Writings of Francis Bacon and Robert Boyle." *Ambix* 9: 102–114.
Zilsel, Edgar. 1941. "The Origins of William Gilbert's Scientific Method." *Journal of the History of Ideas* 2: 1–32.

2

On the Social Evolution of Knowledge

Renée Prendergast

In *Understanding Knowledge as a Commons*, Hess and Ostrom (2007: 4) note that *commons* is a general term referring to a resource shared by a group of people. Traditionally, the word commons has been associated with physical resources such as grazing land or fisheries but more recently it has been applied in the context of the knowledge economy. Both knowledge resources and environmental resources are products of evolutionary processes but knowledge resources differ from natural resources in a number of important respects. While natural resources exhibit a high degree of subtractability – use by one reduces the amount available for others – the use of knowledge by one party does not diminish its availability for consumption by others. This non-rivalrous aspect of knowledge may lead to problems of supply since each potential knowledge producer secures only a small proportion of the total benefits to which his or her innovation may give rise. The standard solutions proposed to address this issue involve either government subsidies or the creation of intellectual property rights which allow the innovator to monopolise the benefits deriving from his or her creation for a limited period of time. But, as has long been recognised, property rights do not necessarily solve the problem of undersupply. They may be costly to enforce effectively and may create opportunities for rent seeking. In general, the increased supply is obtained at the cost of delayed diffusion. Moreover, as Frischmann (2012), has noted, when account is taken of the fact that knowledge is built cumulatively over time, and that present knowledge is an input into future knowledge, it is by no means certain that the long-term impact of intellectual property rights is an increase in knowledge output.[1] Hence, the need to identify new institutional/social frameworks to govern knowledge production.

[1] Concerns relating to the proliferation of intellectual property rights in biomedical research on both upstream and downstream innovation led Heller and Eisenberg to suggest a tragedy of an anti-commons leading to the underuse of scarce resources because too many owners can block each other (Heller and Eisenberg 1998). Subsequent research has indicated that this is less of a problem than originally thought especially with regard to upstream investment

The terms 'knowledge economy' and 'knowledge commons' are relatively new and are motivated by the perception that the role of knowledge in the economy is increasingly important and that technologies such as the Internet are of their nature shared resources. While the shared and distributed features of the Internet have made it natural to think of it as a commons or at least a potential commons, Madison et al. (2009) emphasise that 'knowledge commons' refers not to properties of knowledge itself but to an institutional approach to governing its management or production. What makes something a commons is not inherent in the resource but depends on the relationship between the resource and the relevant user/producer community. If being a commons is not something inherent in a resource but rather built from 'intentional' human activity, it becomes important to understand the histories and narratives that underpin commons management of the resource in question. As Madison et al. (2009: 375) note, we need to ask questions such as: why a commons might be good thing in a particular context, whether perceptions have changed over time and what conflicts were embedded in changes of narrative and perception.

This chapter aims to examine the historical emergence of the main narratives relating to the broad categories of knowledge relevant to economic progress. In doing so, we need to remember that the relevant community depends on the particular context – sometimes it is humankind in general, sometimes a subset in the form of a nation, a particular demographic or specialist group. The narratives that today inform our understanding of knowledge emerged historically. It is therefore important to comprehend the circumstances which governed that emergence and of the changing relationship between knowledge generation, production and economic growth.

Our story begins at the end of sixteenth century with Francis Bacon's challenge to the belief in a classical golden age of knowledge inherited from the ancient world, and with his assertion that the progress of knowledge was continuing and cumulative and depended in large part on practical scientific experiment. It then examines the elaboration of this concept over the following two centuries and the beginnings of an understanding that knowledge evolution takes place within, and is dependent on, a wider social and institutional framework. The initiation of this approach is found particularly in the work of Mandeville and Ferguson in the eighteenth century. Both stressed that knowledge results from a wide collective process of learning derived to a large extent from everyday involvement in the ordinary business of life. This insight was soon lost as the classical political economists made capital the centrepiece of their theory of growth. The change in focus was originally due to Adam Smith who

(Eisenberg 2008). From the rather different perspective of profiting from innovation, Teece (2018) has pointed to the special problems associated with value capture in the case of innovators of enabling technologies and the consequent likelihood of private underinvestment in innovation in these technologies.

for methodological reasons singled out capital as the connecting principle binding together various factors contributing to growth (Thomson 1965; Smith 1980: II.12; IV.19). Although challenged, amongst others by Bentham, List and Rae, this catch-all concept of capital as the driving force of productive change dominated economics through most of the nineteenth and twentieth centuries. Meanwhile, the concept of communally acquired knowledge was either classed as an externality or transferred, with Edmund Burke and the German historical school, into the study of civil institutions where it became associated with preservation of tradition rather than progressive change. Only with the development of the knowledge economy in the later decades of the twentieth century has the focus on knowledge as the driver of progress returned to centre stage.

2.1 KNOWLEDGE: THE PRODUCT OF COMMUNAL EFFORT OVER TIME

Francis Bacon (1561–1626) is widely regarded as the initiator of the modern approach to knowledge with its focus on understanding and shaping natural processes and its vision of knowledge as the product of a communal effort rather than individual effort (Gaukroger 2001). For Bacon, the proper aim of science was the endowment of human life with new inventions and riches. This, however, did not mean that all scientific effort had to be immediately useful or profitable. As Bacon noted, the expectation of future progress required experiments that led to the discovery of causes and axioms that were enlightening as opposed to immediately profitable (Bacon 1902: 80). Bacon was of the view that excessive reverence for the thought of antiquity could hold back progress in the sciences and he challenged the then popular view of a golden age of Greece and Rome and a subsequent degeneration of mankind. Bacon argued that the use of the word antiquity with respect to the Greek and Roman world was misleading. Being earlier in time, the world was younger then and would therefore be expected to have a lower stock of knowledge. Bacon concluded, ‘we have reason to expect much greater things of our own age . . . than from antiquity, since the world has grown older, and its stock has been increased and accumulated with an infinite number of experiments and observations. Truth is rightly named the daughter of time, not authority’ (Bacon 1902: 61–62). While Bacon emphasised that people in his own age had the potential to know more, he did not envisage any simple accumulation of knowledge. Obstacles in the form of idols and false notions needed to be guarded against or removed. New additions to knowledge required the use of appropriate methods (Bacon 1902: 8).

Bacon placed considerable emphasis on the importance of the mechanical arts and discoveries. The invention of printing, gunpowder and the compass had given rise to far-reaching changes in the state of the whole world: first in literature, then in warfare, and lastly in navigation. However, the importance of the mechanical arts for

Bacon lay not just in their impact but in the model they offered for the organisation of scientific inquiry in which the key to progress was collaboration (Eamon 1996).

> In arts mechanical the first deviser comes shortest, and time addeth and perfecteth; but in sciences the first author goes furthest, and time lesseth and corrupteth. So we see artillery, sailing, printing and the like, were grossly managed at first, and by time accommodated and refined; but contrariwise the philosophies and sciences of Aristotle, Plato, Democritus . . ., of most vigor at first, and by time degenerate and imbased; where of the reason is no other, but that in the former many wits and industries have contributed in one; and in the latter many wits and industries have been spent about the wit of some one, whom many times they have depraved rather than illustrated.
>
> (cited in Eamon 1996: 323)

Bacon's distinction between the potential for progress in the mechanical arts as opposed to philosophy was original to him. However, the view that progress in knowledge and invention was the product of communal effort over time was not entirely new. Hayek (1967) cited Cicero to the effect that Roman law was founded on the genius not of one man but of many and not in one generation but in a long period of several centuries and many ages of men. In the early eighteenth century, the physicians Georgio Baglivi and Bernard Mandeville both cited Galen as the original authority for the communal point of view (Prendergast 2014: 90–91). Probably the most influential medical researcher of antiquity, Galen sought a mid-way between pure rationalist and pure empiricist approaches to medicine and based his writings on experiments and dissection as well as theory. These became the mainstay of medical training for well over a thousand years, being superseded only in the mid-sixteenth century. Having defined history as 'an account of what one has perceived oneself or an account compiled from books of those things on which all who have written about the matter agree', Galen argued that the empiricist has to make use of history 'because of the vastness of the art, since one man's life will not suffice to find out everything' (Galen 1985: 33–34).

As Bury (1960: 78–97) notes, the challenge to the prevalent theory of degeneration which began in the early seventeenth century led, in France and England, to a century-long literary war over the comparative merits of the ancients and moderns.[2] It is no accident that the controversy arose at a time when scientific effort was accelerating and a millennium and a half of virtual stagnation was coming to an end. Amongst those who argued that contemporary learning had surpassed that of

[2] Fontenelle's *Digression sur les anciens et les modernes* in 1688 and a work along similar lines by Perrault provoked a response from Sir William Temple in the form of his *Essays on Ancient and Modern Learning and on Poetry* in 1690. Temple's essay focused English attention on the controversy and may have inspired Jonathan Swift's satirical Battle of the Books. Much of this wider literature debated the relative merits of the ancients and moderns and rehearsed Bacon's critique of pure rationalism and pure empiricism.

the ancients were the French polymath Blaise Pascal (1623–1662) and the science populariser Bernard le Bovier de Fontenelle (1657–1757). Pascal's position is set out in the Preface to his *Treatise on Vacuum* first published in 1651. In the said Preface, Pascal explained why knowledge was cumulative in the sciences that are subject to experiment and reasoning and, consequently, why the knowledge of the present generation in these subjects was greater than that of the ancients. Men differed from the animals in that they were capable of accumulating knowledge (Pascal 1910: 448).

> [Man] is ignorant at the earliest age of his life; but he is instructed unceasingly in his progress; for he derives advantage, not only from his own experience, but also from that of his predecessors; ... And as he preserves this knowledge, he can also add to it easily; ... not only does each man advance from day to day in the sciences, but all mankind together make continual progress in proportion as the world grows older, since the same thing happens in the succession of men as in the different ages of single individuals. So that the whole succession of men, during the course of many ages, should be considered as a single man who subsists forever and learns continually.
>
> (Pascal 1910: 449)

The metaphor employed by Bacon and Pascal in referring to their own time as the old age of the world had the drawback that it appeared to exclude the idea of indefinite progress of knowledge (Bury 1960: 109). Rejecting the metaphor, Fontenelle argued that mankind would have no old age because the sound views of scientific men in successive generations would continually add to what was already known.[3] Scientific progress would therefore go on indefinitely. Progress in the sciences was the result of chance but had its own order and rule. Each addition to knowledge happened only when earlier discoveries had laid the foundations for it (Devaille 1910: 215–217; Bury 1960: 110–113). In other words, human knowledge develops in a structured manner with the later possibilities being determined by the earlier achievements. This broad position on the progress of knowledge appears to have become the new orthodoxy. As shown below, in one form or another, a series of writers including Mandeville, Ferguson, Turgot, Condorcet, Babbage and Marx saw knowledge as an ever-growing product of the joint labour of several ages.

Both Mandeville and Ferguson are discussed in later sections of this chapter, so reference to them here will be brief. Mandeville's commitment to a cumulative and collective view of knowledge is evident in a number of his works but especially in the second volume of his *Fable of the Bees*. There, he refers to many useful arts and

[3] While Fontenelle's point is important, it is worth noting that much of Bacon's effort was directed towards removing the obstacles to progress in the sciences. He lamented the fact that men were satisfied by the small amount that had been achieved to date (Bacon 1902, I: A88). He also argued that one of the greatest obstacles to the advancement of the sciences was a lack of hope or the despair of success which, in turn, he attributed to men's perception of the shortness of individual life and the obscurity of nature (Bacon 1902, I: A102).

sciences being the result 'human sagacity in general, and the joint labour of many ages, in which men have always employed themselves in studying and contriving ways and means to soothe their various appetites, and make the best of their infirmities' (Mandeville 1924, II: 128). Likewise, in his *Essay on the History of Civil Society*, Adam Ferguson (1723–1816) wrote: 'men continue their works in progression through many ages together: They build on foundations laid by their ancestors; and in a succession of years, tend to a perfection in the application of their faculties, to which the aid of long experience is required, and to which many generations must have combined their endeavours (Ferguson 1782: 7).

The young Turgot (1727–1781), in his *Philosophical Review of the Successive Advances of the Human Mind*, wrote that 'all ages are successively bound up with one another by a succession of causes and effects which link the present state of the world with all those that have preceded it. The arbitrary signs of speech and writing, by providing men with the means of securing the possession of their ideas and communicating them to others, have made of all the individual stores of knowledge a common treasure house which one generation transmits to another, an inheritance which is always being enlarged by the discoveries of each age' (Turgot 1913, I: 215; Meek 1973: 41). Likewise, in his *Plan of the Discourses on Universal History*, Turgot referred to man transmitting his acquired ideas to his successors 'as a heritage which is always being augmented'. He continued: 'A continual combination of this progress with the passions, and with the events they have caused, constitutes the history of the human race, in which each man is no more than one part of an immense whole which has, like him its infancy and its advancement' (Turgot 1808: 212; Meek 1973: 63).

Written in 1793 while he was imprisoned by the Robespierre faction of French revolutionaries, Condorcet's (1743–1794) *Sketch for a Historical Picture of the Progress of the Human Mind* proposed that humankind progresses continuously towards perfection. Progress would continue in the future due to the destruction of inequality between different nations; the progress of equality in one and the same nation; and lastly, the real improvement of man (Condorcet 1796: 251). Like his mentor, Turgot, Condorcet believed that freedom of commerce would lead to greater equality within countries whereas his expectation of greater equality between countries was due to his belief that once development began in poor countries, it would progress rapidly because they could quickly learn things that had taken Europeans a long time to discover (Condorcet 1796: 254–259). As far as the amelioration of the human race is concerned, Condorcet thought that new discoveries in the sciences and the arts[4] would continue to be made, and, that as a consequence, there would be improvements in the means of individual and general prosperity. As new discoveries are made, they are gradually simplified and integrated with existing

[4] Condorcet believed that the view that progress in the arts was necessarily limited was no more than a prejudice (Condorcet 1796: 282).

knowledge so that they can be grasped by those of ordinary capacity. Hence, the progress of the sciences allowed progress of the art of instruction, which, in turn, accelerated the progress of the sciences. As a result of better organisation of the knowledge that had been achieved, in every generation, 'what may be acquired in a given space of time, by the same strength of intellect and the same degree of attention, will necessarily increase' (Condorcet 1796: 285). Condorcet was also of the view that there would be a real improvement in human beings themselves as a result of better nutrition, housing, sanitation, regular exercise and medical practice (Condorcet 1796: 289–290).

2.2 THE SUBSUMPTION OF KNOWLEDGE WITHIN THE CONCEPT OF CAPITAL

It is evident that, by the late eighteenth century, authors such as Condorcet connected the accumulation of knowledge to wider processes of social change. This perspective was reinforced by the emergence in Scotland and in France of a stages view of history with each stage characterised by a different mode of subsistence and corresponding legal and social institutions (Pascal 1938; Meek 1976; Skinner 1982). Such a materialist and historical perspective implies recognition of the importance of institutions and there is no doubt that Smith, as a leading member of the Scottish branch of this school, was very much pre-occupied with establishing the institutional conditions under which the market mechanism would operate effectively (Rosenberg 1960). However, as Rosenberg has noted, later generations stripped the institutional aspect from Smith's presentation of the role of the price mechanism in resource allocation. Likewise, the relationship which Smith had postulated between capital and growth underwent important changes. Whereas in his discussion of growth issues, Smith used the concept of capital as a connecting principle subsuming other factors contributing to development, in the hands of his successors, capital accumulation came to be seen as the sole driver of development. As a result, the role of knowledge disappeared from view (Prendergast 2010). Although a number of authors criticized Smith and his followers for neglecting the accumulation of knowledge as an autonomous motor of economic growth, their critiques had limited influence and there was no systematic revival of knowledge-based approaches to economic growth until the twentieth century. Authors such as Hodgskin (1825) suggested an ideological motive for the focus on capital. Hodgskin argued that knowledge rather than capital was the source of increased productivity and that consequently capital had no right to appropriate the entire surplus.[5]

[5] Before many of our most useful machines and instruments could be invented, a vast deal of knowledge gathered in the progress of the world by many generations was necessary. At present also a great number of persons possessed of different kinds of knowledge and skill must combine and cooperate, although they have never entered into any express contract for this purpose, before many of our most powerful machines can be completed and

Arguments relating to the importance of the independent role of knowledge accumulation came from other quarters as well. Throughout his career, Charles Babbage consistently maintained that the arts and manufactures of a country were intimately connected with the progress of the 'severer sciences' (Babbage 1835: 379). In *The Exhibition of 1851*, Babbage noted that, in fulfilling their exiting wants and necessities, each generation availed of the knowledge bequeathed to them by their predecessors. They also purified the knowledge which it had inherited and added to it for the benefit of their children. Remember, Babbage argued

> that accumulated knowledge, like accumulated capital, increases at compound interest: but it differs from the accumulation of capital in this; that the increase of knowledge produces a more rapid rate of progress, whilst the accumulation of capital leads to a lower rate of interest. Capital thus checks its own accumulation: knowledge accelerates its own advance. Each generation, therefore, to deserve comparison with its predecessor, is bound to add much more largely to the common stock than that which it immediately succeeds.
>
> (Babbage 1968: 210–211)

Like Smith, Marx is mainly focused on the role of capital but his conception of capital encompassed social relations of production as well as fixed capital in the form of machines, buildings and so forth. In the early draft of *Capital* commonly known as *Grundrisse*, he was explicit that the full development of capital took place only when the machine as the technological application of science dominated the production process. Whereas Hodgskin emphasised that the knowledge which appeared to belong to capital really resided in the engineers and workmen who contributed to the creation of machinery, Marx appears to accept that the general productive forces of the social mind are absorbed into capital. As he put it:

> before they can be used. The labour of the draughtsman is as necessary to construct a ship as the labour of the man who fastens her planks together. The labour of the engineer, who 'in his mind's eye' sees the effect of every contrivance, and who adapts the parts of a complicated machine to each other, is as necessary to the completion of that machine as the man who casts or fits any part of it, without being sensible of the purpose for which the whole is to serve. In like manner the labour and the knowledge of many different persons must be combined before almost any product intended for consumption can be brought to market. The knowledge and skill of the master manufacturer, or of the man who plans and arranges a productive operation, who must know the state of the markets and the qualities of different materials, and who has some tact in buying and selling, are just as necessary for the complete success of any complicated operation as the skill of the workmen whose hands actually alter the shape and fashion of these materials. Far be it, therefore, from the manual labourer, while he claims the reward due to his own productive powers, to deny its appropriate reward to any other species of labour, whether it be of the head or the hands. The labour and skill of the contriver, or of the man who arranges and adapts a whole, are as necessary as the labour and skill of him who executes only a part, and they must be paid accordingly.
>
> (Hodgskin 1825)

> The accumulation of knowledge and of skill, of the general productive forces of the social mind, is thus absorbed into capital, as opposed to labour, and hence appears as a property of capital, more precisely, of fixed capital, to the extent that it enters into the production process as means of production in the strict sense.
>
> (Marx 1987: 84)[6]

Later in the same work, he argued that:

> The development of fixed capital shows the degree to which society's general science, KNOWLEDGE, has become an *immediate productive force*, and hence the degree to which the conditions of the social life process itself have been brought under the control of the GENERAL INTELLECT and remoulded according to it. It shows the degree to which the social productive forces are produced not merely in the form of knowledge but as immediate organs of social praxis, of the actual life process.
>
> (Marx 1987: 92)

Marx is here acknowledging not only that knowledge is a productive force but also that knowledge is bound up and cannot be separated from society's structures and practices. As we shall see this view predated Marx and was to be found already in the work of authors such as Mandeville and Hume.

2.3 DIFFERENT VIEWS OF KNOWLEDGE

2.3.1 *Knowledge Is Not Separate from Artefacts, Practices, Laws and Institutions*

When authors such as Pascal and Fontenelle or even Turgot and Condorcet wrote about knowledge, they primarily had in mind formal scientific knowledge and knowledge of the arts. A very different way of viewing knowledge emerged in the writings of the Dutch born physician Bernard Mandeville (1670–1733). Mandeville agreed with his predecessors that knowledge is the product of communal effort taking place over long periods of time but the knowledge he has in mind is not necessarily embodied in symbols but could instead be embodied not only in artefacts but also in the practices of human beings as they go about the ordinary business of life. Particularly in volume II of his *Fable of the Bees*, Mandeville spelt out the means by which the joint labour of men of ordinary capacity led to progress in many useful arts and sciences.

6 The Anglo Irish 'utopian' socialist William Thompson had earlier noted that 'knowledge was capable of being detached from labour and opposed to it. He saw this separation as something that accompanied progress. However, he was optimistic that the separation would be overcome in the co-operative society of the future (Thompson 1824: 274–275).

> To men who never turn'd their thoughts that way, it certainly is almost inconceivable to what prodigious height, from next to nothing, some arts may be and have been raised by human industry and application, by the uninterrupted labour and joint experience of many ages, though none but men of ordinary capacity should ever be employed in them.
>
> (Mandeville 1924, II: 141–142)

Mandeville's particular example was a ship, specifically 'a first–rate man of war', which he regarded 'as vastly superior to any other moveable body of human invention'. He argued that, provided they had access to proper materials, that there were many 'sets of hands' in the nation that could produce such a ship in less than six months. The division of labour was key to this. The task would not be possible 'if it was not divided and sub-divided into a great variety of different labours; and it is certain that none of the labours require any other, than working men of ordinary capacities' (Mandeville 1924, II:142).

Mandeville emphasised that the progress that had been made in shipbuilding was not the product of genius or deep penetration but instead was due to the cumulative experience of many generations. The Chevalier Reneau had written a book in which he showed the mechanism of sailing and accounted mathematically for everything that belonged to the working and steering of a ship. Mandeville allowed that Monsieur Reneau's reasoning was correct but he insisted that those who first invented ships and who afterwards improved them were ignorant of those reasons. He continued:

> They are seldom the same sort of people, those that invent arts and improvements in them, and those that enquire into the reason of things . . . none succeed oftener in the first, than active stirring and laborious men, such as will put their hand to the plough, try experiments and give all their attention to what they are about.
>
> (Mandeville 1924: 144)

At one level, Mandeville is simply saying that the division of labour – a term which he was the first to use – plays a vital role in allowing the production of complicated objects and also in facilitating experiments and innovation. When people specialize, they not only become useful to one another 'but the callings and employments themselves will in the same number of years receive much greater improvements, than if all had been promiscuously followed' by each person (Mandeville 1924, II: 284). One might also note that a corollary of the division of labour is that knowledge itself is divided up. That gives rise to some advantages in that it facilitates the transmission of knowledge between generations through learning by doing, by means of apprenticeships, and by forms of specialist education (Mandeville 1924, I: 58–61). It also gives rise to the need for co-ordination – 'how to get services performed by others when we have occasion for them, is the grand and almost constant solicitude in life of every individual person' (Mandeville 1924, II: 349). Note also that the references to Reneau's work suggest that scientific understanding of what has been created comes at the end rather than the beginning of creative activity. The full importance of this may be better understood, if we take account of the fact that what Mandeville wrote about ships applied not just to artefacts but to the laws and practices of human society as the following remarks relating to the regulations governing a large city make clear.

> Remember what ... I told you concerning the arts of shipbuilding and politeness. The wisdom I speak of, is not the offspring of a fine understanding, or intense thinking, but of a sound and deliberate judgement, acquired from a long experience in business, and a multiplicity of observations .... It is common now to have clocks, that are made to play several tunes with great exactness: The study and labour, as well as trouble of disappointments, which, in doing and undoing, such a contrivance must necessarily have cost from beginning to end, are not to be thought of without astonishment: There is something analogous to this in the government of a flourishing city, that has lasted uninterrupted for several ages: There is no part of the wholesome regulations belonging to it, even the most trifling and minute, about which great pains and consideration have not been employed, as well as length of time; and if you look into the history and antiquity of any such city, you will find that the changes, repeals, additions and amendments, that have been made in and to the laws and ordinances by which it is ruled, are in number prodigious.
>
> (Mandeville 1924,II: 322–323)

2.3.2 *Knowledge as Problem-Solving Activity*

Mandeville believed in the primacy of practical over theoretical knowledge. This seems to have been in part a reflection of his view that practical knowledge was more comprehensive. In A *Treatise of the Hypochondriak and Hysterick Diseases*, Mandeville argued that the proper teaching of anatomy required more than knowledge of every part of the inside of the body. In addition, the student of anatomy should be 'expert at dissecting ... He ought to know ... the names of every muscle in the body and how to go to them readily and separate them from those they are annexed to, without mangling or injuring the adjacent parts' (Mandeville 1730: 196–197). Likewise, in volume II of *Fable of the Bees*, Mandeville attempted a distinction between different kinds of knowing which has something in common with modern distinctions between information and knowledge. There was, he argued, a great difference between knowledge in the sense of information received and stored and knowledge in the sense of ability to retrieve information and use it for our purposes (Mandeville 1924, II: 171). There were, Mandeville continued, 'Men of prodigious reading that have likewise great memories, who judge ill, and seldom say anything *a propos*'. 'Knowledge must have lain in their Heads, as Furniture at an Upholder's; and the Treasure of the Brain was a Burden to them, instead of an Ornament!' (Mandeville 1924: 171–172).

While those with book knowledge did not always have the ability to use it, Mandeville also pointed out that not all knowledge was expressible in words.[7] In the *Treatise of the Hypochondriak and Hysterick Diseases*, he noted that:

> A curious observer learns in time to distinguish, between things that very nearly resemble one another, have the same name, and seem to those who are less acquainted with them not to differ at all .... A man may know a thing perfectly well, and at the same time not be able to tell you, why, or how he comes to know it.
>
> (Mandeville 1730: 61)

As a further illustration of this point, Mandeville gave the example of his conviction that a certain painting was an original by Van Dyke. Although he was convinced that this was the case, it would be impossible for him to explain why it was so especially to somebody who had no skill in painting (Mandeville 1730: 62).

Consideration of the view that true knowledge related to the ability to act rather than book learning is also to be found in Adam Ferguson's *Essay on the History of Civil Society*, Ferguson (1723–1816) drew parallels between the activities of those engaged in scientific endeavours and those engaged in business. Both sought to 'collect a multiplicity of particulars under general heads, and to refer a variety of operations to their common principle' (Ferguson 1782: 43). They measured their own abilities by their capacity to identify what is important in every subject, and the facility with which they extricate themselves on every trying occasion. Ferguson emphasised that it was these, and not the extent of book learning which were 'the proper test of capacity and force'.

> The parade of words and general reasonings, which sometimes carry an appearance of so much learning and knowledge, are of little avail in the conduct of life. The talents from which they proceed, terminate in mere ostentation, and are seldom connected with that superior discernment which the active apply in times of perplexity; much less with that intrepidity and force of mind which are required in passing through difficult scenes.
>
> (Ferguson 1782: 45)

Men, Ferguson continued, should be estimated based not on what they know but what they were able to perform 'from their skill in adapting materials to the several purposes of life; from their vigour and conduct in pursuing the objects of policy, and in finding the expedients of war and national defence. Even in literature, they are to be estimated from the works of their genius, not from the extent of their knowledge' (Ferguson 1782: 48).

7 Mandeville was amongst the first to devise an evolutionary theory of language. He believed that people would 'make themselves intelligible to each other by signs and gestures, before they would attempt it by sounds: But when they lived together for many years, it is very probable, that for the things they were most conversant with they would find out sounds, to stir up in each other the idea's of such things when they were out of sight' (Mandeville 1924, II: 288).

2.4 THE OWL OF MINERVA?

Earlier, it was noted that Mandeville's references to Reneau's work suggest that a full scientific understanding of what has been created comes at the end rather than the beginning of creative activity. Ferguson made a connected claim, namely that the forms of society 'arise, long before the date of philosophy, from the instincts, not from the speculations of men'. As he put it in the passage made famous by F. A. Hayek:

> Every step and every movement of the multitude, even in what are termed enlightened ages, are made with equal blindness to the future; and nations stumble upon establishments, which are indeed the result of human action, but not the execution of any human design.
>
> (Ferguson 1782: 205)

In a later part of the work, Ferguson explained that the 'establishments of men, like those of every animal, are suggested by nature, and are the result of instinct, directed by the variety of situations in which mankind are placed'. They arose from 'successive improvements that were made, without any sense of their general effect' and which cannot be fully comprehended even when the whole is carried into effect (Ferguson 1782: 304). Ferguson continued:

> Who could anticipate, or even enumerate, the separate occupations and professions by which the members of any commercial state are distinguished; the variety of devices which are practised in separate cells, and which the artist, attentive to his own affair, has invented, to abridge or to facilitate his separate task? In coming to this mighty end, every generation, compared to its predecessors, may have appeared to be ingenious; compared to its followers, may have appeared to be dull: And human ingenuity, whatever heights it may have gained in a succession of ages, continues to move with an equal pace, and to creep in making the last, as well as the first, step of commercial or civil improvement.

It is clear that, as with Mandeville before him, Ferguson was of the view that people act without awareness of the full consequences of their actions with the result that they may produce effects that they did not anticipate. Consequences may be unforeseen due to bounded rationality which, in turn, may be linked to complexity, on the one hand, and specialization, on the other hand. This, however, is not the whole story because, as we have seen, both Mandeville and Ferguson envisage a situation where innovation is taking place and each generation progresses beyond what was achieved by its predecessor. Since novelty of its nature has to be actualised before it can be analysed, an understanding of what has been created comes after rather than before the event. This is not to say that knowledge is unimportant – existing knowledge in whatever form is an input into the creation of the new. But as Hegel wrote in the introduction to *Philosophy of Right*, 'Philosophy, as the thought of the world, does not appear until reality has completed its formative process, and made itself ready' (Hegel 2001: 20). Note, however, Ferguson's qualification that the establishments of men 'cannot be fully comprehended even when the whole is carried into effect'. In other words, human beings cannot even fully understand what they have already created.

2.5 CONTINUITY, REVOLUTION AND THE DIFFICULTY OF PREDICTION

Ferguson's contemporary, Edmund Burke (1723–1792) was also of the view that human beings were unlikely to fully understand the nature of the institutions they had constructed. He particularly emphasised that policy should be based on 'actual circumstances' rather than 'mere abstract principles' (Burke 1981: 193–194). He put this most colourfully and controversially in *Reflections on the Revolution in France* where he wrote of being unable to give praise or blame to anything relating to human actions or concerns 'on a simple view of the object, as it stands stripped of every relation, in all the nakedness and solitude of metaphysical abstraction' (Burke 1989: 58). He insisted that the science of constructing or reforming a commonwealth was an experimental science requiring long experience 'because the real effects of moral causes were not always immediate' (Burke 1989: 111–112). A policy that produced unfavourable effects in the short term might have good long-term consequences and vice versa. Since even a lifetime of experience might not be sufficient to appreciate the remote consequences of actions 'it is with infinite caution that any man ought to venture upon pulling down an edifice which has answered in any tolerable degree for ages the common purposes of society, or on building it up again, without having models and patterns of approved utility before his eyes' (Burke 1989).

Society was a contract but not an ordinary contract for goods which could be dissolved by the fancy of the parties. 'It is a partnership in all science; ... in all art; ... in every virtue, and in all perfection. As the ends of such a partnership cannot be obtained in many generations, it becomes a partnership not only between those who are living, but between those who are living, those who are dead, and those who are to be born'.[8] As such, the present generation were not at liberty 'to dissolve it into an unsocial, uncivil, unconnected chaos of elementary principles' based on speculations of contingent improvement. All of this implied that change should be approached with considerable circumspection because the results of change 'cannot be certainly known beforehand' (Burke 1989: 121). Despite all these strictures about the dangers of change, Burke was very much aware that change was important. He, himself, was a tireless social reformer and he insisted that a state without the means of some change is without the means of its conservation.

8 The difference between Burke's position and that of the American founding fathers is suggested by Thomas Jefferson's letter to James Madison of 6 September 1789 in which he argued that one generation of men did not have the right to bind another.

Burke's *Reflections* was translated into German and was influential amongst adherents of Romanticism and the German Historical School of Law. The school rejected reason-based law and recognised traditional law as the established law. Its most important member was Friedrich Carl von Savigny (1779–1861). Against the philosophical school of natural rights, Savigny argued that true cognition of the human condition could only be established by historical means (Klenner 1989). No era gives rise to a new world arbitrarily. Everything new was derived from the entire past of a nation, and consequently was historically determined. Law emerged and developed not by legislative arbitrariness, but first by usage and popular belief and later by jurisprudence (Klenner 1989).

The main challenge to the historical school of German law came from Georg Friedrich Wilhelm Hegel who regarded the school as an apologia for the existing state of law. Hegel argued that that the law could not be based on mere habit. Everything needed to justify its existence before the tribunal of reason (Klenner 1989). In a criticism of the German historical school of law published in 1842, Karl Marx accused the school of making history self-justifying and of legitimizing the baseness of today by the baseness of yesterday (Kelley 1978). He pointedly criticised its position on knowledge accusing its adherents of supposing 'that because we cannot know what is *true*, we consequently allow the *untrue*, if it *exists* at all, to pass as *fully valid*' (Kelley 1978). It is clear from this that Marx recognised that there were limitations on our understanding of society but that he did not accept that this licenced uncritical acceptance of laws and practices that had been inherited from the past. Marx was not, however, denying the importance of the connection between the past and present or indeed the present and the future. This was already clear in his outline of historical materialism in *The German Ideology* (1845–1846). It was set out more clearly in a letter written to Annenkov in 1846 in which Marx argued that men were not free to choose this or that form of society:

> [M]an is not free to choose *his productive forces* – upon which his whole history is based – for every productive force is an acquired force, the product of previous activity .... The simple fact that every succeeding generation finds productive forces acquired by the preceding generation and which serve it as the raw material of further production, engenders a relatedness in the history of man
>
> (Marx 1982: 96)

For Marx, however, recognition of the continuity between past, present and future was not a reason for inaction. On the contrary, development in one part of the system created the need for changes elsewhere:

> Man never renounces what he has gained, but this does not mean that he never renounces the form of society in which he has acquired certain productive forces. On the contrary. If he is not to be deprived of the results obtained or to forfeit the fruits of civilisation, man is compelled to change all his traditional social forms as soon as the mode of commerce ceases to correspond to the productive forces acquired.
>
> (Marx 1982)

Marx's view on the nature of the choices open to mankind finds echoes in Joseph Schumpeter's *Capitalism, Socialism and Democracy*. There Schumpeter argues that:

> Mankind is not free to choose ... things economic and social move by their own momentum and the ensuing situations compel individuals and groups to behave in certain ways whatever they may wish to do- not indeed by destroying their freedom of choice but by shaping the choosing mentalities and narrowing the list of possibilities from which to choose.
>
> (Schumpeter 1947a: 129–130)

2.6 KNOWLEDGE, GOVERNANCE AND POLICY

In *Dialogues Concerning Natural Religion*, Hume used an argument based on Mandeville's example of a sailing ship to call into question the view that the apparent order of the world necessarily implied the existence of a god or grand designer.

> If we survey a ship, what an exalted idea must we form of the ingenuity of the carpenter who framed so complicated, useful, and beautiful a machine? And what surprise must we feel, when we find him a stupid mechanic, who imitated others, and copied an art, which, through a long succession of ages, after multiplied trials, mistakes, corrections, deliberations, and controversies, had been gradually improving?
>
> (Hume 1779, part 5)

Hume suggested that, rather than postulating one grand designer, one should consider the possibility that the world was the result of efforts by several 'lesser' gods. If a great many men could join together to build a house or ship, to found and develop a city or to create a commonwealth, there was no reason why several gods could not combine in designing and making a world. In other words, the world itself was the product of trial and error by many over a long period of time (Glacken 1967; Alter 2008).

Hume's challenge to arguments for the existence of a grand designer has been appropriated in modern times for a different purpose, namely to challenge arguments for forms of state intervention in the economy. Thus, for instance, Lorenzo Infantino argues that due to an extremism of reason which has lost 'the awareness of its own limits' we moderns have moved from the idea of an intentional order attributable to God to that of an intentional order attributable to the designs of man (Infantino 1998: 1). Infantino cites a passage from F. A. Hayek's *Constitution of Liberty* in which having commented on the subtlety and complexity of the institutions of law, Hayek contended that such institutions are the products of evolutionary processes and have not been deliberately designed. As Hayek put it:

> If it had been deliberately designed, it would deserve to rank amongst the greatest human inventions. But it has, of course, been as little invented by any one mind as language or money or most of the practices and conventions on which life rests.
>
> (Hayek 2011: 216)

There is no issue with Hayek on this point of the single designing mind. However, as Jacob Viner pointed out in his review of Hayek's book, correct statements about strong cases become a problem when they are applied more generally. Viner presciently challenged Hayek's implicit characterization of government as a single, unified entity arguing that government itself may be 'an institution which is in large degree a spontaneous growth, inherently decentralised, experimental, innovating, subject not only to tendencies for costly meddling but also to propensities for inertia and costly inaction' (Viner 1961: 235).

The tendency to consider the state or policy maker as a single actor, which was commonplace in post-war welfare economics, is no longer the mainstream view (Flanagan et al. 2011). For example, Schmitter (1985: 33) refers to the state as 'an amorphous complex of agencies with ill-defined boundaries, performing a variety of not very distinctive functions' while Hay (1999) argues that the state 'comprises a diverse array of specific, but none the less interdependent, agencies, apparatuses and institutions'. These institutions enjoy some degree of latitude which is reflected in their structures, practices, procedures and modes of conduct.

Arguments relating to the proper location of decision making about economic resources have a long history as is evidenced by the contrasting position taken by James Steuart and Adam Smith in the second half of the eighteenth century. Steuart argued that public spirit is as 'superfluous in the governed as it ought to be all-powerful in the statesman' (Steuart 1767: Vol. 1, 164). The reason for this was that everyone might consider the public interest in a different light and join in the ruin of it by endeavouring to promote its advantages. Steuart who was unashamedly interventionist was making the reasonable point that coherence is a requirement of good policy. Adam Smith agreed that there was need for coherence in policy: 'Some general and even systematical idea of the perfection of policy and law, may no doubt be necessary for directing the ideas of the statesman' (Smith 1976a: VI. ii.2–18). However, he castigated the 'man of system' who imagines that 'he can arrange the different members of a great society with as much ease as the hand arranges the different pieces of a chess-board' (Smith 1976a: VI. ii.2–17). Smith was categorical that, 'in his local situation', the businessman was likely to make much better decisions than the statesman and he warned of the danger of intervention by a statesman or even a council or senate who had the folly to presume that they would do better (Smith 1976b. IV. ii).

Smith was living at a time when few important inventions could be either directly attributed to scientific discoveries or were dependent in some way on scientific insights (Smith 1976b: I.1.9; Mokyr 2018: 217). In such circumstances, the specialist knowledge of the manufacturer and his own local situation are the most relevant factors in any investment situation. However, as Mokyr notes, localised specialist knowledge could not continue to give rise to sustained technological revolutions. These required the confluence of scientific method and discovery and artisanal knowledge (Mokyr 2018: 274). Smith acknowledged that philosophers and machine makers sometimes had a role in innovation and that there was a case for granting a temporary monopoly to the inventor of a new machine or to a merchant who opened up trade with a remote nation (Smith 1976b: V.i.3 art1).[9] However, he did not address the problems associated with innovative activity in any great detail.

This task was performed by Jeremy Bentham. Like Smith, Bentham advocated reliance on 'the spontaneous exertions of individuals' (Bentham 1843) and already in 1787 he was critical of what he saw as Smith's inconsistency for having proposed a ceiling on the rate of interest in order to discourage excessive risk-taking. Bentham countered that restraints on pecuniary bargains would act as restraints on the progress of inventive industry by making it impossible for those promoting new and inherently risky projects to obtain funds. Governments could rely on the intelligence and inclinations of individuals to promote economic growth. '[N]othing is necessary to be done on its part but to leave them in possession of *the power*, to insure to them *the right* of enjoyment, and to hasten the development of general knowledge' (Bentham 1843: III. 2.iii§23). In identifying measures to hasten the development of general knowledge, Bentham recommended a substantial list of activities which governments might pursue. These included encouraging study of the sciences, instituting prizes for discoveries and experiments, publishing detail of technological processes employed domestically and in foreign countries, publishing price information and the granting of patents for a limited number of years (Bentham 1843) He also argued that, to ensure the right of enjoyment, exclusive privilege was 'absolutely necessary, in order that what is sown may be reaped'. He explained:

> He who has no hope that he shall reap, will not take the trouble to sow. But that which one man has invented, all the world can imitate. Without the assistance of the laws, the inventor would almost always be driven out of the market by his rival, who finding himself, without any expense, in possession of a discovery which has cost the inventor much time and expense, would be able to deprive him of all his *deserved* advantages, by selling at a lower price.
>
> (Bentham 1843)

[9] Recognition of the value of a temporary monopoly as a means of encouraging innovation goes back at least to the early part of the seventeenth century. Misselden referred to patents as beneficial restraints, which provided the inventor of a new art with 'recompense of his industry and encouragement to others to study and invent things profitable to the public' (Misselden 1622: 60).

Bentham also emphasised that entrepreneurial activity was ultimately valuable for the wider society because successful innovation would be emulated by others who would repeat and multiply the success (Bentham 1818: XIII. 35). Even where ventures turned out to be failures, others might ultimately benefit and could learn from the mistakes made.[10]

Apart from Bentham's contribution, the discussion of the special characteristics of scientific and technical knowledge in late-eighteenth-century Britain was limited with the main focus being on the question of how to prevent leakage abroad of the country's technological knowledge. Restrictions were placed on the migration of skilled artisans and following this the export of machinery was prohibited. Laws restricting the emigration of skilled labour were eventually repealed in 1825 but restrictions on the export of machinery remained in place until the 1840s (Jeremy 1977).

2.7 LAGGING ECONOMIES AND THE TRANSFER OF TECHNOLOGY

Although the classical economists in the early nineteenth century were more aware of technical change than Smith had been in the late eighteenth, the framework of analysis remained one in which growth was conceived as a process of accumulation driven by 'parsimony' (Brewer 1991). As noted earlier, this framework was challenged by a number of authors amongst them, John Rae (1796–1872). Rae did not deny that there was some truth in the accumulation story but he argued that accumulation and innovation did not necessarily go hand-in-hand. An important source of innovation had been neglected, namely 'the progress of arts in other communities and their subsequent transfer to it' (Rae 1834: 76–77). Rae argued that although such transfer was potentially beneficial, it would require costly adaptation. No individual had the incentive to make the necessary investment because, if he did, he would derive no more benefit from his effort than others who copied his innovation (Rae 1834: 56). Rae identified differences in the supply of raw materials, and differences in relative factor prices as factors giving rise to the need for considerable adaptation in the course of technology transfer. An even more serious difficulty was the fact that the information relevant to technology transfer did not exist in a complete and codified form. This meant that the transfer of technology from one country to another necessarily required the migration of skilled personnel, which in turn posed both incentive and selection problems. Rae suggested that these difficulties and his own perception that the majority of men had a strong preference for the tried and tested paths meant that some favourable conjuncture of events was necessary before

[10] But let Titius have found out a new dye, more brilliant or more durable than those in use, let him have invented a new and more convenient machine, or a new and more profitable mode of husbandry, a thousand dyers, ten thousand mechanics, a hundred thousand husbandmen, may repeat and multiply his success: and then, what is it to the public, though the fortune of Titius, or of his usurer should have sunk under the experiment? (Bentham 1787: ch. XIII, 178)

technology transfer could take place. Calamities were favourable to innovation because they disturbed the expected order of events and exposed 'the necessity, or the possibility, of connecting them by some other means' (Rae 1834: 223). However, calamities also diminished the desire for accumulation since they exposed the property of members of society to danger.

Whereas both Bentham and Rae emphasised the public good aspects of technological knowledge, Rae can be thought of as recognising some of the limitations of this perspective, namely the tacitness of technological knowledge and the fact that technology has what Rosenberg described a long umbilical cord and so requires adaptation before it becomes usable in a new situation (Rosenberg 1976: 167). A further limitation was pointed out by Friedrich List in *The National System of Political Economy* [1841]. This was that knowledge was necessary to access existing knowledge.[11] As he put it:

> The present state of the nations is the result of the accumulation of all discoveries, inventions, improvements, perfections, and exertions of all generations which have lived before us; they form the *mental capital of the present human race,* and every separate nation is productive only in the proportion in which it has known how to appropriate these attainments of former generations and to increase them by its own acquirements.
>
> (List 1841: 113)

List attributed to Adam Smith and his followers a cosmopolitan view of political economy which advocated free trade but failed to take adequate account of differences between nations.[12] List was not anti-free trade per se but against free trade in a context where some nations had fallen behind others so that their industrial development would be stifled by foreign competition. This, and the fact that new industries involved considerable risk meant that there was a case for providing them with a temporary monopoly in the domestic market. The interests of consumers would be protected by the gradual introduction of domestic competition and the eventual restoration of free trade (Shafaeddin 2000).

In his introduction to the 1909 edition of *The National System*, J Shield Nicholson drew particular attention to the difference between List's view of capital and that which had been attributed to Adam Smith. While Smith, himself, had taken an inclusive view of capital including within it the natural and acquired abilities of the inhabitants, his successors took a much narrower view focused entirely on material forms. As a result, the importance of immaterial productive forces and powers dropped out of view. List argued that mere accumulation of fixed capital was not enough. 'All expenditure in the instruction of youth, the promotion

[11] For a detailed discussion of the relevance of this issue see the chapter by Kealey and Ricketts in this volume.

[12] As Shield Nicholson (1909) and Watson (2012) have pointed out, List's criticisms of Smith are not altogether reliable. However, whereas some of List's criticisms are wrong as applied to Adam Smith, they are often just as applied to his followers.

of justice, defence of nations, &c. is a consumption of present values for the behoof of the productive powers' (List 1841: 112). This was not all, a long list of institutions, conventions, innovations and reforms were, List argued, rich sources of productive power. These included: the Christian religion; monogamy; abolition of slavery and of vassalage; hereditability of the throne; the introduction of the principle of freehold property, and of means of transport; and invention of printing, of the press, of the postal system, of money, weights and measures, of the calendar, of watches, and of police (List 1841: 113). Elsewhere in Book II, List noted the contribution of financial sector, the importance of science and scientific education as well as the importance of infrastructure such as roads and waterways. List summarised:

> The nation derives its productive power from the mental and physical powers of the individuals; from their social, municipal, and political conditions and institutions; from the natural resources placed at its disposal, or from the instruments it possesses as the material products of former mental and bodily exertions (material, agricultural, manufacturing, and commercial capital).
>
> (List 1841: 181)

The validity of List's distinction between values of exchange and productive powers has been questioned on the ground that the only way to measure the strength of productive powers is to measure the values in exchange of what they actually produce (Winch 1998: 308). However, both the theoretical and empirical literature on economic growth provide strong evidence to support Schumpeter's contention that the gains from technical progress greatly outweigh those that may be achieved through allocational efficiency. As Schumpeter put it:

> A system ... that at every point of time fully utilizes its possibilities to the best advantage may yet in the long run be inferior to a system that does so at no given point of time because the latter's failure to do so may be a condition for the level or speed of long run performance.
>
> (Schumpeter 1947a: 83)

Intimations of several aspects of modern innovation theory can be traced to List. His recognition that knowledge is required to access and use 'the mental capital of the human race' is nowadays discussed under the heading of absorptive capacity (Cohen and Levinthal 1990). List is also acknowledged as a pioneer of the concept of national innovation systems, one of the main frameworks used for the analysis of modern science, technology and innovation policy (Freeman 1995; Lundvall 2010; Schot and Steinmueller 2018).

2.8 THE INNOVATION ECOSYSTEM

The policy issues which had been identified by the mid-nineteenth century have not been assuaged by the passage of time. By the mid-twentieth century, it was increasingly clear that scientific knowledge was important for innovation and growth and questions were posed as to how greater scientific effort might be elicited in market-based economies (Elder and Fagerberg 2017). In an influential paper published in 1962, Kenneth Arrow argued that a free enterprise economy had a tendency to underinvest in invention and research because it is risky, because the product can be appropriated only to a limited extent and because of increasing returns in use. Furthermore, even if a firm did manage to engross the value of its inventive activity, there would be underutilisation of that knowledge compared with the ideal. This analysis, usually referred to as the market failure framework, provided support for three policy approaches: (i) state support for basic research, (ii) use of subsidies to encourage additional research and development (R&D) in the private sector, and (iii) strengthening of intellectual property regimes (IPR).

The market failure framework proved to be resilient and able to identify if not resolve new problems arising from changes in technology and industry structure. However, it has also attracted criticism from a variety of directions. Those concerned about the efficacy of government intervention in the innovation process argued that policy makers lack the information that would enable them to intervene optimally or even effectively. They also argued that policy interventions encourage rent seeking and various forms of unproductive activity (Kreuger 1974). Others maintained that the view taken of innovation in the market failure framework is overly narrow and that a broader systems perspective was required to account of some features of the knowledge economy. These were : (i) that rather than being a pure public good, knowledge is sticky and hence linked to a variety of geographical, organisational and cultural factors (von Hippel 1994); (ii) that the ability to absorb and develop new knowledge depends on prior acquisition of capabilities which are themselves linked to a variety of social capabilities including education, an entrepreneurial outlook and the nature of wider supportive institutions (Cohen and Levinthal 1990); and (iii) that rather than being a linear process in the form of flow from science to R&D to commercialization, knowledge is generated through interactions between users, including end users, and producers at various administrative and geographical levels (Schot and Steinmueller 2018). This broader systems perspective on innovation has the merit of focusing policy attention on a wide range of relationships and emergent organisational forms operating at different geographical levels: international, national and local. Advocates of the national perspective emphasise that countries differ not only in their historical experience, language, culture and legal systems but also in their industrial structure, in the role of the public sector, in their education and training systems, and in the structure of their financial and R&D sectors. Others, emphasising the stickiness of knowledge and the importance of interfirm interaction focus their attention on regions and industry clusters. Advocates of the systems frameworks do not deny that imperfect information and even lack of information is a problem, but they argue that the right way of thinking of industrial/innovation policy is as a discovery process – one where economic actors including firms and the government learn about underlying costs and opportunities and engage in strategic co-ordination (Rodrik 2004).[13]

There is a large literature on the relevance of the national systems of innovation framework to developing countries (Nelson 1993: part III; Kim 1999; Cimoli et al. 2010; Yip and McKern 2016). The perspective also found favour in more advanced industrial countries due to its relevance for the maintenance of the competitive advantages of domestic firms in an era of increasing globalisation (Lundvall 1992, 2016; Nelson 1993; Freeman 1995; Porter 1998; Shot and Steinmueller 2018). However, arguments about the nature and extent of policy interventions did not go away but re-surfaced as arguments about the merits of level playing fields as opposed to discretionary policy. As Lundvall (2016) notes, one drawback of the national systems framework is that the precise implications for policy are difficult to identify. This is partly because most studies are country-specific but, even where comparative analysis has been carried out it often lacks a common theoretical framework.

The Marshallian industrial district as updated by Beccatini and Michael Porter's cluster–based approach shares many features of the systems-based approach (Becattini 1990; Porter 1998).[14] Porter sees the clusters as geographic concentrations of companies and institutions in a particular field. These may include suppliers of specialised inputs and infrastructure; channels to customers; manufacturers of complementary products; and companies in industries utilising similar skills, technologies or other inputs. Clusters involve both competition and co-operation – the former is necessary to prevent stagnation and drive innovation whereas the latter opens up opportunities for the provision of scale-sensitive or collective goods including research, training and testing facilities; the collection of information; the organisation of trade fairs; and managing purchasing consortia.

Overlapping with the notion of industry cluster is Pisano and Shih's (2012) concept of the industrial commons. Commons is seen as consisting of webs of technological know-how, operation capabilities and specialised skills that are embedded in the workforce, competitors, suppliers, customers, co-operative R&D ventures, and universities and often support multiple industrial sectors (Pisano and Shih 2012: 13). Pisano and Shih emphasise that industrial commons are a delicate

[13] Carlsson and Stankiewicz (1991) emphasise that the boundaries of technological systems may or may not coincide with national borders and may vary from one techno-industrial area to another.

[14] Mention should also be made of Porter and van de Linde's (1995) article which suggests that environmental regulation could induce innovation of clean technologies and in doing so make production processes and products more efficient. The article has spawned a huge literature the main contours of which are reviewed in Ambec et al. (2013). While the Porter hypothesis can be regarded as part of the market failure/organisational failure literature that affects all innovation, it has opened up important discussions about whether a Pareto superior global equilibrium fulfilling environmental and other objectives might exist and how it might be reached in practice.

ecosystem which can easily unravel if the private returns of some elements drop below a threshold (Pisano and Shih 2012: 60). Their position is best understood in the context of the arguments which suggest that economies such as that of the United States can benefit from concentrating on R&D and design while subcontracting more routine work to low-wage international providers. This may work in some industries but Pisano and Shih argue that in many, product innovation cannot be readily separated from manufacturing. In such industries, outsourcing firms may be undermining not only their own capacity to innovate but also that of the wider ecosystem. Interestingly, Pisano and Shih's proposed remedies in the face of decline have echoes of List – not in terms of protectionist trade policies but in terms of a clear focus by firms on building capabilities and on appreciating the value of belonging to a strong industrial commons (Pisano and Shih 2012: 105). Likewise, they propose that government should commit to strengthening the scientific and technological foundations of the commons and the development of human capital at all levels (Pisano and Shih 2012: 125–133).

While Pisano and Shih and Porter emphasise the importance of tacit knowledge and localisation in the innovation process, others explore situations in which a firm's ability to innovate depends more directly on assets that it does not own (Iansiti and Levien 2004; Adner 2006; Moore 2006). These authors emphasise not just spillovers from other firms in the ecosystem but situations where any given firm's innovations rely on complementary innovations by some other firms with no one firm possessing all the specialised knowledge and resources required for innovation (Moore 2006). These ecosystems may arise as a result of disaggregation of departments in existing firms or be developed by entrepreneurial leaders who as Moore (2006) puts it 'declare a "space" for invention and investment'. Either way, mechanisms for co-ordination are required. In some cases, these are provided by a lead enterprise or platform where the latter is described as any combination of hardware or software that provides standards, interfaces and rules and support that enable providers of complements to interact with each other and or users (Cusumano and Gawer 2002; Kay et al. 2018; Teece 2018). Apple is regarded as an example of a lead firm. Wikipedia may be taken as an example of an ecosystem/knowledge commons/community of practice without a key player. Wikipedia operates without a centralised review of contributor actions but it is also an evolving sociotechnical system that employs managerial hierarchies, protocols and automated editing systems to orchestrate human and non-human contributors (Niederer and van Dijck 2010). The important point here is that co-ordination mechanisms are always required, though they may take many different forms and evolve in various ways. In their study of innovation by open source software communities, Mateos-Garcia and Steinmeuller (2008) note the tendency to see knowledge-related communities with voluntary organisation of effort and traditional, hierarchically managed organisations as the only alternatives available for organising the production of knowledge in an online context. They suggest, instead, a continuum of possible structures whose shape is determined by the way in which rules of entrance and participation are defined and put into practice.

As has long been recognised, standardisation reduces transaction costs and facilitates the division of labour. The digital economy is no exception; technological standards provide the platform on which rival firms build their product and service offerings (Cusumano and Gawer 2002; Teece 2018: 1380). These standards may emerge as a result of market competition especially in downstream applications. They may also be developed by means of formal processes undertaken by national and international standard setting organisations most of which operate on a not-for-profit basis. Once provided, standards facilitate entry and competition and allow for autonomous innovation without the need for active co-ordination as long as the relevant standards for their module are met (Teece 2018: 1380–1382). Teece distinguishes between standard setting, which is concerned primarily with achieving uniformity and compatibility, and standard development, which takes account of the potential for further innovation not just at the level of the individual actors in the ecosystem but also at the architectural level. This issue of standard development has recently arisen with respect to the Internet itself. It is suggested that the existing protocols are not adequate to underpin new developments such as self-driving cars and the Internet of Things and that a more efficient address system is required to support emerging technologies (Gross and Murgia 2020).

Whereas Teece (2018: 1381) discusses standard development as a technical selection process which begins with firms investing large sums of money in R&D, Potts (2018) and Allen and Potts (2016) focus on information pooling and emerging standards at earlier stages in the innovation process. They postulate a stage zero innovation commons involving peer production of the information required to discover opportunities from which to develop markets, firms and industries. According to Potts (2018: 1026), 'innovation originates in a prior state of non-market coordination among proto entrepreneurs and technology enthusiasts who develop governance rules to facilitate co-operation'. Likewise, emphasising the entrepreneurial function, Malerba and McKelvey (2020) note that knowledge and business opportunities do not exist a priori but instead emerge and come together through the actions of entrepreneurs. In the process, there may be a demand for new knowledge as well as the creation of conditions in which it may emerge. Some of the knowledge relevant to innovation is codified or embodied in artefacts and conventions and institutions but much of it exists as what we nowadays call human capital (Foray 2004). In a situation where there is no innovation (Schumpeter's circular flow), the specialised knowledge is co-ordinated by means of hierarchies and normal market arrangements. These, however, are insufficient when what requires co-ordination is not yet fully known because the new thing is still in the process of creation. It is the need for co-ordination of this type that gives rise to Schumpeter's entrepreneurial function (Schumpeter 1961). It involves bringing together fragmented knowledge and creating the conditions for this knowledge to be actualized in things, in services or in social constructs. The process is likely to be ongoing in time and experimental. Different participants and governing structures may be required at different stages (Dedehayir and Seppänen 2015).[15] It may, therefore, involve a complex and ever-changing array of institutions, standards, conventions and resources to facilitate information exchanges and co-operation by different actors including firms, governmental and non-governmental organisations, education and research establishments, professional bodies, voluntary associations and individuals.

While innovation adds to our stock of knowledge, ultimately our interest must be not just in adding to knowledge but also in its efficient use. The peculiar properties of knowledge mean that these two objectives may be both contradictory and indissociable as Foray (2004) notes. Knowledge is non-subtractable in consumption but at the same time universal access may be an obstacle to its private production. Knowledge is also cumulative so that collective progress may be inhibited by intellectual property rights provided to encourage private production. There are no simple governance solutions to these dilemmas, but the solutions generated in any conjuncture have the potential to be beneficial for society and to enhance the possibilities for further progress.

In the concluding pages of his *The Origin of Species*, Darwin wrote that the study of natural history would become far more interesting when we no longer look at organic things as a savage looks at a ship but instead see every production of nature as one which has a history in the same way as we look at any great mechanical invention as the summing up of the labour, the experience, the reason and even the blunders of numerous workmen (Darwin 1859: 485–486). In this chapter, it is suggested that this perspective might fruitfully be recaptured for knowledge itself. Doing so enables us to see that knowledge is cumulative, tacit, and embedded. It allows us to understand that it is a social product, that it is developed and transmitted socially in the context of a division of labour which makes transmission possible while also shaping access to existing social knowledge. It enables us to appreciate that while the future path of knowledge cannot be predicted with any certainty, it is tethered to the present and not arbitrary and is therefore shaped by present choices. Not least, it forces us to recognise the limitations of our own rationality while appreciating the coherence of what has been communally achieved.

[15] A study of asynchronous design by Delemarle and Laredo (2008) shows that while identifying a space for invention and innovation is important, it needs to be accompanied by standardization if non-hierarchical development of a field is to succeed. They found that European-financed support for conferences and research involving both universities and firms helped to build the credibility of the asynchronous design field as a basis for breakthrough innovation. However, in this case, independent research groups pursued different niche projects and because of this were unable to converge on a dominant architecture or design tool. As a result, no market could be shaped and no product class standards emerged.

REFERENCES

Adner, Ron. 2006. 'Match Your Innovation Strategy to Your Innovation Ecosystem'. *Harvard Business Review* 84 (4): 98–107.

Alter, Stephen G. 2008. 'Mandeville's Ship: Theistic Design and Philosophical History in Charles Darwin's Vision of Natural Selection'. *Journal of the History of Ideas* 69: 441–465.

Allen, Darcy and Jason Potts. 2016. 'How Innovation Commons Contribute to Discovering and Developing New Technologies'. *International Journal of the Commons* 10 (2): 1035–1054.

Ambec, Stefan, Mark A. Cohen, Stewart Elgie and Paul Lanoie. 2013. 'The Porter Hypothesis at 20: Can Environmental Regulation Enhance Innovation and Competitiveness?' *Review of Environmental Economics and Policy* 7 (1): 2–22.

Arrow, Kenneth J. 1962. 'Economic Welfare and the Allocation of Resources for Invention'. In *The Rate and Direction of Inventive Activity: Economic and Social Factors*, edited by R. R. Nelson, 609–628. Princeton: Princeton University Press.

Bacon, Francis. 1902. *Novum Organum*. Edited by Joseph Devey. New York: P. F. Collier.

Babbage, Charles. [1832] 1835. *On the Economy of Machinery and Manufactures*. Fourth enlarged edition. London: Charles Knight.

[1851] 1968. *The Exposition of 1851*. London: Frank Cass.

Becattini, Giacomo. 1990. 'The Marshallian Industrial District as a Socio-economic Notion'. In *Industrial Districts and Interfirm Co-operation in Italy*, edited by Frank Pyke, Giacomo Becattini and Werner Sengenberger. Geneva: IILS, 37–51.

Bentham, Jeremy. [1787] 1818. *Defense of Usury*, 4th ed. London: T. Payne and Son.

1843a. 'The Rationale of Reward'. In *The Works of Jeremy Bentham*, Vol. II, Book III, Chapter ii, edited by J. Bowring. London, Edinburgh: W. Tait.

1843b. 'A Manual of Political Economy'. In *The Works of Jeremy Bentham*, Vol. III, edited by J. Bowring. London, Edinburgh: W. Tait.

Brewer, Anthony. 1991. 'Economic Growth and Technical Change: John Rae's Critique of Adam Smith'. *History of Political Economy* 23 (1): 1–11.

Burke, Edmund. [1769] 1981. 'Observations on a Late State of the Nation'. In *The Writings and Speeches of Edmund Burke*, edited by P. Langford. Oxford: Clarendon Press.

[1790] 1989. 'Reflections on the Revolution in France'. In *The Writings and Speeches of Edmund Burke*, edited by L. G. Mitchell and W. D. Todd, Vol. VIII, 102–180. Oxford: The Clarendon Press.

Bury, John B. 1960. *The Idea of Progress: An Inquiry into Its Origin and Growth*. London: The Macmillan Co.

Carlsson, Bo and Rikard Stankiewicz. 1991. 'On the Nature, Function and Composition of Technological Systems'. *Journal of Evolutionary Economics* 1 (2): 93–118.

Cimoli, Mario, Giovani Dosi and Joseph E. Stiglitz. 2010. *Industrial Policy and Development: The Political Economy of Capabilities Accumulation*. Oxford: Oxford University Press.

Cohen, Wesley M. and Daniel A. Levinthal. 1990. 'Absorptive Capacity: A New Perspective on Learning and Innovation'. *Administrative Science Quarterly* 35 (1): 128–152.

Condorcet, Antoine N. 1796. *Outlines of an Historical View of the Progress of the Human Mind*. Philadelphia: Lang and Ustick.

Cusumano, Michael A. and Annabelle Gawer. 2002. 'The Elements of Platform Leadership'. *MIT Sloan Management Review* 43 (3): 51–58.

Darwin, Charles. 1859. *The Origin of the Species by Means of Natural Selection*. London: John Murray.
Dedehayir, Ozgur and Marko Seppänen. 2015. 'Birth and Expansion of Innovation Ecosystems: A Case Study of Copper Production'. *Journal of Technology Management & Innovation* 10 (2): 146–154.
Delemarle, Aurélie and Philippe Larédo. 2008. 'Breakthrough Innovation and the Shaping of New Markets: The Role of Communities of Practice'. In *Community, Economic Creativity, and Organisation*, edited by A. Amin and J. Roberts, 178–199. Oxford: Oxford University Press.
Devaille, Jules. 1910. *Essai sur l'histoire de l'idée de progrès jusqu'à la fin du 18e siècle*. Paris: F. Alcan.
Eamon, William. 1996. *Science and the Secrets of Nature: Books of Secrets in Medieval and Early Modern Culture*. Princeton: Princeton University Press.
Eisenberg, Rebecca S. 2008. 'Noncompliance, Nonenforcement, Nonproblem? Rethinking the Anticommons in Biomedical Research'. *Houston Law Review* 45 (4): 1059–1099.
Elder, Jakob and Jan Fagerberg. 2017. 'Innovation Policy: What, Why and How'. *Oxford Review of Economic Policy* 33 (1): 2–23.
Ferguson, Adam. 1782. *An Essay on the History of Civil Society*. London: T. Cadell and Edinburgh: W. Creech and J. Bell.
Flanagan, Kieron, Elvira Uyarra and Manuel Laranja. 2011. 'Reconceptualizing the "Policy Mix" for Innovation'. *Research Policy* 40 (5): 702–713.
Foray, Dominique. 2004. *Economics of Knowledge*. Cambridge: MIT Press.
Freeman, Chris. 1995. 'The "National System of Innovation" in Historical Perspective'. *Cambridge Journal of Economics* 19 (1): 5–24.
Frischmann, Brett M. 2012. *Infrastructure: The Social Value of Shared Resources*. Oxford: Oxford University Press.
Galen. 1985. *Three Treatises on the Nature of Science*. Translated by Richard Walzer and Michael Frede. Indianapolis: Hackett Publishing.
Gaukroger, Stephen. 2001. *Francis Bacon and the Transformation of Early-Modern Philosophy*. Cambridge: Cambridge University Press.
Glacken, Clarence J. 1967. *Traces on the Rhodian Shore*. Berkeley: University of California Press.
Gross, Anna and Madhumita Murgia. 2020. 'China and Huawei Propose Re-invention of the Internet'. *Financial Times*, March 27.
Hay, Colin. 1999. 'Crisis and the Structural Transformation of the State: Interrogating the Process of Change'. *British Journal of Politics and International Relations* 1 (3): 317–344.
Hayek, Friedrich A. 1967. 'Dr. Bernard Mandeville. Lecture on a Master Mind delivered to the Academy on March 23, 1966'. *Proceedings of the British Academy* 52: 125–141.
2011. *The Constitution of Liberty*. Chicago: University of Chicago Press.
Hegel, Georg W. F. 2001. *Philosophy of Right*. Kitchener: Batoche Books.
Heller, Michael A. and Rebecca S. Eisenberg. 1998. 'Can Patents Deter Innovation: The Anticommons in Biomedical Research'. *Science* 280 (5364): 698–701.
Hess, Charlotte and Elinor Ostrom. 2007. *Understanding Knowledge as Commons: From Theory to Practice*. Cambridge, MA: MIT Press.
Hippel, Eric von. 1994. '"Sticky Information" and the Locus of Problem Solving: Implications for Innovation'. *Management Science* 40 (4): 429–439.

Hodgskin, Thomas. 1825. *Labour Defended against the Claims of Capital: Or, the Unproductiveness of Capital Proved with Reference to the Present Combinations amongst Journeymen*. New York: Augustus M. Kelly.

Hume, David. 1779. *Dialogues Concerning Natural Religion*. London.

Infantino, Lorenzo. 1998. *Individualism in Modern Thought*. London and New York: Routledge.

Iansiti, Marco and Roy Levien. 2004. 'Creating Value in Your Business Ecosystem'. *Harvard Business Review*, https://hbswk.hbs.edu/item/creating-value-in-your-business-ecosystem.

Jeremy, David I. 1977. 'Damming the Flood: British Government Efforts to Check the Outflow of Technicians and Machinery, 1780–1843'. *The Business History Review* 51 (1): 1–34.

Kay, Neil M., Sohvi Leih and David J. Teece. 2018. 'The Role of Emergence in Dynamic Capabilities: A Restatement of the Framework and Some Possibilities for Future Research'. *Industrial and Corporate Change* 27 (4): 623–638.

Kelley, Donald R. 1978. 'The Metaphysics of Law: An Essay on the Very Young Marx'. *The American Historical Review* 83 (2): 350–367.

Kim, Linsu. 1999. 'Building Technological Capability for Industrialization: Analytical Frameworks and Korea's Experience'. *Industrial and Corporate Change* 8 (1): 111–136.

Klenner, Hermann. 1989. 'Savigny's Research Program of the Historical School of Law and Its Intellectual Impact in 19th Century Berlin'. *The American Journal of Comparative Law* 37 (1): 67–80.

Kreuger, Anne O. 1974. 'The Political Economy of Rent-Seeking Society'. *American Economic Review* 64 (3): 291–303.

List, Friedrich. 1841. *The National System of Political Economy*. London: Longmans, Green, and Co.

Lundvall, Bengt-Åke. ed. 1992. *National Systems of Innovation: Toward a Theory of Innovation and Interactive Learning*. London: Pinter Publishers.

2010. *National Systems of Innovation: Toward a Theory of Innovation and Interactive Learning*. London: Anthem.

2016. *The Learning Economy and the Economics of Hope*. London: Anthem.

Madison, Michael J., Brett M. Frischmann and Katherine J. Strandburg. 2009. 'The University as Constructed Cultural Commons'. *Washington University Journal of Law & Policy* 30: 365, https://openscholarship.wustl.edu/law_journal_law_policy/vol30/iss1/12.

Malerba, Franco and Maureen M. McKelvey. 2020. 'Knowledge-Intensive Innovative Entrepreneurship Integrating Schumpeter, Evolutionary Economics, and Innovation Systems'. *Small Business Economics* 54: 503–522.

Mandeville, Bernard. 1730. *A Treatise of the Hypochondriack and Hysterick Diseases. In Three Dialogues*. London: J. Tonson.

1924. *The Fable of the Bees*, 2 Vols. Edited by F. B. Kaye. Oxford: The Clarendon Press.

Marx, Karl. [1842] 1975. 'The Philosophical Manifesto of the Historical School of Law'. Supplement to the *Rheiniche Zeitung* No. 221, August 9, Marx & Engels, *Collected Works*, Vol. 1. London: Lawrence and Wishart.

1982. 'Letter to Annenkov'. In *Karl Marx, Fredrick Engels Collected Works*, Margarita Lopukhina, Mzia Pitskhelauri and Anna Vladimirova, Vol. 38, 95–106. London: Lawrence and Wishart.

1987. *Karl Marx, Fredrick Engels Collected Works*, Vol. 29. London: Lawrence and Wishart.

Mateos-Garcia, Juan and W. E. Steinmeuller. 2008. 'Open but How Much? Growth, Conflict, and Institutional Evolution in Open-Source Communities'. In *Community,*

Economic Creativity, and Organisation, edited by A. Amin and J. Roberts, 254–282. Oxford: Oxford University Press.

Meek, Ronald L. 1973. *Turgot on Progress, Sociology and Economics*. Cambridge: Cambridge University Press.

1976. *Social Science and the Ignoble Savage*. Cambridge: Cambridge University Press.

Michie, Jonathan and Renée Prendergast. 1998. 'Government Intervention in a Dynamic Economy'. *New Political Economy* 3 (3): 391–406.

Misselden, Edward. 1622. *Free Trade; or the Means to Make Trade Flourish*. London: John Legatt for Simon Waterson.

Mokyr, Joel. 2018. *Culture of Growth: The Origins of the Modern Economy*. Princeton and Oxford: Princeton University Press.

Moore, James F. 2006. 'Business Ecosystems and the View from the Firm'. *Antitrust Bulletin* 51: 31–75.

Nelson, Richard R. 1993. *National Innovation Systems: A Comparative Analysis*. New York and Oxford: Oxford University Press.

Nicholson, J Shield. 1909. 'Introductory Essay'. In *The National System of Political Economy*, edited by Friedrich List, xiii–xxvii. London: Longmans, Green and Co.

Niederer, Sabine and José van Dijck. 2010. 'Wisdom of the Crowd or Technicity of Content? Wikipedia as a Sociotechnical System'. *New Media & Society* 12 (8): 1368–1387.

Ostrom, Elinor. 1990. *Governing the Commons – The Evolution of Institutions for Collective Action*. Cambridge: Cambridge University Press.

Pascal, Blaise. 1910. *Thoughts, Letters, Minor Works*. New York: P. F. Collier & Son.

Pascal, R. 1938. 'Property and Society: The Scottish Contribution of the Eighteenth Century'. *Modern Quarterly* 1(2): 167–179.

Pisano, Gary P. and Willy C. Shih. 2012. *Producing Prosperity: Why America Needs a Manufacturing Renaissance*. Boston: Harvard Business Review Press.

Porter, Michael E. 1998. 'Clusters and the New Economics of Competition'. *Harvard Business Review* December: 77–90.

Porter, Michael and Claas van de Linde. 1995. 'Toward a New Conception of the Environment-Competitiveness Relationship'. *Journal of Economic Perspectives* 9 (4): 97–118.

Potts, Jason. 2018. 'Governing the Innovation Commons'. *Journal of Institutional Economics* 14 (6): 1025–1047.

Prendergast, Renée. 2010. 'Accumulation of Knowledge and Accumulation of Capital in Early Theories of Growth and Development'. *Cambridge Journal of Economics* 34 (3): 413–431.

2014. 'Knowledge, Innovation and Emulation in the Evolutionary thought of Bernard Mandeville'. *Cambridge Journal of Economics* 38 (1): 87–107.

Rae, John. [1834] 1964. *Statement of Some New Principles on the Subject of Political Economy*. Reprints of economic classics. New York: A. M. Kelley.

Rodrik, Dani. 2004. 'Industrial Policy for the 21st Century'. KSG Working Paper No. RWP04-047.

Rosenberg, Nathan. 1960. 'Some Institutional Aspects of the Wealth of Nations'. *Journal of Political Economy* 68 (6): 557–570.

1976. *Perspectives on Technology*. Cambridge: Cambridge University Press.

Schot, Johan and W. Edward Steinmueller. 2018. 'Three Frames for Innovation Policy: R&D, Systems of Innovation and Transformative Change'. *Research Policy* 47: 1554–1567.

Schmitter, Philippe C. 1985. 'Neo-corporatism and the State'. In *The Political Economy of Corporatism. Sociology, Politics and Cities*, edited by Wyn Grant. London: Palgrave.

Schumpeter, Joseph A. 1947a. *Capitalism, Socialism, and Democracy*, 2nd revised ed. London. George Allen & Unwin.
1947b. 'The Creative Response in Economic History'. *The Journal of Economic History* 7 (2): 149–159.
1961. *The Theory of Economic Development*. Translated by R. Opie. Oxford: Oxford University Press.
Shafaeddin, Mehdi. 2000. 'What Did Friedrich List Actually Say? Some Clarifications on the Infant Industry Argument'. UNCTAD/OSG/DP/149.
Skinner, Andrew. 1982. 'A Scottish Contribution to Marxist Sociology?' In *Classical and Marxian Political Economy*, edited by I. Bradley and M. Howard. London and Basingstoke: Macmillan.
Smith, Adam. 1976a. *The Theory of Moral Sentiments*. Edited by D. D. Raphael and A. L. Macfie. Oxford: Oxford University Press.
1976b. *An Inquiry into the Nature and Causes of the Wealth of Nations*, 2 Vols. Edited by R. H. Campbell, A. S. Skinner and W. B. Todd. Oxford: Oxford University Press.
1980. *Essays on Philosophical Subjects*. Edited by W. P. D. Wightman. Oxford: Oxford University Press.
Steuart, James. 1767. *An Inquiry into the Principles of Political Economy*. London: A. Millar & T. Cadell.
Swift, Jonathan. [1704] 1724. *A Tale of a Tub to Which Is Added an Account of the Battle between Ancient and Modern Books in St. James's Library*, 6th ed. London: S. Tooke and B Motte.
Teece, David J. 2018. 'Profiting from Innovation in the Digital Economy: Enabling Technologies, Standards, and Licensing Models in the Wireless World'. *Research Policy* 47 (8): 1367–1387.
Temple, Sir Willam. 1909. *Essays on Ancient and Modern Learning and Poetry*. Edited by J. E. Springbarn. Oxford: The Clarendon Press.
Thompson, William. 1824. *An Inquiry into the Principles of the Distribution of Wealth Most Conducive to Human Happiness*. London: Longman.
Thomson, Herbert F. 1965. 'Adam Smith's Philosophy of Science'. *The Quarterly Journal of Economics* 79 (2): 212–233.
Turgot, A. R. J. [1750] 1913. 'Tableau philosophique des progrès successifs de l'esprit humain'. *Oeuvres de Turgot*, Tome 2, 214–235. Paris: Librarie Felix Alcan.
[1751] 1808. 'Plan de deux discours sur l'histoire universelle'. *Oeuvres de M Turgot*, Tome 2, par P. S. Dupont de Nemours, 209–352. Paris: impr de Delence.
Viner, Jacob. 1961. 'Hayek on Freedom and Coercion'. *Southern Economic Journal* 27 (3): 230–236.
Watson, Matthew. 2012. 'Friedrich List's Adam Smith Historiography and the Contested Origins of Development Theory'. *Third World Quarterly* 33 (3): 459–474.
Winch, Christopher. 1998. 'Listian Political Economy: Social Capitalism Contextualized?' *New Political Economy* 3 (2): 301–316.
Yip, George S. and Bruce McKern. 2016. *China's Next Strategic Advantage: From Imitation to Innovation*. Boston: The MIT Press.

3

Individual Sovereignty and Coproduction of Knowledge Governance*

Edward J. López

How do shared governance rules emerge to sustain the exchange and production of knowledge goods? How are those knowledge governance rules – also known as institutional infrastructures (Frischmann et al. 2014) – established, enforced, and maintained over time? Understanding these questions at a basic level is useful to identifying contexts where efficient institutions tend to emerge organically, versus other contexts where policy or other interventions may bring improvements. If the establishment of governance structure is an exercise in drawing boundary lines and rules, then we might expect a complex society to have an innumerable mix of formal processes such as legislation, bylaws, and contracts, along with informal processes such as norms, customs, and culture. Many in the literature argue that rules in use are emergent, which means that the rules of interaction are the result and outcome of the interaction itself. This particular claim would benefit from further substantiation, further support within the framework of institutional analysis. Here I focus on the general process of establishing these informal and formal rules of knowledge governance, and I argue that, to some extent, coproduction of knowledge governance is endogenous to economizing behavior because in exchanging knowledge goods people also exchange knowledge, and in exchanging knowledge they contribute to the collective processes of forming shared understandings that are the building block of constructing institutions. To approach these questions, this chapter uses a simple scalar approach to specify the degree of knowledge content in

* This chapter was prepared for the volume, *Governing Markets as Knowledge Commons: The New Entrepreneurial History of Shared Social Infrastructures*, edited by Erwin Dekker and Pavel Kuchař. I thank the editors and the other contributors for helpful comments during the March 2019 manuscript conference hosted by Mercatus Center. I also thank James Caton for valuable discussion and collaboration on related work. Finally, I thank members of the "Quarantine Zoom Economics Drinks and Discussion" group, who began meeting on Monday nights during COVID-19 shelter-in-place conditions, and who became a community in the sense borrowed for this chapter. The usual caveat applies.

economic goods, and it adapts the Institutional Analysis and Development (IAD) framework to define community along non-geographic boundaries. Next we introduce individual sovereignty as a concept of power relations within non-geographic communities. The main contribution of the chapter is to utilize the IAD to identify contexts where collective action of community members is likely to perform well in the coproduction of knowledge governance. Namely, in contexts where individual sovereignty is high, and where the degree of knowledge content is high, members of the community contribute to the coproduction of knowledge governance as a by-product of their ordinary economic activity. A second contribution of the chapter is to show where four large areas of literature connect to form a basis for further study of knowledge commons. In this aspect, the chapter does not forge new territory but instead draws attention to some of the intellectual foundations and deep lines of thought that gird emerging scholarship on governing knowledge commons.

The IAD framework (E. Ostrom 1990, 2005, 2010) has been employed to study knowledge commons. The general editors of Cambridge Studies on Governing Knowledge Commons describe recent strands of research on a broad range of knowledge commons including scientific data commons, intellectual property pools, open-source software, wikis, internet protocols, newswire services, medieval guilds, and more. They set forth a research agenda to adapt the IAD framework from its original emphasis on physical goods to the newer emphasis on knowledge goods.

> There are many different knowledge commons. Yet we know very little about them: How do such commons work? Where do they come from, what contributes to their durability and effectiveness, and what undermines them? ... Building on Ostrom ... [we] developed a framework for the systematic study and comparative analysis of knowledge commons ... The underlying nature and structure of the inquiry as well as the focus on complexity, context, communities, and institutions unites our project with Elinor Ostrom's legacy.
>
> (Dedeurwaerdere et al. 2014: 2–3)

In other words, this research agenda seeks to develop systematic understanding of communal governance across all kinds of knowledge goods. How do communal institutional arrangements (which are mostly informal) emerge, how are they defined (access and use rights), how do they function (enforcement mechanisms), how long do they last (status quo survival), and under what conditions do they fail (institutional change)? These are the central questions in advancing IAD to knowledge governance. In this chapter, I contribute to this literature by identifying contexts where human action within market rules itself contributes to the implementation, maintenance, and evolution of those same rules. I combine elements of IAD to provide a way to define a notion of community that draws on social and economic boundaries, contra the usual geographic and political boundaries familiar to physical commons. Central to the contribution are the concepts of knowledge governance, individual sovereignty, community, shared understanding, and, following John Searle, the interaction between constitutive and regulative rules. The general point of the chapter is a comparative static between knowledge content and governance. Drawing on Searle's ontology of institutions and Ostrom's IAD framework, people's everyday expressions of information and sharing of knowledge contribute to the establishment of institutions. By exchanging knowledge goods people are exchanging ideas, and this very exchange of ideas can be sufficient to supply knowledge governance. The main implication for the literature is that entrepreneurial action in knowledge goods space is at once economic entrepreneurship, in the sense of producing and exchanging knowledge goods, while simultaneously it is also institutional entrepreneurship, in the sense of contributing to the establishment and maintenance of the knowledge governance institutional structure. As a corollary, supposing physical and knowledge goods are not binary categories (instead we can situate all goods on a continuum of knowledge content), then the greater the knowledge content in goods exchanged, the closer economic and institutional entrepreneurship approach simultaneous functions of the same human action. In the limit, when economic goods are purely constituted by knowledge content, the act of exchanging goods is sufficient for the coproduction of knowledge governance.

Section 3.1 lays the foundation for the rest of the chapter by making three analytic distinctions: (1) between physical and knowledge goods; (2) between knowledge goods and knowledge governance; and (3) between commons that involves a lack of ownership versus communal or shared ownership. Here we draw heavily from the traditional law and economics literature, which predominantly focuses on the degree of rivalry when formulating policy implications. By focusing instead on the degree of knowledge content in economic goods, we more clearly delineate where inefficiencies might arise. It matters, for example, whether policy correction targets the point of individual production of knowledge goods or the point of collective production of knowledge governance. Section 3.2 migrates the discussion to political theory and the concept of sovereignty. Sovereignty is the fundamental concept used to analyze distributions of power within a territory. It specifically references supreme authority; or, as we will see, it determines who in a territory is "the one who decides on the exception" (Schmitt 1934 [2005]). Sovereignty is distinct from rights, obligations, or duties. A sovereign might have the authority to use coercive force while simultaneously holding a duty not to use it. Venturing in this way into political theory is risky for at least a couple of reasons. First of all, the literature on sovereignty is vast and deep, so I will necessarily have to gloss over important subtleties and areas of fundamental disagreement among scholars.[1] That literature is also contentious and controversial on important issues that are not our focus. And finally, there may arise the question of fit. How does political authority find its way into analyses of knowledge governance? The answer, for purposes of this chapter, is

[1] Later in the chapter we will breach a fault line in the literature on sovereignty by equating territory with non-geographic margins of social proximity and individual identity.

that I use a stylized concept of sovereignty. Most of Section 3.2 is devoted to the particular notion of *individual* sovereignty, which I attribute to Vincent Ostrom (2006) and James Buchanan (1996), and which parallels the analysis of power relations both in Elinor Ostrom's IAD framework (E. Ostrom 2005) and in John Searle's ontology of society (1995). Common to all four of these major scholars is the similar theme that institutions not only shape and make possible human interactions by regulating behavior but also are everywhere a product of collective action. Governance is both produced by individuals in a community and consumed by those same members as a common pool resource. People draw benefits from the relative certainty provided by shared understandings and agreed-upon rules. All members of a community are free to avail themselves of the rules of engagement to structure their associations, form their bonds, make their investments, and engage in quotidian exchanges of sentiments and goods. Governance is both public enterprise dependent on individual contributions-in, and a common pool resources sustaining their extractions-out. This differentiates knowledge governance from more frequently studied natural resource common pools. This focus is similar to Kealey and Ricketts (2014; Chapter 1), who model science as a contribution good, and to Won and Klamer (Chapter 11), who describe shared governance among creative communities within large cities. To generalize, markets can extend beyond spot-trading opportunities only because of the institutions of contract, money, and property. These underlying economic institutions, once constituted, are available for all buyers and sellers to use. In short, the rules themselves, once having been coproduced within a community, then become a shared resource that members of a community utilize to structure their interactions. Communities therefore face a persistent collective action problem, namely, how to continually generate contributions to coproduce the common pool of knowledge governance and to maintain it over time such that the depletion rate of governance does not systematically exceed the replacement rate of governance. Governance is both public enterprise dependent on individual contributions-in and shared resources sustaining their extractions-out.

Sections 3.3 and 3.4 show how institutions are coproduced through systematic processes of idea exchange. Elements of the IAD are used to define community along non-geographic margins of people's social and economic connections. Institutions are fundamentally cognitive and communicative. Some early papers in the development of the IAD help us to see how Elinor Ostrom prioritized the cognitive origin of institutions and the centrality of language and communication to the coproduction of rules. She taught her students and readers to search for data in the language that people use, the expressions they make, and the ideas they trade. Much of this interleaves with, if not anticipates, the same cognitive and communicative foundation of Searle's ontology of institutions. I show these foundational connections between Ostrom and Searle, and use them to emphasize the interaction between constitutive rules, which social scientists tend to neglect, and regulative rules. In contexts of high individual sovereignty and high knowledge content of traded goods, once the constitutive rules are established, they imply and actually feature the regulative rules as well. Finally, in the concluding section I apply this framework of coproduction to communities that exchange goods of high knowledge content. I draw on some empirical results from the literature on intellectual property among magicians.

3.1 KNOWLEDGE GOODS, KNOWLEDGE GOVERNANCE, AND EXCHANGE ACTS AS SPEECH ACTS

In this section I distinguish knowledge goods from physical goods, placing the degree of an economic good's knowledge content on a continuum. I also distinguish knowledge goods from knowledge governance, treating knowledge governance as a coproduced collective good. And third, I distinguish communal ownership from commons. As I will argue, once we incorporate the degree of knowledge content in a good, then the degree of non-rivalry becomes irrelevant to questions of coproducing knowledge governance.

First let us classify economic goods into two distinct categories, physical goods and knowledge goods. A knowledge good derives its economic value from the configuration of ideas that are embodied in it. Knowledge goods do have some form of physical, tangible manifestation (ink on paper, or digital bytes, for example), which serves the function as medium for conveying the good. However, a knowledge good's economic value derives first from the configuration of ideas embodied in it, and secondarily from its physical manifestation. A theorem, a short story, and a radio signal are examples of knowledge goods. More generally, knowledge goods include information, science, creative works, data, and so on.

Many economics and legal scholars have argued that knowledge goods are non-rival by nature. Some argue that non-rivalry presents a market failure, in the sense that a policy intervention would be necessary to optimize producer incentives, otherwise knowledge goods fall under risk of over-depletion or under-provision relative to a social welfare standard. At issue is a *disclosure problem* associated with the supply of knowledge goods. Once an entrepreneur brings a knowledge good into circulation, the ideas behind its design and operation can be detected, and copied, by other entrepreneurs. In the case of celebrity image, for example, the sustainability of a celebrity's economic value to fans could be depleted through overexposure in media play, especially advertising. Disney notoriously manages the image exposure of its cartoon characters, and has vigorously pursued copyright expansion and enforcement. Likewise, entertainers including Bette Midler and Humphrey Bogart have prevailed in what is now a mature body of right-of-publicity cases. Trademark law, more broadly, recognizes the depletable nature of knowledge goods through its explicit rationale of avoiding brand dilution (Landes and Posner 2002). In general, due to the disclosure problem, many knowledge goods are non-rival, at least up to a congestion point. This non-rivalry translates into an incentive alignment problem. On the margin, a single copy of Adam Smith's *Wealth of Nations* might be of negligible marginal value, easily replaced with the next copy. Once Smith releases the particular configuration of words that constitute his brilliant work, that configuration and therefore the recipe for reproducing it becomes known to all. Similarly, a garment design embodies the ideas of the fashion designer. Once presented on the runway, the garment conveys the designer's ideas to all observers. Other fashion designers can therefore imitate or tweak those ideas by observing the garment (*Cheney Bros.* v. *Doris Silk* 35 F2d 279 1929; Raustiala and Sprigman 2006). Likewise, once a chef serves a dish, or once a magician performs an illusion, the ideas behind the good's appeal can be detected and imitated by others (Loshin 2008; Cunningham 2009). Similar dynamics unfold with craft goods, which can blur the lines between physical and knowledge goods. In their chapter, for example, Vachris and Vachris (Chapter 8) show how purveyors of fine Scotch whiskeys historically designated and over time maintained "single malt" standards of quality and production process, to distinguish from cheaper ("blended") and non-Scottish ("foreign") imitators. To negotiate the disclosure problem, these early single malt entrepreneurs took advantage of the fact that fine whiskeys take years to age, giving them a decade-plus first-mover advantage over would-be copyists. Similarly, the global scientific community has historically used attribution rules, such as naming of theorems or celestial bodies, to guard against the disclosure problem (Kealey and Ricketts 2014; Chapter 1). In these and other examples of supplying knowledge goods, the disclosure problem creates at least in principle an adverse incentive structure for achieving the socially optimal mix of knowledge goods produced. Under an expectation of being copied, a producer expects high fixed costs and insufficient marginal revenue to be profitable. Therefore, Adam Smith would have insufficient incentive to write *The Wealth of Nations*, fashion designer Yves Saint Laurent would not bother to pioneer the 1950s "New Look," and chef Roy Choi would not have innovated the Korean Taco. By this non-rivalry and disclosure-problem argument, an exclusive right to sell (e.g., a copyright) would ameliorate this disincentive.

Meanwhile, others have used non-rivalry in knowledge goods to argue the opposite policy prescription; namely that despite non-rivalry, market strategies and informal norms such as attribution can provide adequate producer incentives without a policy intervention. In performance magic, for example, Loshin (2008) argues that magicians need more nuanced rules than formal intellectual property law is capable of providing, so they rely instead on explicit norms for group admission and within-group interaction. A magician's claim to original ownership, for example, is established by performing the illusion publicly. Once ownership is established, enforcement norms are used to punish violators, initially with small and subtle social cues, but eventually by escalating to banishment if necessary.

A physical good, by contrast, derives its economic value from the configuration of materials that are embodied in it. Physical goods do have some forms of knowledge embodied in them (material science, basic design, production processes, etc.). However, a physical good's economic value derives first from its configuration of materials and second from its ideas. A deck of playing cards, a stack of lumber, and a radio receiver/player are examples of physical goods. More generally physical goods include real property (land, buildings), tangible property (vehicles, equipment), personal property (clothing, food), and so on.

Land use contexts also reveal that communities often utilize non-state/non-market governance structures. For example, in California's Shasta County, cattle ranchers establish and enforce boundary rules internally (Ellickson 1994). Similarly, groups of people have often established communal rights to govern shared access to fugitive resources, such as fisheries, elephants, underground water basins, and other resources that naturally migrate across the surface estate boundaries of real property (E. Ostrom 1990). Friedman (2000) describes the practice known as *unitization*, whereby individual property owners collectively govern shared access to subterranean oil reserves that flow across their surface estate boundaries. These and many more examples are better suited to communal rather than private property.

Now here is a puzzle. Even though physical goods are *rival* in use, they still carry a form of the disclosure problem, and this in turn carries social welfare and policy implications similar to those attributed to non-rivalry. Take real property, for example. Land is quintessentially physical and rival in use. However, a very large and mostly game-theoretic literature has accumulated around the disclosure problem in land assembly projects. The essential problem is, once information is disclosed that a developer is assembling parcels in an area, sellers in that area can strategically holdout and holdup to capture surplus. This causes delay and threatens otherwise efficient assemblies, thus creating social losses. Under the paradigm that distinguishes only two sets of policies, market or state, this problem leads to recommendations of eminent domain as corrective policy. By attenuating sellers' rights of alienation, eminent domain removes the option of holdout and thus restores social welfare (Miceli 2014). Notice that the disclosure problem rests a key feature of exchange, regardless whether it occurs in contexts of pure knowledge goods or pure physical goods: the very act of economic exchange itself conveys information. By the action of supplying the good, or assembling the parcel, economic entrepreneurs are communicating and receiving ideas. The argument in this chapter is that the exchange of ideas that is inherent to acts of economic exchange in turn shapes institutional arrangements. Ideas shape institutions, both in pure knowledge goods and in pure physical goods. Many land developers, for example, have eschewed eminent domain and instead have confronted potential holdouts with counterstrategies. These counterstrategies have included contingent contracts, strategic secrecy, holding companies, and more (Benson 2005). When developers seek market strategies, eschewing policy intervention, the role of the state is to recognize

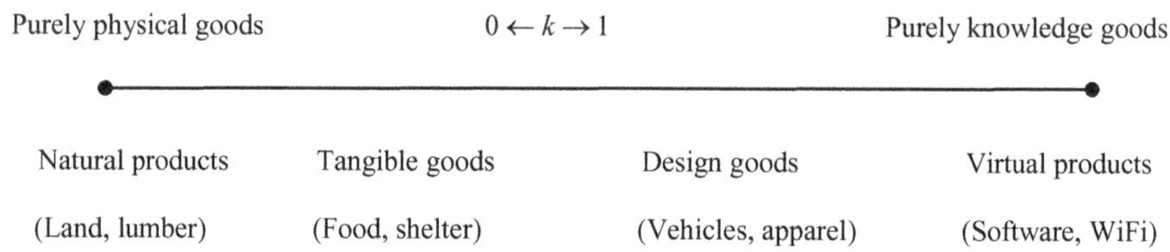

FIGURE 3.1. Intensity of knowledge content in economic goods

and enforce contracts. But when developers instead seek transfer of property through eminent domain, the state becomes an active participant in economic exchanges. These are very contrasting institutional settings, so this illustrates how economic action entails the exchange of ideas and as such it directly influences institutions.

Rather than the degree of rivalry or the disclosure problem and their implications for institutional arrangements, I focus instead on the implications of the degree of knowledge content in economic goods. To that end, let us next classify knowledge goods and physical goods not as separate categories but along a continuum. The economic value of a good in terms of its marginal revenue to the seller can be stated as $MR_q = k(QP)$, where P is the unit price, and the scalar ($0 < k < 1$) measures the degree of knowledge content embodied in unit q of economic good Q. Using the scalar k, we can place economic goods along a continuum that measures the intensity of knowledge content.

Figure 3.1 can be used to describe familiar aspects of economies. For example, the process of economic growth transitions an economy from a simple capital–labor mix, where k approaches zero, through its agricultural and then industrial development all the way to a modern "knowledge economy" where k approaches 1. We can also delineate the intensity of knowledge content within classes of goods. For example, we could construct a knowledge content continuum for food goods, and we would say that molecular gastronomy has a relatively high k while the k for home cooking is low. Similarly, high fashion embodies greater design content than commercial clothing does (Raustiala and Sprigman 2006). We can describe a range of knowledge content similarly for the engineering sophistication of cars, smart features in homes, and literary subtlety in television.

Different economic models become useful as we move to the right along the continuum. In cases of physical goods such as crops and lumber, a model of competitive equilibrium can organize much of the dynamics of the market. But as we move to the right, traditional models do not so readily apply. For example, as economic growth leads to greater k across much of the economy, then we begin to require models that feature endogenous growth or generalized increasing returns. Similarly, at the micro level, as innovative technologies create new markets with greater k than had been experienced before, traditional structure–conduct–performance models perform poorly. In the browser wars of the late 1990s (*United States v. Microsoft Corporation* 980 F.Supp 537), for example, the charge of monopolization was levied at an alleged monopolist for charging a price of zero. Alternative models built on network effects, and emergent competition and non-price competition began to make better account of the new, information-driven, knowledge economy. As greater knowledge content has prompted alternative models of markets, it has led to alternative models of governance as well. Focusing on the degree of knowledge content, rather than the degree of rivalry, enables us to focus on the coproduction process of knowledge governance.

The term *knowledge governance* refers to the formal and informal institutional arrangements that structure the production and exchange of knowledge goods. Discussions of knowledge governance are sometimes obscured by the term *knowledge commons*, which is ambiguous in use because it sometimes means the absence of any governance structure, but in other usages it means a governance structure is present yet it allows open access. Consider how Cole and Grossman (2005) summarize this ambiguity in their textbook, *Principles of Law and Economics*:

> Common property is often conflated with nonproperty/open-access, but it is easy to see that they are distinct institutions .... One apparent reason for the conflation of common property and open access is the use of the term commons to describe any area not owned by private individuals or the public/state. It remains crucially important, however, to distinguish between commons, which are collectively owned by some nonstate group to the exclusion of others, and commons, which are completely open-access so that no one has the right to exclude anyone else.
>
> (Cole and Grossman 2005: 95)

Notice that their discussion can be applied to goods along the range of *k*, from physical to knowledge, and that they trace the ambiguity of the term *commons* to an implicit binary assumption of institutional alternatives – either state regulation or free market (see Frischmann, Marciano and Ramello 2019 for further discussion of *commons*). But, of course, other alternatives include communal governance, absence of governance, and mixed or alternating regimes. Therefore, Cole and Grossman (2005: 94–96) continue by referencing four ancient Roman categories for property. First, *Res privatae* is private property. For example, a majority of land in the United States is held by private individuals or small groups of co-owners. In contexts of knowledge goods, *Res privatae* can be seen in the form of proprietary logo designs and branding slogans under the auspices of intellectual property law such as trademark. *Res private* is what economists typically mean when discussing private property rights. By contrast, *Res publicae* is the joint ownership by all in society as represented by the state. Over 40 percent of land in the United States is held by government entities at the local, state, or federal level. Prior to the use of spectrum license auctions in the mid-1990s, Congress controlled bandwidth under a public ownership regime, but following Coase (1959), spectrum was then partially privatized through auctions (Hazlett 2017). Third, *Res nullis* means the absence of exclusion rules such that no one in the society has property rights; therefore, all members of the public have open access. In Europe and North America, for example, modern-day governments have designated traditional rights of way and certain lakes and rivers as open access, available to the general public as shared common heritage. *Res nullis* can also be found in US copyright law, which continues to reserve for the public domain certain standard elements and gifts of nature, thus denying creative expressionists the exclusive rights to knowledge goods that are "the common heritage of humankind."[2] Whether in real property or knowledge goods space, notice that both *Res publicae* and *Res nullis* define the general public as the principal and the state as agent. The distinction is not whether the state is involved, or whether the governance structure is designed to benefit the public, but instead whether a rule of exclusion exists. And fourth, *Res communes* refers specifically to collective ownership and sharing of access and exclusion rights. A typical example in real property is the neighborhood swimming pool or the homeowners' association (Buchanan 1965). In the vein of Elinor Ostrom's work (e.g., E. Ostrom 1990), many examples of communal ownership have become well known in fisheries, water, and public enterprises. In knowledge space, many examples of open-source code fall into *Res communes*, and communal rights have also been formalized into nonstate institutional arrangements such as Creative Commons licensing (Lessig 2003).

In this chapter, I am primarily focused on *Res communes*. In particular, I seek to identify important implications of treating *knowledge governance* (the institutional structure supporting the production and exchange of *knowledge goods*) as itself a coproduction process of collective action under shared meta-rules of communal ownership. In this vein, I follow Frischmann (2012) in organizing governance as a social structure, and Aligica et al. (2019) in differentiating between joint production and coproduction, both working within the IAD framework. In my treatment, the structure of knowledge governance is itself a collective consumption good, whose production requires some coordination and organization of individual human action into useful collective action. In other words, this chapter simply asks: what determines the process of coproduction of knowledge governance? As we will see in Sections 3.3 and 3.4, shared understandings are the building blocks of social institutions, and communication of speech acts is how people form shared understandings. Therefore, Section 3.2 next describes the importance of individual sovereignty to loosening constraints on speech acts.

2 "Nature gives us ideas of animals in their natural surroundings: an eagle with talons extended to snatch a mouse; a grizzly bear clutching a salmon between its teeth; a butterfly emerging from its cocoon; a wolf howling at the full moon; a jellyfish swimming through tropical waters. These ideas, first expressed by nature, are the common heritage of humankind, and no artist may use copyright law to prevent others from depicting them." *Satava* v. *Lowry* 323 F.3d 805 (2003)

3.2 INDIVIDUAL SOVEREIGNTY, SPEECH ACTS, AND TERRITORIALITY

Sovereignty is a fundamental concept in political theory that refers to assignment of political authority. At its most general level, sovereignty is defined as "supreme authority within a territory" (Philpott 2016). The assignment of political authority amounts to "who sets the rules." For example, following Schmitt (1934 [2005]), the "sovereign is he who decides on the exceptions." The sovereign's authority can be absolute, in the sense that it spans the entire range of human affairs within a territory, or it can be non-absolute, whereby the sovereign is still the supreme authority but within a more narrowly defined scope of activity. For example, a sovereign might have supreme authority over matters of trade and state, but that authority might not extend to matters of family or religion.

Historically, by assigning authority, sovereignty implied responsibility. As a responsibility, it was not equivalent to a right, or a license, or a duty. For example, medieval sovereigns had rights that far surpassed those of subjects, but sovereigns were still bound by justice in their treatment and protection of subjects (de Jouvenel 1957 [1997]). To this point, de Jouvenel emphasizes the "fortunate powerlessness of kings" that prevailed during the medieval periods of the absolute monarch. There we find that kings did enjoy more political rights than subjects did; however, the sovereign could not violate those relatively few rights that subjects did enjoy while still claiming to be just. Furthermore, kings were not all powerful but instead entered contractually into arrangements with subjects to exchange resources for rights protection. Therefore, while kings held supreme authority on most matters, on contracted matters they instead held duties to not infringe. With the gradual decline of kings and the Church, culminating in 1648s Treaty of Westphalia, sovereignty shifts from the crown to what would become the universally dominant form of political organization, the state. Then, with the period of Enlightenment philosophy and American constitutionalism, sovereignty shifts still further, this time from the state toward the individual, who transforms during this process from subject to citizen (de Tocqueville 1835). Then, with the late nineteenth- and early-twentieth-century rise of totalitarianism, sovereignty shifts from individuals to the nation-state. Finally, since about mid-twentieth century, the sovereignty tension has located between nation-states and international federations – a set of battles that plays itself out today in the United Kingdom, Catalonia, Hong Kong, Quebec, and between Washington and the 50 states. Territoriality is usually understood in the geographic sense, which in turn defines the community to which individuals belong. "Territoriality is a principle by which members of a community are to be defined. It specifies that their membership derives from their residence within borders .... It is rather by simple virtue of their location within geographic borders that people belong to a state and fall under the authority of its ruler" (Philpott 2016: 3–4).

The particular notion of sovereignty used in this chapter is based on James Buchanan's concept of *individual sovereignty* (Buchanan 1996) and Vincent Ostrom's *citizen-sovereign* (V. Ostrom 2006), both of which fall in the line of Enlightenment philosophy and liberal constitutionalism. The main differences I add here are twofold. First, I place a more explicit emphasis on territoriality than either Buchanan or Ostrom do, and second I define territory to include cultural, economic, and other social boundaries as well as the geographic and political boundaries that are the traditional emphasis in studies of sovereignty.

In their treatments of sovereignty, Buchanan and Ostrom both fall into a line of liberal thinkers on the topic that includes Bertrand de Jouvenel, Alexis de Tocqueville, James Madison, Adam Smith, and more. For Buchanan, the hallmark of *individual sovereignty* is the protection of inalienable rights against tyranny sourced in the coercive power of the state. Philpott (2016) distinguishes between the mere wielding of coercive power as compared to the right to use it. Buchanan self-identifies as a philosophical anarchist, by which he means there should be a presumption of liberty, and any infringement requires solid justification. In *The Limits of Liberty: Between Anarchy and Leviathan* (Buchanan 1975), he attempts to delineate the scope of human affairs within which the state has legitimate authority to use coercive force. For example, in a key chapter he treats the law as a public good, directly anticipating theories of social capital. In one subset of human interaction, people's activity contributes to the upholding of the law, and to the law's beneficial reform in the direction of liberal constitutionalism. However, in the remainder of human action, people free-ride on others' contributions to the collective production of law. The scope of the latter category forms the basis for the scope of legitimate state authority – to solve the free-rider problem in the collective production of law. However, outside that scope, where no compelling reason can be identified for state infringement on private affairs, the individual is sovereign (Buchanan 1996). In particular, Buchanan prioritizes economic rights and the off-limits status of economic activity.

> It is relatively easy to describe the ideal structure of politics for a large community, defined by territory or by numbers of citizens, if the overriding objective is the protection of individual sovereignty against political coercion. A central government authority should be constitutionally restricted to the enforcement of openness of the whole nexus of economic interaction.
>
> (Buchanan 1996: 265)

In other words, the state's legitimate role is to support and sustain economic activity by enforcing open access to economic activity. In an explicit Tiebout-competition framework, Buchanan concludes that *competitive federalism*, by its virtue of providing each citizen with the power of exit as an enforcement mechanism, also provides the optimal protections against infringement of individual sovereignty. Vincent

Ostrom, in his 2005 John Gaus Lecture, similarly emphasizes the individual citizen's sovereignty, and its implications for the individual's civic responsibilities.

> Rather than sovereign nation-states and associations of nation-states, ... we need to give serious attention to Tocqueville's concept of the principle of the sovereignty of the people reinforced by the assessments of Hamilton and Madison about the essential place of individual responsibility in the exercise of the prerogatives of persons and citizens. Fictions created by the association of individuals are helpful only in light of shared understandings and complementarities of actions amid continuing reflection and choice. Fictions are ways of creating concepts about social realities, not reality as such .... [L]ife in civil society is constituted by how individuals as persons and citizens relate to one another in multitudes of shared communities of understanding in the pursuit of innumerable opportunities. Among these innumerable opportunities are values that we characterize as learning, enlightenment, and scholarship.
>
> (V. Ostrom 2006: 15)

In Ostrom's approach voice rather than exit is the key mechanism. In his Tocquevillian approach, the very processes of social interaction that constitute civil society are processes of communication. People tell stories, learn from each other, and study together, while they simultaneously seek shared understandings and opportunities for mutual betterment. Both James Buchanan and Vincent Ostrom treat human interaction as collective action processes that constitute rules of interaction, and regulate decisions of state and private individuals. Exit and voice are expressions of individual sovereignty, and individuals use them to limit the scope and reach of state infringement. Where exit and voice are curtailed or attenuated, human action threatens to become misaligned with beneficial progress.[3] As applied to knowledge goods, this same line of reasoning reflects the feature that economic action necessarily communicates information. Exchange acts are speech acts, and the general process of exchanging ideas contributes to the collective production of knowledge governance. The following two sections fuse Elinor Ostrom's IAD and John Searle's ontology of institutions to reflect this same collective action implication: economic interaction is exchange of speech acts, and speech acts create the shared understandings used to collectively define institutions.

3.3 NON-GEOGRAPHIC COMMUNITIES, POWER RELATIONS, AND THE COGNITIVE AND COMMUNICATIVE FOUNDATIONS OF RULES: COMBINING ELEMENTS OF THE IAD FRAMEWORK

Neither Buchanan nor Ostrom stresses territoriality in their treatments of sovereignty, although geographic area is clearly implicit. This gap can be addressed using

[3] In the conclusion we return to ongoing literature in this line of thought, for example Aligica et al. (2019) whose approach supports maximizing the space for diversity of viewpoint, and Boettke and Candela (2017) for maximizing the space for economic exchange to realize generalized increasing returns.

elements of the IAD framework, which is designed as a generalized set of nested building blocks that can be modified to study a broad range of social contexts. The IAD framework situates individuals in a dynamic action arena, where participant interactions are linked to potential outcomes and feedback loops. The IAD accommodates models of individuals that go beyond optimizing within constraints. Individuals are assumed to be adaptive, learning, and imperfect agents pursuing usually multiple and often conflicting objectives. Of central importance are the rules of interaction, both "rules in form" and "rules in use." Detailed treatments of the IAD framework originate in E. Ostrom (1990, 2005, 2010), and applications to knowledge commons can be found in Frischmann et al. (2014) as well as in the introduction to this volume. Here I will utilize three key aspects of the IAD framework. First, the framework's boundary rules provide a mechanism to define community, and this notion of community can in turn define non-geographic territory of individual sovereignty. Second, some of Elinor Ostrom's early papers on the elements of institutions emphasize power structure within a situation, and the implied relative freedoms of expression. This early work thus anticipates the concept of individual sovereignty as developed in Section 3.2. Third, as with Vincent Ostrom's emphasis on voice above, Elinor Ostrom characterizes rules of interaction as being formed through communication, thus anticipating the argument that exchange of speech acts is a mode of collective action that contributes to the production of governance. This can be seen, for example, in her work on the evolution of social norms (E. Ostrom 1999). This section, therefore, joins the work that applies the IAD framework not only to physical goods such as fisheries, or to services such as water or security, but also to knowledge goods and to the institutions of knowledge governance that support them (Hess and Ostrom 2007).

Communities are groups of individuals interacting under the same shared understandings about the rules in form and rules in use that govern their situation. Within the IAD framework, communities begin with collectively agreed upon boundary rules. A community's boundary rules govern membership; they determine the individual attributes needed for entry, and they set conditions for entry to and exit from membership (E. Ostrom 2005: 194 ff.). Persons who satisfy the boundary rules are welcome to interact on this side of the boundary, within the community, while those who do not must remain out. Boundary rules may reference geographic space, as with land assembly problems or fugitive resources that we discussed in Section 3.1. Boundary rules may also delineate areas along non-geographic margins, where people on any given occasion might interact each as members of numerous overlapping communities at once. Once inside the boundary, whether defined along geographic lines or not, a nexus of within-group rules governs individuals' interactions with others in the community. These rules determine an individual's stature within the community (position rules), their potential impact on others in the community (scope rules), what authority supports or restricts her actions within the community (authority rules), what knowledge they contribute to and withdraw from the community (information rules), how much weight their decisions carry (aggregation rules), and the costs and benefits to them and others of their actions (payoff rules). These within-group rules also govern members' interactions with non-members. Among these rules are those that determine the degree of control, opportunity, and therefore power held by each individual. With these latter rules, we can use the IAD framework to identify variables that determine the scope of individual sovereignty within a community.

The concept of sovereignty can be recognized in the IAD framework by focusing on Elinor Ostrom's treatment of power in her early working papers on the IAD (E. Ostrom 1983, 1985).[4] As discussed above, sovereignty can be understood in traditional geographic contexts as a right to use coercive force, which might be limited or unlimited in scale and scope depending on the rules of engagement. Ostrom isolates the particular rules that are relevant for sovereignty in communities with geographically or socially defined boundaries, namely those that shape an agent's *opportunity* and *control* within a situation.

> The power of an individual in a situation is the value of the opportunity (the range of outcomes afforded by the situation) times the extent of control. Thus, an individual can have a small degree of power even though the individual has absolute control if the amount of opportunity in a situation is small, or conversely, when the amount of opportunity is large, but the individual has only a relatively small degree of control. Action situations may involve differential distributions of control and opportunity to different individuals in the situation. Consequently, individuals may differ in the amount of power they have in the situation. Concepts of opportunity, control, and power are thus defined as situation dependent. A single individual may have dramatically different levels of control, opportunity, and power in the different action situation[s] in which they participate.
>
> (E. Ostrom 1983: 19)

We can see that her discussion of power mirrors the discussion of sovereignty from above. Sovereignty can be supreme yet non-absolute, as power can similarly extend over a range of opportunities yet still depend on one's degree of control. Furthermore, her focus on the distribution of power among *individuals* in a situation mirrors Buchanan's and Vincent Ostrom's focus on *individual* sovereignty from above. A highly centralized political order is prone to attenuate individuals' opportunities for exit and voice, thus concentrating the political situation's distribution of power. In the IAD, the rules in form and rules in use of any situation will determine the distribution of power in that situation. This naturally raises the question how the rules in form and rules in use take their shape.

Cognition and communication are fundamental to the third feature of IAD used here. The use of language to exchange ideas sustains the process of individuals

[4] I thank Pavel Kuchar and Erwin Dekker for pointing me to these early articles.

coming to shared understandings with others. The exchange of ideas is fundamental, therefore, as "all participants must share some information about the situation before an analyst can even state that the participants are in an action situation" (E. Ostrom 1985: 5). This theme of sharing information, of communicating among others, is therefore antecedent in the IAD framework to people subsequently forming shared understandings. Through repeated interaction within a community, there is a give and take, a back and forth, a dynamic game of knowledge sharing. This leads people in a community to develop ways of doing things. They adapt toward certain behavioral norms with each other, and they adopt certain institutional rules of membership and within-group interaction. All of this is accomplished through the exchange of knowledge and ideas toward the development of shared understandings.

> Two of the key types of building blocks identified in this approach – rules and community – are basically cognitive in nature! One cannot say they are operative, until real people in real situations learn the rules and meld them with their cultural heritage into an ongoing activity with predictability and meaning for the participants. While we can treat rules and community as types of variables in an analytical scheme—as we do in the framework—these variables do not operate in the world unless they are part of the cognitive frame of the participants.
>
> (E. Ostrom 1985: 16)

The main overall application to knowledge goods and knowledge governance that we draw from combining these three elements of the IAD is that rules are cognitive and communicative in nature. Institutions do not form without individuals thinking and talking together to form shared understandings. Elinor Ostrom instructed users of the IAD to study people's discourse, "to discover the linguistic statements that form the institutional basis for shared expectations that influence observed regularities in behavior... Is there an articulated sense of moral or social obligation expressed?" (Crawford and Ostrom 1995: 586). As we will see, these early papers anticipate much of the same emphasis on language and shared understandings in John Searle' ontology of institutions. By delving next into Searle's framework, we better see that institutional rules, once constituted through cognition and communication, also regulate behavior. Searle's framework provides a clear and general notation for making these connections and applying them to questions of knowledge goods governance.

3.4 CONSTITUTIVE AND REGULATIVE RULES AS COPRODUCTIVE COLLECTIVE ACTION: INCORPORATING SEARLE'S SOCIAL ONTOLOGY

Social scientists tend to emphasize institutions as regulative rules – those rules that constrain actions in antecedently existent arenas. In economic exchange, for example, the formalization of rights, duties, and responsibilities through property and contract law came long after people had been pursuing their natural tendencies to truck, barter, and exchange. Similarly, legislation governing organ transplants, genetic modification, ride sharing, and autonomous cars were passed only once these technologies took on actual practice in society. In other contexts, however, people's actions did not precede the establishment of rules, but instead were made possible only by the establishment of new rules. Many board games such as chess fit this description. Searle (1995: 27) describes: "It is not the case that there were a lot of people pushing bits of wood around on boards, and in order to prevent them from bumping into each other all the time and creating traffic jams, we had to regulate the activity." Rules that create new action arenas are *constitutive* rules. Once the rules of chess constitute the play of chess, the same rules now *regulate* the play of chess. In this sense, constitutive rules always imply regulative rules.

Like the IAD, Searle's framework provides highly generalized building blocks for analysis of institutions in diverse contexts. In Searlean terms, institutions are constituted by collective assignment of status functions to social phenomena. People use language to tell stories, exchange observations, and share "beliefs, hopes, desires, emotions, perceptions, and lots of others" (Searle 2006: 56) to express *collective intentionality* about the purpose of a situation, and to *assign function* to the elements of an action situation. This *collective assignment* of function enables people to *constitute rules* that coordinate individuals' actions, both in cooperative and conflictual situations, based on shared understandings of the rules that govern the situation. The collective assignment of status functions is a necessary condition for people to interact on recognized terms, especially in non-physical situations amenable to knowledge goods analysis, where

> the collective assignment of function is imposed on a person or an object where the function is not performed in virtue of the physical features of the person or the object, but rather, in virtue of the fact that the collective intentionality assigns a certain status to that person or object and that status enables the person or object to perform a function which could not be performed without the collective acceptance of that status. An obvious example is money. The piece of paper in my hand ... performs the function not virtue of its physical structure but in virtue of collective attitudes.
>
> (Searle 2006: 57–58)

In all situations, institutional rules and systems of rules follow the form: X counts as Y in context C. The term X is a phenomenon of the physical or social world. It can be an object, an idea, an action, a proposition, or almost any phenomenon that could possibly be considered. The term Y is a status function that represents the status of X as an institutional rule. The phrase "counts as" lies at the heart of institutional formation. This process is what Elinor Ostrom describes as cognitive and necessarily communicative in nature. This is one of many direct parallels between Elinor Ostrom's development of the IAD and Searle's development of the ontology of society. We also see here direct parallels to Vincent Ostrom's emphasis on voice and social interaction that we covered in Section 3.2. In Searle's treatment, people in the community engage in speech acts, and in the process come to shared understandings about the status of diverse phenomena in their physical and social contexts. People express shared understandings as collective recognition, collective acceptance, and collective acknowledgment of all phenomena in the nexus of X, all toward the eventual collective assignment of status to any phenomenon $X_{i,t}$ in context C_t that it serves function $Y_{i,t}$. This process of establishing an institution is cognitive and communicative in nature, as it comes when people use ideas and language to collectively develop shared understandings about various physical and social facts of the world. Through continued exchange of ideas in repeated interaction, people come to collectively assign functions to those physical and social phenomena. As Searle (1995: 40) sums up, "This is the beginning point of all institutional forms of human culture, and it must always have the structure X counts as Y in C."

Consider Searle's structure applied to the boundary and within-group rules of a community that trades in a high knowledge context and features high individual sovereignty. For example, suppose there is an X_a that can be expressed as "a member of the magician community has publicly performed but has not published a novel illusion." According to the collectively coproduced rules constituted in context C_t, "period t in the community where people produce and exchange magic tricks," X_a counts as Y_a, "this magician owns this illusion." As Loshin (2008: 31) reports, "Performance of a trick without publishing it is a magician's strongest signal to the magic community that she intends to keep it for herself." Such a rule is how magicians collectively agree on how to solve the disclosure problem discussed in Section 3.1 and thereby constitute rules to coordinate their behavior toward mutual gain. Now suppose a different X_b could be expressed as, "a member of the magician community has disclosed communally owned magic secrets to non-magicians." Magicians consider this to be a serious offense and therefore this would count as Y_b, "economic value has been permanently lost from magician's common pool of secrets" in the context C "the magician community." Notice that articulating either phenomena X_a or X_b involves an implicit assumption that a boundary rule has been constituted, and that it has determined prior to the emergence of phenomena X_a or X_b who is and who is not a member of the magician community. In short, we can easily see that boundary rules to determine community membership, and within-group rules to regulate member interactions, are as much contained in Searle's ontology as they are in Ostrom's IAD.

Notice also that once established, these constitutive rules also regulate the play of the game. In other words, constitutive rules imply regulative rules. It is striking how easily Searle's framework can be adapted to define and specify many combinations of the elements of an IAD action situation as we have just seen. These include boundary rules that determine membership in a community and within-group rules that regulate interaction among community members. Searle's framework also affords clear distinction between constitutive and regulative rules. Both E. Ostrom and Searle provide that constitutive rules are sourced ultimately in cognitive and communicative processes. Both use similar deontic powers arguments as their general mechanisms that connect the establishment of constitutive rules with the necessarily implied regulative rules that follow. Both also take the further next step in connecting deontic powers with the distribution of power in a community. "The answer is that the status functions are the vehicles of power in society . . . What we have in society is a set of deontic power relations" (Searle 2006: 59). Crawford and Ostrom (1995: 585) argue in parallel, "the meaning of the deontics obliged (*must*) and forbidden (*must not*) fit well into most conceptions of normative statements. . . In many instances, assigning a *may* to an action is the equivalent of 'constituting' that action (Searle 1969)."[5] The interaction between constitutive and regulative rules can be easily expressed using the adapted Searlean framework in Caton and López (2020):

X counts as Y incontext C, therefore if α then β.

The constitutive rule Y is necessarily followed by the regulative rule if α then β. To illustrate, consider again the X_a and X_b examples from the magician community. Social norms that assign rights to valuable goods may require enforcement or inducement norms to achieve compliance. Therefore, the constitutive rule Y_a, "this magician owns this illusion," necessarily implies the regulative rule: if α_a "a second magician performs the illusion elsewhere without attribution," then β_a, "peers in the community reduce their respect and esteem for the second magician." Searle (1995: 104 ff.) frames the implied regulative rules as structuring the power relations within a community. An individual's power in any given situation can always be expressed as "the power to do something or constrain someone else from doing something" (Searle 1995: 104). Therefore, any status function Y implies an agency function whereby person (or group) S has or does not have the power to take action A. There are numerous formulations of this general structure. In the magician community, assigning ownership status through Y_a means that the originator magician S_o is allowed under the rules to take A, "perform the novel illusion."

> [T]his non-exposure norm remains the most strongly and consistently enforced of the bunch. Indeed, it tends to be treated as an absolute, per se rule. Magicians break the norm even when they reveal their own secrets. Any exposure damages the common enterprise of magic; it cheapens the craft.
>
> (Loshin 2008: 30, italics in original)

[5] This is one of several clear ties between the building blocks of the IAD and the ontology of institutions from Searle.

This community's strongest rules of ownership imply that nonowners such as the would-be copyist magician, S_c, are not permitted to take action A. Furthermore, if a person S_c does take action A, then another set of regulative rules, namely enforcement rules that are composed of the same general structure, enable all other persons of the community to enforce Y_a by shunning or reducing their respect and esteem for S_c. All these rules in use emerge as a consequence of the community first constituting the ownership rules. Notice that the regulative rules, which are necessarily implied by the constitutive rules, draw the contours around freedom of expression. Because magical illusions are nearly pure knowledge goods, their performance by magicians and their consumption by the viewing public are acts of economic exchange that are inseparable from the speech acts used to make their exchange.

3.5 CONCLUSION: INDIVIDUAL SOVEREIGNTY AND KNOWLEDGE CONTENT

How do communities coproduce knowledge governance? Traditional approaches treat knowledge governance as non-rival and its production as vulnerable to free riding, which internal mechanisms and policy interventions can be designed to ameliorate. Much of the scholarship on knowledge governance aims to understand these organic community mechanisms and to design effective external interventions to solve free-riding on non-rival resources. Policy discussions often conflate individual production of knowledge goods with collective coproduction of knowledge governance. Substantial scholarly effort has been deployed to clarify this confusion with resort to models of economic entrepreneurship within rules distinct from institutional entrepreneurship to change rules.

This chapter has instead set non-rivalry and free-riding aside, focusing instead on the degree of individual sovereignty enjoyed in a community and the degree of knowledge content in the economic goods that community members exchange. In contexts where the knowledge content of economic exchange is relatively high, and where individuals are sovereign in their expression of ideas, people's ordinary economic activity contributes to the coproduction of knowledge governance. To make the case for this, this chapter has drawn elements from four large bodies of work: law and economics, political theory, IAD, and Searle's ontology of institutions. Salient to these varied approaches are two fundamental features that carry useful implications for governing knowledge commons. First, scholars in all four areas treat social institutions as the shared product of collective action. To varying extents, scholars in all four areas also distinguish between formal and informal institutions. Second, people's use of language and repeated interaction to form shared understandings often contributes directly to this rule-producing collective action. The main contribution of the chapter is to draw attention to an implication of this latter point. Specifically, as the degree of knowledge content in economic goods increases, that is, as the scalar discussed earlier in the paper, $k \to 1$, and as individuals have more sovereignty, then we can expect endogeneity of economic and institutional entrepreneurship, such that people in their ordinary economic behavior simultaneously pursue their individual ends while contributing to the coproduction of the shared governance rules that sustain the community.

How do communities shape their rules? We have focused on the collective action of individuals as a direct outcome of their ordinary economizing interaction within communities. Individuals become members of communities by satisfying various boundary rules, defined along traditional geographic as well as emergent non-geographic margins. Community membership means individuals agreeing to be regulated by the communities. By interacting within those rules, individuals contribute to the process of repeated interaction and trial-and-error evolution of those rules. By contributing to the evolution and creation of new shared understandings, their interaction is constitutive of new rules on the margin. We can see this especially in cases where innovators work within extant rules while exerting pressure on the creation of new and replacement rules. In other words, entrepreneurship within rules often channels innovation toward the margins of a community's shared understanding. This seems to be pronounced in contexts of high knowledge content. Many knowledge commons contexts, for example, self-governing internet communities, have an egalitarian ethos and a presumption that knowledge and ideas are free and mutually shared. In these communities, shared resources are like shared beliefs, and the collective ethos may well be both cause and effect of these underlying shared understandings. For example, cases have been studied in areas of internet governance and self-governing online communities. Harris (2018) presents a case study of online pirate communities who collectively define and enforce effective boundary and within-group rules. Similarly, Gradoz and Raux (Chapter 9) study website communities where members self-define and self-enforce rules and freely enter and leave communities. Members who sufficiently push the boundaries of agreed-upon rules become classified as trolls, and enforcement norms are used to push undesired activity to the margins, sometimes resulting in groups of trolls establishing their own communities and rules. Interestingly, geography is orthogonal to the definition of boundary rules in these communities. Yet geography can still be an advantage to intergroup interactions. Leeson (2008) explains how large populations of diverse individuals and groups use signaling mechanisms (i.e., they convey low-cost information about more subtle knowledge) to solve social distance obstacles to exchange. In contexts of knowledge goods such as creative goods industries, where the disclosure problem discussed earlier in the chapter can deter exchange, within-group norms enforce attribution, and enable sharing. Recent evidence suggests that agglomeration economies are more pronounced where creators are in closer communication with each other, especially by cross-group geographic proximity (Tao et al. 2019). Similarly, the global scientific community spans all geographic boundaries, yet maintains within-group social proximity through certain rules that promote coproduction of governance and outcomes (Kealey and Ricketts 2014; Chapter 1). In these and many similar contexts, future research may further untangle the relationships between people's ordinary economic activity and the coproduction of knowledge governance.

The analysis carries social and policy implications at broad levels. Individual sovereignty is not exclusively about state infringement on the individual sphere of authority as defined by formal rules such as constitutions and legislation. Because economic exchange is idea exchange in contexts of high knowledge content, individual sovereignty reduces to freedom of expression in many of these contexts. Sovereignty can therefore be perturbed by state rules that attenuate otherwise eligible members' access to boundary rules, or by state action that distorts organic within-group rules. Strong exit and voice can be used as mechanisms to avert concentrations of power. As applied to policy, the state's implied role is to provide external structure for knowledge goods communities to maximize internal access for economic exchange (Buchanan 1996; Boettke and Candela 2017) and viewpoint diversity (V. Ostrom 2006; Aligica et al. 2019). Meanwhile, nonstate positions of power in a community can also perturb individual sovereignty. In communities with concentrations of power, individual sovereignty is subject to greater uncertainty and is less extensive in scope. In communities where power is more evenly distributed, however, individual sovereignty is of a larger scope and greater certainty. In summary, individual sovereignty in a community necessarily implies access to the arena in which people exchange ideas. As applied to knowledge goods contexts as identified in this chapter, this open access priority implies a polycentric approach and a reliance on within-group mechanisms to coproduce, enforce, and sustain shared governance rules.

REFERENCES

Aligica, Paul D., Peter J. Boettke, and Vlad Tarko. 2019. *Public Governance and the Classical-Liberal Perspective*. Oxford University Press.

Benson, Bruce. 2005. "The Mythology of Holdout as a Justification for Eminent Domain and Public Provision of Roads." *The Independent Review* 10 (2): 165–194.

Boettke, Peter J., and Rosolino Candela. 2017. "The Liberty of Progress: Increasing Returns, Institutions, and Entrepreneurship." *Social Philosophy and Policy* 34 (2): 136–163.

Buchanan, James M. 1965. "An Economic Theory of Clubs." *Economica* 32 (125): 1–14.

1975. *The Limits of Liberty: Between Anarchy and Leviathan*. University of Chicago Press.

1996. "Federalism and Individual Sovereignty." *Cato Journal* 15 (2–3): 259–268.

Caton, James, and Edward J. López. 2020. "The Cognitive Dimension of Institutions." In *A Companion to Douglass North*, edited by Andres Marroquin and Nikolai Wenzel, 233–260. Francisco Marroquin University.

Coase, Ronald. 1959. "The Federal Communications Commission." *Journal of Law & Economics* 2: 1–40.

Cole, Daniel H., and Peter Z. Grossman. 2005. *Principles of Law and Economics*. Pearson Prentice Hall.

Crawford, Susan, and Elinor Ostrom. 1995. "A Grammar of Institutions." *American Political Science Review* 89 (3): 582–600.
Cunningham, Emily. 2009. "Protecting Cuisine under the Rubric of Intellectual Property Law: Should the Law Play a Bigger Role in the Kitchen?" *Journal of High Technology Law* 9: 21–51.
de Jouvenel, Bertrand. 1957 [1997]. *Sovereignty: An Inquiry into the Political Good.* Liberty Fund.
Dedeurwaerdere, Tom, Brett Frischmann, Charlotte Hess, David Lametti, Michael Madison, Charles Schweik, and Katherine Strandburg. 2014. "An Introduction to Knowledge Commons." Workshop on Governing Knowledge Commons.
Ellickson, Robert C. 1994. *Order without Law.* Harvard University Press.
Friedman, David. 2000. *Law's Order: What Economics Has to Do with Law and Why It Matters.* Princeton University Press.
Frischmann, Brett M. 2012. *Infrastructure: The Social Value of Shared Resources.* Oxford University Press.
Frischmann, Brett M., Alain Marciano, and Giovanni Battista Ramello. 2019. "Tragedy of the Commons after 50 Years." *Journal of Economic Perspectives* 33 (4): 211–228.
Frischmann, Brett M., Michael J. Madison, and Jatherine J. Strandburg (eds.). 2014. *Governing Knowledge Commons.* Oxford University Press.
Harris, Colin. 2018. "Institutional Solutions to Free-Riding in Peer-to-Peer Networks: A Case Study of Online Pirate Communities." *Journal of Institutional Economics* 14 (5): 901–924.
Hazlett, Thomas W. 2017. *The Political Spectrum: The Tumultuous Liberation of Wireless Technology, from Herbert Hoover to the Smartphone.* Yale University Press.
Hess, Charlotte, and Elinor Ostrom. 2007. *Understanding Knowledge as Commons.* MIT Press.
2014. "Modeling Science as a Contribution Good." *Research Policy* 43: 1014–1024.
Landes, William M., and Richard A. Posner. 2002. "Indefinitely Renewable Copyright." John M. Olin Law & Economics Working Paper No. 154: 1–48.
Leeson, Peter. 2008. "Social Distance and Self-Enforcing Exchange." *Journal of Legal Studies* 37: 161–188.
Lessig, Lawrence. 2003. "Dunwody Distinguished Lecture in Law: The Creative Commons." *Florida Law Review* 55 (3): 763–768.
Loshin, Jacob. 2010. "Secrets Revealed: Protecting Magicians' Intellectual Property without Law." In *Law and Magic: A Collection of Essays*, edited by Christine A. Corcos, pp. 123–142. Durham: Carolina Academic Press.
Miceli, Thomas. 2014. *The Economic Theory of Eminent Domain: Private Property, Public Use.* Cambridge University Press.
Ostrom, Elinor. 1983. "The Elements of an Action Situation." Working Paper W83–23. Workshop in Political Theory and Policy Analysis, Bloomington, IN.
1985. "Formulating the Elements of Institutional Analysis." Working Paper W85–15. Workshop in Political Theory and Policy Analysis, Bloomington, IN.
1990. *Governing the Commons: The Evolution of Institutions for Collective Action.* Cambridge University Press.
1999. "Collective Action and the Evolution of Social Norms." Working Paper W99–20. Workshop in Political Theory and Policy Analysis, Bloomington, IN.
2005. *Understanding Institutional Diversity.* Princeton University Press.
2010. "Prize Lecture: Beyond Markets and States – Polycentric Governance of Complex Economic Systems." *American Economic Review* 100 (June): 641–672.

Ostrom, Vincent. 2006. "The 2005 John Gaus Lecture: Citizen-Sovereigns – The Source of Contestability, the Rule of Law, and the Conduct of Public Entrepreneurship." *PS: Political Science and Politics* 39 (1): 13–17.

Philpott, Daniel. 2016. "Sovereignty." *Stanford Encyclopedia of Philosophy* (Summer 2016): 1–24, https://plato.stanford.edu/cgi-bin/encyclopedia/archinfo.cgi?entry=sovereignty.

Raustiala, Kal, and Chris Sprigman. 2006. "The Piracy Paradox: Innovation and Intellectual Property in Fashion Design." *Virginia Law Review* 92 (8): 1688–1777.

Schmitt, Carl. 1934 [2005]. *Political Theology, Four Chapters on the Concept of Sovereignty*. University of Chicago Press.

Searle, John R. 1995. *The Construction of Social Reality*. The Free Press.

2006. "Social Ontology: Some Basic Principles." *Anthropological Theory* 6 (1): 12–29.

Tao, Jin, Chun-Yu Ho, Shougui Luo, and Yue Sheng. 2019. "Agglomeration Economies in Creative Industries." *Regional Science and Urban Economics* 77: 141–154.

Tocqueville, Alexis de. [1835, 1840] 1945. *Democracy in America*, edited by Phillips Bradley, 2 vols. Alfred A. Knopf.

4

Common Sense Commons

The Case of Commonsensical Social Norms

Brett Frischmann

Common sense is fundamental to humanity in two different but related ways. First, it is a basic capability essential to human flourishing.[1] It helps us effectively engage with each other and our complex world. Second, it is social knowledge, often situational and contextual. Though easily taken for granted, common sense functions as critical social infrastructure that shapes and enables various social systems, including markets. This chapter examines this special type of social infrastructure, exploring common sense in general and focusing on the subset of common sense that also constitutes social norms.

Common sense and social norms are concepts with rich histories and hotly contested meanings across different disciplines and contexts. I draw on existing literatures but do not provide a comprehensive literature review, nor do I engage debates about contested meanings of the terms. Instead, in Section 4.1, I define my terms and carefully limit the scope of my inquiry. Section 4.2 explains that commons sense, understood as a body of social knowledge about the common sense world, and commonsensical social norms are forms of social infrastructure, and like most infrastructure, these critical social resources tend to be underappreciated and taken-for-granted by users, producers, and policy-makers. Section 4.3 explores commons governance of common sense and commonsensical social norms. I examine an interesting nesting of knowledge commons: the essential "inputs" for common sense (namely, the shared core knowledge base, language, and social interactions sufficient to generate common understandings and beliefs) are knowledge commons, and the shared "outputs" of common sense also are knowledge commons.

4.1 DEFINING TERMS AND THE SCOPE OF THIS CHAPTER

This chapter explores an important domain of social knowledge. I begin by adopting a definition of common sense, and then I narrow the scope of the resource set in two

[1] See Appendix.

steps: First, by focusing on common sense solutions to everyday life problems, and second, by focusing on social norms. These steps are mainly for expository and analytical convenience. This two-tiered discussion allows me to explore each tier while making connections between them. Rather than comprehensiveness, my aim is to reveal areas deserving exploration in future research, especially systematic empirical research guided by the Governing Knowledge Commons framework (Frischmann, Madison, and Strandburg 2014).

Common sense entails shared knowledge and skills that shape how we perceive, understand, and live our everyday lives. I adopt the following perspective on *common sense knowledge* and the *common-sense world* offered by Philosopher Gerald Erion:

> A more focused notion of commons sense ... [is] virtually universal among typical adults because it concerns an important subset of objective reality that we all live our everyday lives in, the *common-sense world*. As rough approximation, it is helpful to think of the common-sense world as the realm of familiar objects that we become acquainted with during ordinary experience. People, plants, non-human animals, and simple geographic features are all included in this world, while sub-atomic particles, neurons, and galaxies are not .... [We] can understand *common sense* itself as the base of knowledge about common-sense reality that allows each of us to survive and thrive during our everyday lives. Common beliefs about the common-sense world are the most prominent components of this knowledge base. ... common sense also includes the widespread abilities that allow us to act successfully in the common-sense world.
>
> (Erion 2001: 33. italics added)

Erion explains how work in "various cognitive sciences" supports his claim that this type of common sense exists. It entails core knowledge and skills that are shared and "used by all of us (even skeptical philosophers) during our everyday lives." Language is critical to common sense both as knowledge and as skill. That is, competence in using language is a "subset of common sense" (Erion 2001: 36).

"Many cognitive scientists believe that the mind is equipped with innate intuitive theories or modules for the major ways of making sense of the world. These are modules for objects and forces, for animated beings, for artifacts, for minds, and for natural kinds like animals, plants, and minerals" and for much more (Pinker 1997: 314–315). "An intelligent system [...] cannot be stuffed with trillions of facts. It must be equipped with a smaller list of core truths and a set of rules to deduce their implications," which are features of common sense (Pinker 1997: 14). As Redekop (2009: 404–406) explains in the excerpt below, modern research has validated principles of common sense that Thomas Reid articulated in the late eighteenth century (see also Redekop 2020).

> Some facial expressions – such as a smile – have a cross-cultural, universal emotional meaning, pointing to the existence of what Pinker terms an "intuitive psychology" shared by all humans (Ekman 1982; Pinker 1997: 29–30, 63–64).

> Research on infants has shown that we come into the world equipped to perceive cause-and-effect relationships, and to perceive objects as continuous, bounded units that move on coherent paths, affecting each other's motion only if they touch (Leslie 1984; Leslie and Keeble 1987; Spelke 1994). Using sophisticated techniques of habituation and dis-habituation, researchers have concluded that "the idea of cause and effect lies at the heart of both commonsense and scientific thought" (Leslie and Keeble 1987: 265).
>
> We not only come equipped to perceive causality in inanimate objects, but agency or intention in animate ones (Premack 1990; Gelman and Gottfried 1996). And there is good reason to think that we come into the world predisposed to think of things (including living beings) as having essences; according to Gelman and Wellman (1991), "Young children distinguish insides of objects from their outsides, even when the two conflict, and believe that insides can be more essential to an object's functioning and identity" (239; see also Medin and Ortony 1989). Human beings are by nature essentialists; whatever its drawbacks, without the assumption that things have essences that make them what they are, we would be unable to identify and categorize complex entities.
>
> Echoing Reid, educational psychologists suggest that "Education and development is possible because of the existence of [...] primitive 'commonsense' categories and mental operations" in children, for example a "number sense" or the ability to judge relative magnitudes (Olson 1987: 327). Generally speaking, in contrast to previous, more empiricist and behaviorist theories, cognitive scientists now argue that "[Innate] knowledge is central to common-sense reasoning throughout development. Intuitive knowledge of physical objects, people, [numerical] sets, and places develops by enrichment around a constant core, such that the knowledge guiding infants' earliest reasoning stands at the center of the knowledge guiding the intuitive reasoning of older children and adults" (Spelke 1994: 439).

Most of us possess and use common sense and are capable of commonsensical thinking, meaning we can perceive, interpret, and understand each other and our everyday world through our senses and experiences. Yet the knowledge and skills we possess are hardly uniform or uniformly distributed. The intellectual resources vary significantly across people and communities and their shared everyday experiences. For example, members of different communities may have different common sense beliefs about what to do when one's car breaks down on the highway, how long one should wait before repeating a question, or how much to tip in a restaurant, among many other things. Some common sense beliefs conflict with each other and with scientific studies. Common sense – as I have defined it for present purposes – does not mean universal, true, or even accurate; it often is culturally contingent, varied, and mistaken or erroneous.

The definition I adopted from Erion conflicts with Plato's more restrictive definition of knowledge as "justified true beliefs." Plato was critical of the sensory experiences and shared public beliefs as forms or sources of knowledge. He elevated true scientific knowledge. Aristotle, in contrast, saw value in that which Plato disdained. Common sense knowledge was foundational for scientific inquiry and inductive reasoning about the world and how it worked. Take what is given – as intellectual infrastructure (see Section 4.2) – and be willing to question, test, and revise it through reasoned inquiry. Despite recurring Platonic skepticism of common sense as a genuine form or source of knowledge in modern science and philosophy, I, like many others, follow the Aristotelian view.

There is much that common sense does and can do in helping make sense of the world, yet there is much that common sense gets wrong. Again, as Redekop (2009: 408) usefully explains:

> [P]erhaps one of the most important conclusions to be drawn from a study of common sense is that while it is most useful in localized, face-to-face interactions that mirror those of our ancestral hunter-gatherer environment, it is less useful in settings which transcend that environment. As we have seen, with the rise of modern science a gulf began to open between common sense and science, and for good reason. Many of the discoveries of modern science – and particularly those that make use of advanced mathematics – contradict or go beyond common sense. Modern science has been very good at reaching beyond everyday sense experience to uncover truths that seem to go against our basic intuitions, whether we are talking about an earth in motion or the behavior of subatomic particles. We are not constituted to easily make sense of things on the scale of the very large and the very small; large numbers, time frames, and distances pose problems for us, as does the behavior of electrons and quarks (see Oppenheimer 1954, for a classic discussion of this point).

Redekop appropriately notes that scale and scope issues arise with common sense. This may be due to sensory, experiential, or social factors in the generation, curation, and sharing of common sense knowledge. Common sense often is contextual and even situational, and as such, often embedded in culture, norms, and language. One can find common sense lurking beneath the surface of many different philosophical and sociological theories about knowledge and social norms, ranging, for example, from Donna Haraway's work on situated knowledge to Helen Nissenbaum's work on contextual integrity and norms for appropriate information flows (Haraway 1988; Nissenbaum 2009). These theoretical approaches reveal how common sense, as a body of shared social knowledge, often serves as social infrastructure for market and nonmarket systems.

Common sense depends upon a shared core knowledge base, language, and social interactions sufficient to generate common understandings and beliefs about "the realm of familiar objects [and experiences] that we become acquainted with during ordinary experience" (Erion 2001). This statement serves as an important limitation on the scope of our definition and constitutes an important claim. To see why, suppose that one of the essential preconditions or inputs for generating common sense is eliminated. Imagine, for example, that people in a community failed to interact with each other in a manner sufficient to generate common understandings and beliefs about their everyday lives. Maybe they are simply too busy, distracted, or entertained to take the time to discuss the many seemingly mundane aspects of their everyday lives. Bear in mind that this is just a thought experiment. The point is to show the nature of the claim: *common sense is not a given; it is contingent.* "The precursors or inputs to the creation and sharing of common sense are not stable or inevitably accessible and shared" (Frischmann and Selinger 2018: 203).

The quality of common sense as a form of knowledge depends upon the quality of accessible inputs, which typically comprise a body of shared knowledge, as well as the social processes and skills involved with its creation, curation, and distribution within a community.[2] In prior work on knowledge commons, coauthors and I use "knowledge" capaciously to capture a wide range of intellectual resources, recognizing that in many specific contexts we need to differentiate among different types of knowledge resources. In this chapter, I follow that same functional approach and treat common sense as a set of knowledge (or knowledge-related) resources. If we follow Erion and "understand *common sense* itself as the base of knowledge about common-sense reality that allows each of us to survive and thrive during our everyday lives," we have cast a rather wide net that encompasses a nearly limitless range of knowledge. After all, our everyday lives are quite varied and complicated.

To narrow the scope and identify areas where governance dilemmas arise, let us focus on the knowledge domain of problem-solving that encompasses common sense solutions to problems faced in our everyday lives. Many everyday problems involve an element of Knightian uncertainty when trying to figure out what to do (Knight 1921). Think for a moment about many of the problems you encounter daily that require you to use common sense. There are many examples, yet it can sometimes be difficult to identify one because like most infrastructural resources, common sense knowledge often operates behind the scenes, in the background, taken for granted.

Readers of this chapter in early draft offered the following suggestions of everyday problems for which common sense solutions seem appropriate:

- You run out of coffee filters and don't have time to go shopping
- You wake up in the morning with a sore back or throat
- You forgot where you left something
- You forgot someone's name or birthdate

[2] There is much more one could unpack from the history and philosophy of science, epistemology, and other fields that engage in debates about common sense. But I will spare you. (I highly recommend Redekop's book in progress, Common Sense and Science: From Aristotle to Reid.)

What should you do in these or similar situations? Most of us rely on common sense solutions to address these types of problems. In *Re-Engineering Humanity*, Evan Selinger and I explore the following example:[3]

> Suppose Alice gets in a taxicab, gives the driver an address, and then falls asleep. Thirty minutes later, the taxicab driver wakes Alice, takes her money, and leaves immediately after she exits the vehicle. After shaking off her initial grogginess, Alice realizes the cab dropped her off in the wrong location, and she is lost. What does common sense dictate suggest she should do?

Take a moment and think about your answer. For anecdotal data, I turned to Facebook and Twitter to find out what common sense suggested Alice should do. Many commenters suggested she order a cab using Uber. Among other things, they assumed she had a smartphone and felt safe enough to use it in public. After many similar comments, one person expressed surprise that no one had suggested Alice look around and ask someone for help.

Evan and I suggest Alice should get her bearings, formulate a plan, and take action. How would she do this? Presumably by looking around, observing people, reading street signs, and so on. Her senses could provide her with baseline information that would help her evaluate her situation, options, and decide on a course of action. Based on such information about her environment, Alice could form beliefs about her safety, whether she could trust people, whether people would understand her, and so on. Assessing her present situation would include evaluating risks and uncertainties concerning her future (Knight 1921). She might be able to determine the likelihood of another taxi arriving or whether some form of public transportation was accessible nearby. She might be able to figure out her location and then formulate a plan for getting safely from there to her intended destination.

We have assumed Alice possesses the relevant situational and problem-solving common sense. What if she lacks the ability to get her bearings through the various means just described? What if she is unable to take in and translate the various cues and information? Perhaps her incapacity stems from a physical or cognitive disability. Perhaps she has never had the necessary experiences that would have led her to develop the relevant abilities. For example, perhaps her prior navigation of the world was technologically mediated and fully automated. Perhaps she was raised in a town with no street signs and thus would not think to look at street signs for location data. She might lack the relevant situational and problem-solving common sense because she has never discussed the problem of being lost with anyone else or contemplated the situation in which she now finds herself. That may seem hard to fathom but being lost may be a problem of the past, at least in the near future. After all, upon recognizing her plight, Alice need only pull out her smartphone, and she'll be on

[3] The next few paragraphs are adapted from Re-Engineering Humanity.

her way to her intended destination. She need not ask anyone for directions, learn very much about the environment in which she finds herself, or do much planning.

Common sense may dictate using technology in one form or another – be it a map, cellphone, or smartphone. The technologies, however, are not neutral or equivalent. The degree to which a person such as Alice relies on (i) herself, her common knowledge base of beliefs, and experiences, and critically, on other human beings, rather than (ii) a technological device and system that varies quite substantially across different technologies (e.g., from map to cellphone to smartphone). The shift from (i) to (ii) is relevant and important. We might think that common sense becomes embedded in the technological devices and shifting from (i) to (ii) entails a shift in the relevant community of human beings that Alice relies on – that is, from the community of people Alice knows and shares common experiences with to the community of people behind the technological system. Either way, the shift is remarkable and worth examining. It is by no means limited to the thought experiment. One could formulate a similar thought experiment around what common sense dictates in a variety of everyday circumstances, such as when one feels a sharp pain in one's back or when there is a power outage. Doing so would lead to the same observations, shifting from (i) to (ii). The shift affects the nature of knowledge production, curation, and governance. This is an area ripe for systematic study. Though beyond the scope of this chapter, case studies using the GKC framework could focus on different examples where these shifts are taking place.[4]

Let us narrow the scope again by focusing on the intersection of common sense solutions to everyday problems with social norms. These are overlapping sets. Let us call the shared elements *commonsensical social norms*. Social norms have been studied extensively by various disciplines, including philosophy and the social sciences (for a review, see Bicchieri et al. 2018). Social norms are generally defined as the informal rules that govern social behavior. Bicchieri et al. (2018) note that some scholars focus on the *functions* of norms, for example:

> [as] efficient means to achieve social welfare (Arrow 1971; Akerlof 1976);
> [to] prevent market failures (Jules Coleman 1989), or cut social costs (Thibaut and Kelley 1959; Homans 1961);
> [as] either Nash equilibria of coordination games or cooperative equilibria of prisoner's dilemma-type games (Lewis 1969; Ullmann-Margalit 1977), [and thus, solutions to] collective action problems (Bicchieri et al. 2018).

Others put aside functionalism and focus on explaining how social norms emerge, persist, spread, or die. For example, "[n]orms are represented as equilibria of games of strategy, and as such they are supported by a cluster of self-fulfilling

[4] There is an interesting intellectual history that relates Frank Knight's work on common sense in the face of uncertainty to the Ostroms' work on shared communities of understanding. I thank the editors for this observation.

expectations. Beliefs, expectations, group knowledge and common knowledge have thus become central concepts in the development of a philosophical view of social norms" (Bicchieri et al. 2018). Connecting both streams are those who examine *norm conformity*, that is, whether or not individuals (groups) conform to norms. For example, game theoretic accounts suggest "conformity to a social norm is always conditional on the expectations of what the relevant other/s will do" (Bicchieri et al. 2018). In a sense, norms not only specify what one person ought to do but also what one may reasonably expect others (ought) to do. Each of these foci is relevant to the study of commonsensical social norms and commons governance more generally (Frischmann, Madison, and Strandburg 2014).

Commonsensical social norms are often functional solutions to everyday social problems, including those that arise regularly in everyday market contexts. For example, consider the simple problem of an audience member who would like to interrupt a speaker to ask a question. Common sense solutions to this problem range from (i) signaling the speaker, for example, by raising your hand, to (ii) exercising restraint and waiting until the speaker has finished. The appropriateness and effectiveness of solutions vary dramatically according to the context, culture, and community. In some contexts, (i) is acceptable only for clarification questions and (ii) is the default for all other questions. In other contexts, (i) is always appropriate. It may depend upon whether the speaker is a teacher in a classroom (and what type), a public speaker in a large auditorium, an entrepreneur making a pitch to potential investors (or to their roommates). It may depend on the relationships between the speaker and audience members.

Despite the variability, these types of common sense solutions may become normalized within different contexts, cultures, and communities. In the academic context, for example, many rituals are commonsensical social norms that solve simple coordination problems. Take rituals followed during faculty workshops or meetings. These rituals vary considerably across different academic institutions and even among departments within an institution. There is no "correct" solution. What matters is that a group follows a norm and thereby adopts a solution. Though some have suggested that social norms are not planned (Bicchieri et al. 2018), adoption still may be explicit; sometimes, groups recognize, discuss, and debate options. The same analysis applies if we switch to family rituals, conventional market practices at the county fair or corner store, and a host of other everyday coordination problems that require social communications to commit to a norm.

In other cases, commonsensical social norms alleviate or even avoid more difficult collective action problems, for example, those involving prisoners' dilemmas. One relatively cheap means for avoiding tragedy of the commons dilemmas, at least in reasonably small-sized and close-knit groups, is maintaining communications and repeat interactions among members of group. Not surprisingly, social norms requiring attendance at meetings and participation in discussion or deliberation are common (sensical).

Consider a few examples related to privacy, security, and use of technology in social situations:

- *Privacy-related commonsensical social norms*:
  - Wear clothing in public.
  - Respect people's express or implied desire for confidentiality.
  - Be clear if you seek confidentiality.
  - Host of norms arguably derived from the "Golden Rule," such as
    - Don't eavesdrop.
    - Don't surveil others in private or public spaces: Don't record (or post) videos of people, don't take photos and search for them with Google, don't live-cast other people's lives without their permission.
- *Security-related commonsensical social norms*:
  - Be smart about passwords.
  - Don't click on attachments unless you know for sure what it is, who sent it, and why.
- *Commonsensical social norms regarding smartphone use in social settings*:
  - Turn off your phone in theater, classroom, and other public settings.
  - Use headphones when watching videos, listening to music, or having a conversation on public transportation.
  - Don't put your phone on the table during meal.

These off-the-cuff examples are illustrative. I list them to identify common sense solutions to both long-standing and more novel but increasingly common everyday problems. For some examples, it is contestable whether a social norm exists (yet). For example, applying the Golden Rule to an individual's use of a smartphone to surveil others in public is not necessarily normalized. I return to many of these examples below.

4.2 COMMON SENSE AS A FORM OF SOCIAL INFRASTRUCTURE

In this section, I briefly explore the infrastructural nature of common sense knowledge. This requires (at least) two conceptual tasks. First, I explain what I mean by infrastructural. Second, I apply that theory to common sense knowledge.

According to Frischmann (2012), infrastructural resources satisfy the following criteria:

(1) The resource may be consumed nonrivalrously for some appreciable range of demand.
(2) Social demand for the resource is driven primarily by downstream productive activities that require the resource as an input.
(3) The resource may be used as an input into a wide range of goods and services, which may include private goods, public goods, and social goods.

The first criterion captures the consumption attribute of public and impure public goods (Samuelson 1954; Cornes and Sandler 1996). In short, this characteristic describes the "sharable" nature of infrastructural resources. The second and third criteria focus on the manner in which infrastructural resources create social value. The second criterion emphasizes that infrastructural resources are capital goods that create social value when utilized productively downstream and that such use is the primary source of social benefits. The third criterion emphasizes both the variance of downstream outputs (the genericness of the input) and the nature of those outputs, particularly public goods and social goods.

Applying the infrastructure criteria to intellectual resources, such as common sense, delineates a broad set of resources that create benefits primarily through the facilitation of productive activities, many of which generate spillovers – that is, benefits for third-parties not involved in the activities. The three-criteria definition of infrastructure can be reduced: Nonrival input into wide variety of outputs. This seems incredibly capacious. Intellectual infrastructure can be identified and analyzed at various levels of abstraction, ranging from the meta-cultural-environment itself to a discrete general-purpose input, such as a basic idea, to a specific expression that has broad communicative power and social meaning.

Language is an excellent example of intellectual infrastructure with strong public and social components, for language serves as the foundation for the production and exchange of knowledge and the development and operation of social systems and interdependencies. Of course, language is the basic infrastructure for social exchange in markets and nonmarkets, and as noted in the previous section, language is intimately related to common sense.

Common sense likewise qualifies as intellectual infrastructure, particularly when it is conceptualized as a body of knowledge resources used productively to explain, understand, navigate, or otherwise deal with situations people face in everyday life. Social interactions and economic transactions often depend upon countless bits of shared knowledge we take for granted, ranging from expected rituals to initiate a transaction to conceptions of what is (un)fair or (in)appropriate to the shared meaning attributed to gestures, language, and other communicative acts. Frank Knight (1921) emphasized how basic, shared classification schemes and "knowing what to do" when facing genuine uncertainty often depend upon common sense. He recognized the infrastructural nature of such knowledge and the everyday nature of such uncertainty. His early analysis influenced the Ostroms and contributed to their views on shared communities of understanding, rule-in-use, and the relationship between actions and outcomes.

Like all knowledge, common sense is nonrivalrously consumed, meaning that it is sharable and consumed at zero marginal cost. As a body of knowledge, it is generic or general-purpose and not narrowly directed toward one specific use. Like a dictionary, encyclopedia, library, or other collection of knowledge, common sense may consist of many different more specific or applied examples or entries. Even then, the common-ness of the knowledge makes it relevant and relatable to many and thus somewhat generic. We need not choose a level of abstraction, for common sense is infrastructural at multiple levels – for example, the Golden Rule generally or applied in specific contexts.

To appreciate the infrastructural nature of common sense, it is helpful to return to the idea of a *common sense world*. In *Worlds of Common Sense: Equality, Identity, and Two Modes of Impulse Management*, Pauline Nichols Pepinsky (1994) summarizes decades of sociological and psychological research comparing the common sense worlds of Norway and the United States and examines how those worlds shape social attitudes, beliefs, values, and behavior. Persistent, salient characteristics of the environment (e.g., size, scale, and complexity of country; physical conditions; and political history) shape the common sense world, meaning the basic premises of everyday life (e.g., in Norway: everyone knows everybody else, the truth will come out, nature is close and powerful, strangers are suspect, and power seekers are not trustworthy, to name just a few mentioned by Pepinsky) as well as values (e.g., in Norway: virtues, including rational behavior, kindness, honesty, and cooperativeness, *inter alia*, and vices, including impulsivity and loss of emotional control, arrogance and pride, pretense and deception, and exploitation of others, *inter alia*). Pepinsky examines how the common sense worlds shape basic social norms (e.g., in Norway: basic general rule that "no one is better than anyone else" and series of corollaries, such as "avoid making a fool of yourself before others," "think before you speak," and "avoid risk taking"). These commonsensical social norms feed into and become a part of Norwegians' common sense world. The shared body of social knowledge is infrastructural, cultural, and environmental. (Compare Frischmann 2007, 2012 on cultural environment as intellectual infrastructure.)

As a predominantly social infrastructure, common sense knowledge, including commonsensical social norms, often is produced, curated, sustained, and disseminated in social systems that are nonmarket and nongovernment. Families, clubs, communities, and other social groups produce common sense solutions to problems faced in members' everyday lives. Yet in everyday life, actions and interactions in market and political contexts also contribute to the production and distribution of common sense.

There are strong interdependencies among different social systems (market, government, social). People live their everyday lives in environments shaped by all of them, at times moving among these systems and at times directly engaged in all of them. These social systems depend heavily upon the common sense world as social infrastructure. For example, in Norway and the United States, different ideologic orientations toward the role of government and markets in society, reflected in and derived from the different *common sense worlds*, shape how people interact with those social systems (Pepinsky 1994).

At a much more practical level, markets depend on many commonsensical social norms that coordinate behavior and facilitate transactions. For example, similar to the earlier discussion of interrupting speakers, there are plenty of common sense solutions to everyday commercial problems – such as tipping – that vary across contexts, cultures, and communities. Naming and other classification systems are another example (Knight 1921).

The supply and demand logics of market and political systems are not what fundamentally drive the production, sharing, and use of common sense knowledge. People do not manifest their demands for common sense knowledge through prices or votes; entrepreneurs and politicians typically are not competing to supply people with the commons sense solutions they need – if anything, quite the opposite. Yet, as Kuchař (2016) suggests, entrepreneurs might need to propose novel common-sense interpretations and classifications to justify interactions that would otherwise not have been legitimate. Such entrepreneurial epistemic action seems to work with and within the social production model I have suggested. Common sense is produced socially (or jointly) as people communicate with each other about their everyday lives and experiences, including their success and failures in addressing familiar problems. Dekker and Kuchař (2019) relate this to the more conventional economic idea of joint production (see also Cornes and Sandler 1996).

This matters for a few reasons. First, it means that we need to understand how the social systems work to generate common sense knowledge. I have said some and will say some more about this, but I highlight it in this chapter mainly to flag it as an interesting area for further research. Second, we need to appreciate how social systems interact with market and political systems. There are advantages and disadvantages to each in addressing a variety of social issues, but as the series of arguments in Appendix suggested, I wonder whether the market for supposedly smart technological solutions to many of our everyday problems may have a detrimental impact on individual and social capabilities for common sense (e.g., common sense thinking as well as socialization). Third, we need to appreciate how much of the infrastructural value of common sense knowledge is not captured by those producing or disseminating it. There are significant spillovers from its use, yet that does not mean there is a market failure or need for government to intervene and fix something. The flow of externalities can be a social boon.

I do not mean to overstate the third point, however. On the one hand, some value from producing, curating, and disseminating common sense knowledge is captured. Effective commonsensical social norms generate direct benefits for the group via cheaper and more effective cooperation and social coordination. Further, reputational benefits have long been attributed to wise people within communities (e.g., a family, tribe, or village). Reputed wisdom often is based on trusted competence grounded in experience (rather than intellectual prowess or analytical capacity); of course, there are other reasons and factors to consider (e.g., power).

On the other hand, social systems and common sense can fail and lead to negative externalities as well. In fact, social systems can fail in various ways that are analogous to market failures. For example, socially valuable common sense knowledge may not spread as widely as it could or should. There may be various explanations for this, but one reason might be that a social group that arrives at a decent common sense solution to an everyday problem may have little incentive to share the knowledge beyond the group. This may explain why there is market demand for "life hack" books, articles, websites, and so on that collect such knowledge and distribute it more widely.

Plus, common sense can be biased and wrong. It can conflict with scientific evidence, and it can lead people to make terrible decisions. For example, in some communities, it may be common sense that vaccination leads to autism or some other malady, and so community members may refuse to get vaccinated. Yet this erroneous belief contradicts scientific evidence and can harm community members and others.

4.3 GOVERNANCE OF COMMON SENSE

In this section, I explore commons governance of common sense. This is a difficult task. It feels odd to talk about *governing* common sense. There doesn't seem to be an explicit or even implicit institutional framework, but that is only because common sense is so broad a set of knowledge and so ubiquitous yet variable across contexts. Can we really say that common sense worlds are governed? Of course, we can, although the modalities of governance run the gamut. The governance, like the knowledge, is contextual, social, and contingent upon the communities within which the knowledge is generated, cultivated, and shared.

Commons is a mode of governance for resources that can be especially attractive for infrastructural resources (Frischmann 2012). It usually entails governance of, by, and for the community. A core principle is sustainable sharing on nondiscriminatory terms within the community (Frischmann, Madison, and Strandburg 2014). With respect to infrastructure,[5] this usually means nondiscrimination among users and uses, and the corresponding preservation of equality and general purposiveness. The basic functional idea is to leverage nonrivalry and the sharable nature of the infrastructure (first criterion) to sustain the general-purpose nature of the infrastructure and support the wide range of user activities that generate private, public, and social goods (second and third criteria). In an important sense, commons governance engineers a degree of freedom for community members to decide for themselves about how to use shared resources. Frischmann (2012) explains how commons management insulates resource users from the logics and demands of market and political systems.

Common sense is, by definition, knowledge shared among members of the community. But it is not clear that such sharing incorporates nondiscrimination

[5] The defined community may be the public, in which case commons management converges with open access. The community might also be more limited in scope, in which case there may be members and nonmembers. See Frischmann (2012); Frischmann, Madison, and Strandburg (2014).

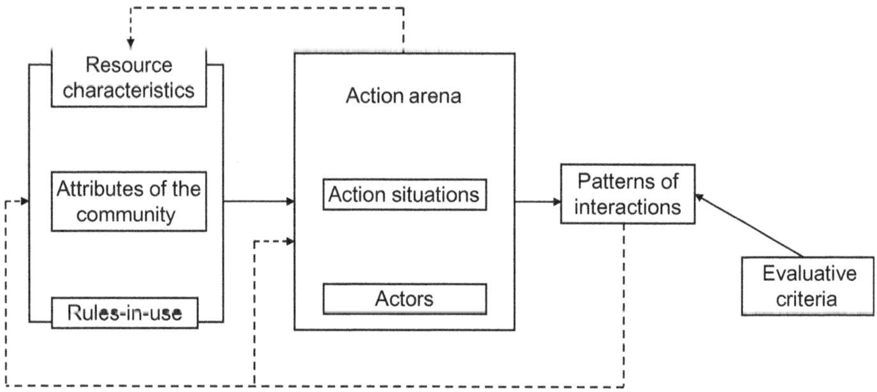

FIGURE 4.1. Governing Knowledge Commons framework

in a meaningful way. Moreover, common sense often implies a specific use rather than expanding members' freedom or range of choices. Commonsensical social norms regulate behavior, after all. But commons governance is more relevant to an examination of how community members produce and share common sense knowledge and how they participate in generating and normalizing what come to be commonsensical social norms.

We can identify different "action arenas"[6] (stages) where commons governance plays a role in the emergence, persistence, and diffusion of common sense knowledge in general and commonsensical social norms in particular. For those less familiar with the Governing Knowledge Commons framework, consider the following diagram (Figure 4.1).

According to Sanfilippo, Frischmann, and Strandburg (2018: 122–124):

> An action arena is simply a recurring type of situation in which community actors interact with one another. Interactions in an action arena produce outcomes, denoted here as patterns of interaction, which can then be evaluated according to some community or socially generated criteria .... [R]esource characteristics, community attributes (including members and roles), and a set of governing "rules-in-use" are inputs to an action arena. Patterns of interactions accumulate, feeding back to create new action situations and influencing resource characteristics, community attributes, and rules-in-use. Knowledge resources are often produced and defined by the community. The knowledge outputs of some knowledge commons action arenas must themselves be managed by the community and may be inputs to further knowledge production .... The "action arena" concept is flexible and can be applied at a variety of levels of generality, depending upon the question of interest to the analyst. The GKC framework thus facilitates examination of resource sharing in dynamic local settings, as well as in broad contexts, and permits study of the ways in which such local settings may combine and nest within a hierarchy of increasingly broad settings in between.

[6] On action arenas, see Ostrom (1990); Frischmann, Madison, and Strandburg (2014).

Here, for purposes of illustration,[7] I focus on the action arena concerning knowledge generation, including experimentation, innovation, and communication, by community members within the relevant social context (system). Success – meaning *only* the emergence of common understandings, beliefs, and possibly norms and not necessarily good ones – depends on a shared core knowledge base, language, and social interactions sufficient to generate commonality or acceptance. Within this action arena, commons governance involves sharing core knowledge and opportunities for meaningful social interaction. Commons may be less relevant in hierarchical social arrangements where, for example, access to knowledge is restricted to a few.

At a high level of abstraction, our common sense worlds are open and shared, even if culturally contingent. We internalize social attitudes, beliefs, and values as we live our lives with others (Pepinsky 1994). But the more relevant action arenas are often situational and contextual (Haraway 1988; Nissenbaum 2009). Consider, for example, the emergence, persistence, and diffusion of the privacy-related commonsensical social norms noted above. Some, such as the privacy norm of wearing clothing in public, are quite old and widespread. Others are contingent, varying across contexts and still emerging or otherwise being shaped by new technologies. For example, digital networked technologies afford users, service providers, governments, and others incredible surveillance capabilities. Commonsensical social norms regarding when and how to use such capabilities depend upon shared understandings and beliefs about what is appropriate (Nissenbaum 2009). Schools, homes, businesses, and other social contexts, including virtual contexts such as social media platforms or online games, serve as action arenas within which such understandings, beliefs, and norms are (re)negotiated. Frankly, the same can be said about commonsensical social norms regarding smartphone use in social settings. It would be inaccurate to suggest that all the action arenas follow commons governance principles. Some do, and some do not. Using the GKC framework to study emerging privacy norms across contexts is a promising research area (Sanfilippo, Frischmann, and Strandburg 2018).

New technology not only leads to (re)negotiation of commonsensical social norms, but it also can be a substitute (see Appendix). Recall the earlier discussion of Alice exiting the taxi at the wrong location. I identified a few ways in which Alice might come to lack the relevant situational and problem-solving common sense. Most involved her lack of access to experiences or social interactions necessary to develop relevant skills and knowledge. As a thought experiment, imagine a world where continuous reliance of geotracking and mapping technologies alleviate any need to develop the commonsensical skills or knowledge. This would be a different common sense world than one without ubiquitous tracking.

Core knowledge essential to developing common sense is not always controlled by the community. It may come from external sources. Thus, diffusion of knowledge and norms across communities and contexts is an important dimension to study. Consider,

[7] For the sake of brevity, I will not explore action arenas concerning persistence and diffusion. This would be a ripe area for future work employing the GKC framework.

for example, the security-related commonsensical norms noted earlier. What does common sense suggest about choosing security passwords? Be smart. OK, fair enough. But what exactly does that mean? For most, common sense indicates one should not use "password" or "qwerty" or one's name as a password; those passwords are easily guessed by another person. But what about "10rangePotato"? No person would guess this password, right? Is it a smart password? No, it is not, but not because another person could easily guess it. It is a bad password because it is easily "guessed" by a bot (a computer program).

What "being smart" about choosing passwords means may seem like common sense for some but not for others. It depends upon one's experience and the communities to which one belongs. Many folks chastise others for lacking common sense about choosing passwords, but those "in the know" typically have specific substantive knowledge, relevant experience, and/or access to community knowledge. *Many people do not have access to the necessary inputs.* For example, some people do not anticipate bot adversaries when choosing passwords, and thus, for them, common sense might support the conclusion that "10rangePotato" is a smart password. For that to change, diffusion of knowledge (e.g., facts about bot adversaries) across communities is necessary.

As security researchers at Carnegie Mellon emphasize, the "first step in evaluating the security of a password is to understand the threat model" (Ur et al. 2012). Critically, and perhaps counterintuitively, being smart about choosing passwords is more nuanced than common sense may imply. In fact, some apparent common sense solutions to the increasingly everyday problem of password management may do more harm than good. For example, common sense suggested people should frequently change their passwords to improve security; to normalize the practice, some employers nudged and others required employees to change passwords on a periodic basis. According to security experts, however, this practice is actually counterproductive (Goodin 2016).

Commons governance of common sense is often more about governing the community and social systems within which common sense knowledge is generated, shared, cultivated, and disseminated than about governing the body of knowledge itself. A key premise is that common sense in general and commonsensical social norms in particular are social constructions generated by humans, and thus, a key aim of commons governance is to sustain some participatory role for people.

***

Common sense is socially valuable as a means for cheaply and effectively solving many problems of everyday life. It is social infrastructure for everyday market transactions and social interactions. But there is much more to common sense than problem-solving. Participating in the social processes associated with common-sense-making generates spillovers to the community through learning and socialization. People share experiences, problems and solutions, and as a social practice, this can strengthen bonds within a community and sustain social capital. But participation is not guaranteed. It depends on, among other things, access to essential resources and opportunities, and this need, in turn, may give rise to social dilemmas and social demand for community governance.

Appendix

In *Re-Engineering Humanity*, Evan Selinger and I suggest there's a risk that our common-sense-making capability and common sense itself could be reduced or depleted if we outsource various thinking tasks to supposedly smart digital tech or if our access to and use of the essential "inputs" (noted in the main text) are constrained. I do not engage these arguments in this chapter because my focus is on the resource conception of common sense rather than the capability conception. Here I briefly explain.

Consider the following set of arguments:

1. Humans face common problems in everyday life ("everyday life problems").
2. Humans develop and rely on common sense solutions to everyday life problems.
   a. Developing common sense solutions necessarily depends on a shared core knowledge base, language, and social interactions sufficient to generate common understandings and beliefs.
   b. Developing common sense solutions depends on experimentation and social innovation.
3. Humans develop technology to solve problems.
   a. Developing technology to solve a problem depends on knowledge, experimentation, and innovation, but not necessarily on a shared core knowledge base, language, and social interactions sufficient to generate common understandings and beliefs.
4. Some technology solves everyday life problems.
5. If technology solves an everyday life problem (more efficiently than existing common sense solutions) then humans will not (are less likely to) develop common sense solutions to that problem.

6. If technology solves all everyday life problems, then humans will lack common sense (or a subset of common sense that concerns problem-solving).
7. Humans without common sense are indistinguishable from machines, at least in one important respect.

The first four statements are uncontroversial. The same is true for the soft version of the fifth statement (read with the parentheticals). The stronger version of the fifth statement is questionable. Surely humans may continue to develop common sense solutions to everyday problems for which there is a technological solution, it is just a cost–benefit calculation.

The sixth statement, however, requires more explanation. The idea that technology will eliminate the need for common sense solutions to everyday problems may seem far-fetched, mainly because it is hard to believe that technology can so comprehensively address human needs. Moreover, perhaps technological solutions to present-day everyday life problems merely shift the demand curve, making a range of problems that were more extraordinary less so and thus potentially amenable to common sense solutions. There also is an intermediate step missing between the fifth and sixth statements; something that would explain the aggregation of incremental substitution of technology for common sense.

These arguments endorse a particular notion of common sense, explained in Section 4.1, and they also suggest a potential zone of conflict between common sense and technology as well as some deeper concerns about humanity. The zone of conflict is a potential source of social dilemmas where commons governance plays an important role.

REFERENCES

Akerlof, George A. 1976. "The Economics of Caste and of the Rat Race and Other Woeful Tales." *Quarterly Journal of Economics* 90 (4): 599–617. DOI: https://doi.org/10.2307/1885324.

Arrow, Kenneth J. 1971. "A Utilitarian Approach to the Concept of Equality in Public Expenditure." *Quarterly Journal of Economics* 85 (3): 409–415. DOI: https://doi.org/10.2307/1885930.

Bicchieri, Cristina, Ryan Muldoon, and Alessandro Sontuoso. 2018. "Social Norms." *The Stanford Encyclopedia of Philosophy* (Winter 2018 Edition), edited by Edward N. Zalta.

Coleman, Jules L. 1989. "Afterword: Rational Choice Approach to Legal Rules." *Chicago-Kent Law Review* 65 (1): 177–191.

Cornes, Richard, and Todd Sandler. 1996. *The Theory of Externalities, Public Goods, and Club Goods* (2nd ed.). Cambridge: Cambridge University Press.

Dekker, Erwin, and Pavel Kuchař. 2019. "Lachmann and Shackle: On the Joint Production of Interpretation Instruments." *Research in the History of Economic Thought and Methodology* 37B, 25–42. DOI: https://doi.org/10.1108/s0743-41542019000037b005.

Ekman, Paul. 1982. *Emotion in the Human Face*. Cambridge: Cambridge University Press.

Erion, Gerald. 2001. "The Cartesian Test for Automatism." *Minds and Machines* 11 (1): 29–39.
Frischmann, Brett M. 2007. "Cultural Environmentalism and the Wealth of Networks." *University of Chicago Law Review* 74: 1083–1911.
2012. *Infrastructure: The Social Value of Shared Resources*. New York: Oxford University Press.
Frischmann, Brett M., and Evan Selinger. 2018. *Re-engineering Humanity*. Cambridge: Cambridge University Press.
Frischmann, Brett M., Michael J. Madison, and Katherine J. Strandburg, Eds. 2014. *Governing Knowledge Commons*. Oxford: Oxford University Press.
Gelman, Susan A., and Gail M. Gottfried. 1996. "Children's Causal Explanations of Animate and Inanimate Motion." *Child Development* 67: 1970–1987.
Gelman, Susan A., and Henry A. Wellman. 1991. "Insides and Essences: Early Understandings of the Non-obvious." *Cognition* 39: 213–244.
Goodin, Dan. 2016. Frequent Password Changes Are the Enemy of Security, FTC Technologist Says, ars technica (August 2, 2016), https://arstechnica.com/information-technology/2016/08/frequent-password-changes-are-the-enemy-of-security-ftc-technologist-says/.
Haraway, Donna. 1988. "Situated Knowledges: The Science Question in Feminism and the Privilege of Partial Perspective." *Feminist Studies* 14 (3): 575–599.
Hausman, Daniel M. 2008. "Fairness and Social Norms." *Philosophy of Science* 75 (5): 850–860. DOI: https://doi.org/10.1086/594529.
Homans, George C. 1961. *Social Behavior*. New York: Harcourt Brace and World.
Knight, Frank H. 1921. *Risk, Uncertainty and Profit*. Chicago: University of Chicago Press.
Kuchař, Pavel. 2016. "Entrepreneurship and Institutional Change." *Journal of Evolutionary Economics* 26: 349–379. DOI: https://doi.org/10.1007/s00191-015-0433-5
Leslie, Alan M. 1984. "Spatiotemporal Continuity and the Perception of Causality in Infants." *Perception* 13: 287–305.
Leslie, Alan M., and Stephanie Keeble. 1987. "Do Six-Month-Old Infants Perceive Causality?" *Cognition* 25: 265–288.
Lewis, David. 1969. *Convention: A Philosophical Study*. Cambridge, MA: Harvard University Press. DOI: https://doi.org/10.1002/9780470693711.
Medin, Douglas L., and Andrew Ortony. 1989. "Psychological Essentialism." In *Similarity and Analogical Reasoning*, edited by Andrew Ortony and Stella Vosniadou, 179–185. New York: Cambridge University Press.
Nissenbaum, Helen. 2009. *Privacy in Context: Technology, Policy, and the Integrity of Social Life*. Redwood City, CA: Stanford University Press.
Olson, David R. 1987. "Schooling and the Transformation of Common Sense." In *Common Sense: The Foundations for Social Science*, edited by Frits van Holthoon and David R. Olson, 327. Lanham, MD: University Press of America.
Oppenheimer, J. Robert. 1954. *Science and the Common Understanding*. New York: Simon and Schuster.
Ostrom, Elinor. 1990. *Governing the Commons: The Evolution of Institutions for Collective Action*. Cambridge: Cambridge University Press.
Pepinsky, Pauline N. 1994. *Worlds of Common Sense: Equality, Identity, and Two Modes of Impulse Management*. Westport, CT: Greenwood Press.
Pinker, Steven. 1997. *How the Mind Works*. New York: W. W. Norton.
Premack, David. 1990. "The Infant's Theory of Self-Propelled Objects." *Cognition* 36: 1–16.
Redekop, Benjamin W. 2009. "Common Sense in Philosophical and Scientific Perspective." *Management Decision* 47 (3): 399–412. DOI: https://doi.org/10.1108/00251740910946679
2020. *Common Sense and Science: From Aristotle to Reid*. London: Anthem Press.

Samuelson, Paul A. 1954. "A Pure Theory of Public Expenditure." *Review of Economics and Statistics* 36: 387.
Sanfilippo, Madelyn R., Brett M. Frischmann, and Katherine J. Strandburg. 2018. "Privacy as Commons: Case Evaluation through the Governing Knowledge Commons Framework." *Journal of Information Policy* 8: 116–166.
Spelke, Elizabeth. 1994. "Initial Knowledge: Six Suggestions." *Cognition* 50: 432–445.
Thibaut, John W., and Harold H. Kelley. 1959. *The Social Psychology of Groups*. New York: Wiley.
Ullmann-Margalit, Edna. 1977. *The Emergence of Norms*. Oxford: Clarendon Press.
Ur, Blase, Patrick G. Kelley, Saranga Komanduri et al. 2012. "Helping users create better passwords." USENIX. www.usenix.org/system/files/login/articles/login1212_ur.pdf.

5

Conventions as Shared Cognitive Infrastructures

*Young Back Choi**

Conventions are ubiquitous in human life. Conventions are certain regularities in human actions and interactions, such as commonly observed practices, customs, and traditions. Conventions also reflect the less observable, namely, the underlying beliefs and implicit theories about the world that people come to share. They are often taken as conventional wisdom or common sense.

Conventions are emergent solutions to knowledge problems in social life. They are the shared cognitive infrastructure, on which all human actions and interactions are built, including economic activities and market transactions. Conventions belong to knowledge commons that people share and contribute to maintain (Hess and Ostrom 2007).[1] The stability of conventions provides a degree of stability of expectations into the future and about others with whom we regularly interact. However, conventions are not immutable. Conventions change over time through cumulative processes of experimentation and learning and their changes represent significant alterations in human affairs.

Given the centrality of conventions in human affairs, any study of human actions and interactions should aim to account for how conventions emerge and how they are maintained and get changed and transformed. Conventions, however, fall outside the purview of the dominant tradition in economics. The reason is that the dominant tradition in economics focuses on the rationality of choices in the context of given ends and means, overlooking the ubiquitous knowledge problems that underlie choices. It is oblivious of the prerequisite knowledge basis of social interaction and cooperation. In acknowledging neither the possibility of learning over time, nor differential learning processes across individuals, nor the possibility of changes conventions (or in the shared cognitive infrastructure in society), the dominant tradition

* This chapter was presented at the conference on "Governing Markets as Knowledge Commons" at the Mercatus Center, Fairfax, VA, March 28–30, 2019.

[1] Knowledge commons is equivalent to Popper's World 3 (Popper 1972).

focuses on analyzing a changeless world (Arrow 1974). In the static framework of economics, therefore, the source of a change must be exogenous, and unexplained. Though the model of rational choice (in a timeless world) has proven to be a powerful tool for some purposes, it has the shortcoming of ignoring the crucial knowledge problem as the basis of social cooperation and the source of change.

Economists in the Austrian tradition are keenly aware of the subjective nature of knowledge and have addressed in various ways the nature of the knowledge problem in human actions and interactions (Hayek 1945). Even so, Ludwig von Mises (1957) issues one of the strongest warnings for economists against delving into the givens in economics qua economist by drawing a bright line between praxeology (the science of human action) and thymology (moral psychology).[2] According to Mises, economics, the most developed of praxeology, is the exploration of the logic of choice. Mises sweeps all the "givens" (not only tastes and valuations, but also ways in which people understand the world, their beliefs and convictions, etc.) under the carpet of thymology and assigns them to historians.

The analysis of rational choice by taking ends and means as given has led economists to treat (or assume) "means" as *commonly known*. The implicit step has enabled economists to treat means (such as capital) in terms of "more or less," and in terms of aggregate quantity. In doing so, economists overlook the subjective dimension of "means," the possibility of different actors perceiving different possibilities, even as they face what appears outwardly the same.[3] It is as if economists never heard of the saying, "one man's trash is another man's treasure." If all knowledge is assumed to be known to all (and shared), there is no room for genuine learning, discovery, or entrepreneurship. Also, the practice of taking goals (preference) as given has led economists to sweep under the carpet, not only tastes, but also crucial elements in social life, namely, beliefs about accepted rules of conduct. The rational choice model, thus, limits economics to timeless and changeless world.

Surely, attempts have been made to overcome the limitations of economics by foraying into what Mises would regard as the thymological realm – economic imperialism, economics of information, economic psychology, behavioral economics, institutional economics (old and new), etc. These have had varying impacts on economics. The degree to which these attempts have been incorporated into the mainstream economics appears to be inversely related to the degree to which they depart from the core premises of mainstream economics. For example, behavioral economics that started out disputing the empirical validity of rationality assumptions of traditional economics has developed a vast literature on how to nudge people into behaving more rationally, as judged by economists and policy makers.

[2] Compared to the majority of modern economists, Mises is less formally committed to constrained maximization as the core theory. He is much more aware of knowledge problems in social life. Yet, he insists on the purity of economic theory, as distinct from psychology, or history.

[3] Austrian economists with a subjectivist approach have largely managed to escape this problem.

One of the most notable of the attempts to address the shortcomings of traditional economics is on entrepreneurship. Frank Knight viewed the entrepreneur as earning economic profit by facing uncertainty (as distinct from calculated risk). Knight's entrepreneur, however, is supra-rational and a breed apart from the economic man who populates the competitive market in equilibrium. In trying to account for capitalist economic development, Joseph Schumpeter tried to graft innovative entrepreneurship onto the static equilibrium of the traditional economics as the agent of change. His entrepreneur is also a breed apart from the economic man who populates the stationary state. Israel Kirzner introduced the concept of entrepreneurship as the arbitrageur by abandoning the concept of equilibrium so that profit opportunities are ever present (or never exhausted or ever newly created for those who are able to notice them). His entrepreneur somehow notices profit opportunities from price gaps that others simply fail to notice. These contributions remain on the fringes of economics, however.[4]

It should be noted that Kirzner adheres to Mises' stricture against delving into thymology. To the question of how the entrepreneur can discover profitable opportunities that others overlook, he replies that it happens somehow, or the entrepreneur simply happens to be more alert to the sweet scent of profit. He declared, along with Mises, that the question of how (or why) some people discover a $100 bill on the sidewalk while others are unaware of their existence belongs not to economics but to psychology, or thymology.

The aim of this chapter is to dare to cross the bright line drawn by Mises and Kirzner and explore conventions as shared cognitive infrastructure on which much of human actions and interactions, including production and exchanges, rest.

Conventions are wide ranging, from languages to shared beliefs about the world (including human beings who populate it), and to rules of acceptable conduct in various situations. Conventions reflect our implicit understanding of the world and are antecedent to rational choice and human action. Human affairs are through and through conventional. Different conventions produce different social outcomes, for good or ill. To a student of society, the questions of how different conventions arise and how they may persist or change, and under what conditions, are worthy of a serious inquiry. I believe that a systematic inquiry into conventions is possible and would yield valuable insights into social tendencies. In addressing the heightened interest in entrepreneurship and innovation, a good understanding of convention as cognitive infrastructure is essential insofar as entrepreneurship and innovation consist of the process of introducing new conventions.

[4] William Baumol's conception of entrepreneurship as the agent of economic productivity improvement obeys the law of supply. He seems to view entrepreneurship as a special kind of human capital that can be employed either productively or destructively (in rent seeking or plunder), depending on the relative expected gains.

What is attempted in this chapter is not the "economics of conventions," explaining conventions as an outcome of rational choice. Conventions, as implicit understanding of the world, are antecedent to the exercise in the logic of choice. What this chapter attempts is an exploration of conventions as knowledge commons; conventions will be presented as the necessary consequence of the human predicament of decision making in the face of uncertainty given the human ability to imagine, learn, and communicate.

The exploration of the nature of convention attempted here turns upside down the theory of the dominant tradition in economics, focusing on the logic of choice, taking as given the ends and means. Instead, we take the logic of choice as given (as nonproblematic) and focus on how human beings cope with uncertainty (with the knowledge problem). With the aim of providing a structure to our understanding of conventions, I now turn to the nature of the knowledge problem.

5.1 THE LOGIC OF CHOICE VS. DECISION MAKING IN THE FACE OF UNCERTAINTY

Economics is often touted as the science of choice. What is meant by this is that the core economic theory is based on the idea that the rational individual would choose the option from which he expects the greatest net value, given ends and means. The idea can be illustrated in the following two cases: (1) an individual in isolation and (2) exchange between two individuals.

(1) Suppose that Mr. A is given a choice between two options, a $10 bill or a $100 bill, no strings attached. Mr. A should choose the $100. (2) Now suppose that Mr. B has one X and Mrs. C has one Y. If their preferences are such that Mr. B values one Y more highly than one X and Mrs. C values one X more highly than one Y. The two then should agree to exchange their goods for mutual benefit. In either case, the choice of the rational actor, or actors, is entirely reasonable.

However, what usually escapes unnoticed in the theoretical setup of the rational choice model is the presumption that the choice situation is clearly presented to the subject (the imagined decision-maker) by the experimenter (the economist) and the subject understands and agrees to the experiment. The presumption sweeps under the carpet, as it were, all things concerning the understanding of the situation, antecedent to the choice.

But how many of our real-life situations are so clearly defined, with a neat list of available alternatives and the conspicuous best choice among them? In the real-life situation, for example, how did Mr. A come to know whether there are only two alternatives of specific value, or whether there are indeed no strings attached to the alternatives, or to the choice situation itself? When and how does he determine that he is faced with a choice situation in the first place?

In a similar vein, how did Mr. B and Mrs. C come to know that there is only one other potential trading partner, or that they each value what the other has more than one's own, or that the exchange can be made safely, or that the expected gain from the exchange is worth the trouble when all things are considered, etc.? The scope and reliability of knowledge necessary, but presumed, in real life is formidable. To portray the logic of choice as the essence of real-life decision making is the proverbial Hamlet without the Prince.

One may wonder, however, that, if the knowledge problem and the problem of understanding a given situation in decision making so formidable, how is it that we are not paralyzed by uncertainty in our daily life? For, in most circumstances, we go on with our lives effortlessly as fish swim in water. I claim that it is because most of life situations we encounter are rendered nonproblematic by a variety of conventions (through an implicit understanding) we acquire in the course of living.

Human beings are not as tightly hardwired as lower animals. Therefore, human beings face, in most situations, immensely open possibilities of action. They have the freedom of action. The other side of the same coin, however, is facing uncertainty. Out of so many possible ways of acting, how should one act? What is the right way? In order to take a definite action in a particular situation, human beings must resolve uncertainty, one way or another.

If human beings are insufficiently hardwired and cursed with attendant uncertainty, they are blessed with endowments needed to cope with uncertainty, namely, the capacity to imagine, learn from experience, and make mental tools. The capacity enables each individual human being to acquire, in the course of growing up and living a life, a whole set of mental tools to cope with uncertainty in recurrent situations he or she faces. The mental tools we fashion reflect our conception of the world around us, in the sense that they reflect our implicit understanding of the world and enable us to act.

The mental tools we acquire and use define who we are; they become our *second nature*. Conventions are but mental tools *certified*, as it were, by others in the group to which one belongs through repeated interactions. What makes possible cooperative interactions among people in a group without constant surprises is the shared conventions. As such, conventions belong in knowledge commons shared among relevant people. Acting conventionally, therefore, is to act according to our second nature. It is no wonder that we are often unaware of what we do. In most familiar life situations we encounter, we are on an autopilot. Ordinary speech in everyday life is a good example.

Incidentally, this is the very reason why we find the economic model of rational choice so appealing. Taking for granted the conventions that have become our second nature, we often judge whatever we do most reasonable.[5] Of course, whatever we do is most reasonable, if the way we understand the given situation is

5 I believe that it is on a similar ground that David Hume in his Treatise (1739–1740) said: "reason is, and ought only to be the slave of the passions." Hayek (1973) also states that what is construed as reasonable rests on the evolved attitudes, values, and institutions.

accepted as given, or if we followed conventions. To believe that rational choice (the logic of choice) is the essential feature of decision making is to believe that the tail wags the dog.

But if we are interested in better understanding the nature of conventions, we should try to see how conventions (as means of coping with the knowledge problem and the problem of understanding different situations, or as resource in knowledge commons, as it were) emerge, are sustained, and evolve over time. To that end, let us turn to explore the ways in which human beings use their capacity to imagine, learn (from experience and from interactions with others), and fashion mental tools to cope with uncertainty.

5.2 COPING WITH UNCERTAINTY

To explore the nature of conventions, we should consider the situation where conventions are absent, the situation in which an individual is facing a completely unfamiliar situation, which he cannot readily understand to ground his decision and act (Choi 1993). In other words, the starting point of analyzing conventions is decision making in the face of uncertainty.

Uncertainty is a state of mind in which one cannot identify appropriate conventions to follow. To identify appropriate conventions to follow is to have an implicit understanding of the situation one is faced with. Since birth, we face a series of situations in which we are uncertain as to how to act. In each of these instances, we are either taught by others how to act, or imitate what seemed to be viable, or act on a hunch. We try a new set of mental tools. Whether taught or guessed, our actions reflect, however tentatively, an implicit understanding of the situations.

We become more confident in the type of actions (and the implicit understanding that undergirds the actions) that brought good outcomes. Over time, the types of mental tools that "worked" for us in a wide variety of situations become our routines and habits. Reflecting each of our individually unique experiences, the set of routines and habits we come to acquire over time is likely to be individually unique. The implicit understanding of the world that undergirds our routines and habits that define who we are is likely to be individually unique, as well.

Life becomes easier to the extent we acquire a repertoire of mental tools (and rules of action) for all occasions we have faced and are likely to encounter in the future. Moreover, to the extent that we live in society of others, many of the rules of action that we acquire will necessarily have been so adapted to produce the appearance of being shared with people with whom we frequently interact. Such apparently shared rules of action are conventions. We become quite conventional by the time we reach a certain age. As we go about our lives in familiar milieus, we are not at all uncertain about how to decide. Indeed, we choose rationally, assuming conventions we follow.

Still, we sometimes run into unfamiliar situations. It could be that we have never been in the situation. Or it could be that our conventional actions fail to produce expected results, leading us to wonder whether our implicit understanding of the situation is adequate. In either case, we would be uncertain about the nature of the situation we are facing and how to act. In an uncertain situation we have an epistemic problem. There will be a great urge (we become anxious) to resolve this uncertainty, inasmuch as our lives are sustained by actions.

In a completely unfamiliar situation, the individual will have to exercise his or her imagination and come up with a hunch (a conjecture and an implicit understanding) about the nature of the situation he or she is faced with. Only with an idea of what the situation is can he or she decide what the appropriate course of action would be. Uncertainty is overcome only when individuals manage to cope with the epistemic problem with a hunch and decide what to do (or when they can make a rational choice).

A hunch (or a conjecture) is a tentative guess at the situation, likely to be based on its suspected resemblance to other situations with which the individual is already familiar (i.e., the situations he or she understands and in which, therefore, he or she knows how to act). The individual will then try out his or her hunch by acting on it. The manner in which the individual comes up with a hunch and trying it out is analogous to the way scientists come up with a hypothesis and subjecting it to tests.[6] Both try to gain an understanding of the hitherto unknown.

Economists versed in model building may be tempted to build a model of decision making in the face of uncertainty. But there is no way to reliably resolve the epistemic problem of uncertainty. If it were possible, there would be no more uncertainty. Let me explain. Uncertainty is resolved with a hunch about the nature of a novel situation we are faced with. That uncertainty is resolved, at least provisionally, with a hunch is of logical necessity. But a hunch with which we resolve uncertainty defies a general description (or a rule). It is because the inferential process by which we produce a hunch is a deeply subjective process of imagination, reasoning, and even a leap of faith, at a specific moment in time. The difficulty of coming up with a general rule for hunch is precisely the same in nature as the difficulty of a generally valid rule for science.[7]

In fact, the difficulty of a generally valid rule for hunch is even greater because our approach to uncertainty in life situations is mostly informal and implicit, with

6 Loasby (1999) refers to the American psychologist George Kelly as seeing certain parallel between the everyman and the scientist.

7 See Hume (1902) and Popper (1934). The manner in which an individual arrives at an understanding of a given situation is not different in kind from how the scientist comes to a hypothesis about some phenomena. Just as there is no proven method of coming up with a scientific hypothesis, there is no proven method of coming to an understanding in daily doings. This fact hasn't prevented some clever people from offering a general rule of decision making. The American quip, "If you are so smart, why ain't you rich?", is apt. See Choi (1999).

the foremost concern for viability. Scientists at least try to state their hypotheses clearly, and to provide their plausibility, by initial test results or other evidences. Students of the history of science may even learn something about how scientists get their hypotheses from their private journals. In contrast, people's hunches tend to be momentary and nearly always unspoken.

Herein lies the difficulty of studying decision making in the face of uncertainty. Uncertainty is resolved with a hunch. But the inferential process leading to it defies a rule.[8] Offering a rule of how to come up with a reliable hunch (or a method of how to deal reliably with uncertainty) is unconvincing. For any rule offered one could easily think of exceptions. In the absence of a generally valid rule of hunch, the process of generating a hunch seems to be chaotic. This, I believe, is the reason why many who might have seriously considered the question of decision making in the face of uncertainty did not pursue it. What is to be done?

One possible way to gain some understanding into the process of resolving uncertainty is not by trying to account for the content of hunches (of which there may be infinite variations), or by trying to formulate the general rule of hunch, but by exploring the patterns of behavior that people would exhibit in the process of hunting for a hunch, or in the process of learning how to cope with an unfamiliar situation.

In Section 5.3 we will try to tease out the behavioral patterns of learning by analyzing the case of decision making in the face of uncertainty in different contexts. The behavioral patterns thus derived would be useful in better understanding the process of the emergence, sustenance, and changes in conventions as cognitive infrastructure for social life.

5.3 THE BEHAVIORAL PATTERNS OF LEARNING PROCESS

To derive behavioral implications of decision making in the face of uncertainty let's conduct a series of thought experiments in which actors face uncertainty. The thought experiments are purely a *logical exploration* of the implications of the facts of decision making in the face of uncertainty.

Life is sustained by actions. Uncertainty is a state of mind in which one is unsure of how to act, or unsure of how to classify the given situation and identify appropriate rules of conduct. When faced with an uncertain situation, therefore, there is a great urgency to resolve it by coming up with a hunch (and an implicit understanding of the situation), without which we cannot act (Nisbett and Ross 1980). People

8 Cognitive psychologists have identified several heuristic rules that human beings use, such as representativeness, anchoring, availability, affect, etc. The trouble with these heuristics is that they could lead to fallacious inferences if used inappropriately. The pertinent question is: what is the rule to decide when to use which heuristic?

will be placed in different settings – in isolation, and in a group with or without interaction and communication – to derive the behavioral patterns of learning.

Before we proceed, let's first consider the logical implications of the necessity of a hunch with which people resolve uncertainty.

1. A hunch, whatever it is, is not predetermined; people cannot predict what hunch he they come up with; otherwise, they could not have been uncertain.
2. The hunch represents a selective understanding of the situation, as it is one of many possibilities.
3. Selected among many possible, however implicitly, people must invest a degree of confidence in, and commitment to, the goodness of the hunch, as their life depends on it.
4. Trying a hunch, nevertheless, is a trial-and-error process. The goodness of a hunch is not guaranteed. If actions based on a hunch lead to a frustrating experience, the actor will classify it as what not to do in the future. If a hunch leads to acceptable outcomes, it will be classified as what to do in the future in a similar situation.
5. Repeated good experience with a hunch would lead the actor to become more confident about the implicit understanding implied in the hunch. In due course, practices based on successful hunches become a part of our repertoire of mental tools, (or routines and habits).
6. Established routines and habits will not be abandoned unless people subsequently experience repeated frustrations with them and can come up with a hunch for a better way. With these, let's now turn to actors faced with uncertainty in different decision contexts.

5.3.1 *A Person Facing Uncertainty in Isolation*

The setting of a person in isolation is only for the purpose of mental experimentation. Of course, human beings are social animals; I believe that even Robinson Crusoe shipwrecked on an uninhabited island was not alone; in his mind, he still had the company of other men with whom he had associated, including his father from whom he fled.[9] The hypothetical person in isolation is thus not a mental blank state; in addition to innate inclinations, he would have a whole set of mental tools (routines and conventions) he has acquired up to the point when he is faced with a novel situation in isolation. The setting implies the following:

9 Robinson Crusoe carried with him all the conventions he had acquired as an Englishman of certain social station of his time and location, with additional experience of his adventures after he ran away from his father.

1. In a truly novel situation, what hunch an actor will come up with (and how he or she will behave as a result) is unpredictable.
2. The hunch will be based on the extant understanding of the world (and the repertoire of mental tools in possession) and the recognition of a resemblance to situations the actor experienced before. History matters.[10]
3. The hunch will be hypothetical and experimental.
4. The hunch is not aimed for universal validity (as a scientific hypothesis might be), but to meet the urgent demand for the resolution of uncertainty at a moment in time. The outcome could be globally optimal, only by a fluke.

5.3.2 *A Person Facing Uncertainty in a Group without Interaction*

Let's suppose that our imagined actor is faced with uncertainty but he or she is no longer alone; he or she can observe a bunch of strangers in a similar situation, (without the possibility of being seen by them, or interacting with them.) If so, there is a possibility of conducting a *vicarious* experiment to come up with a hunch, by using others as the guinea pig, as it were. The group situation should be further divided into homogeneous and heterogeneous, as the nature of vicarious experimentation will differ.

If the group is homogeneous (i.e., if the strangers appear to be very similar to him or her), the actor can more easily learn, by just watching them, what to do and what not to do.

5. The actor could *imitate* examples of success and *shun* examples of failure.
6. If a group of similar individuals faces uncertainty, they, looking to get a hint from one another, may end up imitating the first seemingly successful action, thus create a herding behavior such as a fad or a stampede.
7. A group of similar individuals will persist in the herding behavior, unless shaken by a shock (a disaster, for example).

If some of the strangers whom the actor can observe are dissimilar from him or her, the vicarious experiment must be modified to hope for a better hint. The vicarious experimentation must be controlled (or adjusted) for differences in attributes. For the actor is more likely to get a good hint by imitating the successful action of the similar, rather than that of the dissimilar.

[10] A well-known quote from Confucius is: "One comes to know the new from the old."

8. It follows that, in a heterogeneous group, the actor will make relative comparisons to decide who should be classified as the comparable group, or the reference group, and who should not be.
9. The actor should look for a hint from the actions of individuals in the reference group, expecting similar results from the actions of similar individuals.

5.3.3 *A Person Facing Uncertainty in a Group with Interaction*

This is a social setting where the actor expects interactions with strangers. The actor is no longer playing the game against nature; he or she is transacting with other human beings. Two issues arise in the social setting: how to act in the company of other human beings who may react to one's own actions and how to react to others' actions, to which others may in turn react. He or she is aware (if not, will be made aware) that the goodness of a hint on what to do when faced with uncertainty in a social setting depends on how others respond or react to his or her actions.

In a social setting, the actor should conduct mental experiments of imagining himself or herself in others' shoes to resolve uncertainty concerning how to act toward others and how to react to others' actions. *Empathy* is the human capacity to do so.[11]

10. The actor would seek those actions that he or she believes would meet the approval of others (and seek to avoid their disapproval).
11. Since it is not usually possible to ask others whether they would approve one's action *ex ante*, the everyman will seek the approval of the imagined others, the imagined reference group (and avoid their disapproval).[12] The habitual regulation of one's actions with reference to the imagined reference group is often described as following one's conscience.[13]
12. To avoid reacting inappropriately toward others, the actor will guide his or her response to others' actions in consultation with the imagined reference group.

[11] Adam Smith provided a valuable insight into the process of resolving uncertainty in a social setting in The Theory of Moral Sentiments (1759/1984). He used the term sympathy to mean, in modern usage, empathy. If a person cannot empathize, he or she would be apathetic toward others. Such an asocial individual may find himself or herself in isolation, or in a group without interaction. Confucius would agree as he regarded empathy (恕) as the basis of virtue.

[12] Adam Smith (and David Hume) believed that man naturally seeks the approval of others and avoids their disapproval by acquiring an impartial spectator in the breast. Such natural tendency to develop a conscience may be an outcome of learning or becoming aware that the viability of our actions largely depends on the approval of others.

[13] Adam Smith called the imagined reference group, "a tribunal within the breast, which is the supreme arbiter of all our actions" (1759/1984: 129).

13. Social interactions have the effect of restraining the actor's impulses and make social cooperation possible.[14]

A series of thought experiments, in which the actor faces uncertainty in different settings, has yielded several logical implications of the process of searching for an actionable hunch: unpredictability, importance of precedents, path dependence, local and temporal character of our understanding, relative comparisons, reference groups, empathy, approval seeking, and imagined reference group. These are necessary behavioral patterns of people's learning process.

Life is a series of learning processes, in which we learn how to handle novel situations. Residues of past learning are our individual habits and routines with which we manage our lives. Our habits and routines reflect and engender implicit understanding of the world that gives meaning to life as we experience it. We acquire a unique understanding of the world as the learning processes we have gone through as individuals are unique. But the uniqueness of our understanding of the world and habits and routines that reflect it are tempered, to an extent, through social interactions.

Let's now turn to the question of how the conventional cognitive infrastructure for social interactions emerges and what role it plays in human interactions.

5.4 CONVENTIONS AS COGNITIVE INFRASTRUCTURE

Human beings are social animals. People must live in the company of other human beings, frequently interacting with them in diverse situations. Our behavior in diverse situations depends on our implicit understanding of these situations (which include the operating principles of others, if there are such principles). How well we fare in life depends a great deal on how the relevant others act and react toward us in ways not inconsistent with our understanding of the situation. The same would be true for other individuals in society, as well. Thus, it is necessary that most of individuals in society come, however tentatively and inadvertently, to a commensurable understanding in the diverse situations in which they interact regularly. Otherwise, frustrating experiences will prompt individuals to modify their outlook and conducts.

Over time, frequently interacting individuals in society must arrive at an understanding of situations that they face regularly so that each of their actions would not be surprising or upsetting to others but be agreeable and result in satisfactory

[14] The set of mental tools that a person acquires up to a moment in time defines who they are is in terms of their understanding of the world and their character. Subsequently, they may acquire additional mental tools, or they may modify or replace existing mental tools, reflecting new experience and learning. In general, however, as a person gets older, their ability or inclination to modify or replace their accustomed mental tools diminishes considerably.

outcomes. In other words, individuals imaginatively improvise and eventually adopt mental tools to produce a set of workable rules of conduct, a set of conventions.

Once enough individuals in a group behave conventionally, or come to behave based on shared conventions, those individuals who fail to adopt conventions will face disappointing results, command little respect from others, and fare ill in life. Therefore, all ongoing groups and societies will develop their own set of conventions over time. It is this requirement to resolve uncertainty in social settings that produces conventions over time. The emergence of conventions makes life easier for everyone.

People may simultaneously belong to multiple groups in a society, such as a family, a neighborhood, a workplace, a church, a sports club, a chess club, a reading group, a labor union, a political party, etc. Diverse groups may share overlapping conventions to the extent that they all belong to the same overarching larger group or society – the Ostromian Institutional Analysis and Development (IAD) framework talks about different "action arenas" – but each of the groups may also have its own unique set of conventions, reflecting its history and membership. Conventions that members of a group come to respect and follow are the cognitive infrastructure of the group, in the sense that the problem of decision making in the face of uncertainty (the problem of understanding a given situation) is collectively resolved by their adoption.

Let me hasten to add that conventions as a "collective resolution" of epistemic problems refer only to the observed phenomena of certain patterns of behavior, not necessarily to the process by which conventions are produced. Most of the observed conventions in fact have not been produced at a constitutional convention; instead, they *emerge* over time as individuals in their own ways tried to come to grips with confounding situations they were faced with through guess, imitation, empathy, and experimentation. The process through which conventions emerge is the process of trial and error, at both the individual and the group levels. Once conventions are well established (followed by the majority) in a group the young or the newcomer will have to learn the extant conventions. The young and the newcomers who face uncertainty concerning how to act, and sense social pressure to conform, have a strong inclination to adopt the established conventions.

However, even when members of a group appear to seamlessly conform to conventions, the individual's implicit understanding of the situation and why he or she is conforming to the conventions may not be the same.[15] In other words, diverse subjective understanding of a given situation may nevertheless produce what appears to be a shared pattern of behavior among people in society.[16]

[15] The reason would have to do with the sequence in which different habits and routines individuals come to acquire. One possible piece of evidence is how people who seem to share conventions in total may nevertheless respond differently when a familiar situation is slightly altered and they have to act on a hunch.

[16] In the face of changing circumstances, some of the underlying diversity in understanding may be expressed as unconventional behavior.

A society or a group whose members do not develop a set of workable conventions, or a shared cognitive infrastructure on which cooperative social interactions rest, will fare badly and may even become extinct over time, through attrition. When most individuals in a group come to conduct their affairs by conventions, those few who behave unconventionally will fare badly and die out, (unless they convince others to accept the unconventional as the new convention. In this case, the unconventional are innovators and entrepreneurs. Discussions on the agents of change will follow in the next section where we discuss changes in conventions.)

There is no presumption that conventions are optimal (or the best possible) in their respective situations. A set of conventions are only one of many possible modes of behavior (and an understanding) in a situation. Its relative merit is difficult to judge. For example, think about the convention of eating food with utensils: fork and knife vs. chopsticks. There is no point in arguing which is a better way of eating. Once a convention is adopted, say chopsticks, people develop certain dexterity with chopsticks and cooks will prepare food to be eaten with them. For example, a Japanese wife is not likely to place a T-bone steak (a lump of cooked meat) on the table, to be eaten with small chopsticks. Instead, she is most likely to cut meat into small pieces to be eaten with a pair of small chopsticks. But once established, a convention tends to persist until and unless replaced by another.

In the age of globalization (and inexpensive utensils), it is not uncommon to find both types of utensils are found in a typical urban household, where a family may, on some days, use chopsticks to eat an Asian noodle dish and, on other days, use fork and knife to eat a T-bone steak. A tradition-loving English family may choose to eat all sorts of food (including Asian-style soup noodles, crabs, or corn on the cob) only with fork and knife (supplemented with spoon for soups). Whatever inconvenience they may face, they can manage with enough dexterity that comes with practices. There could be different conventions for different families.

There is no guarantee that different groups will develop equally serviceable conventions. Some group's conventions may be more useful in promoting the well-being (or the survivability) of the group than those of others. A society where people commonly eat raw food may not do as well as another society where people mostly eat cooked food. In isolation, the two societies may persist in their conventions. But when the two come into contact, the latter may dominate the former in terms of numbers. Over time, the convention of cooking food may come to prevail even in the former as people in the formerly raw-food-society learn the benefits of cooking. As the saying goes, "if you cannot beat them, join them."

A historical example of one group's conventions spread through increase in its number is the growth of early church. According to Rodney Stark (1996: 95–128), the spread of early church owed much to the Christian prohibition of infanticide and abortion and a higher status accorded to women that resulted in a higher population growth rate, higher conversion rate among women, and more balanced sex ratio (relative to the pagan world). The convention of female infanticide and abortion in the contemporary Greco-Roman world resulted in a severe sex ratio imbalance and slow population growth.[17] In addition, the congregation of early church was predominantly female. The reason for this was the more balanced sex ratio among Christians relative to pagans and a higher proportion of females among pagan conversions to Christianity.[18] The resultant higher female sex ratio among Christians led to higher population growth, relative to pagans. Given the vastly different sex ratios between Christians and pagans, it was natural that many Christian women ended up marrying pagan men, leading to secondary conversions of pagan husbands, contributing to the further spread of Christianity.

Conventions, applicable in different situation, can be hierarchical or nested. For example, consider the English language spoken by over a billion people – as the native-tongue, as the second language, and as a foreign language. Even among native speakers, there is a considerable variation in different countries and regions, in terms of vocabulary, idiom, cliché, turn of phrase, etc. The same is true even within one country within a region; the conventional use of English among different classes of people, depending on education, occupation, etc. may vary considerably. One may even observe considerable variations among families in the same region with a similar socioeconomic background. All sorts of human activities (such as law, science, literature) are nested on the English language. Also, different styles (conventions) of poems may come and go within the English language. And so on.

5.4.1 *Aesthetic, Coordinative, and Cooperative Interactions*

There are three types of interactions that produce conventions – aesthetic, coordinative, and cooperative.

1. The aesthetic interaction is the type of situation where it does not matter what people do except that what they do is seen and judged by others on aesthetic grounds. For example, consider hairstyle. One may think that, other than having excessively long and loose hair in a hazardous situation (such as a factory with spinning wheels), our hairstyle would not matter much. However, we are keenly concerned about how others may view us. So, we will tend to try to have a hairstyle that in our estimation would meet the approval, or even admiration, of relevant others. We may get a hint from a person whom we regard as attractive. Our choice of a hairstyle is meant to convey an impression of ourselves to others. Since different individuals may consider different people attractive, a few

[17] The estimated sex ratio in the Greco-Roman world was 130–140 males per 100 females (Stark 1996: 97).

[18] The estimated sex ratio among pagan converts was 2 females to 1 male. Fearing a worsening of the sex ratio in the pagan population, Emperor Valentinian ordered Pope Damasus I to stop calling at the homes of pagan women.

distinctive hairstyles may emerge as fashionable and become conventions. Once certain hairstyles are accepted as conventional, a nonconventional hairstyle may surprise or even shock people, unless done by someone regarded by many as indisputably attractive. In this manner fashion leaders introduce a new fashion (new conventions).

The processes by which fashions come and go are evolutionary and may not be easily predicted. Many ancient people (the Picts, the Maoris, the Vikings, the Ainus, etc.) tattooed their bodies and faces. Subsequently, tattooing became generally less popular, that is, the convention of no tattoo came to prevail. Tattooing remained conventional only among much smaller segments of society, such as sailors and gangsters. In the twenty-first century, however, tattooing seems to have become an acceptable convention among an increasing number of American youths, thanks to certain daring musicians and mixed martial art fighters.[19]

2. In situations that require coordination of activities, individuals in society may arbitrarily settle on a convention, as some kind of coordination might be better than none (Lewis 1969). For example, as vehicles became common, it made sense to decide which side of the road vehicles should be driven to allow a smoother flow of traffic. It did not matter which side of the road vehicles are driven, as long as they stay on the same side. So, the American convention is to drive on the right and the British and the Japanese (both island nations), on the left. Sharing a long border with Americans, Canadians have chosen the convention of driving on the right.

Coordinative conventions may emerge spontaneously, but when enough number of people feel that a rule is needed, someone (government, an organization, or an international treaty) may initiate the rules of the road. The International Maritime Organization, for example, published navigation rules *prescribing* that all ships (even British ships) are to pass port-side to port-side, that is, on the right.

In general, people would have little reason to disregard coordinative conventions. Once conventions (such as the rules of the road) are widely accepted, those who do not respect the conventions (and cause accidents) will be found to be at fault and become liable for damages. The emergence of the convention of private property (as fences or landmarks between neighbors) to keep peace and encourage industry is one of the most significant turns in the development of humanity. Increase in population density over time necessitated elaborations of property rights enforced collectively by the state (Hume 1902).

[19] Another interesting example of changing fashions brought on by outsiders is the American corporate dress code. The days of the rigid dress codes of Chase Manhattan, IBM, or GE are gone with the rise of Apple, Google, and Facebook.

When a new situation arises for which no extant convention exists, (e.g., when flying cars become a reality), new "rules of the road" will be needed. Such rules for three-dimensional traffic may be improvised based on a combination of the existing rules of the sky (for airplanes) and the rules of the road (for cars).

Language – a prime example of knowledge commons – is another example of coordinative conventions for communication that emerged spontaneously. If an animal is called a horse, all English-speaking people would understand what is meant. Call it something else, no one would understand. It is almost impossible for a person born into a society with a language to not end up speaking that language. A language is a complex set of conventions – the vocabulary, grammar, idioms, cliché, etc. – for the evolution and maintenance of which an unaccountable number of people contributed, small and large.

The mother tongue is what one is born into. An individual may choose to acquire additional languages, if he or she wishes to communicate with people who speak different languages or learn to translate. The number of people who speak a language may change depending on the fortunes of the people who speak the language. If a language-speaking people produced prosperous societies, the language-speaking people my increase in number through the proliferation of progeny and imitation/adoption.

3. In many social transactions the outcome of one's action depends on others' cooperation (i.e., others doing the expected parts). An act of cooperation need not be intentional; cooperation simply means that independent actions of individuals involved manage to produce the desired outcomes for parties involved. The best-known case of unintended cooperation on a large scale is social division of labor through trade, which depends on a host of conventions, such as language, property rights, promise, contracts, etc.

In a coordinative setting, once a convention emerges, there is little reason for anyone to deviate. In a cooperative setting, as in a teamwork, this is not so. Even after members of a group formally agree to a certain way of cooperation, separate individuals may find a way to do better for themselves by breaking the agreement.[20] A cooperative setting is like the familiar Prisoner's Dilemma (PD) game. Therefore, cooperative conventions that emerge in the course of repeated interactions in a PD-like setting must have the feature of responding negatively to those who do not conform to cooperative conventions. Cooperative conventions, once established, may be more enduring because of its self-policing nature (Axelrod 1984).

20 A cooperative regime without an explicit agreement, resting on an implicit understanding, may be subject to opportunistic actions by some members who are willing to undertake actions not explicitly forbidden.

Regardless of the nature of interaction among individuals in society, conventions are the cognitive infrastructure of a society in the sense that they constitute collective resolutions of epistemic problems. Conventions provide a certain way of understanding frequently experienced situations; they provide a stability in the expectations of individuals in society and enable them to produce the extensive network of social interactions and cooperation, including market transactions. The entirety of prevailing conventions in a society defines its culture.

Conventions emerge through the interaction among people over time. Some conventions are explicitly adopted with the aim of a better coordination. The origin of most of conventions, however, is obscure because they are only the by-products of individuals trying in their own ways to deal with the uncertainty they face. When uncertain about how to act, the young and the newcomer look to others for a hint and they would find conventions. Conventions are reproduced daily through people's conformity. If anyone proposes a new way of doing things, a new convention, its success cannot be predicted because it would depend on others' willingness to follow.

5.5 STABILITY VS. CHANGE

The value of conventions as the cognitive infrastructure of a society lies, to a large extent, in their stability, which in turn depends on how widely the people in the group regard them as the way they should act.[21] For any ongoing society, or any social group, it is necessary that the majority of their members upholds the prevailing conventions in relevant spheres of interaction and the shared cognitive infrastructure is governed as a knowledge commons.

Conformity to conventions may come in two ways: affirmation and expediency. Most individuals who interact overtime will come to have an understanding of the world that leads them to believe that conforming to conventions is the *right* thing to do. Most conventionalists will naturally react negatively to those who do not conform, because they do not do the "right" thing and upset their expectations.[22] People often do not make the distinction between what is and what ought to be.

[21] Some thinkers who notice the flimsy and arbitrary basis of human understanding and expectations see society (and the market) forever on the brink of chaos (Shackle 1972). I believe that they have an insufficient appreciation of the requirement of the stability of conventions, which the shared cognitive infrastructure provides. The stability of conventional order is reinforced by the interrelatedness of conventions. Conventions for different occasions and groups are not fully mutually consistent with one another to seamless whole. Some are more tightly related (horizontally and vertically) to other conventions while others are less so. Herbert Simon's concept of decomposability is applicable here. Conventions that are tightly related to others are likely to be more difficult to change.

[22] To act otherwise is to implicitly admit that one does not have a good understanding of the situation and, therefore, not acting in the best way possible. People who are committed to a view of the world (confident of its validity) tend to view alternative views as either false, or inferior to their own.

It is not necessary, however, that all members in a group or society affirm conventions, especially in cooperative interactions. Among those who outwardly conform to conventions some may do so only because they believe that it is expedient. They may view conventions as arbitrary and irrational. The reason why they nevertheless conform to conventions is on the ground of expediency, that they cannot think of a viable alternative.[23] They are more likely to abandon the pretension of conformity if they perceive a more promising rule of conduct, or if their fear of retribution is lessened.

Not everyone may conform to conventions, either by affirmation or on the ground of expediency, however. In any ongoing society, there are ever-present deviants/nonconformists. Some may have not yet been persuaded of the goodness of conventions. Deviations from conventions usually arise from insufficient proficiency with the prevailing conventions, as with the youth or new arrivals. For many of them it may be a matter of time that they become proficient in conventions. Others may outright disbelieve conventions; for them conventions are neither the right nor the expedient things to do. Instead, they find an alternative mode of action to be the right thing to do. It is because they see the situation differently than the conventionalists; these nonconventionalists may see themselves as mavericks. The rank of deviants is filled with newcomers (the young and the outsider).

The deviant is both the disrupter of the stability of the conventional order; deviants challenge the knowledge commons. At the same time, the deviant is the potential originator of new conventions, as innovators, entrepreneurs, or reformers. The deviant as a disrupter of peace (either in terms of expectations or of economic interests) will, in most cases, face negative reactions from the conventionalist and often fare badly. But, if the deviant somehow, despite odds, achieves an enduring success, he or she will be eventually hailed as an innovator/entrepreneur/reformer.[24] Few would be inclined to argue with success. The imitation of the successful subsequently leads to the emergence of new conventions.

There is a perpetual tension between stability and change, that is, between the conventionalist's conformity to sustain the extant conventional order and the deviant's attempt to reach for something better than what conventions promise. The tension arises from conflicting visions, the conventional and the unconventional, representing a potentially viable alternative. If deviants are kept in the fringes, conventions endure; the stability of the conventional order is preserved. If the

[23] Those who conform because it is expedient may or may not have a firm conception of what alternative course of action they could take. René Descartes (2006) decided to conform to all conventions, (other than the subject of his philosophical inquiries), not because he believed that conformity was the right thing to do, but because it was prudent to do so. Not conforming would bring too much unnecessary difficulties in his life.

[24] When the entrepreneur/innovator introduces a new product or a new way of doing things, for example, people sometimes have to be taught its utilities and values. Once enough number of people are persuaded of its values, a stampede may follow, as in the case of iPhone, Uber, and Amazon.

deviant achieves an outstanding success as the entrepreneur or the innovator new conventions will arise, replacing the old. The nature and the extent (or the magnitude) of change may vary depending on the impact of deviations from existing conventions.

In an ongoing society, the odds of a deviant success are not great. Deviants tend to do poorly. Occasionally, deviants manage to beat the odds and succeed as innovators, entrepreneurs, or reformers. What are the factors that influence the odds of successful deviation? Surely, the quality of their vision (and the quality of their execution) relative to conventions matters, provided that the new practices attract enough support to succeed. What can influence the probability of gaining higher-quality vision and the needed support from others? The odds of success from an unconventional practice would be the greatest where there is no extant convention in the way, in spheres where there is no opposing conventionalist. But there are few such spheres.

One of the most important factors in increasing the odds of successful deviation is the *passage of time*. The reason for this is that as conventions (as collective solutions to knowledge problems in various spheres of human action) persist over time, conventionalists (wearing the conventional blinders) tend to overlook many potentially exploitable opportunities that can be had, only if they were willing to look at them with a fresh pair of eyes.[25] The potential for gains from an alternative understanding of the situation tends to grow over time and become easier to notice for those who cast aside the conventional blinder, or who haven't quite learned to wear one. With a passage of time, new discoveries also become easier to understand for others whose cooperation is needed to succeed from new way of doing things (even then the support for a truly breakthrough innovation is more likely to come from people in the fringes than from the mainstream).

Human beings, as conventionalists, live through numerous experiences in varied contexts and accumulate vast amounts of observations. Most of them would be recorded as consistent with conventional expectations and thus unsurprising. Those experiences and observations that do not easily fit into conventional expectations may be overlooked or dismissed as oddities. Also, some observations in a sphere that could provide a hint for improvements in another sphere may be ignored by people wearing conventional blinders, or through sheer inertia. Over time, as the gap between *what is* and *what is possible* grows, the potential for gains from an unconventional action will tend to grow, to the point that they become more easily noticeable to someone, especially if he or she is not yet fully invested in conventions (such as the young, the newcomer, or the outsider). The growing potential for

[25] Kirzner (1973) argues that the entrepreneur discovers unexploited profit opportunities others fail to even notice. Following Mises' stricture for economists qua economist against foray into thymological inquiry, Kirzner states that entrepreneurial discovery just happens, as a simple fact.

neglected opportunities with the passage of time, I believe, best explains simultaneous discoveries in science or swarming innovations in business.

Conventions are crucial means of reducing uncertainty by fixing expectations (i.e., by adopting certain rules) in human actions and interactions. They enable human beings to coordinate their activities and enable them to build a vast network of cooperation. But the very means by which human beings (individually and collectively) deal with the knowledge problem has the effect of leaving, over time, certain opportunities unexploited. The stability of conventions causes the conventional order to become, over time, less efficient (in the sense that the conventionalists do not pick up the proverbial $100 bills on the sidewalk as they do not see them). In other words, conventions (and institutions) tend to become less in tune with the changing world, including cumulative observations and learning.[26] At some point, no one knows when and where, audacious deviants may succeed in demonstrating how the overlooked opportunities can be captured and exploited, rendering silly certain conventions held by many with religious devotions.

Let us now turn to consider the process of introducing new conventions by the agents of change, namely, entrepreneurs and innovators in introducing new conventions.

5.6 PROCESS OF CHANGE

We have established that conventions are shared cognitive infrastructures by means of which individuals in society cope with uncertainty and render familiar the world they are faced with and that these infrastructures are often governed as knowledge commons. Conventions are both *enabling* (of actions and social cooperation) and *delimiting* of our understanding of the world. Over time, conventions are liable to change as some individuals in groups or society come to face novel situations (i.e., uncertainty) for which they find no suitable conventions to use or recognize the unrealized potentials that can be captured.

A conceptual distinction can be made how novel situations may arise – endogenously or exogenously. (1) Novel situations may arise endogenously as experiences/observations incongruent with the prevailing conventions accumulate over time. When faced with an incongruent experience, the impulse of the majority of conventionalists is to ignore it. A few without strong commitments to the prevailing conventions, without the conventional blinder, may be able to see (discover) a better way of doing things, which escaped the notice of the majority of conventionalists. In other words, when we see the state of affairs with a fresh pair of eyes, it may be easy to notice that "the emperor is naked." Those who acquire this fresh perspective may become entrepreneurs, innovators, fashion leaders/trend setters, or reformers.

[26] Quigley (1979) generalizes the idea as "the tendency of an instrument to become an institution."

They are the agents of change. When they are successful, they manage to persuade others (or convert them) to new conventions. Eventually, people in society come to learn to do things differently. (2) Novel situations may also arise exogenously when individuals in a group or society, with a set of prevailing conventions, encounter (and must interact with) other individuals from another group or society with different set of prevailing conventions, or when individuals in a society experience a change in natural conditions such as a lasting climatic change, or significant demographic changes, or in social conditions such as alterations in legal framework.[27] In this chapter, I focus on endogeneous changes in conventions initiated by the entrepreneur.

Persisting in the prevailing conventions is likely to become dysfunctional and the new circumstances may give rise over time to numerous attempts to deal with the novel situation. Individuals in society may gradually adopt what appears to be a better way of doing things, pioneered by entrepreneurs and innovators. When that happens, the structure of knowledge commons will have been altered and individuals in society come to learn to do things differently. In this chapter, we limit ourselves to the discussion of the role of entrepreneurs and innovators in changing conventions.

Since conventions are either informal or formal, and are nested and hierarchical, entrepreneurial innovations may impact at different institutional levels, ranging from informal rules of conduct and accepted business practices to legal rules and practices.

Elert and Henrekson (2014) distinguish entrepreneurship into three types – abiding, evading, and altering kinds – depending on the relationship of entrepreneurship vis-à-vis the existing *formal* institutions, such as laws and regulations. By this classification, most of entrepreneurship is abiding; entrepreneurs typically accept most of the existing informal rules, as well as laws and regulations as given and seek to maximize profit. In innovation, in other words, entrepreneurs typically break from conventions in a narrow range that is pertinent to their innovations. Abiding entrepreneurship, nevertheless, may still bring about epoch-making changes in society and add a host of new conventions to knowledge commons.[28] Of course, there are also entrepreneurs whose innovations consist of evading the existing laws and regulations, or whose innovations require changing the existing laws and regulations.

Entrepreneurship is motivated by profit. When successful, the entrepreneur captures above-normal profit. But how can anyone earn above-normal profit at a

[27] For example, the liability revolution in the United States initiated by judges committed to the cause of social justice managed to convert tort law into a social insurance (Huber 1990).

[28] For example, Henry Ford's mass production of automobiles by assembly lines, or Malcolm McLean's containerization of shipping are the abiding type that nevertheless had revolutionary consequences for society (Evans 2004).

sustained pace when there are many who are looking for ways to earn a higher rate of return? It is not possible by a conventional method, by doing what others are doing. What may appear to be above-normal profit, on a more careful examination, is likely to be normal returns on implicit labor or implicit capital expanded. In other words, there cannot be the proverbial $100 bill on the sidewalk if everyone thought and acted based on the shared set of conventions.[29]

Entrepreneurial profit, the above-normal profit, is possible only if the entrepreneur sees and exploits profit opportunities that others simply fail to see (or does see but not clearly or soon enough). The entrepreneurial profit opportunities may consist of arbitrage opportunities, or creation of new products through novel combinations, or implementing a new way of doing things that is more efficient. Whatever the nature of profit opportunities is, I contend that others fail to see them because of their conventional blinders, and that the entrepreneur sees them because he or she has adopted an unconventional (an alternative) way of seeing things.

In life, as in the business, we learn to put up with all sorts of inconveniences and problems. Over time we manage to live with them and become so accustomed to them that we are no longer even conscious of them as problems or inconveniences. We come to believe that they are facts of life. That is the power of conventions, as epistemic infrastructure for social interactions. But it is entirely possible for a nonconventionalist to recognize a gap between the actual and the potential and see a profit opportunity (from solving problems that others were not even aware, or if they were, then were vaguely wistful for a better way).

5.7 CONCLUDING REMARKS

This chapter has explored the nature of conventions as emergent solutions to the knowledge problem of society; I have suggested that conventions provide a cognitive infrastructure of society as the basis of social cooperation and that this shared cognitive infrastructure is governed as a knowledge commons. The knowledge problem as examined in this chapter is a subject matter traditionally regarded as noneconomic and untouchable. In the traditional sense of the term, conventions are indeed a noneconomic subject. But it is a subject matter no student of society can ignore because conventions, as shared cognitive infrastructures, are ubiquitous in human life. Ignoring conventions, the bedrock of individual actions and social interactions, leads to erroneous views regarding, especially, entrepreneurship and the process of change.

29 This is the central idea of the dominant tradition in economics, that in a competitive market economic profit (or loss) is a transitory phenomenon through unexpected fluctuations in demand and supply (Knight 1921; Schumpeter 1934; Arrow 1974).

Conventions are ubiquitous in human life because human beings face a predicament of having to act in the face of uncertainty. Human beings face a fundamental epistemic problem. If we are cursed with uncertainty by not being fully hardwired like lower animals, we are blessed with the ability to cope with uncertainty, through the endowment of a large brain to imagine, conjecture, and peek into possibilities.

In the course of growing up and making a living, we encounter numerous novel situations that make us wonder. Each time we try to understand what the nature of a novel situation is we face it by means of conjectures. Over time, conjectures that prove to be viable come to form our understanding of the world around us and enable us to make a living with relative ease. What nature failed to hardwire, human beings wire themselves, acquiring a second nature.

Though a generally valid rule of conjecture (or inference) is not possible, we can nevertheless comprehend the process of our coping with the epistemic problem by recognizing the behavioral pattern of learning, by examining how individuals in different contexts obtain mental tools to cope with uncertainty (which become habits, routines, and dispositions) and how a group of individuals generate conventions, by mutually tempering individual mental tools, as a collective solution to the epistemic problem in society. The emergent conventions become shared cognitive infrastructure that enable cooperative social interactions.

Viewing conventions as a collective solution to the knowledge problem in society makes it clear that there is inherent epistemic tension in society. For conventions are both enabling of social cooperation and coordination, on the one hand, and delimiting of our ability to take advantage of new possibilities, on the other hand. The stability of conventions leaves many new possibilities unexploited, especially in the short run. The potential for change necessarily grows over time.

If an ongoing society appears to be orderly, that is, appears to have stability in rules of conduct and expectations, it is because most individuals in that society conform to conventions. However, it is impossible that everyone at any moment fully shares all conventions. At any moment, it is likely that some of the people in the apparently stable society may have some reservations about this or that convention or believe that they have an idea of how to do things better. This would be especially true of the new generation of people, or newcomers, who must learn to become proficient with the prevailing conventions. Not everyone may learn to become proficient in the prevailing conventions and some may find their own way of doing things. Some of these (as deviants, cranks, wild-dreamers, would-be entrepreneurs, would-be innovators, would-be reformers) may become agents of change. Many will fail in the face of inhospitable reception from conventionalists. But few that do succeed will end up persuading others to change their ways, that is, end up changing conventions.

One of the useful insights from the foregone discussions is that people who fully conform to prevailing conventions (i.e., authorities, experts and interested parties not excluded, fully immersed in the extant shared cognitive structure) usually cannot see beyond the conventional blinder.[30] I believe that the insights of the chapter have important implications. Consider, for example, the national innovation programs that have become globally popular (Hemel and Ouellette 2019).

Who would object to the idea that a national economy should become more innovative, with associated benefit of high value-added industries? The typical approach of traditional economics is to propose various optimal innovation policies for government, assuming away the fundamental problems of knowledge and of the discovery of profitable opportunities. In adopting the rational choice model to innovation, therefore, politicians, bureaucrats, and hired experts are implicitly presumed to have the ability to discern profitable opportunities.

It seems the critical question of whether anyone with such abilities would be content to administer government innovation programs, instead of trying to seize profitable opportunities they see/discover for themselves, is seldom, if ever, asked. Before one rushes to identify this or that industry or firm as promising of innovation for government support through subsidies or tax credits at the optimal level, or how to devise government programs to stimulate innovation, one should ask whether anyone put in charge of the innovation programs in various guises would have the ability to identify, beforehand, when, where, how, and who would innovate, and how much the putative innovations would be worth.

A serious consideration of the problem of knowledge and the question of the discovery of profitable opportunities, as presented in this chapter, would lead to the conclusion that innovation is a social experimentation and no one is in the privileged position to know the outcome beforehand.[31] Channeling public support for one possible innovation may in fact disadvantage other truly potential but unknown innovations (Choi 2011. See also Diamond 2019; Potts 2019). From this one should conclude that the best possible innovation policy is free competition within the bounds of law and conventions, where no one shall be accorded a privileged position.

I hope that the essay is a small step toward a better understanding of the process of the formation, emergence, persistence and change in conventions as cognitive infrastructure of society. I believe useful insights into entrepreneurship (the operation of change agents) are possible. Insights from the exploration of conventions will greatly supplement the static analysis of the dominant tradition in economics.

[30] This view is consistent with the "weird ideas that work" Sutton (2001).

[31] Schumpeter (1942) proposed the idea of the routinization of innovation by large corporations, believing that innovation is a function of investment in R&D. I think he overlooked the fact that most innovations are unconventional in the beginning.

REFERENCES

Arrow, Kenneth. 1974. "Limits of Knowledge and Economic Analysis." *American Economic Review* 64: 1–10.

Axelrod, Robert. 1984. *The Evolution of Cooperation*. Basic Books.

Choi, Young Back. 1993. *Paradigms and Conventions*. University of Michigan Press.

1999. "Conventions and Economic Change." *Constitutional Political Economy* 10: 245–264.

2011. "Institutions for Economic Prosperity." In *Institutional Economics and National Competitiveness*, edited by Young Back Choi, 63–83. Routledge.

Descartes, Rene. 2006 [1637]. *Discourse on the Method*. Oxford University Press.

Diamond, Arthur M. Jr. 2019. *Openness to Creative Destruction*. Oxford University Press.

Elert, Niklas, and Henrekson, Magnus. 2014. "Evasive Entrepreneurship." IFN Working Paper No. 1044.

Evans, Harold. 2004. *They Made America: Two Centuries of Innovations from the Steam Engine to the Search Engine*. Little, Brown & Co.

Hayek, Friedrich. 1945. "The Use of Knowledge in Society." *American Economic Review* 35: 519–530.

1973. *Law, Legislation, and Liberty*. Vol. 1. University of Chicago Press.

Hemel, Daniel J., and Ouellette, Lisa L. 2019. "Innovation Policy Pluralism." *Yale Law Journal* 128: 544. www.yalelawjournal.org/pdf/HemelOuellette_d8kwup4i.pdf

Hess, Charlotte, and Elinor Ostrom. Eds. 2007. *Understanding Knowledge as Commons*. MIT Press.

Huber, Peter. 1990. *Liability*. Basic Books.

Hume, David. 1902 [1777]. *Enquiries Concerning the Human Understanding and Concerning Principles of Morals*. Online Liberty Library Project, Liberty Fund.

Kirzner, Israel. 1973. *Perception, Opportunity and Entrepreneurship*. University of Chicago Press.

Knight, Frank H. 1921. *Risk, Uncertainty, and Profit*. Houghton Mifflin Co.

Lewis, David. 1969. *Convention*. Harvard University Press.

Loasby, Brian. 1999. *Knowledge, Institutions and Evolution in Economics*. Routledge.

Mises, Ludwig von. 2007 [1957]. *Theory and History*. Ludwig von Mises Institute.

Nisbett, Richard, and L. Ross. 1980. *Human Inference*. Prentice-Hall.

Popper, Karl. 1934 [1959]. *The Logic of Scientific Discovery*. Routledge.

1972. *The Objective Knowledge*. Oxford University Press.

Potts, Jason. 2019. *Innovation Commons*. Oxford University Press.

Quigley, Carroll. 1979. *The Evolution of Civilization: An Introduction to Historical Analysis*. Liberty Fund Press.

Schumpeter, Joseph. 1934. *The Theory of Economic Development*. Harvard University Press.

1942. *Capitalism, Socialism, and Democracy*. Harper & Brothers.

Shackle, George. 1972. *Epistemics and Economics*. Cambridge University Press.

Smith, Adam. 1984 [1759]. *The Theory of Moral Sentiments*. Liberty Fund.

Stark, Rodney. 1996. *The Rise of Christianity*. HarperOne.

Sutton, Robert I. 2001. *Weird Ideas That Work*. Free Press.

6

Property Rights, Knowledge Commons, and Blockchain Governance

*Darcy W. E. Allen, Chris Berg, Sinclair Davidson, and Jason Potts**

Shared knowledge about ownership – that is, knowledge about property rights – facilitates market exchange and economic coordination. Knowledge about property rights is necessary because participants must believe that the seller owns the goods or services being offered for sale in order to complete the contract. Without that belief, they put themselves at risk of fraudulent sales: this is the infamous 'I have a bridge to sell you' problem, named after the con man George C. Parker, who repeatedly sold the Brooklyn Bridge to gullible buyers at the turn of the twentieth century (Cohen 2005). But while this knowledge about property rights has value, and supports markets and economic coordination, it needs to be produced. Today we rely on a complex mix of formal and informal norms, institutions, and practices to ensure knowledge about property rights is both shared and trusted. In this chapter we ask how this shared knowledge resource is governed through shared infrastructures; how those rules shift due to advances in distributed ledgers; and the implications of this for our broader understanding of robust political economy.

The institutions supporting our knowledge of property rights are a core part of the 'scaffolding' that sustains the market economy (see North 2005: xi). This scaffolding is a mix of norms, technologies, and both formal and informal institutions. Hodgson (2015) has identified the elision in the property rights literature about the distinction between 'economic' property rights – those derived from possession and the ability to use or dispose goods one possesses – and 'legal' property rights – the ability to have those rights recognised in law, which allows for property holders to make complex financial exchanges (such as a business loan) using their legal property as collateral (De Soto 2000; Hoffmann 2013). Further, different classes of property are governed

* Darcy W. E. Allen, Chris Berg, Sinclair Davidson, and Jason Potts are with the RMIT Blockchain Innovation Hub. We would particularly like to thank Mark Miller and Bill Tulloh of Agoric for discussions that have led our research in this direction, and Erwin Dekker and Pavel Kuchař for their comments on an earlier version.

through different institutional mechanisms. Berg et al. (2019) argue that small-value property tends to be governed through a complex process of heuristics and norms, where the observation that an individual (or firm) possesses a good is taken as a proxy for legal ownership. Opportunism in this environment is mitigated by market institutional mechanisms such as reputation and discounting. Where the costs of opportunistic behaviour are larger, the task of governing shared facts about property tends to be assumed by hierarchical organisations, particularly the state – consider, for instance, registers of property ownership in land, or intellectual property (such as patents). Even further, the institutional mechanisms by which property rights are governed are themselves the subject of entrepreneurial innovation – they change as new technologies emerge, including institutional technologies (Allen et al. 2020).

Our approach in this chapter is to view knowledge about property rights as a knowledge commons, with various types of infrastructure to govern that commons. We aim to begin to understand this institutional complexity through Elinor Ostrom's Institutional Analysis and Development (IAD) framework (Ostrom 1990), and to place these understandings within a broader political economy context. Since Ostrom's pioneering work on natural resource commons, the IAD framework has been modified and extended in the context of knowledge, information, and cultural commons (see Hess and Ostrom 2005; Ostrom 2005; Madison et al. 2009; Frischmann et al. 2014). Knowledge commons need to be understood differently to physical comments because they "usually must create a governance structure within which participants not only share existing resources but also engage in producing those resources and, indeed, in determining their character" (Frischmann et al. 2014: 16). For property rights, that knowledge commons involves creating ledgers that are updated accurately and enforced – whether by government, hierarchy, norms, or other technologies.

Our aim is not to analyse a particular 'action arena' where participants interact – we leave that for later empirical work – but rather provide theoretical attention to several parts of the IAD framework, including the underlying social dilemma at the heart of property rights knowledge commons, the nature of the shared infrastructure that helps to sustain the commons, and the 'rules in use' that maintain property rights knowledge commons. Indeed, the challenge of property rights knowledge commons is underpinned by a range of social dilemmas. That knowledge not only needs to align with community norms (so that those property rights are enforced), but that knowledge needs to be trusted by market participants to be accurate, and it must do so in the context of potentially hostile actors seeking to undermine property rights (see Potts 2019: ch 9). The research programme that we reveal focuses on the evolution in the 'rules in use' in the property rights knowledge commons, particularly as new technologies such as distributed ledger technology (including blockchain) change how the property rights knowledge commons are created, protected, and enforced.

We also seek to understand these contributions from a broader political economy perspective. To do so we connect two previously unconnected areas: robust political economy and Byzantine consensus. Economists have developed a framework – robust political economy – for thinking about policy design in the context of information and incentive constraints for government planning (Boettke and Leeson 2004; Leeson and Subrick 2006; Pennington 2011). A system is (more) robust if its institutions deal comparatively well with incentive and information problems – that is, by better coordinating distributed information or by better aligning the incentives of people within a complex system. Computer science also provides a new way of looking at the economic problem of coordinating distributed knowledge about property rights. Byzantine political economy takes its name and inspiration from the Byzantine Generals' Problem in computer science (Lamport et al. 1982). Solutions to this problem are said to be Byzantine fault tolerant, describing a class of methods of maintaining consensus over shared facts in the presence of possible miscommunication – in other words, scaffolding for the maintenance and consensus over knowledge either non-hierarchically, or where hierarchy is incomplete. Our understanding of information about property rights as a knowledge commons – and how such commons governance shifts in the context of technological disruption can be understood through this 'Byzantine political economy' connection: the study of the coordination of shared knowledge by distributed consensus mechanisms at the intersection of economics and computer science.

6.1 BLOCKCHAINS, PROPERTY RIGHTS, AND KNOWLEDGE COMMONS

Our understanding of knowledge about property rights is usually analysed in relation to search costs (Stigler 1961), but there is also a cost of identifying who owns what. Does the counterparty who offers a good for sale actually own that good? Market participants require knowledge about property rights – who owns what and who can trade it – to make exchanges and to coordinate. This is in *addition* to other knowledge, such as knowledge about the rules of contract (see Epstein 2009). A transaction consisting of goods that are not lawfully owned is a risky one – opening the risk of later disputes with the rightful owner, or legal liabilities around trafficking stolen goods. In jurisdictions with low-quality legal infrastructure those who possess land, without holding formal title to that land (i.e., a formal record of ownership), are unable to fully exploit the value of their ownership (De Soto 2000). Therefore, we can identify a kind of 'social dilemma' underpinning property rights knowledge commons – that knowledge about property rights might be underproduced or might be of low quality.

Ideally, knowledge about property rights is easily accessible (to facilitate widespread coordination) and also trusted (mapping to the 'general ledger' – a concept that we introduce below). Blockchains are a subcategory of distributed ledgers that were first developed by Nakamoto (2008a) for the cryptocurrency Bitcoin. While other distributed ledger technologies exist (the word 'blockchain' describes a data structure rather than a consensus mechanism), blockchains are currently the dominant technology, and here we use the word blockchain as a stand-in for all distributed ledger technologies (for a more general survey see Rauchs et al. 2018). As Berg et al. (2019) argue, blockchains are an institutional technology that allows groups to record, and come to consensus over, property rights (see also Davidson et al. 2018) – acting as additional 'rules in use' for the property rights knowledge commons that will shift commons governance at the margin. Importantly, we do not suggest that blockchains will act as a complete substitute to existing infrastructure to maintain the commons, but rather that blockchain represents a technological disruption of those rules at some margins. Precisely on what margins blockchains will improve the governance of the knowledge commons is an entrepreneurial question that will be revealed through time, and one that will manifest differently across jurisdictions and in relation to the quality of existing commons infrastructure. In the same way that there is no regulatory or institutional panacea for other commons, the property rights knowledge commons are maintained through a complex range of nested institutional 'rules in use'. How those commons are maintained and updated – such as through the transfer of property rights – will depend on the particular 'action arena' and the participants in it.

What are the underlying 'resource characteristics' of knowledge about property rights? Understanding knowledge as a commons sits alongside a range of other 'new commons' that examine underlying resources such as culture, science, or intellectual commons (e.g., see Boyle 2003; Hess and Ostrom 2005; Bollier and Helfrich 2014). These 'new commons' differ from early natural resource commons because the resource at hand does not have distinct biophysical characteristics. Rather than natural resource commons, the resource in the property rights knowledge commons has different characteristics. The problem is less that the underlying resource will be depleted through overuse, such as in a fishery. But rather that individuals will underprovide the resource – that is, by free riding – or that there will be a lack of coordination, because the effective production of the knowledge resource requires joint participation by many parties. The knowledge about property rights necessary to exchange and coordinate is similarly a commons where having widespread, trusted and enforced knowledge is a critical input. Our focus below is on the institutional governance arrangements that help to maintain the knowledge about property rights – that is, the infrastructure that is a "form of community management or governance of a shared resource" (Madison et al. 2018: 2). These knowledge commons are governed through a complex set of informal norms and more formalised hierarchical governance structures (e.g., legal enforcement, public registries).

What are the 'rules in use' by which we manage the property rights knowledge commons? One common way is to use possession as a heuristic for ownership (see Berg et al. 2018, 2019). That is, in most exchanges, the fact that a counterparty holds a good (or money) works well enough as an indication that they are the rightful owner of the item. Another common mechanism is through legal documentation that identifies a person or entity as the owner (see De Soto 2000; Hodgson 2015). This approach corresponds to a ledger, whether real or imaginary, that maps relationships between property and individuals (or any other property-owning entity). From an Ostromian perspective – utilising the IAD framework – we can understand these institutional mechanisms as 'rules in use' that shape various action situations of economic, social, and political exchange and coordination.

We can understand each of these governance mechanisms as attempts to govern the underlying property rights knowledge commons, and we can understand the effectiveness of those mechanisms in relation to what Berg et al. (2018, 2019) call a *general ledger*: a hypothetical map of all owned items and property relationships. Possession is a heuristic for the navigation of this general ledger, but possession is also coexistent with formal property ledgers – paper titles to (for example) vehicles that are mapped in centralised (usually government) vehicle registrations databases, and centralised ledgers of titles to land. To understand potential discrepancies between different infrastructures for managing property rights knowledge commons we can think of a *perfect ledger*. From this perspective we can see that better 'rules in use' – or institutional infrastructure – for managing property rights knowledge commons will tend us towards more widespread and more trusted information, facilitating market exchange and making the knowledge commons more robust.

Distributed ledgers, including blockchains, have the potential to more closely align the property rights knowledge commons to the perfect ledger. Blockchains are a technology for the distribution, maintenance, and verification of social facts. This is the basic feature of their design. At their most essential they are databases (ledgers) to which participants propose modifications (make/announce transactions) that are accepted, or not accepted, by other participants (the transaction is included in a new block adopted by the majority of the network). Once those modifications have been accepted by all participants, they are *in effect* rendered immutable – a permanent addition to the shared ledger. What makes (some) blockchains unique is that they achieve this consensus without a single, central authority to manage that process. Acceptance and synchronisation of new transactions occur without the use of a trusted third party to validate those transactions. For a full public blockchain (such as Bitcoin or Ethereum) no one needs permission from a given authority to access and make transactions on the chain. In their ideal or maximalist type, blockchains are thus open-access systems where openness is written into the protocol, rather than norms or laws.

The social facts that blockchains record are property rights (Berg et al. 2018). More specifically, they record the outcome of contractual agreements for the creation and transfer of property rights. In this way blockchains can be understood as a new infrastructure for maintaining the knowledge commons of information about property rights. Blockchain tokens can be inherently (i.e., intersubjectively) valuable on their own right, such as Bitcoin or other cryptocurrencies designed to be money substitutes. Alternatively, tokens can be markers pointing to other digital or material property – such as intellectual property in the case of blockchain applications that manage and track information about cultural or patentable goods, or real-world items like goods travelling across a supply chain. The use, disposal, and exchange of property rights is managed through a public key/private key infrastructure that requires publicly visible transactions on a public key to be signed by a corresponding, secret, private key (Rauchs et al. 2018). The network treats the use of the private key as the endorsement that the owner of the relevant tokens has initiated the transaction. This places a lot of reliance on individual token holders protecting their private keys from theft or loss, particularly given the fact that transactions are irreversible.

Blockchains offer an infrastructure for the social verification of information and access to knowledge about property rights. Blockchains are not the only technology required for secure exchanges in all circumstances – for example, distributed-ledger-managed supply chains rely on significant Internet of Things (IoT) infrastructure and alternative technologies of trust (such as government enforcement of rights). Nonetheless, they offer a publicly accessible record of property ownership with a built-in payment (i.e., transaction) system for exchange. Alongside other centralised or informal ledgers and enforcement mechanisms, the immutability and accessibility of blockchain infrastructure might act as additional 'rules in use' for the underlying knowledge commons.

There are several ways that blockchain infrastructure might augment existing infrastructure. By being freely accessible, distributed ledgers reduce the cost of consulting the ledger representation of the knowledge commons and reduce the risk that information of the ledger has been tampered with by the authority that manages it. Blockchains also offer the potential for the 'tokenisation' of more real-world assets and the association of those assets with ledger entries, allowing for significantly lower transaction costs in the exchange of those assets. Blockchains not only contribute to the scaffolding or infrastructure of the property rights knowledge commons, but also to the contracts underpinning the transfer of those resources. Even further, a decentralised sharing economy might organise more than just houses and drivers, but also ledger entries of lower value assets like hardware and moveable furniture (Catalini and Gans 2016; Munger 2018). Such knowledge about property rights facilitates exchanges on/with those goods in the same way that De Soto (2000) identified the opportunities for capital markets on top of more secure property titling in land.

There are limitations of blockchain-based property rights. This reality raises important questions about their interaction with other mechanisms – whether informal or centralised mechanisms – that also facilitate the knowledge commons. Blockchains sit alongside a range of other institutional mechanisms to maintain knowledge commons. Blockchains add to the complex ecosystem of different ways we manage the property rights knowledge commons, and should not be thought of as a complete substitute for existing institutions of property rights. Rather, different 'action arenas' wherein market participants interact will variously rely on different sources of underlying knowledge, and rights will be exchanged according to different rules. For instance, the potential for blockchain to augment property rights knowledge commons will differ depending on the nature of those rights. For some property rights they are native digital items. Digital tokens (such as Bitcoin) are enforced endogenously by the blockchain itself (Ishmaev 2017) and are less reliant on other institutions to maintain the commons. On the other hand, tokens that refer to property outside the blockchain – physical property whose ownership is governed by a distributed ledger – has no such endogenous enforcement mechanism. Ensuring that a digital exchange is reflected by a change in ownership in the real world faces the same challenges as any other property transfer; that is, it relies on the institutional mechanisms (such as legal rules, policing, and norms) that govern other property rights systems (Djankov et al. 2003). The extent to which blockchains are entangled and reliant on existing structures is a function of several factors, including whether those rights come into disputes and how those disputes are resolved (see Allen et al. 2020). The norms of disputes around blockchain-created and blockchain-enforced property rights are still developing, including where, for instance, there have been malicious hacks of blockchain tokens, and the community governing the blockchain has reversed those transactions.

'Onboarding' existing property rights frameworks onto a distributed ledger is a non-trivial problem. The real-world property rights systems studied by De Soto feature contested rights in environments where owners do not trust a central authority to recognise those rights. However, to realise the benefits of a blockchain-based property system, those contested rights need to be adjudicated by an authority – so that the definitive ownership can be recorded on the ledger. This need for a trusted authority to facilitate the move to a 'trustless' ledger is a common theme of bootstrapping decentralised systems (Berg et al. 2019; Saadatmand et al. 2019). Further, customary and informal property rights systems are not always amendable to the sort of formalisation that a digital ledger requires – a challenge faced by all property formalisation movements from the English enclosure movement (McCloskey 1972) to contemporary Papua New Guinea (Stead 2017). In this sense, blockchain offers a complement, not a replacement, for the existing institutional framework around property rights (Allen et al. 2019). Identifying where blockchain is most valuable at the margin for the governance of shared knowledge is the entrepreneurial task that has been ongoing since Nakamoto (2008a). Blockchains are a complement to existing governance structures of the property rights knowledge commons; they are governance frameworks that can coexist – and interoperate – with other knowledge commons about property rights. Blockchain infrastructure also serves as an input to processes and exchanges that might otherwise not occur. It expands the feasible number of trades that can or could occur within an economy. The open nature of blockchain as a distributed ledger ensures that they constitute shared goods or information that facilitates trade.

Blockchain innovation and diffusion is driven by complex dynamics that are not readily subject to the usual replicator dynamics and adoption-diffusion models that we are used to seeing with production technologies (Allen et al. 2020). Blockchains are an institutional technology – a competing technology in the mainline institutional schema of markets (Smith 1976), firms (Coase 1937), governments (Buchanan and Tullock 1962), clubs (Buchanan 1965), and the commons (Ostrom 1990) – which is subject to the evolutionary pace of production and communication technologies. They are network technologies, subject to network effects and adoption curves, but in which not only the object of exchange (the technology) is rapidly changing but also the institutional framework in which the exchanges occur.

Our aim here is not to describe the complexity of blockchain governance – itself a rapidly evolving field (Allen and Berg 2020). Indeed, the IAD framework has already been applied specifically to distributed ledgers to understand blockchains themselves as common pool resources (see Howell and Potgieter 2019). Blockchains deal with challenges of consensus over property rights in different ways – trading off various features such as privacy and permission in recording and enforcing property rights. The way that any given blockchain governs the knowledge shared within it can also be understood as evolutions in its 'rules in use'. An open permissionless public blockchain, for instance, has murkier resource boundaries than a permissioned one, where read and write access to the distributed ledger is restricted. The 'rules in use' differ across blockchains – depending on the code and the relationship between exogenous and endogenous governance. The question of whether blockchains are private, commons, or club-like depends on how that protocol is designed and the nature of the applications built on top of the blockchain infrastructure. Decentralisation and distribution occur on many margins in blockchain infrastructure. The validation of the network might be decentralised (i.e., there are many miners in Bitcoin) yet the governance of the networks (decisions about how the underlying protocol is modified) might be highly centralised. Private or permissioned blockchains such as IBM's Hyperledger Fabric trade-off the open and public features of decentralised systems for speed or privacy. It is for this reason that we have elsewhere described blockchains as a 'universal Turing institution' – a meta-institution that can be structured to simulate any other institution, just as a universal Turing machine can simulate any other Turing machine (Berg et al. 2019). Nevertheless, on the margin blockchains augment the broader understanding of property rights as knowledge commons.

Why did blockchain-based property rights emerge? Blockchain innovation can be understood as a form of self-governance (Leeson 2009; Skarbek 2011; Stringham 2014) – where they are forms of governance that are developed from the bottom-up with the intention of enabling better coordination. We can therefore understand the process of formalising and developing mechanisms of property rights in a similar way to Demsetz (1967), who argued that the emergence of property rights occurred where the marginal benefits exceeded the marginal costs – that is, where the costs of developing the institution were lower than the potential benefits from trade. The parallel here for knowledge about property rights is that this is a process of discovery over the most effective way to maintain that knowledge commons – whether through government registries, informal norms, private protection, or 'ledgerisation' using blockchains. New mechanisms of governance for the knowledge commons will emerge where the benefits of those new rules in use exceed the costs to maintain them – or, put another way, where demand for knowledge about property rights increases, whether in market or other forms of non-market coordination.

The extent to which blockchain governance is effective is a comparative question, relating to how protocol design solves coordination problems – in this case the recording and verifying of knowledge about property rights – compared to other governance structures. In a public permissionless blockchain those rules are social and communal – just as individual transactions are subject to consensus, so too is the protocol. This goes beyond the voluntary choice to participate or withdraw from participation on the network. Users (and developers) can at any time choose to 'fork' the code or even the history of the chain itself in order to vary its rules. These are complex events within 'action arenas' that are deserving of empirical studies. Proposals for upgrades to the protocol (to deal with, for instance, security problems, or to increase transaction throughput) require the ascension of a (usually) super-majority of users – in the Ostrom schema these are more "collective choice" rules. Bargaining power around these upgrades is unevenly distributed between classes of users (such as 'core' developers, miners, application developers and token holders – see Allen and Berg (2020)), each of whom claim a degree of legitimacy and influence over the choices to upgrade. This dynamic has brought about the crisis in blockchain governance, where these self-organised communities have disputed how decisions about protocol changes (i.e., constitutional level changes) should be made (De Filippi and Loveluck 2016).

What we have seen in this section is both that knowledge about property rights can usefully be thought of as a commons, and that there is a complex range of infrastructural rules that seek to maintain that commons. We have also seen that advances in blockchain technology – as a technology for recording and transferring property rights – are new 'rules in use' for those commons. Now we turn to the implications of this for our broader political economy understanding of knowledge commons and market infrastructure, combining the dual lenses of 'robust political economy' from economics and the 'Byzantine Generals' Problem' in computer science into what we call Byzantine political economy. The upshot from our analysis is that to the extent blockchains augment and complement existing hierarchical and norms-based governance of property rights, they will contribute a more robust political economy.

6.2 TOWARDS MORE ROBUST KNOWLEDGE COMMONS

Thomas Hobbes described governments as *automata* – machines that move itself, like a watch – and the metaphor of government as machine has been a deep thread throughout political thought (Agar 2003). When Walter Bagehot offered his vision of government as divided into the efficient (bureaucracy and administration) and the dignified (the monarch), he did so through an elaborate machine metaphor: the dignified part provided the power, regulator, and safety valves (as required by a steam engine), for the efficient part which 'works and rules' (Bagehot 1872: 4). As the potential and power of computing became evident, Oskar Lange (1967) declared that the socialist calculation debate was now an anachronism. The state's management of the socialist economy could be now delegated to the electronic computer, which would perform better than the market had done. Planning was a matter of extremely complex (although still linear) calculations. In the industrial age, 'machinery' was deployed as a metaphor; in the digital age it could now be a practicality.

What connects these visions together is government as a single apparatus that chooses and acts. The government is seen as *a* single machine – it is a single hierarchical authoritative mind that produces, allocates, and moves resources. To the extent that it has diverse centres of implementation – multiple machines, ministries, or domains of action – they are organised hierarchically (i.e., top-down, according to a command and control system). Orders are passed through the system and implemented by fiat. This approach to government is subject to the Hayekian (Hayek 1945) and public choice critiques (Buchanan and Tullock 1962) – governments do not work like that; in fact, they may be better conceived as orders (see Eusepi and Wagner 2011). Decision makers and bureaucrats do not smoothly, efficiently, and selflessly direct and implement policies in full knowledge of relevant trade-offs. But it is also the case that *machines* do not work like that either. Machines, especially those that interface with hardware might break, erode, deteriorate, fail to communicate, experience noisy communication channels, or even be hacked for malicious or malign purpose.

The Byzantine Generals' Problem is just one of a group of problems around the reliability of communications in decentralised systems. The question facing engineers is how to build reliable computation systems out of components that have non-zero failure rates. Improving the reliability of a component was subject to diminishing returns: eventually it was uneconomical or just impossible given technological limitations to improve reliability further. Thus, engineers accommodated the non-zero failures rates of components by ensuring a degree of redundancy in systems. If one part failed, another could take its place (Pierce 1964; Short 1968).

Such fault tolerance was particularly sensitive in the fields of aviation and space exploration, where it was proposed in the post-war years that an increasing amount of the control of avionics be handed off to computers and where the consequences of failure were, and remain, severe. Two separate research projects into fault-tolerant systems was supported by NASA, Software Implemented Fault Tolerance (SIFT) at SRI International and Fault Tolerant Multiprocessor (FTMP) at C. S. Draper Laboratory (Lee and Anderson 2012). Each approach relied on providing at least three times redundancy in components. In SIFT, for example, processes were run in parallel on three separate components and an executive function reconciled the outputs based on a majority vote (Wensley 1972; Wensley et al. 1978). Establishing how such 'voting' schemes would function and ascertaining the minimum required level of redundancy led to the conceptualisation and construction of the Byzantine Generals' Problem (Lamport 1978; Pease et al. 1980). This is a computer science equivalent to the knowledge problem that we have alluded to before: How does a buyer know that the seller actually owns the good being offered for sale?

The description of the Byzantine Generals' Problem in Lamport et al. (1982) is as follows. The Byzantine army surrounds an enemy castle. The army is divided into divisions, each of which is led by a general. The generals need to come to a consensus over a plan to attack the castle. But not all generals are loyal – a certain number of the generals are traitors, who want either to prevent consensus or for the generals to come to consensus around a bad plan. The messengers that pass information between the generals could be killed – and information therefore does not get through – or they could be late – which we describe as asynchronous messaging. In the simplest set-up of the problem, consider an army with three generals and a binary decision about whether to attack or retreat. Each general sends a message to the other two about their proposed action, and listens for messages from the other. If the traitorous general shares contradictory messages (i.e., recommending to one that they attack, and the other that they retreat) then coordination will fail, risking defeat on the battleground. To deal with the fact that a 'bad plan' is hard to formalise, they designated one general as a commanding general who formulates the plan and distributes orders to the others. Any general, commander, or lieutenant can be a traitor. In business, any seller could be selling unowned goods.

The Byzantine Generals' Problem is thus that: (1) all loyal generals need to obey the same order and (2) if the commanding general is loyal, then all loyal generals obey the order of the commanding general. Metaphorically, traitorous generals are unreliable components that report inconsistently to other distributed components, impeding consensus. Lamport et al. (1982) wanted to know what proportion of loyal/traitorous generals a distributed system could handle. Their finding was that, contrary to prior belief, under the simplest set-up three generals were not tolerant to one of their members being traitorous. This finding has generalised to the statistical expectation that decentralised Byzantine fault-tolerant systems cannot sustain more than one-third of nodes failing or acting maliciously.

The Byzantine Generals' Problem, therefore, describes a class of engineering failures where a system needs to come to consensus but fails to do so because of inconsistencies in communication (a Byzantine fault). The original problem statement gives an anthropomorphic implication to the problem – where generals betray their comrades – but the motive for misreporting is not the key. Whether the fault is the result of faulty reporting, faulty communications links, or capture by hostile actors, Byzantine faults are endemic to distributed systems (Driscoll et al. 2003, 2004).

Some parallels between consensus requirements in the presence of Byzantine faults and the economic coordination problem should be already apparent. Hayek (1945) describes the economic problem as the coordination of activity in an environment where information is "dispersed . . . incomplete and frequently contradictory" (519). Williamson (1985) argues that economic institutions are structured around the contractual problems of opportunism ('self-seeking with guile') and bounded rationality (leading to risks around investment in specific assets). Boettke and Leeson (2004), Leeson and Subrick (2006), and Pennington (2011) all describe the economic problem as being a dual challenge of structuring social institutions to handle information problems, and motive problems in public and private choices, leading to the agenda of robust political economy. These approaches, which can be loosely grouped around the transaction cost and Austrian schools, coalesce around the same problem of social organisation in the presence of disagreement and inconsistent, incomplete, and unreliable communication. In that sense, Byzantine fault tolerance is a parallel conceptualisation of this same class of problem. Nakamoto (2008a) designed the blockchain to operate under these very conditions – creating incentive structures to promote cooperative behaviour in the presence of unreliable trading partners and incomplete information.

The relevance of Byzantine consensus is more apparent when we consider this engineering problem in the context of blockchains – and particularly in relation to the governance of property rights. As we have seen, blockchains offer a shared database that can be updated – recording individual transactions and account states and allowing for complex economic organisation. Blockchains achieve Byzantine fault tolerance through their consensus mechanisms. Gramoli (2017) frames the Byzantine consensus problem in blockchains as "(i) agreement: no two correct processes decided different blocks; (ii) validity: the decided block is a block that was proposed by one process; (iii) termination: all correct processes eventually decide". Nakamoto's (2008a) innovation was to use a group of pre-existing technologies – peer-to-peer networking, asymmetric cryptography, and proof-of-work hashing algorithms – to come to distributed agreement over the state of a shared ledger (Narayanan and Clark 2017). The possible Byzantine faults range from the dramatic (hostile users of the ledger who seek to disrupt agreement and thereby allow for cryptocurrency tokens to be 'double spent') to the seemingly mundane (devices disconnecting from the network, disagreement about the order in which transactions are logged on the ledger due to geographic distances and a lack of synchronised clocks). Unlike in the example of the Byzantine Generals' Problem, there is no 'commander'. Each participant in the network that wants to keep a copy of the ledger and register new transactions must both listen to orders and announce orders.

While the Bitcoin white paper (Nakamoto 2008a) did not make explicit reference to Byzantine consensus, Satoshi Nakamoto's later forum posts argue that the consensus mechanism, part of which involves 'miners' solving a computationally difficult proof-of-work puzzle, gives Bitcoin characteristics which solve the Byzantine Generals' Problem (Nakamoto 2008b). Blockchains order their transactions through a majority agreement mechanism. Each 'miner' (in the case of the classic proof-of-work system in Bitcoin) wants to ensure that their mined block is accepted by the rest of the network, so they only extend the longest chain of blocks that they can observe on the network. Proof-of-work blockchains are vulnerable to '51 per cent' attacks, which allows a single attacker to interrupt honest behaviour if that attacker gains control of more than 50 per cent of the 'hash power' (computational resources directed at the proof-of-work puzzle) of the network (Budish 2018).

Where the anthropomorphic structure of the original Byzantine consensus set-up was somewhat misleading – components do not choose to be loyal or disloyal – Nakamoto consensus is distinct by adding incentives to the consensus mechanism. In Lamport et al. (1982) and the subsequent literature on consensus between unreliable components, reliability is exogenous. Whether a general is honest or dishonest is not affected by the operation of the consensus mechanism. In a real-world system of components this abstraction cannot be entirely true – the probability of component fault increases with the frequency of use due to aging. Nonetheless, generals can choose to betray their comrades, but components do not 'choose' to be faulty. Under Nakamoto consensus by contrast, each general faces distinctly economic incentives as to whether to be honest. Bitcoin is structured to reward miners for acting in the interests of the network (i.e., updating the ledger according to predetermined rules) and to punish other miners forwarding invalid transactions by orphaning chains that do not meet majority agreement. To our knowledge, Narayanan and Clark (2017) were the first to point out that this incentive mechanism made Bitcoin distinct from prior approaches to Byzantine consensus. It is this distinction that brings the study of Byzantine faults squarely into the realm of social science.

6.3 CONCLUSION

In this chapter we have made three interrelated points. First that a knowledge of property rights is a shared resource. Importantly, however, that this is a shared resource that must be produced in the economy. Second that 'rules in use' are an important component of those shared resources and those rules and the governance of those rules are subject to technological disruptions. Finally, we point to distributed ledger technology – blockchain – as an innovation that can better provide a robust political economy solution to existing knowledge commons governance problems.

To the extent that blockchains are adopted as an alternative social organisation for knowledge, how those blockchains are governed and how they interact with the existing set of institutions will become increasingly important. Their creation by Nakamoto (2008a) has opened up a large field of investigation, underlining the role that centralised ledgers play in the economy, and the long-run possibilities brought about by more and more decentralised ledgers. While we have suggested a research programme that examines blockchains as an innovation in how we govern the property rights knowledge commons – using the IAD framework for instance – these studies should also be laid within a broader conception of Byzantine political economy. That is, how can new systems of decentralised governance of knowledge about property rights – and their decentralised enforcement – be understood in the context of the robustness of the knowledge commons that fundamentally underpin our market system?

In this chapter we have laid out the principles at stake – what we have not provided is any empirical validation of these principles. This is largely due to the empirical applications currently being the subject of entrepreneurial discovery. Unlike previous innovative disruptions to the economy, we are seeing the disruption occurring in real time and not over the course of decades. Governance structures and institutions that have evolved over decades, if not centuries, to inform rules in use and resolve commons problems could be disrupted in a matter of years.

REFERENCES

Agar, Jon. 2003. *The Government Machine: A Revolutionary History of the Computer*. Cambridge, MA: MIT Press.

Allen, Darcy W. E., and Chris Berg. 2020. "Blockchain Governance: What We Can Learn from the Economics of Corporate Governance". *Journal of the British Blockchain Association* 3 (1): 1–10.

Allen, Darcy W. E., Chris Berg, Brendan Markey-Towler, Mikayla Novak, and Jason Potts. 2020. "Blockchain and the Evolution of Institutional Technologies: Implications for Innovation Policy". *Research Policy* 49 (1): 1038–1065.

Allen, Darcy W. E., Aaron M. Lane, and Marta Poblet. 2019. "The Governance of Blockchain Dispute Resolution". *Harvard Negotiation Law Review* 25: 75–101.

Bagehot, Walter. 1872. *The English Constitution*. London: Henry S. King & Company.

Berg, Chris, Sinclair Davidson, and Jason Potts. 2018. "Ledgers". *SSRN*. https://ssrn.com/abstract=3157421

2019. *Understanding the Blockchain Economy: An Introduction to Institutional Cryptoeconomics*. Cheltenham: Edward Elgar.

Boettke, Peter J., and Peter T. Leeson. 2004. "Liberalism, Socialism, and Robust Political Economy". *Journal of Markets & Morality* 7: 99–111.

Bollier, David, and Silke Helfrich, Eds. 2014. *The Wealth of the Commons: A World beyond Market and State*. Amherst, MA: Levellers Press.

Boyle, James. 2003. "The Second Enclosure Movement and the Construction of the Public Domain". *Law and Contemporary Problems* 66(1–2): 33–74.
Buchanan, James M. 1965. "An Economic Theory of Clubs". *Economica* 32: 1–14.
Buchanan, James M., and Gordon Tullock. 1962. *The Calculus of Consent, Logical Foundations of Constitutional Democracy*. Ann Arbor: University of Michigan Press.
Budish, Eric. 2018. "The Economic Limits of Bitcoin and the Blockchain". Working Paper 24717. Working Paper Series. National Bureau of Economic Research. https://doi.org/10.3386/w24717.
Catalini, Christian, and Joshua S. Gans. 2016. "Some Simple Economics of the Blockchain". Working Paper 22952. Working Paper Series. National Bureau of Economic Research. https://doi.org/10.3386/w22952.
Coase, Ronald H. 1937. "The Nature of the Firm". *Economica* 4: 386–405.
Cohen, Gabriel. 2005. "For You, Half Price". *The New York Times*, 27 November.
Davidson, Sinclair, Primavera De Filippi, and Jason Potts. 2018. "Blockchains and the Economic Institutions of Capitalism". *Journal of Institutional Economics* 14 (4): 639–658.
De Filippi, Primavera, and Benjamin Loveluck. 2016. "The Invisible Politics of Bitcoin: Governance Crisis of a Decentralized Infrastructure". *Internet Policy Review* 5 (4): 1–28.
De Soto, Hernando. 2000. *The Mystery of Capital: Why Capitalism Triumphs in the West and Fails Everywhere Else*. New York: Basic Books.
Demsetz, Harold. 1967. "Toward a Theory of Property Rights". *The American Economic Review* 57 (2): 347–359.
Djankov, Simeon, Edward Glaeser, Rafael La Porta, Florencio Lopez-de-Silanes, and Andrei Shleifer. 2003. "The New Comparative Economics". *Journal of Comparative Economics* 31: 595–619.
Driscoll, Kevin, Brendan Hall, Håkan Sivencrona, and Phil Zumsteg. 2003. "Byzantine Fault Ttolerance, from Theory to Reality". In International Conference on Computer Safety, Reliability, and Security, 235–248. Springer.
Driscoll, Kevin, Brendan Hall, Michael Paulitsch, Phil Zumsteg, and Håkan Sivencrona. 2004. "The Real Byzantine Generals". In The 23rd Digital Avionics Systems Conference. IEEE Cat. No. 04CH37576, 6. D. 4-61. IEEE.
Epstein, Richard A. 2009. *Simple Rules for a Complex World*. Cambridge, MA: Harvard University Press.
Eusepi, Giuseppe, and Richard E. Wagner. 2011 "States as Ecologies of Political Enterprises". *Review of Political Economy* 23 (4): 573–585.
Frischmann, Brett M., Michael J. Madison, and Katherine J. Strandburg, Eds. 2014. *Governing Knowledge Commons*. Oxford: Oxford University Press.
Gramoli, Vincent. 2020. "From Blockchain Consensus Back to Byzantine Consensus". *Future Generation Computer Systems* 107 (June): 760–769. https://doi.org/10.1016/j.future.2017.09.023.
Hayek, Friedrich A. 1945. "The Use of Knowledge in Society". *The American Economic Review* 35 (4): 519–530.
Hess, Charlotte, and Elinor Ostrom. 2005. "A Framework for Analyzing the Knowledge Commons". In *Understanding Knowledge as a Commons: From Theory to Practice*, edited by Charlotte Hess and Elinor Ostrom, 41–82 (Chapter 3). Cambridge, MA: MIT Press.
Hodgson, Geoffrey M. 2015. "Much of the 'Economics of Property Rights' Devalues Property and Legal Rights". *Journal of Institutional Economics* 11: 683–709.
Hoffmann, Sabine. 2013. "Property, Possession and Natural Resource Management: Towards a Conceptual Clarification". *Journal of Institutional Economics* 9: 39–60.

Howell, Bronwyn E., and Potgieter, Petrus H. 2019. "Governance of Blockchain and Distributed Ledger Technology Projects: A Common-Pool Resource View". Workshop on the Ostrom Workshop (WOW6) Conference, Indiana University Bloomington, June 19–21, 2019.

Ishmaev, Georgy. 2017. "Blockchain Technology as an Institution of Property". *Metaphilosophy* 48: 666–686.

Lamport, Leslie. 1978. "The Implementation of Reliable Distributed Multiprocess Systems". *Computer Networks* 2: 95–114.

Lamport, Leslie, Robert Shostak, and Marshall Pease. 1982. "The Byzantine Generals Problem". *ACM Transactions on Programming Languages and Systems* 4: 382–401.

Lange, Oskar R. 1967. "The Computer and the Market". In *Capitalism, Socialism and Economic Growth: Essays Presented to Maurice*, edited by C. Feinstein, 158–161. Cambridge: Cambridge University Press.

Lee, Peter A., and Thomas Anderson. 2012. *Fault Tolerance: Principles and Practice*. New York: Springer.

Leeson, Peter T. 2009. *The Invisible Hook: The Hidden Economics of Pirates*. Princeton, NJ: Princeton University Press.

Leeson, Peter T., and J. Robert Subrick. 2006. "Robust Political Economy". *The Review of Austrian Economics* 19: 107–111.

Madison, Michael J., Brett M. Frischmann, and Katherine J. Strandburg. 2009. "Constructing Commons in the Cultural Environment". *Cornell Law Review* 95: 657–709.

Madison, Michael J., Katherine J. Strandburg, and Brett M. Frischmann. 2018. "Knowledge Commons". In *Routledge Handbook of the Study of the Commons*, edited by Blake Hudson, Jonathan Rosenbloom, and Dan Cole. Abingdon: Routledge.

McCloskey, Donald N. 1972. "The Enclosure of Open Fields: Preface to a Study of Its Impact on the Efficiency of English Agriculture in the Eighteenth Century". *The Journal of Economic History* 32: 15–35.

Munger, Michael C. 2018. *Tomorrow 3.0*. Cambridge: Cambridge University Press.

Nakamoto, Satoshi. 2008a. "Bitcoin: A Peer-to-Peer Electronic Cash System". www.bitcoin.org.

2008b. "Re: Bitcoin P2P e-cash Paper". In *The Book of Satoshi: The Collected Writings of Bitcoin Creator Satoshi Nakamoto*, edited by Phil Campagne. E53 Publishing LLC.

Narayanan, Arvind, and Jeremy Clark. 2017. "Bitcoin's Academic Pedigree". *Communications of the ACM* 60: 36–45.

North, D. C. 2005. *Understanding the Process of Economic Change*. Princeton, NJ: Princeton University Press.

Ostrom, Elinor. 1990. *Governing the Commons: The Evolution of Institutions for Collective Action*. Cambridge: Cambridge University Press.

2005. *Understanding Institutional Diversity*. Princeton, NJ: Princeton Uuniversity Press.

Pease, Marshall, Robert Shostak, and Leslie Lamport. 1980. "Reaching Agreement in the Presence of Faults". *Journal of the ACM* 27: 228–234.

Pennington, Mark. 2011. *Robust Political Economy: Classical Liberalism and the Future of Public Policy*. Northampton, MA: Edward Elgar.

Pierce, William H. 1964. "Redundancy in Computers". *Scientific American* 210: 103–113.

Potts, Jason. 2019. *Innovation Commons: The Origin of Economic Growth*. Oxford: Oxford University Press.

Rauchs, Michel, Andrew Glidden, Brian Gordon et al. 2018. "Distributed Ledger Technology Systems: A Conceptual Framework". *SSRN*. https://ssrn.com/abstract=3230013.

Saadatmand, Fatemeh, Rikard Lindgren, and Ulrike Schultze. 2019. "Configurations of Platform Organizations: Implications for Complementor Engagement". *Research Policy* 48: 1037–1070.

Short, Robert A. 1968. "The Attainment of Reliable Digital Systems through the Use of Redundancy – A Survey". *IEEE Computer Group News* 2: 2–17.

Skarbek, David. 2011. "Governance and Prison Gangs". *American Political Science Review* 105: 702–716.

Smith, Adam. 1976. *An Inquiry into the Nature and Causes of the Wealth of Nations*. 2 Vols., edited by R. H. Campbell, A. S. Skinner, and W. B. Todd. Oxford: Oxford University Press.

Stead, Victoria. 2017. "Landownership as Exclusion". In *Kastom, Property and Ideology: Land Transformations in Melanesia*, edited by Siobhan McDonnell, Matthew G. Allen, and Colin Filer. Canberra: ANU Press.

Stigler, George J. 1961. "The Economics of Information". *Journal of Political Economy* 69: 213–225.

Stringham, Edward. 2014. *Private Governance: Creating Order in Economic and Social Life*. Oxford: Oxford University Press.

Wensley, John H. 1972. "SIFT: Software Implemented Fault Tolerance". In *Proceedings of the December 5–7, 1972, Fall Joint Computer Conference*. Part I, 243–253. New York: ACM.

Wensley, John H., Leslie Lamport, Jack Goldberg et al. 1978. "SIFT: Design and Analysis of a Fault-Tolerant Computer for Aircraft Control". *Proceedings of the IEEE* 66: 1240–1255.

Williamson, Oliver E. 1985. *The Economic Institutions of Capitalism*. New York: Free Press.

7

Knowledge Commons, Social Infrastructures, and Informal Markets

The Case of Informal Trade Credit in India

*Yugank Goyal**

7.1 THE VISIBLE STORY

Agra is the north-Indian city famous for the Taj Mahal. But beyond the beautiful structure of the Taj lie swathes of 'unstructured' markets of a particular item that Agra is more famous for in the local context – shoes. Agra is the most important centre of (leather) footwear manufacturing in India, and has remained so for centuries. The city produces for about 55 per cent of the Indian domestic markets and 22 per cent of total footwear exports from India (Hashim, Murthy, and Roy 2010). Around 40 per cent of the city's 1.7 million people are directly or indirectly involved with the footwear industry. The National Sample Survey Office (a government organization that collects large-scale sample surveys in India) reveals that Agra fares second in the share of population that is self-employed.[1] A good reason for this is the massive footwear cluster it has had historically.[2]

While there are huge export houses and medium-scale businesses, an overwhelming majority of work takes place in households, with traditional artisans making shoes by hand. These shoemaker artisans (also called *dastakaar*), who work in their homes with their family members making shoes by hand and selling their produce the next day in the wholesale market, employ a significant part of the city's population. By some estimates, more than two-thirds of manufacturing units are located in

* The author would like to thank the editors for their extensive suggestions on the earlier drafts which helped refine the argument greatly. Comments from the participants, particularly from Brett Frischmann and Terence Kealey, at the Mercatus Center Workshop on Governing Markets as Knowledge Commons that took place in Washington DC in March 2019 were invaluable. The author also thanks Aseem Prakash, Pauline Westerman, Amrit Raj, Abhinandan Malik for the insights they brought to his work, and Shiv Swaminathan for the unending joint pursuits in trying to discern polycentricity around us.

1 NSS 2004-05 suggests that for every 1,000 males, 603 are self-employed. The national figure is 395 per 1,000 people.

2 Despite the importance of this cluster, it has escaped a scholarly scrutiny. Knorringa (1994, 1999a, 1999b) and Lynch (1969) are the only two reliable works on this industry till date.

household artisan-dominated communities (Knorringa 1999b). According to some estimates, around '50,000–60,000 production workers, employed in around 4,000–5,000 mostly informal small-scale manufacturing units would produce approximately 300,000 pairs of shoes' (Knorringa 1994: 311), although these have significantly increased in last two decades.

The wholesale market in Agra is called *Hing ki Mandi*. It is a huge, bustling bazaar with hundreds of trading shops and small factory units where artisans come in the evenings with carts and rickshaws laden with shoes to sell. These wholesale shops are run and maintained by traders. Every day, the bazaar comes alive in the evening, with hundreds of shoemakers and traders busy haggling, negotiating, and finalizing prices, and in parallel are sights of loading, unloading, and hundreds of people chatting away. In a matter of a few hours, transaction worth millions of rupees will have taken place in one of the most congested markets one can witness.

A closer look reveals something interesting. Traders buy the footwear but do not make the payment upfront. They purchase shoes on credit. This credit is passed on to a wholesaler in another city, or a retailer. The retailer further buys the shoes on credit. Only when the retailer has made some sale, and received cash from customers, will he fulfil his debt to the trader. And only when all the traders in this supply chain have been paid, will the shoemaker receive his payment. Typically, traders ask three months' credit from the shoemakers.

Businesses around the world run on trade credit. That is not new. But there remain two issues that encourage me to pry into this market further. Firstly, how do traders offer credible commitments to the shoemakers, namely why do shoemakers trust the traders' promise. Secondly, trade credit is offered by shoemakers whose cost of liquidity is very high. They need cash today to buy raw materials for making tomorrow's shoes. How do they access capital for themselves today if the trader pays in three months?

The fieldwork (both participant observation and unstructured interviews) for the study took place between December 2012 and January 2013 and during April–August 2013. I sat in two of the traders' establishments during the day for several weeks, in order to observe how the trade works. This way, without divulging specific financial knowledge, they explained the trade business. My initial understanding of the market emerged through interviews with six traders. These traders took extensive time to explain the functioning of the shoe market, its structure, dynamics, and history. Two of the traders had worked in the market for more than four decades and all of them were second- or third-generation traders. With each trader I had around four to five sessions lasting on an average between one and two hours.

During my stay in the footwear cluster, I met 27 traders, 45 shoemakers, and 4 intermediaries. The meetings with shoemakers were in larger groups, while the meetings with traders and intermediaries were one-on-one. My observations in the footwear cluster were rather consistent over the months. I validated my impressions by repeated conversations with different actors. This validation was further achieved by few unstructured interviews I conducted with those outside the market (with a banker, an industrialist manufacturing footwear packaging, three journalists in local newspapers of which one was a veteran), but with deep knowledge about the market and its actors. During off-days (Mondays), I had the chance to visit shoemakers at their homes and chat with them informally. This intimate setting allowed me to collect richer narratives. Many of these conversations took place with several shoemakers sitting together at one house. I had three of those collective sessions, each lasting about an hour. In these private settings the coherence of my impressions was underscored.

Finally, I met with the leader of the association of shoemakers, where shoemakers informally convene to discuss their business. He explained to me in greater detail the government's and banks' disengagement with the artisans/shoemakers and often lack of understanding and support at the public level. Questions of caste and politics became important in this conversation. In 2011, the association of shoe traders produced a list of 446 shoemakers in the market that year, which was made available to me. Through one trader and one intermediary (*aadhatiya*), who had several decades of experience in the market, I compiled the discount rates of these traders to get a sense of overall market discount rate. The responses from the two respondents yielded small deviations so qualitative conclusions could be drawn with confidence. With the help of that list I could determine the average discount rate of 312 traders, since not all of those in the list were prominent.

Through my fieldwork I discovered that the problem of informal trade credit is solved with the help of an institutional artefact, the *parchi*, which literally translates into a paper-slip. When shoes are sold, the trader takes out a *parchi*, which bears his name, the amount due and the payable date, and hands it over to the shoemaker. The *parchi* is signed by the trader, and the understanding is that when his *parchi* is brought to the trader on the mentioned date (which is usually three months later), the trader will pay the said amount. He will pay his debt obligation to whoever brings him the *parchi* on the due date. Every trader makes such a promise. With sufficient trust in the market (which I discuss below), this aims to solve the problem of credible commitments.

How does the *parchi* solve the problem of liquidity? This is done because *parchis* assume the status of a promissory note, a negotiable instrument, informally within the market. Informal intermediaries have evolved in the market, known as *aadhatiyas*. They buy the *parchis* at a discount. On the due date, they go to the trader whose *parchi* they had purchased and claim the amount. They earn the discount, the shoemaker gets his liquidity and the trader gets his credit. This structure is illustrated in Figure 7.1. In many cases, the *parchis* act as currency as well, when shoemakers can buy raw materials in the market through a *parchi* – again at a discount.

One may wonder, what is the discount rate? It depends *only* on the creditworthiness of the trader. If a trader is known to delay his payments or renege on his *parchi*

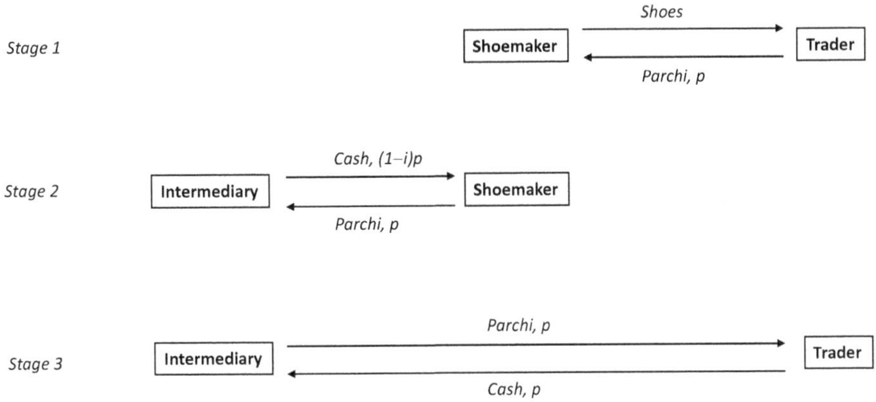

FIGURE 7.1. Transfer of credit in Agra footwear industry. p denotes value of parchi and i is the discount rate of the parchi that aadhatiya (intermediary) charges the shoemaker. (*Source*: Author's fieldwork)

promise, his discount rate would be high. For those with high trust ratings, discount rates are lower. And since shoemakers want to sell the shoes to a trader with low discount rates, they will go to the most trustworthy ones. This means, if a trader wants to attract good shoemakers, he better be trustworthy, and have a record of payment in time.

My primary survey revealed that the mean monthly discount rate is 1.41 per cent, ranging from 0.75 per cent to 3 per cent. This annual interest rate of about 17 per cent is almost 5 per cent points higher than the bank's interest rate. But people don't go to the bank. Even in moments of disputes, the local association of shoe traders arbitrates. These are community elders who have also been successful shoe businessmen. They will draw from their own experience, integrity, and knowledge of the market participants.

7.2 THE INVISIBLE INFRASTRUCTURE IN THE STORY

Surely, this complex and delicate institution could not exist without an appropriate, advanced, and elaborate infrastructure of norms and knowledge. An institutionalized sharing of resources between the community members is essentially the idea behind commons (Madison, Frischmann, and Strandburg 2010: 841). This governance method itself is a kind of knowledge that is driven by formal and informal rules and norms. It becomes important to examine what holds informal markets in such high state of trust that without the means of any legally structured contract or property rights regime, market participants are able to engage with each other and constantly negotiate their positions with respect to market institutions? How do they know what rules, infrastructures, and artefacts (for instance, interest rates) are in place and when and how is it changing? How do they create and simultaneously use this knowledge? If this knowledge is a resource, how is it governed and arranged? Is the absence of any anxiety on the part of market actors in the uncertain environment they operate, any indication of some form of culture that prevails in this market? How is the knowledge and culture shared, consumed, and absorbed?

Through the example of Agra's footwear cluster case, I observe the invisible socio-cultural infrastructure,[3] which helps me theorize on the instruments of classifications and interpretations done through a shared knowledge resource.

7.2.1 *The Nature of Product*

The shared knowledge of creditworthiness is the crucial resource that is used by market participants to allocate credits and discount rates. This creditworthiness – and consequently the discount rates on *parchis* of each trader – is the product in question. It is produced and consumed simultaneously as knowledge commons by an intricate network of knowledge-sharing mechanisms like gossip, rumour, and everyday interactions. Presence of this close-knit network – both physically as well as psychologically – allows a great deal of flexibility in the markets, at the same time arresting an otherwise expected uncertainty in a decentralized credit. The product is produced by physical presence in the market, by chatting away with hundreds of people every day, by closely observing the traders and their public (even private) dealings. Since creditworthiness cannot be directly observed by looking at traders' bank account details (anyway most of the trade happens in cash), market participants must rely on a range of other variables that act as useful proxies for the product.

For instance, knowledge of trader's financial health, his social relationships, his record of past promises, his reputation in the market, his ongoing trade deals, and so on become important. But also important are floating knowledge details on traders' exposures to high debt, business health, their future contracts, inventory size, downsizing processes, purchase of a new machinery, sale of their plot of land, and family marriages (girl's marriage as increasing liability and boy's marriage as enhancing asset provided the bride comes from a rich family). News of, say, cancelling of a large order or important meeting abroad or participating in a trade fair will also become crucial. Factors that affect a trader's financial health are embedded in their

[3] Frischmann's work (2012) in this context is instructive, and forms the bedrock of this concept. He uses cultural infrastructure as an umbrella category to include social, intellectual, and legal infrastructure. Cultural resource in some sense, 'captures the contextual, contingent, and social/relational aspects of the resources that constitute the meta-environment; the resources are resources vis-à-vis their meaning to and among people' (Frischmann 2012: 258). For the purposes of this chapter, I use cultural and social infrastructure interchangeably since they follow the same spirit as his scholarship suggests. This social/cultural infrastructure will capture the ideas of intellectual infrastructure – manifested in ideas and language – but not legal infrastructure since the market does not use the formal or written legal institutions for its governance (legal infrastructure could be visible in patents for example).

day-to-day functioning both within and outside the market. It depends on their linkages and relational associations that they may have. Therefore, knowledge about a trader's personal life and that of his debtors and creditors becomes paramount to keep an eye on his financial health. This type of information sharing also means that rumours could be risky. Hence, market participants have to be extremely cautious about anything they do in the public domain, lest a fake news is spread.

Further, since every action of the market participants (particularly the traders) is being observed, they do not want to be caught engaging in what would otherwise be morally repugnant. Whatever the market participants do must have a cultural sanction, because moral judgements carry strong bearing on one's character, and consequently one's creditworthiness. For instance, market may not take kindly to a trader who is known to have, say, thrown his old parents out of the house. Scholars have shown extensively how morality and markets have often intersected on cultural junctions (Fourcade and Healy 2007). The various mental models and even social artefacts of culture become useful components of the social infrastructure on which knowledge commons breed. It deters them from engaging in activities which are socially undesirable. And since what is socially undesirable keeps changing with times, this knowledge is also dynamic in nature.

And extraction of this knowledge is possible by self-presence and absorption of tacit knowledge (Polanyi 1966) through 'being' in the market and network. The close-knit community ensures near-to-perfect information symmetry. There is very low likelihood of misinterpretation because the tacit knowledge for market participants here locates within existing mental models that are formed over time. And as the knowledge is produced, it is quickly shared by participants, through word-of-mouth. As soon as the news of discount rates spiking up reaches one person, almost everyone gets to know about it. The more the word spreads, the more certainty this knowledge assumes. In consuming this knowledge, people produce it. This means, unlike a physical resource (Klamer 2017), this knowledge commons is anti-rival. When the knowledge commons on creditworthiness is produced, it enhances its value and often transforms its applicability as and when more and more people use it. As Hess and Ostrom (2005) illustrate the concept of contribution to a shared resource, I see the market participants in Agra's footwear cluster do the same – they have the right to change the content of the resource, and add or remove knowledge attributes that yield various layers of the knowledge about creditworthiness. The interesting thing is that the change in the shared knowledge resource of creditworthiness can be triggered by anyone. Everyone safeguards the shared resource collectively.

This information readily hovers in the market within the participants but will be extremely difficult for an outsider to collect. Incremental elements of the knowledge will be worthless for someone who does not have the cumulative knowledge endowment. Consequently, non-market actors, from outside, usually would not have any bearing or the right to change the knowledge commons. Such an exclusion is seen simply in the shared knowledge of community networks, group (caste, as shown later) loyalty, and continuous interaction between the market participants, and not the outsiders.

All of this means that the knowledge structure of creditworthiness is built on a range of shared knowledge pillars. Put together, the entire volume of knowledge commons is shared and used by market participants every moment while they are in action. The value of this resource is dependent on the value of the entire socio-cultural infrastructure that makes the shared resource valuable (Madison, Frischmann, and Strandburg 2010: 689; Frischmann 2012). But such an infrastructure itself relies on various technological features that enable governing the knowledge commons.

7.2.2 *Enabling Technology*

The shared understanding of various items mentioned above forms the inventory of socio-technical imaginary that enables the knowledge resource to be shared and utilized in the market. A valuable platform in this context – to establish credible commitments – is the high level of information symmetry in the market. Almost every market participant knows every other participant, and news of non-payment (or delayed payment) spreads fast. If a trader reneges on his payment, this is quickly known in the entire market (even to stakeholders outside), through informal channels of information dissemination in the form of discussions, gossip, chats, rumours, and informal gatherings. The market is very cohesive and close-knit; relational and trust-based conversations are invoked in everyday transactions. This builds a fertile environment of reliable tacit knowledge (Goyal and Heine 2021). Such tacit knowledge develops as knowledge is inherently created by those who use it. Its amorphous form also makes the exercise of putting the contract onto paper meaningless. Those within the market cannot escape it anyway, and those outside cannot acquire it easily.

The group cohesion becomes stronger because of the Indian caste system (explained in the next section). Most traders come from the *Punjabi* community, while artisans and workers are either Muslims or belong to the backward castes (*Jatavs*). If one looks at their dwelling pattern, traders reside in certain premium locations in Agra (like *Jaipur House*), and hence they meet often during local social gatherings. They have conjugal alliances and are members of the same city clubs. The artisans live in ghettos and after work they get together for local drinks and food. They share stories, rumours, and build and disseminate information. Idiosyncratic knowledge develops from within the community and dynamically alters itself through these gatherings. The convergence in interpretation has brought about the tacit knowledge structures, shared by the community and which are characteristic features of the marketplace experience. If the news of a trader not paying his dues or having a contract cancelled is revealed to one of them, in short time almost every shoemaker will know about it. The market allows everyone to keep a keen eye on the worth of the traders. Hence, if a trader issues *parchis* higher than their estimated worth, artisans receive the alert instantly through gossip and street rumours.

This allows us to see the physicality of space through an analytical aperture. The fact that the market is physically a cohesive space (note more than 3–4 km^2), coupled with the interwoven habitats in the localities participants live, makes the shared resource produced and consumed easily. Participants benefit from the tacit knowledge by simply being physically located around each other. A videoconferencing or remote access to information is of no use. The physicality of the shared infrastructure is the reason market participants are able to draw the resource much better than a bank or another financial intermediary located outside. Cultural resources are distributed spatially, and cultural experiences are linked with accessibility and proximity (Cohen 2007). Since the social infrastructure is culturally embedded (Frischmann 2012: 256), this part of knowledge commons governance – as visible in Agra's case – must be recognized.

The shared resource relies on a certain type of social infrastructure in order to cultivate itself and grow.[4] Formal markets have written laws that enable, inter alia, shared goods to be reproduced and utilized. Laws often act as normative coordinating points around which people converge their behavior through a shared understanding of the law (McAdams 2015). In the absence of written formal laws, people discover or invent normative private orders, which may or may not be as efficient as a formal legal order. Nevertheless, absence of formal order does not mean transactions will take place in an institutional vacuum. New normative orders will develop. The informal footwear cluster in Agra does the same. Shared resources draw from an inventory of social infrastructures constructed on the edifices of shared understanding of caste, familiarity, hierarchy, group-loyalty, conjugal alliances, social embeddedness, gossip, conversations, cohabitation, informal rules, norms, beliefs, and many such aspects. These attributes construct, consume, and coordinate the shared pool of knowledge as common good. They allow interdependencies that go far beyond just the agreement on price; they share a variety of expectations, which is possible through the tools offered by the social infrastructure in place (Kuchař and Dekker 2017).

All of this social infrastructure – in addition to various other artefacts that I discuss below – exists in the form of a knowledge commons. It acts as a cohesive social glue that is manufactured in the everyday interactions and community characteristics. Agra's footwear cluster not only produces shoes but also jointly produces the infrastructure that makes shoe production possible. It is able to do so through a sense of coherence manifested in the beliefs, ritualistic negotiations, observance of

[4] I synonymize social and cultural here, because each society has its own cultural characteristics, and often defining ones. Hence, for the Agra footwear cluster, the sustenance of shared resource takes place through various cultural practices (which go beyond just social).

reciprocity, formal rules and shared knowledge about the product, and various other characteristics of the knowledge resources. North's imagination of structuring interactions comes to mind (North 1990). The social infrastructure is indeed the key resource which ensures that the shared good is a common resource, and that it is produced and consumed – and in consuming, further produced.

7.3 PLUGGING THE STORY IN A FRAMEWORK

Elinor Ostrom has offered theoretical beacons that can shed light on the designs of institutions which govern the commons (1990, 2005). Her extensive work across the world (for instance, lobsters in Maine, high meadows in Switzerland, forests in Sri Lanka, fisheries in Alanya, Turkey, and water in Nepal) helped her design a framework that can potentially explain the commons governance at a general level. The framework – known as Institutional Analysis and Development (IAD) framework – offers a very effective toolkit to understand community managed resources.

If knowledge is a common resource in question in Agra's footwear cluster as I show above, perhaps the IAD framework may illuminate my case as well. Just as Ostrom thought of tangible resources like lobsters or fish, one can think of intangible resources, like knowledge. But the two products are not the same, exactly. For starters, lobster fisheries are rival resources and may get depleted by overfishing (for argument's sake). Knowledge, on the other hand, would not; on the contrary, it will grow with more consumption. In that it will be anti-rival. Further, the lobsters occur naturally and are truly exogenous. Knowledge, on the other hand, is produced by the consumers themselves, displaying an interplay between them (as well as the rules which emerge out of the manner in which community produces and consumes the resource). One may say that the knowledge, in many cases may not be cumulative as in lobsters because of the heterogeneity of the product or service at hand. In that sense, it could be a specific kind of situational knowledge that must be appropriate for the stock of knowledge to 'grow' meaningfully. Regardless of this – and I need more space to dwell on this question – the IAD framework must be appropriately tweaked to incorporate a new type of resource: the knowledge commons.

This tweaking must absorb such social infrastructure which becomes the bedrock for informal markets to emerge and persist over time. This has been done creatively in Madison, Frischmann, and Strandburg (2010), which I draw on. The authors examine patent pools, open source software, Wikipedia, Associated Press, medieval guilds, and modern research universities to show how Ostrom's framework can be suitably modified to capture knowledge as a commonly held good. I attempt to locate the case of Agra's footwear cluster in the same modified-IAD framework.

Two modifications of the IAD framework encourage me to use that framing. *Firstly*, in the modified framework, the resource characteristics (biophysical features), community attributes and rules-in-use continuously co-evolve, rather than existing as three separate exogenous variables. In other words, the independence and exogeneity of the three variables is suspended. In the context of knowledge commons prevalent in informal markets like Agra's footwear cluster, as I show, I observe that the three variables co-produce each other. They are also continuously fed from the patterns of interaction, as is the provided for in the modified IAD framework. *Secondly*, the distinction between patterns of interaction and the outcome is collapsed. The patterns of interaction in market resting on social and cultural infrastructure are itself the outcome which will be used as one of the inputs in manufacturing and consuming the resource.

We have discussed the resource characteristics in the preceding section. It is also clear why patterns of interaction would be the outcome itself, feeding back into the resource creation and usage – it is through gossip and endless chats and conversations that the knowledge resource of creditworthiness gets created, and it is through the community attributes that the conversations take place the way they do, under the rules which are drawn based on community networking in the first place. This knowledge about the creditworthiness is interrelated and dependent on the patterns in which informal contract and property rights are recognized, and which explain who can sell and be part of the transactional frame. I shall now examine the community attributes and the rules-in-use to help theorize the idea of governing knowledge commons, particularly in cases of informal clusters that are hinged on some shared knowledge to sustain and evolve, and in doing so, help locate the suitability of the modified-IAD framework for examining our case.

7.3.1 *Community Attributes Folded in Culture and History*

Hess and Ostrom (2005) propose that for any self-organized commons to be successful, in addition to collective action and self-governance, what is really needed is social capital. These again form part of the social infrastructure. This means, then, that knowledge commons may have a strong cultural construct. Evolution of any marketplace relying on informal social norms will exhibit development of social infrastructure over time, which in turn ought to explain the community attributes. These attributes become part of the functional identity through which the resource gets produced and disseminated. Knowledge remains nested in the social relationships. It is therefore culturally constructed.

Cultural constructions take time to build. Hence, understanding the evolution of the market through history offers a useful starting point to appreciate the social infrastructure in place, which enables the patterns of interaction to feed back into the resource, community, and rules. As Hall and Jones (1999) have shown, historical design of social infrastructure is crucial to understand economic performance in the long run. I show that through history, caste dynamics and their skillsets become necessary community attributes, and this in turn evolves the market and its interactive patterns in the way they are manifested today.

Hindus are generally divided into several castes, vertically and roughly segregated on the basis of occupation. Work on dead animal's hides or leather is considered polluting and forbidden to upper castes (Khare 1984). Hence, historically, leather goods could be made mostly by Muslims and a particular lower caste called the *chamars* (also called as *Jatavs*). Only those born as *chamars* could 'occupy the status of shoemaker without breaking caste rules' (Lynch 1969). Agra has had a huge *Jatav* population (as well as Muslims) historically,[5] and during the sixteenth and seventeenth centuries, Agra was the capital of Mughal dynasty, which was a great connoisseur of art, craftsmanship, and embroidery – as well as leather footwear. Availability of skilled labour and high demand from the elites led Agra to assume importance in leather footwear making. Later, the British brought in English designers and enhanced the skillsets of the artisans in Agra, which was the capital of one of their provinces for a good part of the nineteenth century. At around 1900, in fact, the first central shoe market was set up in *Hing ki Mandi*, which facilitated the trade significantly by allowing wholesale traders to sit at one place where both manufacturers and other merchants could come directly (Knorringa 1999b). My interviews with local elders reveal there was no *parchi* system at that time since the market never needed any. But more interestingly, I learn that the artisans would occupy specific localities and work used to happen in clusters of neighbourhoods. This is something we still see today. And as discussed in the preceding section, the physicality of the presence of participants together generates a cohesiveness which enables sharing the knowledge resource.

The India–Pakistan partition, which took place in 1947, uprooted around 30 million people on both sides, in one of the largest displacements in recent human history (Bharadwaj, Khwaja, and Mian 2008). A good part of Agra's Muslim footwear merchants migrated to Pakistan, leading to a decline in the shoe industry in the city (Knorringa 1999b). At the same time, the city saw a huge influx of Punjabi migrants from the other side of the border.

Punjabis, usually Hindus or Sikhs, however, do not observe the strict forms of caste-based segregation. Consequently, they have no qualms working with leather. They observed the market flooded with skilled craftsmen and quickly became their commissioning agents. Slowly, trust began to develop between Punjabi merchants and *Jatav* shoemakers. This trust and close-knit cohesiveness built knowledge structures about each other, tacitly produced, enriched, and shared between the parties. Migration led to various community interactions that led to the emergence of new forms of trade. *Punjabis* were migrant communities, and remaining closely knit was a social necessity. Old records of their settlements in Agra don't exist, but urban patterns of their dwelling show homogenous, affluent, gated communities in

[5] Imperial Gazetteer of India. Oxford, Clarendon Press, 1908–1931 [v. 1, 1909] v. 5, p. 76. Available at http://dsal.uchicago.edu/reference/gazetteer/pager.html?objectid=DS405.1.I34_V05_085.gif, last accessed on 5 December 2019.

which *Punjabis*, *Baniyas*, and other upper castes live together. In the same way, *Jatav* artisans live in poor ghettos of the society. Sticking with each other, and working in the same cluster, trading communities gather idiosyncratic knowledge by virtue of their presence in the market. This physicality was indeed crucial to build the initial level of trust.

This trust, slowly enabled credit to emerge in the market. Punjabis began purchasing shoes from *Jatav* artisans on credit. They would sell them off in markets outside Agra, give the shoemakers their due and keep the rest for themselves. The only difficulty was remaining penny-less for the first round of the cycle. Once the second round began, the chain of credit was triggered. This led to the emergence of early signs of *parchi* system in the industry.

Perhaps another factor led to the creation of this institution, and that is, the caste system itself. Note that Punjabis occupy a much higher status in India compared to lower castes. *Jatavs*, at the bottom, could easily have been subdued by the higher cultural and feudal status of Punjabis. Punjabis could have garnered various forms of caste-based subservience from lower caste people and 'used' *Jatav* artisans. Bremen (1974) observes the caste-based societies in India and identifies that both patronage and exploitation often coexist in such places. Indeed, records suggest that the pre-partition relations between Muslim distributors and *Jatav* producers were 'smooth' and amicable (Lynch 1969: 36). The former would purchase shoes in cash and also give favourable loans to *Jatavs*. All this changed when Punjabis replaced Muslims after the partition. Punjabis' approach was much harsher and more antagonistic towards *Jatav* artisans (Knorringa 1999b). Using their institutional power of caste, Punjabis, over time, expanded the markets through credit.

Be that as it may, creation of the institution of *parchi* was hinged on the community attributes which enabled certain type of characteristics for the resource to emerge. Physicality and the caste-system are two useful takeaways. The community attributes are very clear in terms of their identity, in terms of castes that occupationally segregate them. Such types of community attributes therefore can be seen to give rise to certain form of knowledge sharing to happen automatically. When knowledge is used as a resource, the governance of that shared knowledge evolves around the same community attributes which helped trigger its production. The consumers, producers, and coordinators of the knowledge are the community, through their own characteristic features that developed historically.[6] We can observe this in the way participants discriminate prices, discount rates, and, most importantly, switch between traders. The shared infrastructure allows for an extremely low level of loyalty between artisans, traders, and intermediaries, but at

6 Some of my interviews revealed that some of the first ones to invoke the idea of *parchi* were the big traders themselves, who wanted a credit on their payment. This was done through their own relatives standing outside their shops buying the *parchi* which shoemakers would come out with. More investigation is needed on this narrative, but it does make sense when one talks to market veterans.

the same time, a very high level of loyalty within the market as a whole. The social infrastructure in this case was historically as well as culturally constructed. Such a construction crystallizes the community (cultural) attributes which also enables certain rules to evolve. And it is the combination of the community and the rules that effectively utilizes the resource in question.

7.3.2 *Salient Features and Rules*

Market in Agra and, more specifically, the trade credit institution in the market, as we have seen, was not a purely natural or a purely artificial construction. It was born in the cultural intercourse that happened as a result of friction between different communities engaging with each other. And the community engagement led to peculiar and complex rules to emerge in the market. In fact, Karl Polanyi (1944) has remarked how trade is an external affair between different communities rather than the same tribe. The story of Punjabi–Jatav interactions triggering a new layer of trade explains this vividly. Trading with strangers would have required new intellectual and legal infrastructures and new tools, which are indeed visible today. It also encapsulates the general order of how things work in the market with respect to trade credit, and centralizes the importance of trust, reciprocity, and various forms of monitoring and sanctions, as illustrated in Dietz, Ostrom, and Stern (2003). This now needs to be understood in an extensive form, that is, what these rules are used for and how they achieve the purpose.

The real aim for which rules-in-use are to be conceptualized here include continued production of shared knowledge, reducing transaction costs to access and use it and ensuring the accuracy of the knowledge resource. Production and dissemination of the knowledge commons happens through continuous engagement of the communities amongst each other, manifested in their daily interactions, gossips, rumours, and being part of the market. The continuous engagement helps screen accurate from inaccurate knowledge. Since any new piece of knowledge goes through the test of confirmations, with dialogical testing, it will die out soon unless it can be validated and re-validated through the market participants in their regular conversational use. When the knowledge may pertain to an actor in the market, he is incentivized to arrest spread of any untrue knowledge. Beliefs aside, an untrue knowledge, without being continuously tested and legitimized, soon dies out. In addition, caste-based loyalty enforces the spread of rumours, news and other such material information that then gets carried far and wide and takes the shape of a templatized form of discount rates.

The rules-in-use, therefore, underscore respecting promises of *parchi*, which acts as a promissory note, credit rationing, dispute resolution, and imposing multilateral punishment strategy. Perhaps the most important is the idea of keeping promises. When a trader issues a *parchi*, his reneging is sure to attract penalty and this disciplines the market to observe the promise. It is such a strict rule that the market has practically no sympathy for any delayed payment, no matter the reason behind the delay. The day of the payment witnesses massive exchange of cash between traders because they have no qualms in borrowing money to pay off their dues on the payment date. In one of my interviews it was revealed that on the day of the payment, even if a dog comes to the trader with his *parchi* stuck in its mouth, the trader will take the *parchi* and shove the money in its mouth.

Actors make their own networks, operate within, and rely on their own caste and community networks for accessing the knowledge commons, and reusing it to share with others. Punjabis do it amongst themselves, *Jatavs* in their own community and so do the intermediaries. And since all of them talk to each other, there is hardly any difference or arbitrage in the knowledge commons. The caste networks bring them closer – they all share stories, rumours, gossip, and build information within their respective groups. This also puts one group against the other. The usual narrative among the traders is that the shoemakers are a lazy lot and they spend their money in gambling and drinking. The other group laments how traders exploit them, squeezing them off any surplus. This makes each of these groups loyal to each other.

The rules-in-use have also evolved on the manner in which trading on some *parchi* will exhibit credit rationing. This means that discount rates do not keep on rising with increasing risk. Beyond a point, people simply stop dealing with the trader, instead of selling shoes on credit with high interest. Stieglitz and Weiss (1981) in their seminal work showed that it will often make sense for the banks to ration credit and not keep on raising interest rates indefinitely, because through this, they avoid adverse selection problems. Something similar happens in the market here. The reputational impacts are strong and any reneging on the *parchi* payment will bring down the credibility of the trader massively. If this happens more than once, his *parchi* may simply not run in the market and will lose all value, thereby forcing him out of the credit business. In fact, one can see the traders frantically trying to arrange cash a day before the *parchi*-payment date, so that none of their creditors have a reason to return. In financial terms, one can see an interesting credit rationing happening in the market.

These rules often guide the manner in which dispute resolution in the market takes place. Cases of bankruptcies are dealt with informal dispute settlement, organized by local associations of traders. These bodies are headed by veterans of the trade who mediate and order how much the creditors need to be paid, assessing the leftover worth of the bankrupt trader. The settlements are not done with documentary evidences but exploit the existing local knowledge about the matter. People know the story and lying is not possible by and to a market participant. Judgements of association members are usually adhered to, and State's judiciary and courts are seldom invoked. This is also possible because many of the unwritten norms are followed with great adherence. For instance, Mondays are no-working days. Payment days are always the 5th, 10th, 15th, 20th, 25th, and 30th of each month (or the next day if the payment date is a holiday/Monday). These rules are not wavered from, and this keeps everything around them also in a strict normative order.

Running away with a huge credit on your head is very rare. This is because the market runs through family units and those players have relational ties, hence arriving at such an end-game (exit) situation is not very likely. Cheating traders' sons, sons-in-law, and other relatives still continuing in the market may have to suffer the repercussions. The threat of foregone earnings, not just for yourself, but for your near-ones arrests such cheating tendencies.

More interesting is the multilateral punishment strategy. News of nonpayment spreads like wildfire and discount rates spike up instantly. Regardless of who is cheated, once such a trader is discovered by market participants, almost everyone stops going to the trader. This creates a huge cost to the trader and he would not likely try to dupe anyone. If shoemakers stop coming to him, he will have to rebuild his reputation, which will not only take a long time, but no one will sell the shoes to him on credit. Since this news will become public in the market, arranging for cash to regain the trust in the market could be very difficult. And so the threat of future losses disincentivizes the trader from engaging in any dishonest act. This threat of sanction is similar to Greif's (2006) conception of multilateral punishment.

7.3.3 *The Story Cast in the Modified-IAD Framework*

One should now be able to connect Agra's story to the the modified-IAD framework. Informal markets are rugged petri dishes to observe knowledge commons embedded in a social infrastructure. In other words, we can make considerable sense of how informal markets are collectively governed if we observe their social infrastructure and the knowledge commons associated with it. These infrastructural elements, as we saw, are embedded in the history, society, and culture of the place, in which many aspects of knowledge commons are created by some shared goods, manifested in friendships, gossip, and caste-based structures. And having arrived at this point, I can now swiftly slide some of the routine observations about the social infrastructure that enables knowledge commons governance in the modified-IAD framework.

Figure 7.2 illustrates the foundational features of the modified-IAD as it would appear for an informal market like Agra's footwear cluster. The creditworthiness as the crucial knowledge resource will be a shared, anti-rival resource which is governed like commons. Caste-based loyalty and spatial proximity are crucial community attributes that enable the production, coordination, and consumption of the resource, and corresponding institutional structures have all evolved historically. The rules-in-use are evident in adopting *parchis* as promissory notes, along with the threat of multilateral punishment strategy (with credit rationing and dispute resolution methods that are not reflected in the figure). Each of these variables – resource, community, and rules – co-produces the other. The knowledge resource exists because the community necessitates its sharing, and that happens through the rules-in-use, which in turn, are by-products of the community's governance of knowledge commons. The range of interactions, gossip, and knowledge-building exercise which feeds directly into the resource-community-rules collection, themselves act as the outcomes on which the market thrives.

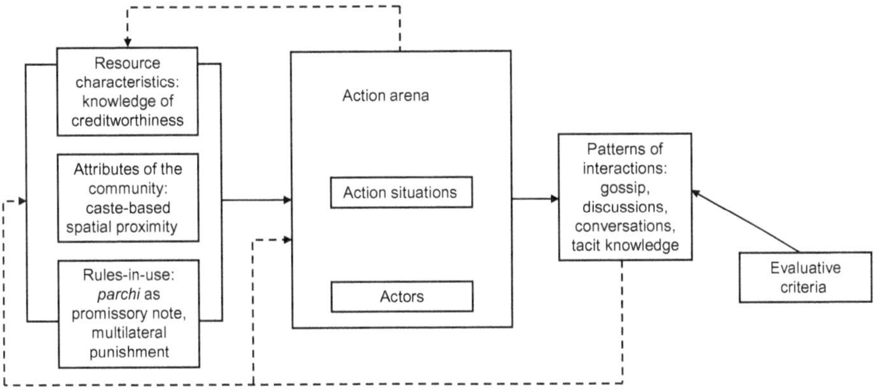

FIGURE 7.2. The footwear cluster, as located in the GKC framework (Frischmann, Madison, and Strandburg 2014: 19)

Note that looking at the social infrastructure and knowledge commons governance architecture as proposed in the model allows us to understand why this institution of *parchi* has remained immutable over time. A more formal approach could have enhanced the economic scale of this credit, which would have attracted banks to offer higher credits on lower interest rates. They could have pooled in the risks associated with *parchis* and offered much better and more voluminous credit instruments. But over several decades, the design of this institution has remained unaltered.

This is because the very social infrastructure that makes knowledge commons governance possible is not easy to formalize. Banks, for instance, simply lack knowledge about the community and are incapable of following their rules. The cost of knowledge for any formal, third party is very high. Knowledge about creditworthiness of the traders is a tacit knowledge embedded within the social infrastructure and known to market actors instantly; securing the information for anyone outside is difficult, including banks. The knowledge of group members, their identity, financial exposure, credit history, social capital, and social embeddedness as valuable repository of the knowledge resource comes easily through the patterns of interaction of the community, which is both the user and producer of the resource. Scaling it up by any formal body will break down these necessary ingredients which make the resource and its use. And should such an effort be considered, it will require an exhaustive understanding of the market to develop some design principles.

7.4 CONCLUSION

That markets are cultural is not a remarkably new idea. They emerge and evolve within cultural infrastructures. Both Michael Polanyi (1958) and Karl Polanyi (1944) had argued how economic dynamics are part of larger socially embedded attitudes – a sentiment shared by Karl Popper as well who celebrated open societies to build and share scientific knowledge (1945). The social background is the necessary institutional framework that allows certain types of economic performance and disables the others. Schumpeter was of the view, for instance, that capitalism requires unrestrained democratic space to flourish (1976). Bardhan (1989) reminds us of Carl Menger's (1883) distinction between *organic* and *pragmatic* institutions, where the former are a result of individual pursuits, undersigned, while the latter emerge from conscious contractual design. Both these institutional frameworks inspire heavily, the type of market-based activities that will emerge in time to come. Economic sociology has constructed valuable ideas to explain this as well (Smelser and Swedberg 2010).

It is in this larger context of resuscitating the link between markets and culture that the chapter locates itself. And the necessary theoretical link is offered by the knowledge commons. By looking at the centuries' old footwear cluster in Agra, and locating its institutional framework in the theory of knowledge commons, the chapter not only empirically tests the theory and surfaces the importance of socio-cultural infrastructure but also advances a conceptual apparatus to understand informal markets from a knowledge commons perspective. If (1) Strandburg, Frischmann, and Madison (2017: 10) suggest that knowledge commons is an 'institutionalized governance of sharing and, in many cases, creation of … intellectual and cultural resources' and (2) informal markets are constructed on cultural edifices as I show in this chapter, then it is not difficult to expect knowledge commons framework manifested in a large number of informal market behaviors around the world. And that is why, the generality of the idea cannot be overstated. A vast majority of markets in developing countries operate through knowledge commons, created, and shared on the basis of social, legal, and intellectual infrastructures.

This also calls for a renewed interest not just in informal markets, but also the knowledge commons project. Indeed, if one uses the lens of institutional change to focus on existing informal clusters, one is welcomed by a fascinating array of actors ingeniously producing and consuming knowledge resources to build and rebuild these markets. Knowledge commons are often the building blocks on which foundations of informal spaces are built. And informal spaces employ a majority of the populations in Africa, South Asia, and Latin America. Understanding their structure is, therefore, understanding more than half the world.

REFERENCES

Bardhan, Pranab. 1989. 'The New Institutional Economics and Development Theory: A Brief Critical Assessment'. *World Development* 17 (9): 1389–1395.

Bremen, J. 1974. *Patronage and Exploitation: Changing Agrarian Relations in South Gujarat, India*. Berkeley: University of California Press, 44.

Bharadwaj, Prashant, Asim Khwaja, and Atif Mian. 2008. 'The Big March: Migratory Flows after the Partition of India'. *Economic and Political Weekly* 43 (35): 39–49.

Cohen, Julie E. 2007. 'Cyberspace as/and Space'. *Columbia Law Review* 107: 210.

Dietz, Thomas, Elinor Ostrom, and Paul C. Stern. 2003. 'The Struggle to Govern the Commons'. *Science* 302 (5652): 1907–1912.
Fourcade, Marion, and Kiearan Healy. 2007. 'Moral Views of Market Society'. *Annual Review of Sociology* 33: 285–311.
Frischmann, Brett M. 2012. *Infrastructure: The Social Value of Shared Resources*. Oxford: Oxford University Press.
Frischmann, Brett M., Michael J. Madison, and Katherine J. Strandburg. 2014. *Governing Knowledge Commons*. Oxford: Oxford University Press.
Goyal, Yugank, and Klaus Heine. 2021. 'Why do Informal Markets Remain Informal: the Role of Tacit Knowledge in an Indian Footwear Cluster'. *Journal of Evolutionary Economics* 31 (2): 639–659.
Greif, Avner. 2006. *Institutions and the Path to the Modern Economy: Lessons from Medieval Trade*. Cambridge: Cambridge University Press.
Hall, Robert E., and Charles I. Jones. 1999. 'Why Do Some Countries Produce So Much More Output per Worker Than Others?' *Quarterly Journal of Economics* 114 (1): 83–116.
Hashim, S. R., M. R. Murthy, and S. Roy. 2010. 'SME Clusters in India: Identifying Areas for Intervention for Inclusive Growth'. Institute for Studies in Industrial Development, Working Paper.
Hess, Charlotte, and Elinor Ostrom. 2005. *Understanding Knowledge as a Commons: From Theory to Practice*. Cambridge, MA: MIT Press.
Klamer, Arjo. 2017. *Doing the Right Thing: A Value Based Economy*. London: Ubiquity Press.
Khare, R. S. 1984. *The Untouchable as Himself: Ideology Identity and Pragmatism among the Lucknow Chamars*. Cambridge: Cambridge University Press.
Knorringa, Peter. 1994. 'Lack of Interaction between Traders and Producers in the Agra Footwear Cluster'. In *Flexible Specialization – The Dynamics of Small-Scale Industries in the South*, edited by P. O. Pedersen, A. Sverrisson, and M. P. van Dijk, 71–83. Rugby: Practical Action Publication.
1999a. 'Agra: An Old Cluster Facing the New Competition'. *World Development* 27 (9): 1587–1604.
1999b. 'Artisan Labour in the Agra Footwear Industry: Continued Informality and Changing Threats'. *Contributions to Indian Sociology* 33 (1–2): 303–328.
Kuchař, Pavel, and Erwin Dekker. 2017. 'Emergent Orders of Worth: Must We Agree on More than Just Price?' *Cosmos+ Taxis: Studies in Emergent Order and Organization* 4 (1): 23–34.
Lynch, Owen M. 1969. 'The Politics of Untouchability'. In *Structure and Change in Indian Society*, edited by Milton B. Singer and Bernard S. Cohn. New York: Columbia University Press.
Madison, Michael J., Brett M. Frischmann, and Katherine J. Strandburg. 2010. 'Constructing Commons in the Cultural Environment'. *Cornell Law Review* 95: 657.
McAdams, Richard H. 2015. *The Expressive Powers of Law: Theories and Limits*. Cambridge: Harvard University Press.
Menger, Carl. 1883 [1963]. *Problems of Economics and Sociology*. Translated by F. J. Nock. Urbana: University of Illinois Press.
North, Douglass C. 1990. *Institutions, Institutional Change and Economic Performance*. Cambridge: Cambridge University Press.
Ostrom, Elinor. 1990. *Governing the Commons*. Cambridge: Cambridge University Press.
2005. *Understanding Institutional Diversity*. Princeton, NJ: Princeton University Press.
Polanyi, Karl. 1944. *The Great Transformation: The Political and Economic Origins of Our Time*. Boston: Beacon Press.

Polanyi, Michael. 1958. *Personal Knowledge: Towards a Post-Critical Philosophy*. London: Routledge & Kegan Paul

1966. *The Tacit Dimension*. Garden City, NY: Doubleday.

Popper, Karl R. 1945. *The Open Society and Its Enemies*. Routledge.

Schumpeter, Joseph A. 1976. *Capitalism, Socialism and Democracy*. Routledge.

Smelser, Neil J., and Richard Swedberg (eds.). 2010. *The Handbook of Economic Sociology*. Princeton, NJ: Princeton University Press.

Stiglitz, J. E., and A. Weiss. 1981. 'Credit Rationing in Markets with Imperfect Information'. *The American Economic Review* 71(3): 393–410.

Strandburg, Katherine J., Brett M. Frischmann, and Michael J. Madison. 2017. *Governing Medical Knowledge Commons*. Cambridge: Cambridge University Press.

8

Entrepreneurship and Governance in the Scotch Whisky Knowledge Commons

*Michelle Albert Vachris and Kyle Vachris**

The Scotch whisky industry is centuries-old and steeped in tradition. Indeed, "it has long been used as a symbol of Scottishness" (Baxter 1985: 77). Recently, distillers in other countries have adopted the Scotch whisky process and have successfully imitated single malt Scotch whisky. Legally, they cannot call their product "Scotch" unless it was made in Scotland, so, instead, it is whisky in the style of Scotch or peat malt whisky. The increased competition from these non-Scottish distilleries caused quite a stir. While at first it was proclaimed that these liquors would never hold a candle to the true Scotch, Japanese and Australian spirits won acclaim and even surpassed some Scottish bottles in worldwide spirits awards (World Whiskies Awards n.d.) and single malt guides (Roskrow, Smith, and Jackson 2015). As early as 2003, a Japanese single malt earned gold medal status (Kageyama 2017). By 2008, a Japanese single malt was named the best in the world (Yan 2014), and in 2014 an Australian single malt earned that honor (World Whiskies Awards n.d.). Japanese whiskies are showing up as a category of their own on the spirits menus of high-end restaurants in the United States, signaling that consumers have accepted the newcomer as a status drink.

The development of a Scotch whisky industry in places other than Scotland resulted in Scottish producers fiercely defending their legally protected geographic indication for "Scotch." Such exclusion of competing producers is traditionally analyzed using rent-seeking theory, but the case of Scotch whisky is more complicated. This chapter will provide a case study of entrepreneurial history in the Scotch whisky market using the framework of Governing Knowledge Commons focusing

* Michelle Albert Vachris is Professor of Management, Business, and Economics at Virginia Wesleyan University and Professor Emerita at Christopher Newport University. Kyle Vachris is an Economist in the Producer Price Index program at the U.S. Bureau of Labor Statistics. The author wrote this article in his personal capacity. Any opinions, findings, conclusions, or recommendations expressed in this article are those of the author and do not represent the views of the Bureau of Labor Statistics or the US Government.

specifically on the attempts of the entrepreneurs to legitimize their entry into the product category of Scotch. The category of Scotch, especially single malt Scotch was developed and given credence by a small group of Scottish distillers at considerable cost. These distillers, thus, invested in an exclusionary knowledge commons between the producers and the consumers who value the spirit. On the one hand, Scottish producers understandably want to protect this investment and wish to maintain the quality of this shared resource. On the other hand, the exclusionary nature of this commons serves to restrict access to the shared resource and has limited the amount of innovation allowed. This trade-off between maintenance of and access to the shared resource will be the focus of this chapter.

8.1 SCOTCH WHISKY AS A KNOWLEDGE COMMONS

The Governing Knowledge Commons (GKC) Framework described by Dekker and Kuchař (Introduction) is useful to analyze Scotch whisky. This framework, developed by Frischmann, Madison, and Strandburg (2014), is an adaptation of the Institutional Analysis and Development (IAD) framework earlier developed by Elinor Ostrom and colleagues for governing common pool resources such as fisheries and water sources. Frischmann, Madison, and Strandburg (2014) modify the IAD Framework to make it more generalizable to the variety of knowledge commons. They describe a knowledge commons as "the institutionalized community governance of the sharing and, in some cases, creation, of information, science, knowledge, data and other types of intellectual and cultural resources" (2014: 3). We present the case of Scotch whisky, especially single malt Scotch, as a cultural knowledge commons.

8.1.1 *Resource Characteristics*

The resource studied is the knowledge commons surrounding high-quality single malt Scotch. To the Scots, this reputation is a source of national pride, indeed Scotch is referred to as *aqua vitae* or "water of life." The market for Scotch, then, is cultural in nature. What *is* and what *is not* Scotch is determined in the minds of consumers and producers. In this way, the category of Scotch is a "jointly produced" resource (Dekker and Kuchař, Introduction). In order to better understand the cultural nature of this resource, we will provide a very brief introduction to the history of how producers and consumers developed the single malt category of Scotch into a premium beverage.[1]

On the production side, distilleries produce a private good, single malt whisky, that goes beyond mere production to create a product category that serves as a point

[1] For more extensive treatments of the history of Scotch whisky, see Storrie (1962); Tedlow and Jones (1993); Dietz (1997); Lyons (2003); Driver (2014); and Gordon (2014).

of reference for quality. It took hundreds of years for single malt Scotch to attain this status, and the niche market for single malt Scotch is a relatively recent development. How, then, did single malt Scotch obtain its high-quality reputation?

The first official record of Scotch production is found in the Scottish Exchequer Rolls in 1494 (Lyons 2003). From the beginning, a sense of origin was an important characteristic (Driver 2014). Early Scotch production was characterized by single malt distillation in small pot stills for local consumption, but the invention of the continuous still in the 1830s made possible larger, more efficient production processes and blending of Scotch (Storrie 1962). As their names imply, continuous stills distill the spirit on a flow basis; they employ two separate columns for the process and allow for blending of several whiskies. Pot stills, on the other hand, process each batch separately in a single pot, so these are used for single malt Scotch production.[2] The new technology resulted in a more consistent quality for Scotch and allowed for the development of a new profession in blending (Gordon 2014). In 1877, the formation of the Distillers Company by six distilleries transformed the cottage industry into a more modern commercial endeavor capable of distribution beyond the local level (Gordon 2014). Further cooperation among distillers began in 1912 with the formation of the Wine & Spirit Brand Association, which morphed into the Scotch Whisky Association in 1942 (SWA n.d., *Story of Scotch*).

On the demand side, consumption of Scotch was first used for medicinal purposes, but the technical advances in the 1800s led to an increase in the quality of the spirit as a result of blending (Driver 2014). The blended Scotches were very popular due to the predictability from year to year that blending affords. Blends were also more palatable to non-Scots than single malts, which according to conventional wisdom were "too intense, flavorful, or complex for the English and other foreigners" (Roskrow, Smith, and Jackson 2015: 219). Tedlow and Jones (1993) explain how demand for whiskies including Scotch exploded in the 1880s when vineyards in Europe were destroyed by the phylloxera beetle and consumers switched from wine to whisky. The authors point out that Scotch gained further prestige from Queen Victoria who visited distilleries and promoted the industry.

It is widely noted that the popularity of blended Scotch reached America when US soldiers returned home from World War II having been exposed to the drink while in the United Kingdom (see, e.g., Storrie 1962; Tedlow and Jones 1993; Driver 2014). In America, Scotch had an "import cachet" relative to domestic whiskies

[2] The U.K. Statutory Instruments (2009) define the following categories of Scotch: (1) Single Malt Scotch Whisky: distilled in one or more batches at a single distillery, from water and malted barley and no other cereals, in pot stills; (2) Single Grain Scotch Whisky: distilled at a single distillery and is not a Single Malt Scotch Whisky or a Blended Scotch Whisky; (3) Blended Malt Scotch Whisky: a blend of two or more Single Malt Scotch Whiskies distilled at more than one distillery; (4) Blended Grain Scotch Whisky: a blend of two or more Single Grain Scotch Whiskies distilled at more than one distillery; and (5) Blended Scotch Whisky: a blend of one or more Single Malt Scotch Whiskies with one or more Single Grain Scotch Whiskies.

(Driver 2014: 349), but single malt Scotch had not yet been established as a premier spirit. As liquor connoisseur and author wrote in 1948, "Nobody drinks single malt" (Embury, Hess, and Saunders 1948); blended Scotch was all there was at that time.

Scotch was revolutionized with the introduction of the "single malt" category as a premier whisky to international markets in the 1960s. W. Grant and Sons gets credit for pioneering the sale of single malts outside of Scotland (see Driver 2014; Gordon 2014; ScotchWhisky.com n.d., *Glenfiddich*). The Scotch industry had been facing declining demand, and the Grants were facing competition from larger firms buying up independent distillers. In response, W. Grant and Sons introduced their unique triangular shaped bottle, designed to reflect "[w]ater, air and malted barley. A trinity expertly crafted to make a Glenfiddich whisky" (Glenfiddich n.d., *Our History*). The Grant family also began to focus on the single malt category.

One story has it that the distillery had a contract dispute with its grain supplier; and with no grain whisky with which to blend, they decided to bottle the malt whisky by itself (Mennie 2018). Their Glenfiddich distillery was only equipped with pot stills, as they purchased the grain whisky for blending from a distillery that used continuous stills. The Grants went on a marketing blitz, advertising the product as a craft good from the mists of history (not unwarranted, as prior to the industrial revolution and the invention of the continuous still, single malt *was* the only kind of Scotch). Given that Scotch takes time to age, Grant and Sons were able to establish "a ten year first mover advantage" in single malts (MacLean 2016: 18). The Grants expanded their sales to international markets through duty-free stores. Suddenly Scotch whisky had a newly popular category and an entirely new distribution structure. In this way, the Grants can be classified as entrepreneurs who went against convention as described by Young Back Choi (Chapter 5). To this day, W. Grant and Sons remains under the control of the original family (Roskrow, Smith, and Jackson 2015: 219). While the Grants were the first movers, "[c]onsumers loved it, so other producers followed suit" (Mennie 2018). Soon firms such as Glenlivet, Macallan, and Glenmorangie also marketed their own unique single malts (Driver 2014).

This newly marketed category of single malt began to serve as the exemplar of the Scotch industry, and, it can be argued, of whiskies in general. Dekker and Kuchař (2016) develop a theory of exemplary goods to explain how quality distinctions emerge as part of the competitive process. Among whiskies, Scotch, especially single malt, is an exemplar – a standard by which other whiskies are judged and one which other whiskies want to imitate, as the Japanese and others have attempted. According to the head of the Scotch Whisky Association, "Scotch remains THE aspirational spirit, the whisky that everyone, all over the world, wants to drink" (Scotch Whisky Association 2018).

That the country of origin is such a distinguishing signal of the quality of the spirit leads us to conclude that Scotch is also a kind of "credence good." Andersen and Philipsen (1998) provide a theory of credence goods in which the credence characteristics of the good are difficult to ascertain both before and after purchasing the good. A consumer cannot tell for sure if the spirit is Scottish just by looking at the product. Likewise, given that award-winning Scotch-like spirits are also produced in other countries, the Scottish nature cannot perfectly be determined by tasting the spirit. Andersen and Philipsen (1998) conclude that consumers may often rely on third-party verification of the quality of credence goods. Producers have an incentive to pursue that third-party credentialing in order to give consumers reason to believe in the quality of their product. The community of actors help to define and maintain that credentialing.

8.1.2 *Attributes of the Community*

The Scotch community is comprised of consumers around the globe, whisky reviewers and awarding organizations, non-Scottish producers, Scottish producers (organized by the Scotch Whisky Association), and the governments of the United Kingdom (UK) and the European Union (EU). The producers and consumers alike coproduce the category of Scotch.

Consumers contribute to this commons by participating in the culture surrounding Scotch. Learning about and enjoying Scotch is communal in nature, much like the example of the culture of appreciation for opera described by Benzecry (2009). Building on the model for cultural affiliation presented in Becker (1953), Benzecry (2009) describes how opera fans are passionate about the art, in part, "as a result of their belief that opera is something that needs to be learned in order to be properly enjoyed" (134). People come to learn about and appreciate opera through informal, formal, and experiential means. Likewise, Scotch involves a learning curve that consumers enjoy. The distilleries provide formal and experiential educational opportunities in their tours and tastings. There is even a "Scotch Whisky Experience" attraction in Edinburgh that was developed by nineteen Scotch companies in the 1980s to promote the heritage of Scotch (The Scotch Whisky Experience n.d.). This attraction includes a museum, tours, tastings, and a Scotch school where students can earn a "Certificate of Expertise recognised by the Scotch whisky industry." Informally, consumers learn from each other and from bartenders in bars and pubs. Consumers also learn about quality from whisky reviewers who rate the different spirits and from worldwide whisky awards recognition.

Whisky reviewers and awarding organizations add to the knowledge commons by providing signals of quality. Scotch drinkers rely on these ratings much like wine drinkers look for high ratings from, say, Robert Parker. A signal that Japanese and Australian whiskies have gained acceptance in the community is that a popular guide has included "new world whisky" as a section for non-Scottish distillers beginning with their sixth edition published in 2010 (Roskrow, Smith, and Jackson 2015: 393).

The highly rated and award-winning non-Scottish producers today include the Suntory company in Japan and Sullivans Cove distillery in Australia. Suntory's adoption of the production process for blended Scotch began in the 1920s with Masataka Taketsuru who apprenticed in Scotland and brought the craft of blended whisky back home (McNeill 2019). In Australia, Bill Lark recognized that the abundance of natural resources and the climate made Tasmania a perfect fit for whisky and his efforts led to the repeal of distillery prohibition in Tasmania in the 1990s and the development of the whisky industry there (Frost 2014).

The large number of small and large Scottish producers are organized by the Scotch Whisky Association (SWA), which is dominated by the large firms. The purpose of the Scotch Whisky Association "is to safeguard the Scotch Whisky category and prevent unfair competition" (Scotch Whisky Association n.d., *What We Do*). Thus, the SWA maintains the knowledge commons in part by restricting access to it. Acting as a standard setting enterprise, the SWA helped to develop the governance structure described in the next section surrounding the geographic indication protection that is backed by the UK and (until Brexit) the European Union governments. The SWA employs a staff of lawyers that handle legal cases and trademark cases protecting the Scotch commons. The geographical indication protection is the system that producers use to validate the hidden credence characteristics (Andersen and Philipsen 1998) of their Scotch to consumers in order to mitigate the asymmetrical information problem regarding quality.

8.1.3 *Rules-in-Use*

The reputation of Scotch is non-rival (non-subtractable), in that all producers can benefit from it at the same time, but only if it is used appropriately. If lower-quality whiskies were sold under the Scotch name, that would dilute the value of the common resource. For example, Gordon (2014) explains how in the late 1800s, after the introduction of continuous stills allowed the industry to mass produce, there was a glut of lower-quality Scotch offered for sale that damaged the reputation of the industry. The quality of Scotch improved after the passage of the Immature Spirits Act of 1915 that was part of the temperance movement to reduce drunkenness in society (Lady Astor 1923; Weir 1988). The Act sought to reduce the supply of low-quality liquor by requiring that spirits be aged for 2 (and then later 3) years (Gordon 2014). This restriction did rid the market of cheap liquor, but it had the unintended consequence of creating a better quality product that future consumers demanded.

One goal of the knowledge commons is to preserve the high-quality reputation of Scotch whisky. To protect this resource, the Scottish producers have developed a formal governance scheme revolving around laws of geographic indication that have successfully turned this resource into an exclusive "collective monopoly right" (Rangnekar 2004: 1). The evolution of similar reputational protections in the Hungarian wine industry is analyzed by Megyesi and Mike (2016). While they do not utilize the more generalized Frischmann, Madison, and Strandburg (2014) modification of the IAD Framework, they use Ostrom's general model to conclude that the commons literature is useful in studying business organizations' attempts in collective reputations. These reputational rules surrounding Scotch have roots in a tradition of shared values and have evolved from rules-in-use to become rules-in-form.

Distillers cannot call their product "Scotch" unless it was made in Scotland using a specific process. Producers in Scotland have invested resources in the Scotch designation as a signal of the quality of their spirit. Consumers also have a vested interest in the exclusive nature of its reputation because consumption of single malt Scotch distinguishes them as whisky connoisseurs. Thus, the Japanese and Australian entrepreneurs face social and institutional barriers as they enter the industry. If they could adopt the name "Scotch," they could more easily signal to consumers the high quality of their product.

O'Conner (2006) provides a comprehensive history of geographic protection law. He explains that initially two specific designations were protected by law (O'Conner 2006: 22). "Indications of source" merely specified where the product was made, for example, "Made in the USA." The more stringent designation of "appellation of origin" specified the region of production, but also indicated that there is something special about that particular region that makes the product unique, for example, "Gorgonzola cheese." This type of designation, then, included some reputational capital as a cultural phenomenon. In theory, the purpose of the geographical indications protection is twofold: (1) "the protection of consumers from false and misleading information" and (2) "the protection of producers from unfair competition" (O'Connor 2006: 123).

Geographic indications (GIs) are legally different from two other types of designations, namely, trademarks and generic names. Mantrov (2014) explains that sometimes a geographic designation is included in a trademark, such as "Philadelphia cream cheese" (2014: 45), which does not mean it is made in Philadelphia. The purpose of the trademark is to differentiate one product from another, and usually trademarks are owned by a single entity. In contrast, a GI is open to anyone in the geographic area. Generic names, such as "French bread," do not imply any link to a geographic area, although it may be the case that the product originated in the particular geographic area of the same name (Mantrov 2014: 101). Products protected by GIs can lose that protection if, over time, consumers come to view the name as referring to the product generally, as opposed to having a tie to the particular geographic area. Such was the case with "Camembert" cheese and "London Gin" (Mantrov 2014: 103). Scotch producers are vigilant in protecting the classification of the geographic indication so that "Scotch" does not devolve into a generic name.

The World Intellectual Property Organization (WIPO) promotes the benefits of geographic indication protection, arguing that GIs help producers "in developing collective brands" that differentiate their product (World Intellectual Property Organization n.d.). Consumers are usually willing to pay more for a differentiated higher-quality product. The WIPO concludes that protection of geographic indications can lead to "competitive advantage, more added value, increased export opportunities [and] a strengthened brand" (World Intellectual Property Organization n.d.).

Of interest for this chapter are the current protections of the Scotch whisky designation at the international level by the World Trade Organization (WTO), at the regional level by the EU, and at the national level by the UK. International protection of geographic indication is provided by the Agreement on Trade-Related Aspects of International Property Rights (TRIPs Agreement) included in the Uruguay Round of the General Agreement on Tariffs and Trade (GATT). The TRIPs Agreement contains rules for the geographical indications related to all products generally, as well as specific rules pertaining to wines and spirits and to wines separately. The higher level of protections for wines and spirits was especially pushed for by the European Commission at Uruguay (Schloder (1996) as cited in O'Connor 2006: 56, fn 84). The extra provisions in Article 23 (World Trade Organization 1994), relating to the spirits industry prevents the non-Scottish distillers from promoting their spirit as "Scotch" or even as "Scotch-style."

Long before the TRIPs Agreement was approved at the international level, European countries protected geographical indications. As O'Connor (2006: 123) explains, the formation of the European Union standardized these diverse long-standing national protections and made them applicable in all member states. Currently, the general rules protecting geographic indications at the European level are found in Regulation 110/2008 that "lays down rules on the definition, description, presentation and labelling of spirit drinks as well as on the protection of geographical indications of spirit drinks" (European Union 2008). Included in these regulations are the various characteristics (ingredients, proof levels, processes, etc.) and geographic origin that must be met for spirits. For example, the regulations delineate the production methods that must be used for "Gin" versus "Distilled Gin" versus "London Dry Gin." Despite the differences, London Dry Gin is not registered for geographic indication protection, but merely refers to a style of distillation. Those spirits that are registered for geographic indications, such as Scotch whisky, are protected against any "practice liable to mislead the consumer as to the true origin of the product" (European Union 2008).

Under EU law, individual countries that have products with registered geographic indications must have a "technical file" and a "verification scheme." Scotch's technical file was submitted by the UK in 2013 and it includes the definition of the product and details about the minimum standards for production. The technical file, then, defines "what is Scotch" from a legal perspective. For example, Scotch whisky may not include added enzymes, must be made from malted barley, must be aged in oak casks, and must be produced and aged in Scotland (Department for

Environment, Food and Rural Affairs 2013). Single malt Scotch must be both produced and bottled inside the country.

The technical file also summarizes the links between Scotch and Scotland that form the basis of the geographic indication. One such factor is the abundance of peat, important in the flavoring of Scotch. Another is that the geology of Scotland, influenced by ancient seismic activity, has resulted in especially distinct sources of water that vary with the type of rock in the area. Another important factor is the climate. Eastern Scotland's climate is prime for growing the barley and wheat for use in Scotch production and the moistness of the climate where the Scotch is aged, is optimal. Interestingly, Japanese whisky producers also credit Japan's "clean and tasty ground water" and "four distinct seasons" for their success (Kageyama 2017); and Tasmania, Australia is described as having "just about everything you need to make good whisky: water, barley, even peat (although it's different to that found in Scotland)" (The Whisky Exchange n.d.).

Physical conditions are not the only important link between Scotch production and Scotland. The technical file also outlines the "[s]kills and processes developed in Scotland and handed down over the centuries [that] also have a significant effect on the quality and character of Scotch Whisky" (Department for Environment, Food and Rural Affairs 2013: 14). These include the skills of the distillers and blenders and the quality of the stills and casks. In sum, "[i]t is the combination of human and natural factors which contribute to the reputation, character and quality of Scotch Whisky" (Department for Environment, Food and Rural Affairs 2013: 17). These human factors are what distinguishes Scotch from the Japanese and Australian spirits. Japan and Australia may have similar climates, water, and peat, but they are not part of the knowledge commons created and shared by Scottish distillers and consumers of Scotch.

Along with the technical file, the UK also had to submit a verification scheme to the EU. Introduced in 2014, the verification scheme is the enforcement mechanism for ensuring that all Scotch that is sold is in compliance with the specifications in the technical file. Verification is overseen by the Commissioners of Her Majesty's Revenue and Customs (HMRC). Any firm involved with the production of Scotch must register with the HMRC, and staff from the bureau make periodic inspections of the facilities to ensure compliance. The initial fee is 1,630 pounds per production process, so a firm that both ferments and distills would pay twice the fee (HM Revenue and Customs 2014: 22). Even firms involved with blending and bottling outside of Scotland must register and be inspected, although they face a lower fee (520 pounds) since the processes being verified are simpler (HM Revenue and Customs 2014: 22). The total annual cost of implementing the verification scheme is estimated to be 350,000 pounds (Scotch Whisky Association 2014).

In addition to international and European Union level protection, Scotch Whisky has long enjoyed protection at the national level in the United Kingdom, most recently by the Scotch Whisky Regulations of 2009. These regulations were developed upon the recommendations of the Scotch Whisky Association (MacLean 2016, 32). Like the EU technical file, these regulations spell out in detail the production requirements that must be met in order for a spirit to legally be called Scotch, the first of which is "'Scotch Whisky' means a whisky produced in Scotland" (U.K. Statutory Instruments 2009). These most recent regulations even include the specific requirement that single malt Scotch be produced using a pot still, the method already used by the large companies. It is rumored that the pot still requirement was targeting Loch Lomond Distillery, the second largest family-owned Scotch producer, which did not use this method, and was not a member of the Scotch Whisky Association who supported passage of the law (Hansell 2009). In 2014, Loch Lomond was bought out by a private equity group (ScotchWhisky.com n.d., *Loch Lomond.*), and has since joined the SWA.

The SWA summarizes the many ways to infringe on the geographic indication protection. Descriptions such as "Scotch like" or "Scotch style" are expressly forbidden, as is the use of Scottish themed names or pictures (such as tartan or bagpipes) in the marketing of a non-Scotch spirit. Use of an identical label for both Scotch and a non-Scotch spirit is also outlawed. In non-English-speaking export markets, even the use of the English language on a label may imply that the product is from Scotland, when it is not. If the spirit is actually a blend of Scotch with a local spirit, the use of the phrase "Blended with Scotch" can be interpreted as an attempt to mislead the consumer into thinking the product is true Scotch. Some producers may attempt to mislead consumers about the age of the spirit, so the regulations prohibit the use of numbers on the labels unless they truly reflect the number of years the spirit has aged in the cask.

A recent case brought and won by the SWA involved a US distillery in Virginia. The Virginia Distillery Company imports aged malt whisky from Scotland, blends it with single malt made in Virginia, and then finishes it in port, cider, beer, or chardonnay casks (Virginia Distillery Company n.d.). They call their series Virginia Highland Whisky, which has won Best American Blended Malt from the World Whisky Awards for the past three years. The use of Highlands in the name, however, garnered the attention of the SWA. The case has since been settled, with the Virginia Distillery Company agreeing to stop using the Highlands name once current stocks are depleted (Scotch Whisky Association 2019a).

The SWA supported and welcomed the verification scheme, claiming that it "ensures that every part of the Scotch Whisky supply chain, from distiller to consumer, within Scotland or beyond, is mapped by the industry, registered with the U.K. Government and inspected to ensure it complies fully with all the rules on the production of Scotch" (Scotch Whisky Association 2014). According to Magnus Cormack, Scotch Whisky Association Director of Legal Affairs,

> [t]he value of the brand Scotch whisky is really incalculable. At the moment Scotch whisky can only be produced in Scotland. If the geographic description Scotch

> whisky came to mean simply that it was just a type of whisky which could be distilled anywhere, that would be a disaster for the Scottish economy and for the British economy. It's what happened to London Gin. At one time it was only produced in London – now it just means a type of gin which is produced worldwide, and London distillers have missed out on an opportunity. So I think the value of protecting Scotch whisky is essential. But for a protected name, there would be no industry.
>
> (Bennett 2015)

Of course, these protections of quality only make sense if consumers perceive Scotch as a superior drink. Producers and consumers jointly co-create the reputation of Scotch. These protections illustrate the trade-off between maintaining the knowledge commons and allowing access to the shared resource.

All of the Scotch protections refer to geography, not ownership. The largest producer of Scotch, Diageo, who produces more than one-third of all Scotch in the world, is headquartered in London, and the second largest producer of Scotch is Pernod Ricard, a French company (Whisky Invest Direct n.d.). Other distilleries are owned by Japanese, Cuban, Italian, and South African companies (Roskrow, Smith, and Jackson 2015). These foreign ownerships all came about via mergers. While we know of no example of a foreigner obtaining a license to open a distillery in Scotland from scratch, there do not appear to be barriers to foreign entry.

8.1.4 *Valuable Commons or Rent-Seeking Scheme*

As mentioned earlier, Japanese and Australian whiskies have attained ratings and won awards traditionally reserved to single malt Scotch; therefore, these could be seen as at least substitutes for traditional Scotch. Why then, shouldn't they be called Scotch? To answer that question, we can turn to political economy to describe how the members of the Scotch community interact in the action arena of the GKC framework. As Meloni and Swinnen (2013) explain using the wine industry, European regulation resulted from political pressures from countries and producers seeking to protect their monopolistic rents. The same has happened in the Scotch whisky industry. What began as a communally governed craft commons has turned into a vast protection scheme for large industrial producers.

As Wenzel (2012) has pointed out in his analysis of the *Appellation d'Origine Contrôlée* system for French wine, Tullock's (1967) rent-seeking model can be useful here. In this case, the rent-seekers are the members of the Scotch Whisky Association, dominated by the large producers. It serves as the primary lobbying group for the industry and supported passage of the Scotch regulations. The stricter production regulations passed in 2009 not only protect Scottish producers from foreign competition, but also make it harder for small independent firms to compete with the larger corporations. The large firms are better situated to comply with the stricter regulations and indeed may have purposely supported the inclusion of a certain technology, the pot still requirement, to target the smaller Loch Lomond. The structure of the fees for the verification visits also benefits the large producers. The Scotch Whisky Association maintains that the cost of inspections "is being shared across the Scotch Whisky industry" (Scotch Whisky Association 2014), but by charging a flat fee per visit, the smaller producers are relatively harder hit.

McChesney (1987) extends the economic theory of regulation to provide an active role for politicians in extracting rents. He uses the example of "firms' fixed-cost investments in brand-name capital or reputation" (112). The brand name provides a quality signal to consumers and allows the firm to earn a price premium and economic rent. Government regulators, in McChesney's model, can threaten to intervene in the market by passing "legislation to have administrative agencies guarantee quality or truthful information by imposing minimum quality standards or mandatory information-disclosure regulations" (113). Threatened firms would pay up to the brand name rent in order to prevent the legislation from being passed.

The EU requirement that all geographic indications be documented with a technical file and enforced by a verification scheme provides a way for the regulators to extract rents as McChesney's (1987) model predicts. As discussed earlier, the British government now has responsibility for regular inspection of the Scotch producers costing about 350,000 pounds per year. Firms that do not comply will lose their geographic indication and will no longer be able to market their product as "Scotch." The Scottish producers, organized by the SWA, agreed to this rent extraction.

The successful rent-extraction in the Scotch industry can be contrasted to that of London Dry Gin. Remember that Magnus Cormack, the SWA Director of Legal Affairs, lamented that the producers of London Dry Gin missed an opportunity to protect its brand. The gin producers seem to think otherwise. London Dry Gin was traditionally made in London, but the producers never applied for geographic designation status, so the term "London Dry Gin" refers to a specific production method, rather than place. In contrast, a gin that had geographic indication protection is Plymouth Gin; it can only be made in Plymouth, England. Interestingly, the sole producer of Plymouth Gin, the French company Pernod Ricard, declined to renew their protected status once the new regulations required a costly technical file and verification scheme. According to a company spokesperson, the "definition of GI has changed" and they "realised it's not in the best interest of Plymouth Gin" to retain it (Blackledge 2014). That the company was not interested in retaining its GI is not surprising. As the sole producer of Plymouth Gin, Pernod Ricard owns the trademark to the name so other producers may not market a Plymouth Gin (Evans 2014). Pernod Ricard does not need to succumb to the new regulations and pay for the now required inspections in order to maintain their economic rents. The regulators, however, tried to maintain the chance for rent-extraction.

> The Department for Farming, Agriculture and Rural Affairs (DEFRA) says it will push to secure the future of Plymouth Gin's GI status. A spokeswoman said: "Spirit drink geographical identification provides a boost for the UK economy, with products commanding premium prices around the world – our biggest GI Scotch Whisky is worth around £4.3bn in exports to the UK. We are supporting the industry to help them secure the future of Plymouth Gin's GI."
>
> (Blackledge 2014)

In this case, the rent-extractors did not prevail.

Wenzel (2012) argues that the French wine industry suffers from the transitional gains trap described by Tullock (1975). There, the initial gains from obtaining the *Appellation d'Origine Contrôlée* system have been fully capitalized into the land values, and Wenzel argues that keeping the system in place is stifling innovation. The industry has passed a tipping point where maintenance of the commons takes priority over access to the commons. We use the new entrepreneurial history literature in the next section to explore whether the Scotch Whisky Association can escape that trap. Entrepreneurs in foreign countries and within Scotland are trying to alter the knowledge commons but face barriers due to the evaluative criteria set out in the 2009 Scotch whisky technical file. More recent evaluative criteria come from the whisky award and rating organizations. More importantly, consumers evaluate the spirits and vote with their dollars. Scotch's worldwide volume market share has fallen since 2008, while Japanese whisky has gained market share over the same time period (Chaudhuri 2019). All of these evaluative criteria may provide a feedback loop enabling entrepreneurs to succeed.

8.2 NEW ENTREPRENEURIAL HISTORY OF SCOTCH WHISKY

Wadhwani and Lubinski (2017) "propose to reinvent entrepreneurial history as a research field," defining it "as the study of the creative processes that propel economic change" (769). These processes are: "(i) envisioning and valuing opportunities, (ii) allocating and reconfiguring resources, and (iii) legitimizing novelty" (769). All three of these processes are evident in the case of entrepreneurship in the Scotch whisky industry.

The political economy of Scotch described above results in a closed cultural knowledge commons that hampers innovation and change by restricting the right to contribute to the commons. Ostrom and Hess (2007: 52) include the "right to contribute" as a relevant property right. For example, the knowledge commons of Wikipedia is enhanced in value by the ability of users to contribute to the articles. In contrast, entrepreneurs who see opportunity in stretching the boundaries of Scotch are often stymied by the status quo. Producers of Scotch do not have the right to alter the legal definition of Scotch, say, to include whisky made in Japan or Australia. As Andersen and Philipsen (1998: 9) point out, "innovation per definition involves a degree of novelty" that creates uncertainty about quality. The Scotch Whisky Association attempts to preserve the certainty of the high-quality reputation of Scotch, as currently defined, at the expense of possible quality improvements. As was the case with French wine, maintenance of the Scotch commons now takes priority over access.

In addition to discouraging novelty from abroad, the closed commons also limits entrepreneurial activity within Scotland. One of the largest Scotch producers, Diageo, was reined in by the Scotch Whisky Association in the early 2000s when it changed its recipe in order to meet high export demand. Since it takes so long to produce and age Scotch, it is difficult for producers to nimbly respond to changes in demand. Diageo found that it could not meet foreign demand for its single malt Scotch, Cardhu, in 2002. It's solution to this problem was to blend Cardhu with 12-year old malts from other distilleries that it owned. This product was presented as "pure malt" Scotch. They planned to use their old distillery name, Cardow, for the single malt version (MacLean 2016: 131) because traditionally, only single malt Scotch carry the name of the distillery. Unfortunately, Diageo used packaging and labeling that was very similar to that used for the single malt Cardhu, thus a "quality scandal" over the credence characteristic (Andersen and Philipsen 1998) ensued. "The resulting dispute saw threats of legal action and a rival company, W. Grant and Sons, wrote to every Member of the Scottish Parliament, accusing Diageo of 'gambling on might being right'" (BBC News 2004). One of these Parliament members even reached out to Prime Minister Tony Blair for assistance (Chaudhuri 2018). Diageo tried to appease the complainants by changing the color of the bottle, and including more explicit explanations to consumers. In the end, the Scotch Whisky Association intervened and Cardhu Pure Malt was discontinued. Diageo, then, was unable to legitimize the novelty of its product. This Cardhu controversy and the rift it caused within the SWA set the stage for the development of stricter definitions and regulations for Scotch, which finally culminated in the Scotch Whisky regulations of 2009. In fact, these regulations stipulate that

> The name of a distillery mentioned in Schedule 1 must not be used as a brand name, or as part of a brand name of a Scotch Whisky, or be used in a similar fashion in terms of its
>
> positioning or prominence, unless the whisky has been wholly distilled at that distillery.
>
> (U.K. Statutory Instruments 2009: 7)

and

> A person must not label, package, sell, advertise or promote any Scotch Whisky in a way that includes . . . the phrase "pure malt" or any derivation of that phrase.
>
> (U.K. Statutory Instruments 2009: 9)

Scottish distillers and Scotch consumers both have a stake in protecting the high quality of Scotch from dilution. Remember that the glut of low-quality Scotch in the late 1800s damaged the reputation of the whole industry.

In 2018, Diageo again tried to innovate by proposing to age its Scotch in casks previously used for its tequila production (Chaudhuri 2018). That is, it engaged in "envisioning and valuing opportunities" and "allocating and reconfiguring resources" (Wadhwani and Lubinski 2017). Not surprisingly after the Cardhu Pure Malt incident, the legitimacy of this novelty was questioned. Their request was discouraged by the legal affairs director of the SWA at the time. Note that the 2009 Scotch Whisky technical file only stipulates that the finishing cask be made of oak, nonetheless, according to the rules-in-use the tequila casks defied convention (see Choi, Chapter 5). Diageo also proposed creating new flavored infusion and low-alcohol blends of Scotch to meet current consumer tastes, but these changes were not welcomed either. Earlier, in 2016, Eden Mill Distillery and Brewery tried to use chocolate malt in their Scotch, but was also struck down by the SWA (Chaudhuri 2018). In response to these defeats, Diageo created an internal task force to examine potential reforms to the technical file to allow for more entrepreneurship (Chaudhuri 2018, 2019).

There may be optimism in Scotland, however, as the relatively new (appointed in 2017) chief executive of the Scotch Whisky Association, Karen Betts, seems to be open to a reassessment of the regulations (Hopkins 2018). Beginning in 2016, W. Grant and Sons, the same company that pioneered single malts and fought against Cardhu Pure Malt, accomplished what Diageo could not. They began introducing "experimental" lines under the Glenfiddich brand including single malts finished in unconventional casks previously used for India Pale Ale, ice wine, and rum (Glenfiddich n.d., *Experimental Series*). While Diageo has not experimented again with infusions, they have recently partnered with Home Box Office (HBO) to successfully introduce the Game of Thrones Single Malt Scotch Whisky Collection, a limited edition line of single malts packaged with themes from the show (Alindahao 2018).

Finally, in 2019 the use of different types of casks was approved as an amendment to the Scotch whisky technical file. Now, distillers may age Scotch "in casks previously used to make wine, beer or spirits so long as these haven't been made using stone fruits, and they haven't had fruit or other flavoring added after fermentation or distillation" (Chaudhuri 2019). According to Betts, "This amendment provides clarity and some additional flexibility on the range of casks in which Scotch Whisky can be matured. The change is consistent with Scotch Whisky's heritage and traditions, and strengthens our foundations into the future" (Scotch Whisky Association 2019b).

This new openness to change may be analyzed using the GKC framework described in the introduction to this volume as well as in Frischmann's chapter (Chapter 4). The patterns of interactions among participants in the Scotch action arena led to some transactions being deemed repugnant (calling Japanese whisky Scotch) and others being deemed as valuable (aging Scotch in different casks). This feedback then gets transmitted back into the resource characteristics to change what is and is not Scotch, and the rules-in-use and rules-in-form get changed accordingly. Within these new rules, then, the Scottish entrepreneurs are "envisioning and valuing opportunities, allocating and reconfiguring resources, and legitimizing novelty" (Wadhwani and Lubinski 2017: 769).

Entrepreneurs in the United States are innovating with respect to the aging process. The UK and EU regulations require Scotch to be aged (in Scotland) for at least three years, but a new technology has been developed that speeds up this process from years to days. Flash-aging involves pressure and vibration in steel vats with pieces of wooden casks thrown in for flavor (Greenblatt 2013). Initially used for bourbon production, this technology has been used for other spirits, including a Scotch-like whisky. The company Lost Spirits imports unaged Scotch from Scotland and then flash-ages it in California. They call their product a "peated malt" under the tongue-in-cheek brand name "Abomination" (Lost Spirits n.d.). Abomination won Wizards of Whisky's American Craft Whiskey of the Year in 2019 (Haruta 2019).[3] The consumers and whisky reviewers, thus, are more flexible in their acceptance of these novelties than the traditional Scottish producers and the SWA. To the extent that the consumption side of the commons values these nontraditional spirits, Scotch may cease to be seen as the lone prestige drink. If that happens, then the legal protections and other rules-in-form will be useless.

One recent innovation in blended Scotch has been perceived as potentially damaging to the prestige reputation. In October 2019, Glenlivet partnered with a London bar to create "The Glenlivet Capsule Collection," a limited edition of Scotch cocktails served in small biodegradable pods made of seaweed (Pomranz 2019). Consumers pop the pod into their mouths and bite down to release the cocktail. While Glenlivet maintained it was trying to be true to the entrepreneurial bent of its founder, many industry commentators mocked the pods. "An overarching criticism of the whiskey pods was that the capsules would 'cheapen' the mystique of the Glenlivet brand and ruin the experience of drinking whiskey" (Warren 2019). Specifically, part of the Scotch experience is to smell the spirit and sip it slowly. None of this experience is available with the pod. As one critic put it "As soon as you treat it like tequila or cheap hooch, your brand is dead" (Warren 2019).

The entrepreneurial innovations described above provide an illustration of the analysis of institutional evolution presented by López in Chapter 3. Lopez amends Ostrom's IAD framework to include Searle's (1995) institutional theory. Institutions can be regulative (rules that govern actions in an existing arena) or constitutive

[3] Wizards of Whisky awards were created by noted whisky reviewer Dominic Roskrow and they purposely exclude "large established distilleries in Scotland, Japan, or Kentucky" in order to "highlight smaller world distillers and distilleries from non-traditional areas."

(rules that create new action arenas). Lopez uses Searle's concept of "status functions," a special type of constitutive rule that is important to include in the Ostrom's action arena. When Scottish or foreign entrepreneurs innovate, they are attempting to alter the status function of Scotch. Given the high value producers and consumers place on the reputation and exclusiveness of Scotch, it is not surprising that attempts to alter the status function are sometimes met with resistance. Successful innovations are those that are able to alter the shared understandings that surround Scotch.

Remember, the shared understanding of Scotch embodies Dekker and Kuchař's (2016) explanation of exemplary goods. Scotch, especially single malt, is a category unto itself. The Japanese and Australian versions, and the new experimental and flavored Scotches can be seen as "border-line cases" (247) that do not quite fit into the Scotch category. The current definition of the single malt category, however, appears to be changing as a result of the competitive process. Foreign whisky and the new flavored Scotch are the newcomers that may "challenge the existing market categories or shared understandings of the good" (Dekker and Kuchař 2016: 254). Both foreign and Scottish entrepreneurs face cultural and legal obstacles to legitimizing their innovations. These entrepreneurs are attempting to change the shared social infrastructure of the Scotch knowledge commons.

Dekker and Kuchař (2016) further explain that exemplary goods "teach" consumers about the quality of the good "even when we cannot always fully describe or articulate what that quality consists of." In this way, "exemplary goods and practices contain tacit knowledge about the dos and don'ts that is often hard to codify" (10). One example of the tacit "dos and don'ts" for Scotch Whisky is that traditionally only single malts bear the name of the distillery, a "do" that was encoded with the 2009 regulations passed in the aftermath of the Cardhu controversy. The Japanese and Australian distillers faced a huge "don't" by not being able to label their whisky as Scotch after they painstakingly replicated the Scotch process. Despite the similar climate and purity of water and ingredients used by these foreign distillers, only whisky made in Scotland may be called Scotch. Scottish producers maintain that there is tacit knowledge involved with the Scottish culture passed down from generation to generation that is impossible to replicate in other countries.

8.3 IMPLICATIONS AND CONCLUSION

This edited volume is built upon four building blocks, as Dekker and Kuchař explain in the book's Introduction. "First, a market is a form of a culture" (9). We have described the cultural aspects of Scotch whisky and we have argued that single malt Scotch is an exemplary good with credence characteristics. We have used the GKC framework to analyze Scotch as a knowledge commons, which is part of the second building block. Thirdly, our political economy case study examines the "intellectual and legal infrastructures" in Scotch, including the protection of geographic indications that is protected by law and the Scotch Whisky Association.

Finally, we explore how "the shared intellectual infrastructure is produced and reproduced by entrepreneurs who sustain and marginally change these shared infrastructures through breaking rules, slight evasions, and through justification" (9). Specifically, we examine entrepreneurial processes from Scottish and foreign producers who are attempting to alter the definition of Scotch to legitimize their innovations. Because of the closed nature of the Scotch knowledge commons (backed by the geographic indication protection), these foreign entrepreneurs do not have the full "right to contribute" to the knowledge commons that Ostrom and Hess (2007) stress as important.

Prendergast (Chapter 2) uses the example of the "industrial commons" that is relevant for Scotch. All of the actors in the community – distillers, consumers, judges, reviewers, governments – contribute to what is and what is not considered as Scotch. While the legal definition is maintained in the technical file required by the European Union for geographic indication protection, the cultural definition is more flexible. Scotch can be seen as an example of the "delicate ecosystem" Prendergast (Chapter 2) describes, consisting of "webs of technological know-how, operation capabilities and specialised skills." Since the community of actors all contribute to the Scotch knowledge commons, Kealey and Ricketts' (Chapter 1) example of a "contribution good" is also applicable. Once new technologies (such as the continuous still) or new processes (like aging in tequila casks) are contributed, all have access to this knowledge.

In the case of Scotch there remains the tension between access to the Scotch commons and maintenance of the shared resource of the Scotch reputation. On the one hand, producers and consumers wish to maintain the high-quality reputation of the Scotch experience. On the other hand, open access to that resource can dilute the quality, so some actors, like foreign distillers, are shut out. The incumbent Scottish distillers, in particular, have a vested interest in protecting their brand.

The geographic indication system developed, first as rules-in-use and now as rules-in-form, as the craft industry of single malt emerged. W. Grant and Sons were the first movers with their revival of the ancient single malt tradition in response to declining demand for blended Scotch. Consumers bought into the exemplary nature of single malt and other Scottish distillers soon followed suit. As Wadhwani and Lubinski (2017: 779) explain, "new entrepreneurial history highlights the cumulative entrepreneurial processes across multiple actors and over time." Without the buy in of consumers and other large Scottish distillers, Grant's single malt venture may have been short-lived.

The prestige of the Scotch experience was initially enhanced by the closed nature of the cultural knowledge commons. At first, the Scotch Whisky Association and predecessors fostered the development of the commons by organizing the producers, educating consumers, and coordinating the communal effort to raise quality standards. Over time, however, the closed nature of the commons under the SWA has served to inhibit innovation that may benefit the commons. While some progress has been made within Scotland with regard to the acceptance of entrepreneurial activity, the foreign distillers are still left out. It remains to be seen whether Japanese and Australian whiskies will gain acceptance into the existing commons, or, as the number of awards won by foreign whisky continues to increase, they will develop their own knowledge commons.

REFERENCES

Alindahao, Karla. 2018. "A Collection of 'Game of Thrones' Single Malts Is Coming." *Forbes*, October 18. www.forbes.com/sites/karlaalindahao/2018/10/18/diageo-and-hbo-release-game-of-thrones-single-malt-whiskies-2018/#66f4a1c71268

Andersen, Esben Sloth, and Kristian Philipsen. 1998. "The Evolution of Credence Goods in Customer Markets: Exchanging 'Pigs in Pokes.'" Working Paper. DRIUD Winter Seminar.

Baxter, Lynne. 1985. "Political Economy of Scotch Whisky." In *The Scottish Government Yearbook*, edited by David McCrone, 77–106. Edinburgh: University of Edinburgh.

BBC News. 2004. *Diageo Admits Cardhu Malt Defeat*, March 9. http://news.bbc.co.uk/2/hi/uk_news/scotland/3546321.stm

Becker, Howard S. 1953. "Becoming a Marijuana User." *The American Journal of Sociology* 59 (3): 235–242.

Bennett, Magnus. 2015. "Tackling the Scotch Whisky Imitators." *BBC Scotland News*, May 10. www.bbc.com/news/uk-scotland-scotland-business-32500059

Benzecry, Claudio E. 2009. "Becoming a Fan: On the Seductions of Opera." *Qualitative Sociology* 32: 131–151.

Blackledge, Sam. 2014. "Plymouth Gin to Lose Protected Status under New EU Law." *Plymouth Herald*, November 18.

Chaudhuri, Saabira. 2018. "For Scotch Whisky Purists, This Might Be Hard to Swallow." *The Wall Street Journal*, January 24, A1–A12.

2019. "Scotch Makers Relax Rules to Woo Drinkers." *The Wall Street Journal*, June 19, B1–B2.

Dietz, Vivien E. 1997. "The Politics of Whisky: Scottish Distillers, the Excise, and the Pittite State." *Journal of British Studies* 36: 35–69.

Dekker, Erwin, and Pavel Kuchař. 2016. "Exemplary Goods: The Product as Economic Variable." *Schmollers Jahrbuch* 136: 237–255.

Department for Environment, Food and Rural Affairs. 2013. *Technical File for Scotch Whisky*, August 29.

Driver, Jonathan. 2014. "Marketing Scotch Whisky in the 21st Century and Previously." In *Whiskey: Technology, Production and Marketing* (2nd edition), edited by I. Russell and G. Stewart, 343–357. Amsterdam: Elsevier Academic Press.

Embury, David A., Robert Hess, and Audrey Saunders. 1948. *The Fine Art of Mixing Drinks*. New York: Mud Puddle Books, Inc.

European Union. 2008. "Regulation 110/2008, Article 1. Regulation on the Definition, Description, Presentation, Labelling and the Protection of Geographical Indications of Spirit Drinks and Repealing Council Regulation (EEC) No 1576/89." *Official Journal of the European Union*, January 15.

Evans, Peter. 2014. "Plymouth Gin Sails Away from Its 'Geographic Indication.'" *Wall Street Journal Corporate Intelligence Blog*, November 19.

Frischmann, Brett M., Michael J. Madison, and Katherine Strandburg. 2014. *Governing Knowledge Commons*. Oxford: Oxford University Press.

Frost, Vicky. 2014. "Tasmania's Latest Export: The Best Whisky in the World." *The Guardian*, April 2. www.theguardian.com/lifeandstyle/2014/apr/02/tasmanias-latest-export-best-whisky-world-australia

Glenfiddich. n.d. *Experimental Series*. www.glenfiddich.com/us/explore/experimental/

Our History. www.glenfiddich.com/us/family-story/

Gordon, Grant E. 2014. "Marketing Scotch Whisky." In *Whiskey: Technology, Production and Marketing* (2nd edition), edited by I. Russel and G. Stewart, 359–398. Amsterdam: Elsevier Academic Press.

Greenblatt, Alan. 2013. "How a Distillery Ages Bourbon in Days, Not Years." *NPR*. www.npr.org/sections/thesalt/2013/05/02/180661986/how-a-distillery-ages-bourbon-in-days-not-years

Hansell, John. 2009. "New Scotch Whisky Regulations Take Effect." *Whisky Advocate*, November 30.

Haruta, Joanne. 2019. "'Wizards of Whisky' World Whisky of the Year 2019 Awarded to Lost Spirits." *Market Watch Press Release*, March 25. www.prnewswire.com/news-releases/wizards-of-whisky-world-whisky-of-the-year-2019-awarded-to-lost-spirits-300817651.html

HM Revenue and Customs. 2014. "Spirit Drinks Verification Scheme – Technical Guidance: Scotch Whisky Verification." October 1. www.gov.uk/guidance/spirit-drinks-verification-scheme

Hopkins, Amy. 2018. "SWA Chief: Interpretation of Scotch Laws 'Could Change.'" *The Spirits Business*, January 4. www.thespiritsbusiness.com/2018/01/swa-chief-interpretations-of-scotch-laws-could-change/

Kageyama, Yuri. 2017. "Japan Beating Scotland at Its Own Game to Become Whisky World Leader." *The Independent*, March 15.

Lady Astor. 1923. "The English Law Relating to the Sale of Intoxicating Liquors." *The Annals of the American Academy of Political Science* 109: 265–278.

Lost Spirits. n.d. *Homepage*. www.lostspirits.net/home

Lyons, T. Pearse. 2003. "Production of Scotch and Irish Whiskies: Their History and Evolution." In *The Alcohol Textbook* (4th edition), edited by K. A. Jacques, T. P. Lyons, and D. R. Kelsall, 193–222. Nottingham: Nottingham University Press.

MacLean, Charles. 2016. *Charles Maclean's Whiskypedia: A Compendium of Scotch Whisky*. New York: Skyhorse Publishing.

Mantrov, Vadim. 2014. *The EU Law on Indications of Geographic Origin: Theory and Practice*. Cham: Springer International Publishing.

McChesney, Fred S. 1987. "Rent Extraction and Rent Creation in the Economic Theory of Regulation." *Journal of Legal Studies* 16: 101–118.

McNeill, David. 2019. "Care for a Wee Dram of Japanese Whisky?" *The Economist 1843*, Japan Travel Supplement. www.1843magazine.com/japan-travel-supplement/drinks-cabinet/care-for-a-wee-dram-of-japanese-whisky

Megyesi, Boldizsár, and Károly Mike. 2016. "Organising Collective Reputation: An Ostromian Perspective." *International Journal of the Commons* 10: 1082–1099. https://doi.org/doi.org/10.18352/ijc.657.

Meloni, Giulia and Johan Swinnen. 2013. "The Political Economy of European Wine Regulations." *Journal of Wine Economics* 8: 244–284.

Mennie, Alex. 2018. "What Is Single Malt Scotch Whisky? Focus on Glenfiddich." *Winerist*, December 11. www.winerist.com/magazine/drink/what-is-single-malt-whisky-focus-on-glenfiddich

O'Connor, Bernard. 2006. *The Law of Geographical Designations*. London: Cameron May.

Ostrom, Elinor, and Charlotte Hess. 2007. "A Framework for Analyzing the Knowledge Commons." In *Understanding Knowledge as a Commons: From Theory to Practice*, edited by Charlotte Hess and Elinor Ostrom, 41–81. Cambridge, MA: The MIT Press.

Pomranz, Mike. 2019. "The Glenlivet's 'Capsule Collection' Is Sort of Like Gushers, but Whisky." *Food and Wine*, October 4. www.foodandwine.com/news/glenlivet-capsule-collection

Rangnekar, Dwijen. 2004. *The Socio-Economics of Geographical Indications*. Geneva: International Centre for Trade and Sustainable Development.

Roskrow, Dominic, Gavin D. Smith, and Michael Jackson. 2015. *Michael Jackson's Complete Guide to Single Malt Scotch*. New York: Dorling Kindersley Limited.

Scotch Whisky Association. n.d. *Discover: Story of Scotch*. www.scotch-whisky.org.uk/discover/story-of-scotch/

n.d. *What We Do: Protecting Scotch*. www.scotch-whisky.org.uk/what-we-do/protecting-scotch/

2014. *Industry Welcomes Verification Scheme*, January 10. www.scotch-whisky.org.uk/news-publications/blog/industry-welcomes-verification-scheme#.XGxRIrhOm70

2018. *Karen Betts Speech to Scotsman Food and Drink Cconference*, September 4. www.scotch-whisky.org.uk/newsroom/karen-betts-speech-to-scotsman-food-drink-conference/

2019a. *Scotch Whisky Association and Virginia Distillery Reach Resolution on Whisky Labelling Case*, August 29. www.scotch-whisky.org.uk/newsroom/scotch-whisky-association-and-virginia-distillery-company-reach-resolution-on-whisky-labelling-case/

2019b. *Scotch Whisky Technical File Amended*, June 15. www.scotch-whisky.org.uk/newsroom/scotch-whisky-technical-file-amended/

ScotchWhisky.com. n.d. *Glenfiddich, History*, https://scotchwhisky.com/whiskypedia/1856/glenfiddich/#/

n.d. *Loch Lomond, History*, https://scotchwhisky.com/whiskypedia/1877/loch-lomond/#/

The Scotch Whisky Experience. n.d. *About Us*. www.scotchwhiskyexperience.co.uk/about-us/about-us-company

Searle, J. R. 1995. *The Construction of Social Reality*. New York: The Free Press.

Storrie, Margaret C. 1962. "The Scotch Whisky Industry." *Transactions and Papers (Institute of British Geographers)* 31: 97–114.

Tedlow, Richard S., and Geoffrey Jones. 1993. "The Marketing of Scotch Whiskey: An Historical Perspective." In *The Rise and Fall of Mass Marketing*, edited by R. Tedlow and G. Jones, 116–131. London: Routledge.

Tullock, Gordon. 1967. "The Welfare Costs of Tariffs, Monopolies and Theft." *Western Economic Journal* 5: 224–232.

1975. "The Transitional Gains Trap." *The Bell Journal of Economics* 6: 671–678.

U.K. Statutory Instruments. 2009. *Scotch Whisky Regulations*. No. 2890.

Virginia Distillery Company. n.d. *Virginia Highland Whisky Series*. https://vadistillery.com/products/virginia-highland-whisky

Wadhwani, R. D., and C. Lubinski. 2017. "Reinventing Entrepreneurial History." *Business History Review* 91: 767–799.

Warren, Katie. 2019. "Glenlivet Is Trying to Get Customers on Board with Drinking Whisky Out of Little Pods That Dissolve in Your Mouth – and People Have Questions." *Business Insider*, October 7. www.businessinsider.com/glenlivet-whiskey-pods-capsules-reactions-2019-10

Weir, R. B. 1988. "Alcohol Controls and Scotch Whisky Exports (1870–1939)." *British Journal of Addiction* 83: 1289–1297.

Wenzel, Nikolai G. 2012. "Rent-Seeking and Decline in the French Wine Industry." *The Journal of Private Enterprise* 27: 63–81.

The Whisky Exchange. n.d. *Australian Whisky*. www.thewhiskyexchange.com/c/453/australian-whisky

Whisky Invest Direct. n.d. *Top 15 Scotch Whisky Companies*. www.whiskyinvestdirect.com/about-whisky/top-15-scotch-whisky-companies#

World Intellectual Property Organization. n.d. *Frequently Asked Questions: Geographical Indications*. www.wipo.int/geo_indications/en/faq_geographicalindications.html

World Trade Organization. 1994. *TRIPS: Agreement on Trade-Related Aspects of Intellectual Property Rights. Annex 1C, 1869 U.N.T.S. 299, 33 I.L.M.* 1197, April 15.

World Whiskies Awards. n.d. www.worldwhiskiesawards.com/

Yan, Sophia. 2014. "Japan Rivals Scotland in Race for Best Whisky." *CNN Money*, November 24.

9

Trolling in the Deep

Managing Transgressive Content on Online Platforms as a Commons

Julien Gradoz and Raphaël Raux

The figure of the *Ship of fools* is representing, in a symbolic manner, a reality of the fourteenth century: social exclusion from cities faced by the mads, left adrift on rivers (Foucault 2001). On these boats, the fools could freely express their madness in a restricted space, as underlined by most paintings representing the *Narrenschiff* (see Figure 9.1). The mad, in this iconography, could be the one who loses Reason, or the one whose actions, especially laughter, are likely to disturb an established order (Erasmus 2003 [1511]).

There are many commonalities between the Ship of Fools of the fourteenth century and some contemporary websites, where some users called "trolls," due to repeated marginalization for sharing transgressive content, end up gathering on specific forums, where they can express their taste for transgression.[1] Transgression can be understood here as an extreme region of the action space of individuals, in which formal as well as tacit moral rules are violated, and contributing to add an element of spontaneity to social interactions. Because they generally prove to be a threat to the normal functioning of online forums, they tend to be shunned by most communities, and come together in specific forums such as the one we propose to study in this chapter, the "Blabla 18-25" forum of *jeuxvideo.com*.

This extreme case of a "forum for trolls" will allow us to highlight the fact that trolling is a relative concept, defined insofar as it transgresses behavioral and moral rules established within the community at hand. In this perspective, trolling can't be considered as inherently negative.[2] In fact, it depends on the way the community conceives its action space. For example, some creative communities can appreciate

[1] "Trolling may be understood as nonconstructive messages designed to provoke a reaction, to draw targets (and others) into fruitless argument, and to disrupt the avowed purpose of the group gathering" (Coles and West 2016: 234).

[2] Unlike many contributions in the literature: "Trolling is a conceptually fuzzy term and it is often applied indiscriminately to describe various types of negatively evaluated online behaviour" (Hopkinson 2013: 8).

FIGURE 9.1. Pretmakers in een mossel op zee, Pieter van Der Heyden (1562)

the spirit of transgression provided by trolls, and of course forums well-known for rallying trolls have a very specific conception of the action space, in which transgression can even be encouraged. On these forums (e.g., 4chan, the Blabla 18-25, as well as numerous subreddits), we can talk of a "transgression space," corresponding to the action space in which interactions between members take place. Depending on its prevalence, transgression in the case of online forums could range from criminal offense (such as racial hatred or cyber-harassment) to controversial statements (such as advocacy of reactionary views).

Our case study will find its structure in the *Governing Knowledge Commons framework* (Hess and Ostrom 2007; Madison, Frischmann, and Strandburg 2009a, b). This framework considers knowledge commons as "arrangements for overcoming social dilemmas related to sharing and producing information, innovation and creative works" (Larson and Chon 2017: 168).[3]

In our particular case, the *resource* requiring these "arrangements" we will consider is the transgression space allowing members to share the content described above. The main interest of our case lies in the nature of the resource: while regular knowledge commons exist so as to exploit a universally valuable resource (such as knowledge, in

[3] Moreover, knowledge is defined as "a set of intellectual and cultural resources" (Larson and Chon 2017: 168).

the case of Wikipedia), transgression is by essence controversial, and is generally considered as a threat to online communities. A transgression space, therefore, might be considered at large as something to be destroyed were it to rise. But some communities, which the 18-25 is an example of, come to structure themselves around this possibility of transgression, gathering outcasts from other communities.

Thus, this resource will entail specific *rules-in-use* that allow for its durable exploitation. Rules-in-use can be defined as "shared normative understandings of what a participant in a position must, must not, or may do in a particular action situation, backed by at least a minimal sanctioning ability for noncompliance" (Hess and Ostrom 2007: 50). In other words, rules-in-use represent what is considered acceptable to do within the community. *The community gathered around the transgression space, along with its rules-in-use that allow its sustainable exploitation, will form the "common" of our case.* We might abuse language and sometimes refer to the transgression space as the common, but it should be envisioned as an overarching concept, including those who exploit the resource.

The 18-25 community includes several types of participants, who have a different impact on these rules-in-use. First of all, the website hosting the resource will implement a set of measures in order to maintain transgression within a specific range (like a charter and a sanction system), constituting the frontier of the "transgression space." The tension for these websites is encapsulated in the fact that they need to attract as many users as possible (to maximize revenue, the bulk of which is advertisement and data resale) by allowing them to develop a transgression space, while avoiding a shutdown by legal authorities. In other words, the main issue for them is not to prevent transgression, but rather to maintain it at an acceptable level to preserve interactions within the forum without putting it in jeopardy with regard to both the law and public opprobrium. This set of measures is applied through the presence of a moderation team, whose role is detailed in Section 9.3.

The second type of participants are the regular members who engage in various kinds of (possibly *trollesque*) behavior. They have a central role in the definition of the rules-in-use. As a matter of fact, if the website will determine the formal rules delineating the transgression space according to the law, members will determine for their part if they respect these rules and if they participate in implementing them, through social coercion and the report of content that is considered outside the range of the transgression space. More than reporting problematic content, they also actively engage in encoding the transgressive content they share through a complex self-referential culture (Section 9.2), in order to prevent public controversies from arising. This common culture also enables them to exert social coercion toward members who do not respect the rules-in-use.

Finally, on the fringes of the forum, we find what we will call "outside observers," which are nonmembers who scroll by the forum. They represent the main danger for the resource, as they can contribute, through public opprobrium, to shutting the website down.

Thus, social coercion and the formal system of sanction will be considered as the rules-in-use allowing the monitoring of the interactions within the transgression space. The emphasis on the formal and tacit sanctions system is consistent with several contributions to the knowledge commons framework (Gordon 2009), and the seminal work of Elinor Ostrom (Ostrom 1990; Hess and Ostrom 2007) that underlined the central role of "a system for self-monitoring members' behavior" and "a graduated system of sanctions" (Hess 2012: 21).

In this perspective, we propose in this chapter to study, through the *Governing Knowledge Commons* framework, the rules-in-use on a transgressive forum as a governance process ensuring the sustainability of interactions within a transgression space. To be more precise, in order to analyze the specific governance structure of those forums built around a transgression space, we present a case study focused on the *Blabla 18-25* forum hosted by the website *jeuxvideo.com*, one of the most active and transgressive forums in France (Section 9.1). The study of transgression spaces is of particular interest because we argue it can be applied to more general situations, constituting the discussion of this chapter (Section 9.4).

9.1 A CERTAIN IDEA OF TRANSGRESSION: TROLLING ON THE 18-25

9.1.1 *A General Presentation of the Forum and Its Business Model*

The "Blabla 18-25" (hereafter 18-25) is a forum in which registered users can initiate a topic or contribute to existing ones. When a topic is created, the *original poster* is invited to give a title that will indicate the general orientation of the discussion. Everyone accessing the website, even without an account, can browse through topics.

The 18-25 forum is hosted by *jeuxvideo.com*, the main French online video games media.[4] It was founded in 1997 by three friends, Sébastien Pissavy, François Claustres, and Jerôme Stolfo, within the company L'Odyssée Interactive. The company was initially in a very precarious financial situation, barely surviving thanks to the founders' contributions. Around the year 2000, however, Internet usage was growing at an ever-faster pace, and quickly began to supplant specialized video games magazines due to its bottomless pool of knowledge and the possibility to interact through forums.

In this growing market, *jeuxvideo.com* distinguished itself by its responsiveness to the newest trends, and quickly established itself as the reference for video games news (Pissavy 2013). Already in 2000, the site caught the eye of some investors, as Sébastien Pissavy sold 80 percent of his shares in the company to Gameloft, while remaining in charge of the company. In 2006, the French company Hi-Media

[4] "In February, jeuxvideo.com was consulted by 6 369 000 unique users across all supports, according to Médiametrie, the French institute which measures medias' audience" (Laura Motet for *Le Monde*, April 2, 2017, authors' translation).

acquired 88 percent of L'Odysée Interactive for €22.6 mn. In 2012, Sébastien Pissavy stepped down as CEO, and was replaced by Cédric Mallet. At this time, the company was one of the biggest video games online media, employing 40 people and hosting 4 million unique monthly visitors.

The website took a major turn in 2014 when Webedia bought L'Odysée Interactive for €90 mn: alongside undergoing a complete reform, named *Respawn*, the website became tied with a company of a quite different caliber. Webedia is a subsidiary for French holding group Fimalac, owned by billionaire Marc Ladreit de Lacharrière. The company owns substantial interests in Germany, Spain, the United States, and Brazil, among other countries. It displays a broad range of activities, such as cinema, cooking, video games, culture, and tourism. In 2018, Webedia ranked third in French media groups, with 27.1 million unique monthly visitors.

Like many forums and social media platforms, *jeuxvideo.com* makes a profit through the display of advertisement and the resale of personal data.[5] This allows to ensure free access to content on the website for its users.

Jeuxvideo.com hosts numerous specialized forums on various subjects such as politics, sport, music, finance, and many others: there are more than 200 forums, in which there are thousands of topics containing dozens of contributions. "18-25" refers to the suggested age range (although there is no verification of any sort), without predefined topics of conversation. Thus, on the 18-25, everyone can talk about anything, as long as the forum charter is respected.[6]

Before exploring the different aspects of the governance of the transgression space of the 18-25, we have to understand how a transgression space has progressively emerged on a website initially devoted to video games.

9.1.2 *From a Community of Gamers to a Community of Transgression: The Evolution of a Website*

When *jeuxvideo.com* was created in 1997, it quickly became a reference for all video games enthusiasts, as it was the place where they could find reliable information for their gaming sessions. Since the creation of the website, forums were implemented to allow members, most of them teenagers, to discuss various subjects, thus constituting a major place of interaction.

The integration of an interactive component to the website could be easily explained by the fact that many elements of *gaming culture* are so specific that it was sometimes hard to find peers in "real life" also passionate about these subjects, while communities gathered around these topics are likely to encourage interactions

[5] In June 2018, jeuxvideo.com was selling the data to more than 400 partners.

[6] We decided to focus on the 18-25, and not on the 15-18 or the 25-35 because the 18-25 perfectly embodies the spirit of transgression that we aim to analyze through this article.

and creativity. Moreover, as gaming culture was not as widely integrated in society in the 1990s as it is today, "gamers" could be discriminated against or mocked for their passion and perceived as misfits; these forums provided an alternative form of socialization and integration for them.

As a result, online gaming communities often defined themselves *negatively* with regard to society at large, in the sense that they proudly embraced their common interests and sought to clearly distinguish themselves, even if they were sometimes mocked, from what was "mainstream" culture at the time (which did not include video games). Peers came to gather around common interests, and stayed for the welcoming, like-minded people they found. This situation naturally led discussions to lose their exclusive focus on video games and to embrace all aspects of teenager life. This explains why the most popular forums on the website tend to target a specific age range rather than a specific topic.

In this perspective, the 18-25 members can be considered as a *community* (with the social dimension it implies), and not simply as the gathering of individuals around a specific topic, as medical forums or computer troubleshooting discussions. The most striking evidence of a *communal* belonging to the forum is the fact that users call themselves "kheys."[7] This name is a powerful means of rallying members. Many shared references on the forum are based on this word, and it is a common way to hail other users: "thank you khey," "he's a high-quality khey," "how are you my kheys?." Moreover, the spelling of the word is often diverted, implying that those who recognize themselves with these alternative characterizations could be considered as valuable members of the community, or more precisely as *up-to-date* users, underlining their active participation.

Concerning the progressive assimilation of transgression as a core constituent of the 18-25 forum, it first became associated with the website through one of its forums, the 15-18, the younger version of the 18-25. In the years 2000, it was known as a place where young, and sometimes marginalized, people could meet to prattle about literally anything that could be of interest to them. Due to the young age of the average user and the frivolity of discussions, moderation was known for its leniency, as would be appropriate for a small enclosed community that meant no particular harm.[8] Particularly so, since all moderators were also members of the 15-18 that

7 The Arabic word for "friend, brother."

8 For example, under the direction of Sébastien Pissavy and L'Odyssée Interactive, a minimalist approach was taken vis-à-vis moderation instructions: it was a way to attract teenagers by allowing them to debate and exchange with many liberties. Since Sébastien Pissavy himself was both rather young and a video games enthusiast, he understood the intrinsic frivolity of this forum, hence did not see the need for strict moderation. This vision drastically changed in 2014, when Webedia bought jeuxvideo.com. The main objective for Fimalac behind this operation was to create a leading network of online media in France. This ambition, contrasting with the one of Sébastien Pissavy and his company, calls for an entirely different attitude with respect to the "excesses" of the 15-18 or the 18-25. Notably, the risk aversion of big companies pushes them to adopt a non-extreme position regarding social and political matters.

volunteered for it, and faced intense pressure from regular members of the community to sustain this specific transgression space. Many things were stupid, gross, wanton, but served the purpose of the community, in quest for some mindless entertainment. As a result, none of the moderators wanted to act as a killjoy, and their effective power was very much limited, especially since members could easily get back at them through the spreading of rumors and the frequent doxxing.[9]

These peers of roughly the same age played a wide array of games to divert boredom, and submitting transgressive content in order to catch the attention of other members was one of them.[10] Moreover, as anonymity of online participation tends to disinhibit users, transgression is more likely to occur in these forums than in groups of peers in real life, and its intensity likely to be higher.

The establishment of a transgression space on the 18-25 could also be explained with *infrastructural* issues that the forum experienced. As a matter of fact, as underlined by the staff of *jeuxvideo.com*, substantial moderation failures in 2008 can explain the durable development of a transgression culture on the forum:

> But why did the forum become as big, and as frequent a source of polemics? "In 2008, the forum was left without moderation during several weeks, it was a chaotic situation, as Gwendal Lerat recalls.[11] The moderator who arrived at last tried to recover control over the forum, but it was too late". Thousands of users found here a space for expression and, starting from 2007–2008, a particular "culture" was born. Fictions, memes, websites... During many years dozens of references emerged from the forum. It actually was a group of cybernauts who had found here the pretext to gather behind a common culture.
>
> (*Le Monde* 2016, authors' translation)[12]

This event, along with the other factors we mentioned, seems to have accelerated the constitution of a common culture that gathered many trolls of the French web on the 18-25 forum. For a brief moment, the transgression space as a resource had the opportunity to emerge, and users immediately saw the associated benefits; not

To answer the numerous critiques made of the "unruly" members of these forums, a crackdown was performed on practices and language. Along with harsher moderation, the words filter was implemented. However, this kind of policy had very little effect in practice, and new "derivatives" were found for the banned words within a day.

9 Doxxing "is the Internet-based practice of researching and broadcasting private or identifying information (especially personally identifying information) about an individual or organization" (Wikipedia, doxxing, accessed the June 2, 2019).

10 A similar remark was made for the 4chan community: "Trolling is itself a game, one steeped in riddles, deceptions, and misleading other users; other games played on 4chan, often to fight boredom, involve asking questions, guessing answers, 'gaming' the medium itself by predicting post numbers, incorporating reCAPTCHA phrases into discourse, or relating narratives, as in >greentexting or bait-and-switch stories" (Manivannan 2012: §38).

11 Manager of the communitarian forum of jeuxvideo.com.

12 Florian Reynaud for *Le Monde* February 15, 2016.

only the possibility for transgression in itself, but the complex by-products it allowed to generate, especially this common culture shared by the members.

Gradually, trolling came to be a cornerstone of social interactions on the 18-25. As a consequence, it is not only tolerated, but even encouraged:

> On *jeuxvideo.com*, the practice (of trolling) is constant, and consists in writing messages considered as stupid, provocative or obscene to generate reactions, but also sufficiently credible so that some users will respond. The aim could be to "trap" a user who would take the troll's message seriously: it is in this case a sort of a schoolboy prank. The troll wants his message to generate a reaction of indignation or on the contrary adhesion from a gullible user. Sometimes, the idea is just to make other users laugh. A specificity of the forum is that the trolling practice is community-wide: far from being criticized, trolling is encouraged and contributes to the community's identity. Thus, we are not simply talking about some users who would come to disturb the forum: an important part of the posts is trolling.
>
> (Marignier 2017: §10, authors' translation)

In a broad sense, all forms of trolling that aim to entertain the community are valued on the forum, or at least considerably more tolerated than on any website of this size in France. However, some practices are still considered as inappropriate, and can be qualified as *flame trolling* (Bishop 2014), in other words harmful for the community. These practices mainly concern trolling actions affecting the readability of the forum, *ad hominem* transgressive humor or the submission of problematic content that is likely to alert authorities and endanger the common and its resource (posting child pornography links is an obvious example). These types of behavior will be frowned upon by members (through tacit coercion) and sanctioned (through formal moderation), constituting the system of rules-in-use that we present in the following parts.

9.2 SHARED REFERENCES AS A TOOL OF TACIT MODERATION

In this section, we argue that shared references between members of the 18-25 play a pivotal role in the management of the resource represented by the transgression space. Most of those shared references have emerged from repeated interactions within the space, contributing to build a strong sense of community, and therefore increasing members' commitment to protect it.

9.2.1 *Shared References as a Barrier to Entry: The Role of Hermeticism*

In a forum like the 18-25 that is freely accessible to everyone, we could expect transgressive content to reach not only well-integrated members of the community but also "outside observers"; in other words, nonmembers that happen to scroll by the forum (either casual users or people drawn to the forum following one of the numerous public controversies it generated).

While integrated members are aware of the potential transgressive nature of the content, outside observers might be caught off-guard and get offended by it. Indeed, they are not supposed to be aware that they are interacting in a transgression space, and might (rightfully) deem such content to be unacceptable for what they consider to be a regular interaction space.

In order to prevent the multiplication of public controversies, integrated members tend to "encode" transgressive content by using a shared body of references proper to the forum and its community. Due to the community being close-knit, this allows the emergence of quite complex common references that are hermetic for the uninitiated user. They reduce the risk of transgressive content being reported and subject to public outrage, since at best the outside observer will not know that he or she is facing controversial content, and at worst he or she will have to judge intent rather than explicit statements, considerably weakening his or her accusation.

We might remark that what we call here "hermeticism" is closely related to the concept of esotericism developed by Melzer (2014), defined as the "practice of communicating one's unorthodox thoughts primarily 'between the lines,' hidden behind a veneer of conventional pieties, for fear of persecution or for other reason." Hermeticism here serves a dual purpose: to protect the community from society at large, and to protect society from the particularly transgressive culture of the forum, that is not meant to be displayed to the outside observer. These motivations correspond to the defensive and protective forms of esotericism. Melzer demonstrates in his work the consistency of esotericism through classical and modern times, and its sudden decline during the nineteenth and the twentieth centuries, which he explains partly through the expansion of freedom of expression. What makes this comparison interesting in our case is that the rise of hermeticism on the forum was precisely caused by what is considered as restriction of freedom of expression, as attitudes of society toward transgression became more hostile. There suddenly was a need for the community not only to defend itself, but to avoid harming others in perpetuating its culture and catering for its resource.

A typical example on the 18-25 would be the diversion of the word "Arab" in order to express controversial statements with other (innocuous) words. On the 18-25, the word "Arab" first became "tree" (because of its proximity with the French word "arbre"). Then, when "arbre" became polemic (because people knew what this word actually meant), it became "foliage," and so on: many words linked with the semantic field of arboriculture emerged in relation with this kind of controversial issue. The same technique is used for a wide array of potentially sensitive words, contributing to the hermetic nature of discussions.

This kind of substitution is not limited to single words, and can also concern general statements and opinions. Although the variety of opinions on the 18-25 is surprisingly rich, a lot of users tend to share controversial views on thorny issues such as migration policies, feminism, or national identity (since such views are not welcome everywhere on the Internet, many of these users end up gathering on the 18-25, implying a strong selection bias). Many threads that share a highly controversial news item and ask for users' opinions will induce a number of standardized replies based on diversion, which are seemingly benign but carry a very precise meaning that is collectively acknowledged by the community.

For example, the forum takes great pride in having a set of smileys proper to the forum and thousands of homemade stickers (pictures used as reaction faces in discussions) that constitute a significant part of its culture (using smileys from other websites is frowned upon). One of the most common smileys used to react in an elliptic way to controversial news is the 18-25's ":)," which, contrary to its counterparts on other platforms, is not meant to signify a positive reaction, but implicitly carries controversial statements that are largely shared by the community, but that would be censored if stated explicitly. Another example of an elliptic reply consists in the following "pavé" (the 18-25's equivalent of a "copy-paste"):

> This societal issue is interesting to me and I have an opinion on the question. Unfortunately, I am prevented from sharing it with you due to, on the one hand, laws restricting freedom of speech in France, and on the other, jeuxvideo.com's conditions of use that I had to accept to create my account on this site. As a result, the simple expression of my opinions on this discussion space could entail sanctions from this forum's administrators and possibly from legal institutions. It is therefore with great regret that I will content myself with reading your exchanges, without participating beyond this message.

The massive use of diversion encapsulates the tension that suffuses the forum as mentioned in the introduction: members want to have the possibility to share transgressive content, but are aware of the fact that it is bounded by moral and legal rules, therefore opt for elliptic forms of transgression, denouncing society's "doxa" restricting what they consider to be a simple application of freedom of speech. Without entering the normative debate on this issue, we may remark that the line separating freedom of speech from punishable statements is quite blurry, and this is precisely why a transgression space can coexist along with a legal system.

This set of references acquired by users with the practice of discussions on the forum is a strong *barrier to entry* for newcomers, as topics could appear cryptic (18-25) or off-putting (as on 4chan), while discussion is generally considered as a contribution good. This limitation to openness by words diversion with shared references has a double function: on the one hand, it is a way for users to understand their value in the community ("I have observed during a sufficient time the discussions to understand them")[13] and, on the other hand, to be able to talk about controversial subjects without threatening the existence of the transgression space.

[13] This is also the case on 4chan: "Most of these rules encode the obverse of their literal meaning, making it impossible for outsiders to distinguish between the literal and the implicit without consistent lurking and absorption of institutional memory. It is through lurking that 4channers

Once these diversions become a part of the forum's culture, users are able to exert tacit coercion on users that do not use this hermetic way of expressing themselves. In other words, transgression has to be "tamed" for the resource to be durably exploited, and regular members play a complementary role to the one of moderators. Through tacit coercion (usually through the form of scathing or mocking remarks) as well as direct reports to moderators, unacceptable kinds of transgression are shunned by the community.

> Conceptually, informal moderating behaviours are related to the idea of community justice, which refers to the processes by which members of geographically bound communities take responsibility for self-policing and responding to crime via social control mechanisms that enhance community life.
>
> (Bateman, Gray, and Butler 2011: 845)

The culture of the 18-25 has another central function: more than a barrier to entry, it is a way to keep in memory content posted before their disappearance in the thousands of pages of archives not read anymore by the users.

9.2.2 *Shared References as a Way to Prevent Disappearance of Content*

The specific body of shared references of the 18-25 could also be understood as a way, in a platform characterized by ephemerality of content, to preserve a collective memory among users. By ephemerality, we mean that, due to the profusion of messages posted on the 18-25, the time of exposition for a topic, with a few exceptions, is no longer than several minutes.

In this perspective, the integration of some fragments extracted from discussions into elements of language, their possible transformation into *memes* (Bernstein et al. 2011: 56), is a way to preserve collective references that would otherwise quickly fade away due to the endless production of content.

Ephemerality is a common feature of forums, but its management takes numerous forms. On 4chan, threads are systematically deleted upon reaching ten pages, and they are ranked by popularity. On the 18-25, content is not systematically removed. However, existing content quickly fades into oblivion, as most of the activity is concentrated on the homepage, containing the 20 most recently refreshed threads. Most users have integrated the specific rhythm of the forum, that is, the high-paced simultaneous interactions on the most recent topics, by constantly refreshing the homepage.

Facing the issue of ephemerality, users of the 18-25 safeguard the best moments of the discussions by integrating them in the collective references of the forum. This is why the language of the 18-25 is so self-referential: the most interesting contributions

are exposed to institutional memory and acquire collective knowledge and cultural capital for themselves" (Manivannan 2012: §30).

are turned into catchphrases in order to be used by members. Moreover, these contributions are included in archives that have been created to preserve these ephemeral references. We may cite the user-managed *wiki.jvflux.com* that references all "key moments" of the forum, maintaining its collective memory.

More than the overproduction of messages, another aspect of the disappearance of content is linked to the fact that as discussions grow longer, the likelihood that they will transgress the rules-in-use rises, implying a removal by the moderation team. This "law of charter violation" was observed by a current moderator of the 18-25 forum, Odoki, interviewed by *Le Monde*:

> (Far-right members of the 18-25) have perfectly internalized a characteristic of online debates, quite close to Godwin's law:[14] the longer the discussion, the less inhibited it becomes. They do not even need to do their propaganda themselves, only to sow the seeds for a toxic debate and reap the benefits.[15]

As a matter of fact, when a discussion grows longer and users are invited to express their opinion about an ever-growing subject matter, the probability of referring to transgressive ideas approaches one, as one of the very links that bind this community together is precisely this disposition for transgression.

This disposition for transgression implies that while the bulk of the content that is shared is not exclusive to the forum, its interpretation often is. To put it differently, the transgression space allows for an alternative view on current events and societal issues, and from the many interactions stem fundamental ideas about how to perceive and reflect upon the world. These ideas and attitudes vastly differ from the ones produced on other discussion spaces and challenge them, whether they want it or not. These alternative attitudes become constituent of the community's identity, and quite logically are reflected in its alternative culture. Thus, elements coming from what is considered as the "mainstream culture" will be rejected. For instance, Instagram smileys and Twitter links will be frowned upon, popular pastimes such as Netflix ridiculed. This is to prevent culture from falling into oblivion, or worse, being somewhat integrated into mainstream culture, which would cause the destruction (or restriction) of the resource, the transgression space.

Obviously, a great deal of the shaping of the rules-in-use and culture is the prerogative of regular members themselves, using tacit coercion with regard to what is to be accepted and what is not. A functioning hermetic culture as a barrier to entry is enough to contain most transgressive behavior within the transgression space, but not all of it. Over the last years, antisemitic or misogynistic content has become relatively frequent on the 18-25, leading newspapers to denounce this toxic

[14] "Godwin's Law of Nazi Analogies states, 'As an online discussion grows longer, the probability of a comparison involving Nazis or Hitler approaches one'" (Ip 2011: 218). This reductio ad hitlerum that dismisses an opinion or a person by associating it or him or her with Hitler is especially present in online forums.

[15] Laura Motet for *Le Monde*, April 2, 2017.

environment, such as *L'Obs*,[16] *Libération*,[17] or *Le Monde*.[18] As a result, moderation ended up being questioned on its efficiency, and frequent calls were made for Webedia to enforce stricter and stricter rules, thus threatening the transgression space as it was defined initially by members of the forum. We will see in what follows how moderation evolved over time, under pressure from Webedia and civil society, progressively transforming the contour of the transgression space through a formal sanction system.

9.3 IN THE KINGDOM OF TROLLS, THE MODERATOR IS KING

Now that we have described the construction of the transgression space of the 18-25, and how the shared references are operating as a set of tacit rules preserving this common resource, we will touch upon the formal system of sanctions, which is a central feature in the *Governing Knowledge Commons* framework (Gordon 2009).

The moderation team of the 18-25 has a double function: to promote content by pinning it on the homepage of the forum, for example, and to remove content that is incompatible with the charter. This *two-pillar* moderation is a common feature of online forums. However, promoted content is generally one that embodies the *editorial line* of the forum while content that gets removed is broadly considered as harmful for the sustainability of interactions on the forum. In other words, there is usually a *clear* distinction between what should be highlighted and what should disappear. In a community of transgression however, the situation is more complex, as what should be removed is often close to what the users are interested in (i.e., what they would like to see promoted). This tension is precisely why the study of transgressive forums is interesting, and could be applied to many other kinds of platforms sharing transgressive or illegal content: P2P networks, Sci-hub, 4Chan, etc.

Moreover, this tension calls for the greatest possible care in the moderators' selection process. The moderation team of the 18-25 (five members in September 2019), composed of volunteers, is under the supervision of a team of *administrators*, employees of *jeuxvideo.com*, and the tasks are clearly divided between them:

> First at all, the moderator cannot ban. If he is connected as a moderator, his requests are prioritized by administrators (who are able to ban), it is not guaranteed they will be accepted. Then, the moderator is not untouchable, he is before anything else a user. A moderator can be dismissed if administrators judge that he is no longer worthy of his role.
>
> ("La modération," JVFlux, authors' translation)

[16] Thibaut Petit for L'Obs, September 27, 2015.

[17] Libération, January 6, 2017.

[18] William Audureau for *Le Monde*, March 31, 2017.

However, both moderators and administrators' main focus is to cleanse the forum of unacceptable content; this entails punishing users who share such content. *Jeuxvideo.com* possesses a quite complex formal system of sanctions, called the *system of management and treatment of alerts*, along with a reputational score for users, the "karma score," that acts as a criminal record, and which is used as a basis for the "graduated set of sanctions," defined by Charlotte Hess as a core component of the knowledge commons (2012: 21).

On the forums of *jeuxvideo.com*, the selection of moderators is based on elections. To be more precise, users can ask on the forum devoted to moderation of *jeuxvideo.com* to organize the ballot in the forum they would like to manage. The request is examined and accepted if there is a need for additional moderators, and if the applicant's motivations and vision of the forum are judged compatible with the website's. During this voting procedure, users vote by regular message posting: in other words, users have to post a message on the forum with the name of the candidate in order to vote, implying that the vote is not anonymous. In this configuration, more than voting, users can also argue about the election, sparking massive debates on the applicant or the general orientation of the forum. Relatively inactive accounts are ruled out of the election process, to avoid ballot stuffing (by the creation of thousands of ghost accounts). This access restriction to the vote can be legitimized by the fact that active users are those who are the most able to understand what kind of qualities are required to manage the transgression space.

After the voting procedure, the winner has to be approved of by administrators. This last control is implemented to ensure that no "troll" winner has emerged, which could easily occur on a forum such as the 18-25, and in fact has already happened in the past. These trolling moderators are characterized by *trolling in the speech* and/or *trolling in the acts* (using moderation tools). In the first case, as users must regularly interact with moderators to remove a sanction or to contest a decision, the moderator can mock a user to entertain others (some moderators are indeed known for their caustic behavior). In 2018, a user was brought up for trial for an offensive post on the 18-25, and was ironically thanking moderators for this mishap.[19] A moderator then answered by asking him for a *dedication in court.*[20] The second case corresponds to various abuses of power against the community: systematic suppression, arbitrary sanctions, or benevolence to obvious charter infractions, etc. A remarkable example of such form of trolling is the *new year eve scandal of 2017*. A popular *fad* on the forum is to post the message "*post at the same time*" when two or more users are posting a message during the same second. On New Year's Eve, users try to post simultaneously at midnight. This communal action is

[19] Topic entitled "Je passe au tribunal le 27 Novembre à cause du forum," November 20, 2018.

[20] The dedication practice in the 18-25 consists in asking a user to mention his or her pseudonym while performing a real-life action, such as during a classwork presentation about the forum. In this context, it was of course a sarcastic request.

particularly important for users, as some of them present on the forum at this time are alone during this time of celebration. That day, 800 users were connected to the topic. But, just before midnight, the topic was closed by a moderator called Oswild with an arrogant message mocking users. This incident initiated an important controversy about the election of moderators, and proved that even the moderation team is no stranger to transgressive behavior, which is quite logical on a forum like the 18-25.[21]

Even if these cases are marginal, they nicely capture the tensions in the governance of a transgression space. As a matter of fact, moderators, as members of the community, carry the inherent tension characterizing the common at hand. While they also display a taste for transgression, and recognize the fact that it is one of the core constituents of the community, they were elected precisely to control it, so that the resource could continue being exploited, and by-products such as shared references could keep being generated by interactions on the forum. Even though one could argue that, since the Webedia takeover, and following the numerous controversies, moderation has become increasingly strict, resolute attitudes toward free speech still stand among members of the moderation team. We may take the recent example of the *numéro anti-relous* ("anti-creep phone number") scandal. In October 2017 two feminist activists, Clara Gonzales and Elliot Lepers, set up an automated phone number that women could give to admirers who would not take no for an answer. An automated reply would then let the suitor know that they made the person feel uncomfortable and ask them to reconsider their behavior. They announced their action on Twitter.[22] Members of the 18-25 quickly picked up on it ("raided" it, in their terms), and flooded the line with more than 26,000 messages over the course of three days, forcing the activists to temporarily shut the service down.[23] The affair caused significant public outrage, and while most recognized the wrongdoings of said members, many still stood by the free speech argument, including a moderator that we quote here:

> Nobody tackled this issue, but in many of these raid-like situations, we remark that the victims call for the government to regulate the Internet. It is funny how the very same persons that need freedom of speech, demand it to be restrained. I am not in France and there is no actual regulation on the Internet where I am. It represents a free space of discussion for people to grow. Why would you want to regulate that?
>
> (authors' translation)

We observed similar reactions from the host of the forum. As a matter of fact, during the controversy, *jeuxvideo.com* as well as Webedia were asked to break their silence about the issue of cyber-harassment and moderation on the 18-25. Cédric Page, head

[21] Regularly, some topics are created and called "Oswild, never forgive, never forget."
[22] @Claranote on Twitter, October 27, 2017.
[23] Renée Greusard for the Nouvel Obs, October 30, 2017.

of the "gaming" division of *Webedia* and director of *jeuxvideo.com*, while condemning the situation, defended the website nonetheless:

> (In reaction to 18-25 members boasting about spamming the *numéro anti-relou*) This is not very clever, and *Webedia* obviously condemns these schemes, even if all the people that claimed affiliation with the forum were not necessarily among its members. I refute the idea that this humor of questionable taste is specific to *jeuxvideo.com*. This forum is the largest social media for young people in France, and what one finds in there is simply this youth's expression. On this forum, as in the rest of society, the most extreme positions often provoke the most reactions, hence are the most visible.
>
> (Vincent Matalon for France Télévision, October 31, 2017, authors' translation)

Moderators on the 18-25, as part of the knowledge commons, are there to design and implement sanctions for behavior violating the rules-in-use of the community but aim above all at preserving the resource that binds the community together, and allows the commons to exist in the first place. Their task is not easy, especially since the delimitation of free speech is blurry as we mentioned. Also, their actions are limited as they are mere volunteers, that still depend on Webedia's approval, whose motivations do not fully align with the community.

This last point hints that, in order for a transgression space to be sustainably exploited as a resource, there has to be a conjunction of several factors that do not depend exclusively on the community itself (defined as users of the forum). We now propose to discuss the conditions for this peculiar kind of resource – the transgression space – to thrive.

9.4 TRANSGRESSION SPACES IN SOCIETY

In every particular social situation people may find themselves in, they see their action space limited in two ways: by legal restrictions, which prevent them from engaging in any illegal action (without fear of consequences at least), and by restrictions based on social norms (most of them tacit), which stem from the collective acknowledgment of what is expected of a man, for example, when he is engaged with a given group of people. We should rather say, what is *not to be expected of him*. These tacit social norms can be observed in any social group, and effectively restrain the action space, often more compellingly than the law does: indeed, while no police officer will watch every move of the individual, he will systematically be judged on his actions by his environment, often leading to strong coercion, namely, due to the threat of exclusion.

We can consider these "etiquettes" as *restrictive norms*, which are constructed and acknowledged norms restricting the action space further than simple legal frontiers. This concept immediately calls for its opposite, that we might call *permissive norms*, which, instead of restricting the action space further, extend it in some selected aspects beyond legal frontiers. An action space equipped with a permissive norm is what constitutes a *transgression space* in our approach.

The specific combination of permissive norms will also define what is socially accepted in the transgression space: some aspects of the transgression space might be perfectly legal, but considered unacceptable in it. Moreover, not every type of illegal behavior will be deemed appropriate. As we have shown for the specific transgression space of the 18-25, transgression still needs to be "controlled," in the sense that not every kind of trolling will be tolerated on the space. It has to abide by specific codes, which are part of the forum's culture.

The key point here is that transgression spaces are not fundamentally different from traditional action spaces, but they just happen to take a different stance on what are considered "acceptable" actions. This notion of transgression space is therefore meant to be *local*, in the sense that it has relevance for a subset of the action space. This locality concept nicely extends into the GKC framework that structured this chapter: transgression spaces can be considered as *local commons*, since the only people that will deem them valuable are precisely members of the community acknowledging the permissive norm governing the space. Outside observers, either abiding by a restrictive norm, or even a different kind of permissive norm, would consider some behaviors taking place in the transgression space as unacceptable, and quite logically would advocate for its closure.

These peculiar types of commons call for an entirely different type of organization around them. A central point is related to the *openness degree* of the transgression space compared to other action spaces: due to the common being "local," the community around it, unlike other common-centered online communities (such as Wikipedia for example), has a substantially lower interest in expansion or even visibility. As a matter of fact, while more visibility might attract more contributors and expand the pool of knowledge (i.e., enrich the common) in the case of Wikipedia, it endangers the common in the case of the 18-25, because it increases the probability that problematic content oozes out of the transgression space, for (most likely hostile) outside observers to see.

Transgression therefore needs to be confined in some way, to increase the stability of the transgression space, and because members of the community do not want to expose unprepared outside observers to transgressive content or activities. In the case of the 18-25, it takes the form of a complex and elliptic culture as we saw, combined with a general hostility (through mockery) toward those who did not internalize it.

Some general properties of transgression spaces can be highlighted from the case study of the 18-25. First of all, most of the time, a transgression space exists due to an ambiguity vis-à-vis the legal context. In the 18-25, with the exception of a few obviously illegal posts, most content is actually implied rather than explicitly stated, as we have underlined, making any legal stance blurry, as a result. Of course, judging intent rather than acts is indeed much trickier. Moreover, even if online hate speech is now starting to be condemned with the same gravity as its "real life" counterpart, the law is still faced with a plethora of new cases that it has yet to fully integrate, meaning that there is still quite a lot of uncertainty with regard to what is or is not legally punishable on the Internet.

Then, the transgression space is the result of tolerance with regard to activities within the space. This tolerance can be explained by the fact that the increase in opportunities for interactions, due to the extension of the action space, is not too costly for the rest of the society. To a lesser extent, it can be tolerated because the situation would be even worse for the rest of a society with a traditional action space. On the 18-25, internal moderation of transgressive content, with no systematic report to legal authorities, can be understood as tolerance for the sake of some mindless entertainment.

Finally, we want to remark that the existence of a transgression space is always threatened, due to its very nature. Sooner or later, the transgression space's existence will come to be questioned, usually through public outrage caused by transgression oozing out of the space. As a result, there are eventually only two outcomes for the evolution of a transgression space: either the law will be amended to integrate the transgression space, which makes it disappear as a transgression space, or tolerance will be found inappropriate, in which case coercive measures will be taken to shut down the space. Thus, transgression spaces mainly exist due to this *status quo* with regard to tolerance in a particular context: some might argue that yes, it is illegal, but some positive aspects emerge out of it (at least locally), so maintaining it for now would be still profitable. This tacit agreement can always be questioned, and if it is the status of the transgression space will be threatened.

A famous example might also help us understand these issues related to transgression spaces: it concerns the legalization of prostitution in the Netherlands in 2000. It gave cities freedom to decide on which forms of prostitution would be allowed and more importantly their location. In most cities, prostitution came to be concentrated in a specific district (De Wallen in Amsterdam for example). Many other illegal activities, which often gravitate around prostitution, also came to cluster around these districts. Cities displayed varying levels of leniency regarding these activities, but very few actually showed the will to eradicate them, as they considered it as somewhat inevitable. Restricting prostitution to a specific space leads other criminal activities to be confined there, and allowed to "buy peace" for other parts of cities. Showing tolerance with regard to some illegal actions, like money laundering, provided they happen in a strictly delimited space, is exactly the attitude one would have with regard to a transgression space, which is indeed what these districts quickly came to be. But these areas are constantly threatened by officials who are concerned about the lack of security in these parts of the city, and are at the center of numerous heated debates. A parallel can be drawn to the 18-25: allowing this transgression space, on which trolling is acceptable to a larger extent than most of the websites, might be a way to confine transgression to a specific space. One might fear that in the case of a shutdown, the 18-25 trolls would spread to other online platforms, provoking much more damage than the actual configuration of the transgression space.

As a final remark, the combination of a functioning barrier to entry and a tolerant host appears to be necessary conditions for durable transgression spaces to emerge. We see a delicate balance at play in the case of the 18-25, allowing the common to exist. As we saw, the elliptic culture of the forum is not enough to contain transgression within the transgression space, and moderation must compensate for its limitations. Moderators, as members of the community built around the commons, want on the one hand to implement harsher control, but on the other hand to stay moderate in their action, in order to preserve the commons that binds this community together.

9.5 CONCLUSION

In the literature on knowledge commons, the commons at hand is considered as a *good* (as opposed to a *bad*), in the sense that it is universally understood that this resource has value, and that infrastructures should be built around it in order for the community to enjoy it to the fullest while protecting it.

What makes the case of the 18-25 interesting in this context is the fact that the transgression space and its community – the *local commons*– is controversial by essence: while it is highly valued within the community, society at large does seem to consider it detrimental, and would like to see it reformed, or shut down.

Moreover, if the common culture as the by-product resulting from the management of this resource is anti-rival by definition, it only takes its full meaning when it is enjoyed and developed by a community that defines itself negatively vis-à-vis society at large. Hence, the tension that suffuses the whole infrastructure around the transgression space is also found in its culture.

On the one hand, there is a general will for members to promote the development of the commons and of the community around it, in order to increase the opportunities of interactions. But, on the other hand, there is a collective acknowledgment that the very existence of the commons is only possible because its community is marginal, destined to stay on the fringes. Indeed, the commons here is not threatened by the usual rivalry concerns but rather by a rivalry between its proponents and its detractors. Promoting the uncontrolled development of the commons increases the chance of putting it under the scrutiny of its detractors: the outside observers. As we saw, every mechanism involved in the exploitation of the commons includes this additional concern.

From this case study we proposed a more overarching concept of *transgression spaces*, to explain what would be the characteristics displayed by any community centered around a local commons characterized by an extension of the action space. Through our analysis, two fundamental points emerge with regard to the governance of the commons: the need for some kind of *barrier to entry*, effectively containing transgression within the transgression space, and the crucial importance of the host's attitude toward the transgression space, which allows to preserve the *status quo* in which the space can survive. Tolerance, in this regard, is a central notion that could be justified through a number of arguments from both the host and the community: libertarian values, freedom of expression, or even the more pragmatic "containment" argument would be some of them. Through more research on similar online and physical transgression spaces, these reasons could come to be refined, which could enrich the analysis of transgression spaces in society.

REFERENCES

Bateman, Patrick J., Peter H. Gray, and Brian S. Butler. 2011. "Research Note – The Impact of Community Commitment on Participation in Online Communities." *Information Systems Research* 22: 841–854.

Bernstein, Michael S., Andrés Monroy-Hernández, Drew Harry, Paul André, Katrina Panovich, and Gregory G. Vargas. 2011. "4chan and /b/: An Analysis of Anonymity and Ephemerality in a Large Online Community." In *Proceedings of the Fifth International AAAI Conference on Weblogs and Social Media*, 50–57. Palo Alto, CA: AAAI Press.

Bishop, Jonathan. 2014. "Representations of 'Trolls' in Mass Media Communication: A Review of Media-Texts and Moral Panics Relating to 'Internet Trolling.'" *International Journal of Web Based Communities* 10: 7–24.

Coles, Bryn Alexander, and Melanie West. 2016. "Trolling the Trolls: Online Forum Users Constructions of the Nature and Properties of Trolling." *Computers in Human Behavior* 60: 233–244.

Erasmus, Desiderius. 2003 [1511]. *The Praise of Folly*, edited by Clarence H. Miller. New Haven, CT: Yale University Press.

Foucault, Michel. 2001 [1964]. *Madness and Civilization*. London: Routledge.

Gordon, Wendy J. 2009. "Discipline and Nourish: On Constructing Commons." *Cornell Law Review* 95: 733–756.

Hess, Charlotte. 2012. "The Unfolding of the Knowledge Commons." *St Antony's International Review* 8: 13–24.

Hess Charlotte, and Elinor Ostrom. 2007. *Understanding Knowledge as a Commons*. Cambridge, MA: MIT Press.

Hopkinson, Christopher. 2013. "Trolling in Online Discussions: From Provocation to Community-Building." *Brno Studies in English* 39: 5–25.

Ip, John. 2011. "The Dark Knight's War on Terrorism." *Ohio State Journal of Criminal Law* 9: 209–230.

Larson, Maja, and Margaret Chon. 2017. "The Greatest Generational Impact: Open Neuroscience as an Emerging Knowledge Commons." In *Governing Medical Knowledge Commons*, edited by Katherine Strandburg, Brett M. Frischmann, and Michael J. Madison, 166–192. Cambridge, MA: Cambridge University Press.

Madison, Michael J., Brett M. Frischmann, and Katherine J Strandburg. 2009a. "Constructing Commons in the Cultural Environment." *Cornell Law Review* 95: 657–710.

2009b. "Reply: The Complexity of Commons." *Cornell Law Review* 95: 839–850.

Manivannan, Vyshali. 2012. "Attaining the Ninth Square: Cybertextuality, Gamification, and Institutional Memory on 4chan." *Enculturation* 15 : 1–21. www.enculturation.net/attaining-the-ninth-square

Marignier, Noémie. 2017. "'Gay ou pas gay?' Panique énonciative sur le forum jeuxvideo.com." *Genre, sexualité & société*, 17. https://journals.openedition.org/gss/3964#entries

Melzer, Arthur M. 2014. *Philosophy between the Lines: The Lost History of Esoteric Writing*. Chicago: University of Chicago Press.

Ostrom, Elinor. 1990. *Governing the Commons*. Cambridge, MA: Cambridge University Press.

Pissavy, Sébastien. 2013. *Jeuxvideo.com – Une Odyssée Interactive*. Houdan: Pix'n Love.

10

Crowdfunding the Queer Museum

*A Polycentric Identity Quarrel**

Carolina Dalla Chiesa

This case study illustrates how identities can be conceived as knowledge commons and how they can develop and be mobilized in situations of public contestation. The chapter uses the case of an art exhibition project carried out during 2018 in Brazil that portrayed a large number of queer- and LGBT-related visual artworks from Latin America. The exhibition was not merely an artistic project, but also inaugurated a public debate around underrepresented voices and their relationship to contemporary visual arts. The organization and disputes around the "Queer Museum: Cartographies of Difference in Brazilian Art" serve to elaborate how agents seek public legitimation by relying on shared resources, namely, identities and alternative infrastructures.

Unlike most art exhibitions, the Queer Museum (QM) combined the quest for representation with bottom-up ways of curation using alternative funding tools. Out of necessity, crowdfunding became the most viable route when market-state bodies refused to continue the exhibition after extensive conservative protests against its queer content. Facing barriers within cultural institutions and governments, it's organizers sought to channel their frustration toward alternatives available to them: an open funding mechanism, a process of open curation of events, and a diverse institutional setting. That resulted in a situation where markets intertwined with the pursuit of social and political goals.

Given the importance of the case for these interpretations, the chapter starts with a comprehensive description of the project development in two main phases: (a) the first public exhibition and the emergence of conservative protests and (b) the crowdfunding alternative and the reintegration in a semi-public institution.

* The author would like to express gratitude with the extensive comments provided by the editors and the support of Felipe Caruso, whose personal experience with the Queer Museum project was vital to write the chapter.

After the presentation of the case, the chapter discusses the museums' role in governing identities and how this role has gradually changed along with the notion of these identities themselves (Canclini 1995; Witcomb 2007). Amongst other relevant concepts, the chapter draws on the curators' understanding of "dispersed and deviant museums" to illustrate their current role in society (Esche 2005; Fidelis 2018).[1] I start from the idea that identities are socially governed resources that fuel social life in many ways. Even if they can be managed by traditional institutions, the concept is sufficiently open to absorb disputes and new expressions (e.g., queer identities represented through art) often recognized by museums (Adair and Levin 2020) but not without public disputes (Fidelis 2018).

The next section identifies the alternative institutions that allowed the QM to continue after the conservative protests and the initial termination by government and private organizations. The organizers of the QM opted to create a crowdfunding campaign where the general public was invited to contribute and take part in the process of legitimizing identities. Crowdfunding and related strategies are conceived as alternative routes toward building more polycentric and diverse institutional spaces (Aligica 2019; Hess and Ostrom 2007; Ostrom 2010).

The last part of the chapter addresses the combination of bottom-up and top-down governance (i.e., traditional institutions in combination with collective-organized fund-raising) that allows identities to be publicly governed and disputed. In this sense, the chapter argues that cultural commons (identity expression, artistic expression, lifestyles, etc.) are more likely to flourish where there is a capacity for bottom-up organization and institutional polycentricity. The resulting knowledge commons allows agents to draw on this resource and enables new initiatives by other cultural institutions, firms, and also state-run bodies, based on the newly recognized identities.

The Queer Museum represents the combination of two distinct debates: on the one hand, how institutions allow for the diversity of representations in their actions; and, on the other hand, the role of shared infrastructures in articulating knowledge commons that include actors' identities. By setting these observations analytically apart, the chapter concludes that identities are not restricted to governing rules by one or a few institutions. Instead, dispersed voices can construct identities and manage commons even in disagreement. This insight fundamentally contributes to understand complex forms of knowledge commons where *a priori* given sets of rules do not apply and where agents seek legitimation through dispute rather than stability.

10.1 THE STORY OF THE QUEER MUSEUM

The Queer Museum project marked the start of a major public debate in Brazil on which kinds of arts are legitimate. This case became a further evidence of the

[1] Dispersion and deviance in museums emerge mostly from the literature on curatorial practices produced by curators themselves (e.g., Hebert and Karlsen 2013).

country's political polarization, from which the art world is typically somewhat insulated. This section briefly describes the exhibition's unusual path, how it started, was terminated, and managed to restart.

10.1.1 *The First Phase: Exhibition and Protests*

Queer manifestations have caused controversy worldwide, and in many countries LGBT rights are still insufficiently realized. The recent resurgence of conservative politics in Brazil embodied by the rise of Jair Bolsonaro, has further endangered tolerance for diverse modes of living. Alarming data reports show that after the increase of conservative-leaning politicians, many places such as Brazil suffered a spike in deaths related to homophobia. The country even leads the ranking of crimes against various transgender groups (Benevides and Nogueira 2020). Such data contrast sharply with the popular image of Brazil as an open, tolerant, and diverse country. And indeed, not all tendencies point in one direction. The country has also seen the rise of same-sex marriage in recent years and cultural expressions in favor of diversity, especially in metropolitan areas. Precisely the opposing tendencies are a sign on the "wall" of the highly polarized and conflictual nature of the public debate, news, and, most importantly, daily life situations.

The "Queer Museum: Cartographies of Difference in the Arts" was a project hosted by the Santander Cultural institution (a banking corporation branch for the arts) whose exhibition took place from the 15th of August until the 10th of September, 2018, when it was abruptly terminated. The exhibition was enabled by the Brazilian Ministry of Culture, which financially supports art projects in partnership with the artistic branch of Santander Bank. Using a subsidy mechanism through tax exemption for private companies (the so-called "Rouanet Law") the project took place via a private–public partnership.

The project initially aimed at portraying a collection of public and private artworks from around 1950 until the present by representing the diversity of gender and expressions within artistic movements in Latin America. The exhibition relied on a nonchronological disposition of artworks curated by Gaudêncio Fidelis, who intended to promote a democratic discussion of gender diversity through art (e.g., paintings, sculptures, illustrations, audio-visuals, and photography). And to promote the ideals of nondeterminism and queerness (Fidelis 2018). The Queer Museum was a provisory exhibition in which the inclusion of difference was practiced beyond restrictive patterns of the artistic canon. The QM consisted of 270 artworks of 85 artists exhibited in the building owned by the cultural office of Santander (located in the city of Porto Alegre, south of Brazil). Influential local Brazilian artists were represented in this exhibition, such as Lygia Clark, Alfredo Volpi, Candido Portinari, Pedro Americo, and Leonilson Dias.

The exhibition was inspired by other queer-related projects organized by institutions such as the National Portrait Gallery in Washington, the National Museum in Poland, and the Queer British Art exhibition at Tate Britain. In social theory, the term "queer" comprises various gender and sexual identities that refuse the traditional binary representation of males and females (Callis 2014). The exhibition's stated goal reflects the "thinking outside the norm" (Benfeitoria 2018) very well. This outsider or deviant component (see Choi, Chapter 5) of the project caused discomfort among traditional sectors of the society represented by movements like MBL (Liberal Brazilian Movement) and the Christian League in Brazil who started a defamatory campaign through social media to call attention to the exhibition which was argued to be "incentivizing pedophilia, zoophilia, and blasphemy" (Carneiro 2018).

As a response to the protests, the curator joined efforts with artists and local figures to publicly speak in favor of the exhibition to explain the artworks and show their relevance to the public before its closing (VEJA 2017). Approximately one month before the official final date of the exhibition, on the 10th of September 2017, Santander decided to close the doors of the exhibition due to ongoing protests, both online and offline. With a small note, the cultural branch of the bank justified the early closing due to the fact that some artworks "disrespect symbols, beliefs and people" and that this was not the intention of Santander Cultural (Carneiro 2018). A few days later, a public prosecutor assessed the exhibition and concluded that nothing in the artworks was particularly problematic. The Federal Public Ministry, thus, recommended the reopening of the QM. Santander Cultural did not follow this recommendation. Both decisions were the cause for a new set of protests, this time also against censorship and in favor of the freedom of artistic expression. At this stage, the quarrel reached comprehensive national and international media coverage: *Folha de São Paulo* (Erber 2018), *Sul 21* (2017), *The Guardian* (Phillips 2017), *The New York Times* (Londoño 2018), *Le Monde Diplomatique* (Sant'Ana 2017), and *Free Muse* (2017) – most of them came out in favor of the project. This meant that a new dimension became associated with the QM. The exhibition was no longer only about queer identities but had also became about artistic freedom and identity representation more generally.

Following the closure of the exhibition in the southern city of Porto Alegre, the Rio Art Museum (in Portuguese, Museu de Arte do Rio de Janeiro) attempted to mobilize resources to reopen the QM in Rio de Janeiro. This attempt was, however, blocked by the city mayor, Marcelo Crivella, an evangelical preacher. He claimed that the artworks posed a threat to the "family values" that traditional groups held dear. Having faced hindrances from public and private institutions, the QM organizers then decided to search for alternative routes.

10.1.2 *The Second Phase: The Crowdfunding Campaign as an Alternative Strategy*

To reopen the QM, the organizers opted for a strategy that would foster legitimacy and visibility to the project whilst bringing independent funding. The crowdfunding campaign thus inaugurates the second phase that ends with the new exhibition located in the Parque Lage School of Visual Arts (EAV) of the city of Rio de Janeiro – a semi-public institution. It accepted to host the Queer Museum on the condition that the exhibition space would be reconstructed to allow for future projects in the same space.[2] Parque Lage's headquarters is a heritage building, a former home to Brazilian businessman Henrique Lage, later transformed into an open school partially funded by the Rio de Janeiro state government. Other funds usually come from corporations such as banks and petrol companies that direct tax money to cultural institutions via the so-called Rouanet Law (Dekker and Rodrigues 2019). Even in the dictatorship period, when many artistic expressions were censored, Parque Lage remained a relatively independent institution that historically thrived on showcasing established and emergent art (Parque Lage 2020). During the Queer Museum quarrel, Parque Lage's representants remained supportive of artistic voices that had long been part of the school's curriculum. After having the state's approval, the project could be carried on in this institution, if the basic costs were covered.

As Felipe Caruso (project manager of the campaign) says, crowdfunding was then suggested as a fast route for financial support and audience engagement, especially in a situation of institutional restrictions. By using this funding model, people support campaigns often in return for a product, a service, or a public acknowledgment, but sometimes without a tangible return (Belleflamme et al. 2014). Generally, cultural and artistic projects rely on this type of crowdfunding model, where supporters do not share in eventual future profits or become part of the venture in any other way (Dalla Chiesa 2020).

Some technical details about the crowdfunding campaign are worth mentioning.[3] The campaign was hosted on the website *Benfeitoria*, lasted approximately 60 days and succeeded in its goal with the support of 1678 backers.[4] The mean contribution of an individual was about 620 Brazilian Reais (USD 168), a relatively high amount if compared to similar campaigns on platforms like Kickstarter. Beside typical online communication strategies, offline activities were set up to engage with the community, such as music concerts with famous local musicians and a series of roundtables

2 The campaign requested funds to deliver the restoration, preparation, and painting of the *liveries* at Parque Lage. The goal of approximately USD 212k was reached at the end of forty days. The budget also included the production of the exhibition, the platform fee (of 12 percent), and consultancy services.

3 These details were both found in the online project available at Benfeitoria (2018) website as well as in conversations with Felipe Caruso, one of the crowdfunding consultants and project managers.

4 In English: "betterment." Projects hosted by this crowdfunding website are often not-for-profit ones, driven by nonpecuniary motivations. In terms of legal regulations, reward-based crowdfunding, such as this website, is the least restricted one as risks are proportional to the amounts pledged on the platform.

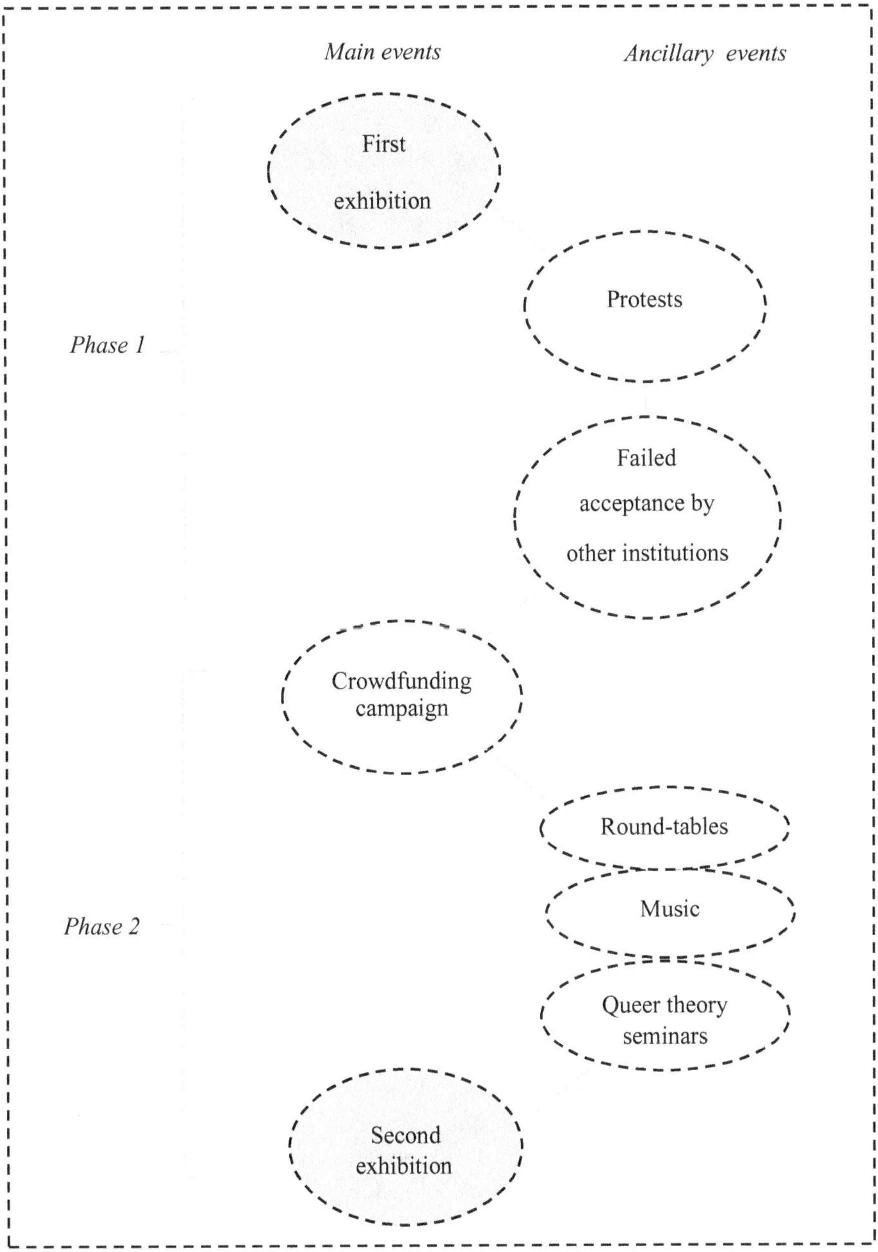

FIGURE 10.1. The sequence of events in two phases

discussions, which enhanced the attention devoted to this project. Figure 10.1 depicts the main sequence of events and the turning point as reported by media articles, the informal interviews, and the event's official publication (Fidelis and Escola de Artes Visuais do Parque Lage 2018).

During the second exhibition, the QM could no longer rely on established formal public or private organizations. This means that the QM increasingly adopted a different governance style: more open, from the funding to the execution, which (in the view of one of the organizers, Felipe Caruso) reinforced the support of diverse identities and art expressions by the QM. By not having typical state-market funds anymore, conservative protesters suddenly changed their agenda to a moral message. It was not the case anymore that funding this kind of art through mandatory tax-payment is wrong, but that the art itself was inappropriate. This shift was provoked by a switch of underlying social infrastructures, which had undermined the previous critique about the misuse of public funds. Identities remained in dispute even when the underlying social infrastructures became more plural, which shows the importance of immaterial resources in the making of social life. As art museums historically play an essential part in the making of legitimized identities (Halbwachs 1992), it is vital to observe how their role has changed alongside the notion of identity itself.

10.2 THE IDENTITY COMMONS RESOURCE AND ITS INFRASTRUCTURE(S)

In this section I argue that identities are cultural commons (i.e., a subset of knowledge commons). I explain how these commons are socially governed. While identity management is traditionally attributed to museums, that role has evolved over time, including the recognition of the importance of artistic and social movements in shaping cultural commons.

10.2.1 *Identity Representation in Museums*

Any description of how institutions deal with identities should first observe how identity became part of practical rationality that is subject to governance structures. As Taylor (1989) argues, identity is an elastic term used to describe the qualities and characteristics of personalities and groups. The concept of identity gradually emerged from philosophical and literary culture to express the inwardness and the original selfhood, not only of individuals but also of institutions. Part of this modern epistemology described by Taylor entails that people as well as countries, regions, and nations *have* an "identity" as long as these entities can communicate "power-relations in societies" (Bennett 1995). In the process of legitimizing recognized identities, it is usual that societies develop a moral compass about what is accepted and what pertains to the realm of "outsiders" (Becker 2018).

Identities have historically been an important element in the governance of societies, through identity-based rules (Koyama and Johnson 2019). And from the nineteenth century onward, many states have explicitly sought to strengthen their own position through the identification and promotion of somewhat coherent sets of historical narratives around the idea of national and local cultures (Anderson 1991; Hobsbawm and Ranger 1993). Museums and art institutions have long been prominent in representing these overall cultural values; they have played a critical educational role as a moral compass of values and heritage (Bennett 1995; Hoogwaerts 2016).

Since the nineteenth century, when many museums were founded, these traditional organizations have been key actors in defining national cultures. Museums typically sought to develop a unifying and homogenous identity and collective memory (Huyssen 1995). More recently, this rather essentialist agenda has been upset by a redefinition of museums' purposes and goals. Under the influence of developments in cultural studies, museum research, and the social sciences, museums now seek to be more heterogeneous, self-reflective, and critical. As Sokefeld (1999) observed, the concept of identity has undergone an unprecedented shift based on the anthropological insight that identities do not necessarily reflect a harmonious consensus but can consist of conflicted and unstable tendencies. The "narrative turn in social sciences" (Hyvärinen 2010) has helped to turn identity into a more hybrid and diverse concept where otherness is part of cultural agency (Canclini 1995; Bhabha 2012).

In this sense, museums have had to rethink their place in society. Traditionally they were often founded and funded by the state to create collective identities and shape a shared memory. In recent years they have increasingly realized that they need to incorporate a more diverse set of narratives and identities into their practices. The resulting "new museology" (Vergo 1989; Witcomb 2007) seeks to remain relevant to society as a cultural product by adapting the way museums organize exhibitions and engage with different communities. Some practices for transforming museums into more welcoming environments discuss the notion of a "dispersed museum" (Esche 2005; Teixeira 2016) or "deviant museum" (Fidelis 2018) in which institutions serve as "hubs" driven by values of equality, inclusion, social justice, and participation (Sandell 1998; Marstine 2017; Simon 2017). The goal is no longer the transmission of a relatively linear story to visitors. Instead, visitors are invited to engage with the art and develop their own interpretations rooted in their personal experiences (Hebert and Karlsen 2013). While these advancements are fundamental for museum management and the intra-institutional landscape, it is crucial to realize identities are collective resources rather than stable assets of organizations. Museums are one among a far broader set of agents that attempt to curate this valuable cultural resource. Identities are just as much created and shaped by social movements, grassroots organizations, artists working outside of traditional institutions, and various subcultures. Some of these developments have been already observed by museums as the work of Adair and Levin (2020) in the particular case of representing gender expressions shows.

10.2.2 *Interpreting Identities as Cultural Commons*

Like other cultural commons, identities are valuable infrastructural resources in making various aspects of social life possible. The expression and coproduction of these identities is certainly not limited to museums. This chapter argues that identities are cultural commons as long as they are a part of self-governing communities (Madison, Frischmann, and Strandburg 2019). Unlike most examples, identities are not bound by a specific institutional framework or set of rules. That is precisely what sets them apart: identity representation can be conflictual, dynamic, and highly contested, as, for example, anthropological studies demonstrate (Cohen 2000). Rather than focusing on the harmonious elements, anthropologists have attempted to show the variations of identity expressions and the dynamic processes that is identity formation (Sokefeld 1999).

Identities are a part of shared knowledge commons because they are key in establishing a collective reputation (Megyesi and Mike 2016), cooperation, and social capital (Bulte and Horan 2010). They fuel state, markets, and public life in general. Therefore, seeing identities as a shared resource implies that not only traditional public art museums benefit from it, but also that in facilitating transfers of goods and services, market interactions rely on these infrastructural resources. In this sense, besides using identities to "present the self in everyday life" (Goffman 1990), agents also seek to acquire them, modify them, make them visible or invisible. Think, for example, of identitarian movements, groups seeking citizenship, migrants and refuges (or the appellation of origin for goods and services, etc.). Ultimately, these immaterial resources help coordinate economic exchanges and create rules that guide social life, religion, and cultural institutions (Koyama and Johnson 2019).

10.3 MAKING A DISPERSED MUSEUM: A WAY TOWARD POLYCENTRICITY

This section discusses how the organizers and participants made the QM an event of increasing dispersion aided by open infrastructures. First, I highlight the resourceful features of the infrastructures they chose. Second, I discuss the new institutional space that comes as a result of this choice: a more dispersed and polycentric environment.

10.3.1 *Using Online Infrastructures as a Shared Resource*

After the protests that resulted in both private and state actors backing out, the organizers sought alternatives and decided to opt for a crowdfunding scheme. Unlike other options available at that moment, crowdfunding offers features that help bring the "freedom of art expression" message across while calling attention to this particular case. As an open shared infrastructure (Frischmann 2014) like other online types of "new commons"[5] (Hess 2008), these funding websites provide a

[5] Wikipedia entries, computer coding, hacker-space communities, online shared infrastructures, public art, music "jam sessions," and culture in a broad sense became part of what has been defined as "cultural commons."

digital space for various purposes such as niche markets, political agendas, individual projects, charitable initiatives, start-ups and various other uses (Cumming and Hornuf 2018). If other options were favored (e.g., more corporate funding, state subsidies, or even international support), visitors might have ended up acting less as active participants and more as passive consumers of the art installation.

For example, the funding campaign created the opportunity for various artists (queer or not), academic practitioners, and activists to curate ancillary events themselves prior and during the new exhibition at Parque Lage. Suddenly, being a supporter of this project also meant the opportunity to contribute to a cause and experience its events. This meant that the second phase emerged as more dispersed and aligned with new museology principles.

10.3.2 *An Open Institutional Space*

A polycentric system consists of a diversity of governing institutions: markets, voluntary organizations, for-profit firms, governments, and partnerships of various types between these entities (Aligica 2019). The more institutional variety there is in societies, the more agents can rely on different channels for their specific purposes. In some situations, monocentric arrangements may be preferable. That is the case for most established art museums in which a stable combination of state-funding, market-action, and volunteerism provides a relatively permanent framework. However, when public contestation arises, agents benefit from having access to more options to fulfil their identity-representation needs, moral compasses, or disputes, and, thus, seek alternatives themselves.

Self-governance typically requires a consistent institutional arrangement available to agents (Hess and Ostrom 2007). In the QM case, this arrangement was relatively unstable as the sequence of events was not initially planned. Instead, the events unfolded as various obstacles appeared, and while the exhibition started and finished in similar conditions (i.e., within a semi-public run institution with a mix of state and market funding), it followed a peculiar process. For example, while the set of artworks was curated and set since the first exhibition by Fidelis (2018), most of the ancillary activities that took place during and after the fund-raising campaign emerged from bottom-up initiatives. This development can give a new meaning to the idea of dispersion and deviance in museums (Esche 2005; Fidelis 2018). No longer are established organizations seeking to disperse their activities; rather, alternative organizational forms emerge on the scene. And in the case of the QM these organizational forms themselves had a dispersed nature, although under a collective umbrella of the QM. This also contributed to further blurring the distinction between a curator and a visitor, which is usually very strict in more traditional museums. In this way the QM allowed a plurality of ideas to emerge and provided an institutional space for them.

The overall combination of the crowdfunding campaign through digital platforms, the reliance on semi-public institutions, and dispersed bottom-up actions

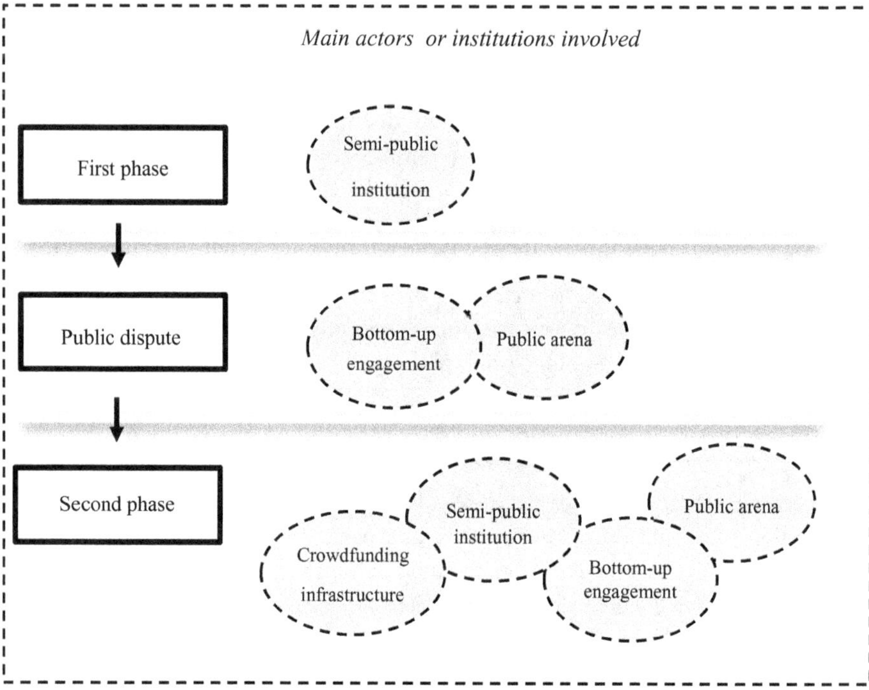

FIGURE 10.2. Visual representation of the flexible institutional arrangement
Even though the figure shows a certain linearity of events, in reality these moments largely intertwine as event schedules overlap. As such, these moments are distinguished for analytical purposes.

shows how the institutional space became increasingly polycentric with the project's advancement. Figure 10.2 reinterprets Figure 10.1 in this light.

Despite the fact that QM was successful within a specific institutional landscape, we should not search for the best combination of institutions and actors that bring about identity commons best. There are no panaceas. The particular institutional landscape does not provide a blueprint for an optimal set of institutional arrangements to be replicated elsewhere. It does, however, highlight the importance of available alternatives. In fact, using alternative funding schemes and open-source premises seems to have benefited the project from an "economics of attention" point of view (Lanham 2007). Dispersion and polycentricity brought more visibility to an otherwise overlooked lack of representation of queer art.

10.4 SOCIALLY GOVERNED IDENTITIES IN THE PUBLIC ARENA

This section elaborates on the previous analysis to further illustrate that identities are not the property of institutions but socially managed resources that become visible when disputes arise. Secondly, I contend that identities as a type of knowledge commons provide an important resource for future actions by private, social, and public actors. As such the QM feeds back into the resources that it has originally drawn from.

10.4.1 *The QM as Arena of Contestation*

Identities sometimes become more evident when they are under dispute. In these situations, as Holder and Flessas (2008) suggest, it is crucial to clarify the stories and remarkable events to better understand the knowledge commons in question. A discussion about identities can be centered on how people relate and give meaning to their resources, ownership, social practices, and disputes. The extract below shows the QM actors' view concerning the value of their campaign to cultivate artistic freedom:

> The campaign moves forward because of the power of society. It is a democratic instrument that will enable access to freedom of choice. No one can be prevented to access knowledge and artistic expression. It is exactly because of this freedom that no one should be prohibited to think, see, appreciate, criticize, talk, and have their own opinions. This campaign is about freedom of choice, expression, and opinions, rights so hardly conquered and that was restricted to us. This is about democracy.
>
> (Benfeitoria 2018: 1)

Queerness (i.e., the act of being queer or representing a queer identity) is historically bounded; it has become more evident in recent years despite being frequently suppressed. More recently, queerness has become the subject of social activism (Butler 2006; Meghani and Saeed 2019). The public debate around queer art seems to follow a similar path, where, first, individuals seek recognition. There were extensive efforts to counteract that search for recognition, which in turn provoked a stronger counterreaction. As a result, antagonistic relations become public. In our case, the quarrel revolved around a museum, its original funders, and a funding campaign, but these can vary as agents may find a channel to express their purposes elsewhere (e.g., music, literature, movies, clothing).

Figure 10.3 elaborates on the previous figures to further clarify the process of identity contestation. These figures show in sequence how queer identities were incorporated into the existing institutional framework and highlight the second moment when an alternative arrangement emerged from a confrontation. The image depicts that once agents debate the right to draw on specific identities as resources, a public arena of contestation emerges where there was only a top-down alternative before (the public–private art museum).

Let me elaborate on the diagram, and the transition from the left-hand initial stage, to the right-hand second stage of the QM. First, official public institutions become less relevant in the overall public debate. Second, bottom-up voices (pro and against queer identities) have a crucial role in any change in the existing setting.

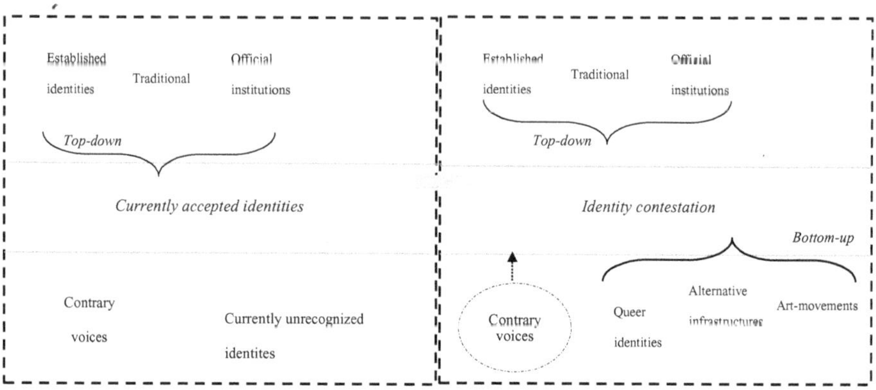

FIGURE 10.3. The development of contestation

Third, with the interplay of bottom-up and top-down institutions, identities such as these become more visible. The very contestation as such makes the alternative identities more visible. At this point, it is not yet clear whether this process of contestation will also lead to a successful (long-term) contribution to the knowledge commons of Brazilian identities.

Figure 10.3 highlights that initially, the existing identities were more or less shared and represented by the official institutions. Then a contestation broke out, both about the content of the knowledge commons (the recognized identities), and the right to contribute and exclude others from contributing to this knowledge commons. In this sense, the notion of "dispersion" often utilized to represent curatorship practices (Esche 2005; Teixeira 2016; Fidelis 2018) can also be used to characterize the way in which identity governance evolved. Dispersion in the case of the QM did not merely mean that the boundaries between the curator and the audience were blurred, but also that the content of the exhibition was publicly disputed, and finally that a more open institutional space was created. If the desired contribution of the QM becomes more widely accepted, art expression might benefit from a more stable situation in which the official institutions would then recognize queer identities and, some of them, incorporate queer art into their artistic practices.

10.4.2 *Identity Contestation and Feedback*

Every society has controversies and disputes. These controversies highlight at the same time what is (presumed to be) shared as well as what is contested and changing (Boltanski and Thévenot 2006). Many controversies and disputes are resolved in favor of the status quo, and do not lead to lasting changes. As newly proposed "contributions" they fail. The case of the QM, however, is an instance of a (partial) success. Although attempts were made to suppress the contribution, alternative ways were found to organize the QM. In this process it was important that alternative infrastructures were available, and the museum itself also become more dispersed, more polycentric.

The underlying effect of an "economics of attention" (Lanham 2007) also explains the campaign's success and its later repercussions. Whilst many similar projects (art and nonart related) are put forward by marginalized groups every year, not all of them reach wider attention from the general public. That a certain level of contestation exists benefits identity legitimation. This legitimation process generates awareness of additional opportunities opened up by the contribution from other actors in markets, governments, and society. Although it must be said that not all forms of identity need or should depend on disputes to exist, this has been the case for queerness worldwide.

Besides the meeting point of supply and demand, markets can also be fruitful sources of knowledge and culture as they result from accumulated beliefs (Storr 2015). Markets are part of cultures and sometimes cultures in themselves. They rely on various kinds of knowledge, some of which are shared goods that may eventually turn into economic inputs and outputs (Dekker and Kuchař, Introduction). Eventually, markets can take over the challenge of representing identities alongside other institutions such as, for example, transforming queerness into big festivals, gay parades, pubs, restaurants, or specialized tourism that all seek to cater to differentiation. These can ultimately help people to self-govern, give meaning to their identities, and be accepted. More critical views could see this as commodification of human culture (Rifkin 2000) or even a way to stabilize a dynamic concept such as queer identity into tradeable goods and services. Either way, the recognition of new identities provides an important resource. And the recognition of these identities is fostered by polycentricity.

In the case of state-induced action, public art museums and semi-public institutions can also "re-imagin[e] their role beyond the mausoleum of artworks" (Witcomb 2007) and draw on the opportunity to build up environments where identity expression is not seen as a threat, but rather as an asset. Although the set of recognized identities is not easy to change, the QM case demonstrated that there are opportunities for doing so and a few contemporary examples in museums already emerge (Adair and Levin 2020). The next step in this process would be to observe if and how other established institutions change their practices into more diverse and welcoming settings.

10.5 CONCLUSION

This chapter used the case of the exhibition "Queer Museum: Cartographies of Difference" to analyze how identity is governed as a knowledge commons. The case allows us to highlight different ways of governing this commons, in both monocentric and polycentric ways. Because of the resistance the Queer Museum encountered from the state government and private actors, it had to seek alternative exhibition spaces and funders. This led to a more dispersed museum, with a greater involvement of its backers. The chapter has argued that the resulting contestation was important in generating attention and recognition for queer identity. Rather than stressing the shared meanings, I have thus sought to demonstrate the importance of conflicts over meaning, and recognized identity, for the making of contributions to the knowledge commons.

For this contestation to happen it was important that alternative social infrastructures were present. In particular the crowdfunding technology was an important resource for the organizers of the QM, but this was also true for the Parque Lage School of Visual Arts. By using these existing infrastructures in new ways, the QM also contributed to the value of these infrastructures. The crowdfunding campaign was a novel way to organize an exhibition in the Brazilian context, and the Parque Lage School had not been previously used for such large-scale exhibitions. If accepted the queer identity, and queer art, QM will provide an important shared resource for the development of new initiatives in Brazilian society. In that sense this chapter has highlighted how knowledge commons are altered, and how they could give rise to other entrepreneurial acts by private, social, and public actors.

A critical remark is in order about the alternative institutional solution of the QM. Crowdfunding is particularly useful as short-term funding solution. Even if the infrastructure itself is relatively permanent, studies have demonstrated that it can often not be successfully used for the long-term financing of an organization.

Important lessons can be learned from this case: (a) the access to diverse cultural goods can be enhanced by diverse institutional landscapes, to which I referred to as polycentric governance; (b) identities can be regarded as knowledge commons in the sense that they can be self-governed and act as resources that further fuel social life through markets, state, and collective action; (c) knowledge commons such as these can become more evident when disputes and public contestations arise, hence allowing agents to recognize themselves, their agendas and take part in social legitimation processes.

This chapter does not seek to suggest that solutions like the ones implemented by the QM are in themselves optimal or even desirable in the medium term. Instead it sought to analyze a moment of contestation in which temporary alternative institutional forms were developed. The possibility for developing such solutions is especially relevant for minority groups in a society. As such the case of QM museum can be informative for other minority groups whose identity is not (fully) legitimized, and that face constraints from more established or official channels.

One consequence of this case is that artistic expressions intertwine with political quarrels in the public space. The meaning of the artworks also changed through this process: their meaning was made more political by it, and they reached new audiences because of it. Ultimately, the QM represents the combination of two debates: on the one hand, how institutions allow for the polyphony of representations in their actions; and, on the other hand, the role of new financial tools as both a resource whose properties agents can openly rely on and as an infrastructure that helps to articulate commons such as identities.

REFERENCES

Adair, Joshua G., and Amy K. Levin. 2020. *Museums, Sexuality, and Gender Activism*. London: Routledge.

Aligica, Paul Dragos. 2019. *Public Entrepreneurship, Citizenship, and Self-Governance*. Cambridge: Cambridge University Press.

Anderson, Benedict. 1991. *Imagined Communities: Reflections on the Origin and Spread of Nationalism*. London: Verso.

Benevides, Bruna G., and Sayonara N. B. Nogueira. 2020. "Dossiê assassinatos contra travestis brasileiras e violência e transexuais em 2019." Accessed August 10, 2020. https://antrabrasil.files.wordpress.com/2020/01/dossic3aa-dos-assassinatos-e-da-violc3aancia-contra-pessoas-trans-em-2019.pdf.

Becker, Howard S. 2018. *Outsiders: Studies in the Sociology of Deviance*. New York: Free Press.

Belleflamme, Paul, Thomas Lambert, and Armin Schwienbacher. 2014. "Crowdfunding: Tapping the Right Crowd." *Journal of Business Venturing* 29 (5): 585–609.

Benfeitoria. 2018. "Queermuseu No Parque Lage." *Benfeitoria: Crowdfunding Com Comissão Livre e Metas Múltiplas*. Accessed September 2019. https://benfeitoria.com/queermuseu.

Bennett, Tony. 1995. "Art and Theory: The Politics of the Invisible." In *The Birth of the Museum: History and Theory Politics*, edited by Tony Bennett, 59–87. Oxford: Routledge.

Bhabha, Homi K. 2012. *The Location of Culture*. Hoboken, NJ: Taylor & Francis.

Boltanski, Luc, and Laurent Thévenot. 2006. *On Justification: Economies of Worth*. Princeton, NJ: Princeton University Press.

Bulte, Erwin, and Richard D. Horan. 2010. "Identities in the Commons: The Dynamics of Normsand Social Capital." *The B.E. Journal of Economic Analysis & Policy* 10 (1): 1–35.

Butler, Judith. 2006. *Gender Trouble*. New York, London: Routledge.

Callis, April Scarlette. 2014. "Bisexual, Pansexual, Queer: Non-Binary Identities and the Sexual Borderlands." *Sexualities* 17 (1–2): 63–80.

Canclini, Néstor García. 1995. *Hybrid Cultures: Strategies for Entering and Leaving Modernity*. Minneapolis: University of Minnesota Press.

Carneiro, Júlia Dias. 2018. "'Queermuseu', a Exposição Mais Debatida e Menos Vista Dos Últimos Tempos, Reabre No Rio." *BBC News Brasil*. Accessed August 16, 2018. www.bbc.com/portuguese/brasil-45191250.

Cohen, Anthony P. 2000. *Signifying Identities: Anthropological Perspectives on Boundaries and Contested Values*. New York: Taylor & Francis.

Cumming, Douglas, and Lars Hornuf. 2018. *The Economics of Crowdfunding: Startups, Portals and Investor Behavior*. Cham: Palgrave Macmillan.

Dalla Chiesa, Carolina. 2020. "From Digitalisation to Crowdfunding Platforms: Fomenting the Cultural Commons." In *Cultural Commons and Urban Dynamics: A Multidisciplinary Perspective*, edited by Emanuele Macri, Valeria Morea, and Michele Trimarchi, 173–186. New York: Springer.

Dekker, Erwin, and Ana Carolina Rodrigues. 2019. "The Political Economy of Brazilian Cultural Policy: A Case Study of the Rouanet Law." *Journal of Public Finance and Public Choice* 34 (2): 149–171.

Erber, Laura. 2018. "Crítica: Mostra 'Queermuseu' Só é Transgressora Para Conservadores." *Folha de S.Paulo*. Accessed September 12, 2018. www1.folha.uol.com.br/ilustrada/2018/09/mostra-queermuseu-so-e-transgressora-para-conservadores.html.

Esche, Charles. 2005. *Collectivity, Modest Proposals and Foolish Optimism*. Accessed September 2019. www.neme.org/texts/collectivity

Frischmann, Brett M. 2014. *Infrastructure: The Social Value of Shared Resources*. Oxford: Oxford University Press.

Fidelis, Gaudêncio. 2018. "The Museum of Deviance." In *Queermuseu: Cartografias Da Diferença Na Arte Brasileira*, edited by Fidelis, Gaudêncio and Escola de Artes Visuais do Parque Lage, 137–141. Rio De Janeiro: AMEAV.

Fidelis, Gaudêncio, and Escola de Artes Visuais do Parque Lage. 2018. *Queermuseu: Cartografias Da Diferença Na Arte Brasileira*. Rio De Janeiro: AMEAV.

Goffman, Erving. 1990. *The Presentation of Self in Everyday Life*. London: Penguin.

Halbwachs, Maurice. 1992. *On Collective Memory*. Chicago: University of Chicago Press.

Herbert, Stine, and Anne Szefer Karlsen. 2013. *Self-Organised*. London: Open Editions.

Hess, Charlotte. 2008. "Mapping the New Commons." *SSRN Electronic Journal*. DOI: https://doi.org/10.2139/ssrn.1356835.

Hess, Charlotte, and Elinor Ostrom. 2007. *Understanding Knowledge as a Commons: From Theory to Practice*. Cambridge, MA: MIT Press.

Hobsbawm, Eric, and T. Ranger. 1993. *The Invention of Tradition*. Cambridge: Cambridge University Press.

Holder, Jane B., and Tatiana Flessas. 2008. "Emerging Commons." *Social and Legal Studies* 17 (3): 299–310.

Hoogwaerts, L. 2016. "Museums, Exchanges, and Their Contribution to Joseph Nye's Concept of 'Soft Power.'" *Museum & Society* 14 (2): 313–322.

Huyssen, Andreas. 1995. *Twilight Memories: Marking Time in a Culture of Amnesia*. New York: Routledge.

Hyvärinen, Matti. 2010. "Revisiting the Narrative Turns." *Life Writing* 7 (1): 69–82.

Koyama, Mark, and Noel D. Johnson. 2019. *Persecution and Toleration: The Long Road to Religious Freedom*. Cambridge: Cambridge University Press.

Lanham, Richard A. 2007. *The Economics of Attention: Style and Substance in the Age of Information*. Chicago: University of Chicago Press.

Londoño, Ernesto. 2018. "In Brazil, 'Queer Museum' Is Censored, Debated, then Celebrated." *The New York Times*, August 26, 2018. www.nytimes.com/2018/08/26/world/americas/queer-museum-rio-de-janeiro-brazil.html.

Madison, Michael J., Brett M. Frischmann, and Katherine J. Strandburg. 2019. "Knowledge Commons." In *Routledge Handbook of the Study of the Commons*, edited by Blake Hudson, Jonathan D. Rosenbloom, and Daniel H. Cole, 76–90. New York: Routledge.

Marstine, Janet. 2017. *Critical Practice: Artists, Museums, Ethics*. Abingdon: Routledge.

Meghani, Shamira A., and Humaira Saeed. 2019. "Postcolonial/Sexuality, or, Sexuality in 'Other' Contexts: Introduction." *Journal of Postcolonial Writing* 55 (3): 293–307.

Megyesi, B., and Mike, K. 2016. Organising Collective Reputation: An Ostromian Perspective. *International Journal of the Commons* 10(2): 1082–1099.

North, Douglass C. 2005. *Understanding the Process of Economic Change*. Princeton, NJ: Princeton University Press.

Ostrom, Elinor. 2010. "Beyond Markets and States: Polycentric Governance of Complex Economic Systems." *American Economic Review* 100 (3): 641–672.

2015. *Governing the Commons*. Cambridge: Cambridge University Press.

Parque Lage. 2020. "International." *Escola de Artes Visuais do Parque Lage*. Accessed October 15, 2020. http://eavparquelage.rj.gov.br/international/.

Phillips, Don. 2017. "Brazilian Queer Art Exhibition Cancelled after Campaign by Rightwing Protesters." *The Guardian*. Accessed September 12, 2017. www.theguardian.com/world/2017/sep/12/brazil-queer-art-show-cancelled-protest.

Rifkin, Jeremy. 2000. *The Age of Access: The New Culture of Hypercapitalism Where All of Life Is a Paid-for Experience*. New York: J. P. Tarcher/Putnam.

Sandell, Richard. 1998. "Museums as Agents of Social Inclusion." *Museum Management and Curatorship* 17 (4): 401–418.

Sant'Ana, Tiago. 2017. "Queermuseu: A Apropriação Que Acabou Em Censura" *Le Monde Diplomatique*. Accessed September 12, 2019. https://diplomatique.org.br/queermuseu-a-apropriacao-que-acabou-em-censura/.

Simon, Nina. 2017. *The Participatory Museum*. Santa Cruz, CA: Museum 2.0.

Sokefeld, Martin. 1999. "Debating Self, Identity and Culture in Anthropology." *Current Anthropology* 40 (4): 417–448.

Storr, Virgil Henry. 2015. *Understanding the Culture of Markets*. Abingdon: Routledge.

Sul-21. 2017. "Ativistas LGBT Protestam Contra Fechamento de Exposição No Santander e Por Visibilidade." *Sul 21*. Accessed September 12, 2019. www.sul21.com.br/ultimas-noticias/geral/2017/09/ativistas-lgbt-protestam-contra-fechamento-de-exposicao-no-santander-e-por-visibilidade/.

Taylor, Charles. 1989. *Sources of the Self: The Making of the Modern Identity*. Cambridge, MA: Harvard University Press.

Teixeira, Mariana Roquette. 2016. "Do 'Museu Aberto' Ao 'Museu Disperso': Desafios Ao Poder." *Midas*, no. 6 (March). DOI: https://doi.org/10.4000/midas.1016.

VEJA. 2017. "Em Protesto, Obra de Lygia Clark é Apresentada Fora Da Exposição | Rio Grande Do Sul." n.d. Accessed April 15, 2019. https://veja.abril.com.br/blog/rio-grande-do-sul/em-protesto-obra-de-lygia-clark-e-apresentada-fora-da-exposicao/.

Vergo, P. 1989. *The New Museology*. London: Reaktion Books.

Witcomb, Andrea. 2007. *Re-imagining the Museum: Beyond the Mausoleum*. London: Routledge.

11

Understanding Different Qualities of the Knowledge Commons in Contemporary Cities

Youn Sun Won and Arjo Klamer

In the past ten years, many (local) policymakers and entrepreneurs have been fascinated with the economic potential of so-called creative industries and smart cities. This fascination was stirred by the conviction that creativity boosts the (local) economy. And because the urban economy accounts for 70 per cent of the global GDP, and as more than half of the total world's population lives in cities, creative industries are all the more relevant both socially and economically. Based on principles of generating creative attractors in city centres, stimulating the creative class, fostering creative communities and developing creative spaces in local areas – blocks, districts, towns and cities – scientific and political practices began to focus on creative urban transition. So did the entrepreneurs.

An important force in all this has been the contribution of Richard Florida with his work on the economic impact of the creative class (Florida 2002). Policymakers across the globe are trying to do spatial transformation to attract creative workers and high-skilled people. They do so by means of developing cultural amenities in cities or local areas. Following what they thought Florida's message to be, they assumed that the congregation of people employed in the creative industries would bring about in a spontaneous way local economic prosperity and an improvement of social qualities. Accordingly, many towns hastened to construct cultural centres and innovation hubs in order to attract creatives and encourage the development of creative industries.

In recent years there has been a backlash. People began to see the shadowed side of the focus on creativity and creative industries. Critical scholars began wondering whether the promised economic returns materialised, how the vulnerable neighbourhoods fared in this new regime, how the quality of the urban environment was affected overall, and, more particularly, whether the sources that were poured into creative sites came at the expense of the sources for affordable housing.

The suspicion arose that when the urban landscape and the local economy improved due to the influx of creatives, not all inhabitants profited and some even lost in terms of the quality of jobs, of their housing and their neighbourhoods. Many people actually felt forced to leave their neighbourhoods and their towns, mainly because they could not continue to pay the rent in their "regenerated" neighbourhoods. A policy directed at creativity may, therefore, have an increase in inequality as the unintended consequence.

Moreover, a loss of local identity is another critical issue. This happens when people from the outside move in and change the environment. Or it happens when areas are overtaken by tourism. The tourists, attracted by a creative atmosphere, cause overcrowding and a flux of commercial activities to satisfy their wants.

It seems vague to understand what the influx of creative activities contributes to the way people live together, apart from the financial outcomes. Does the quality of social life change indeed as is now surmised? In what way do cultural qualities change? Social and cultural qualities become increasingly important in a new economy focused on urban qualities and a meaningful life. City planners and politicians need to determine what works and they need to understand the dynamics of social and cultural qualities. Entrepreneurs and people who seek a place to do their (creative) thing want to be well informed as well of the qualitative characteristics of such a space, and that on the basis of data. Unfortunately for them, standard (economic) accounts of city life do little to meet their needs.

This chapter, therefore, explores a new approach to making sense of the social and cultural qualities of cities in the new economy. This is the so-called Value-Based Approach (VBA) with novel concepts such as shared goods and practices, willingness-to-contribute (WTC) (Klamer 2016), and – a key notion in our application – a commons, more precisely, the knowledge commons.

For the sake of understanding the notion of the commons, this study attempts to elaborate how the commons are generated, organised and appropriated in local neighbourhoods and how they can be studied empirically. By characterising different qualities of the commons in contemporary cities, this study attempts to identify certain qualities of the shared goods that specific neighbourhoods in Seoul and Amsterdam provide. Those neighbourhoods were the subject of urban regeneration programmes by way of cultural and creative interventions. One case that appears to exemplify what is precisely meant by a different understanding of the notion of the commons is the knowledge commons. In order to find out whether the different qualities of the knowledge commons can be compared in significant ways, we will use the Governing Knowledge Commons framework as inspired by the work of Elinor Ostrom (1990) and developed further by Frischmann, Madison and Strandburg (2014).

This chapter consists of four sections. The first section is an overview of what is happening in contemporary cities and what is missing in the current perspective on what people do in the new economy. The second section presents a new framework for analysing urban economies, the value based approach. The third section reflects on the methodological implications of these different perspectives. The fourth section applies this framework to an empirical exploration of the commons in Amsterdam and Seoul. This study also shows how city government can contribute to or damage environments that are conducive and supporting for generating and refining relevant commons in a society.

11.1 WHAT IS IMPORTANT TO CITIES IN THE NEW ECONOMY?

By and large, the question of what makes some cities better than others has been addressed with the standard economic paradigm. According to this paradigm, success denotes economic success and is evident in the form of the growth of the production goods and services as measured with GDP, financial returns, and the number of jobs. It follows that urban development is about the development of markets; governmental interventions are directed at the advancement of market activities. Schools prepare citizens for the labour market, museums strive to attract tourists, and so do shopping centres and nightclubs. The city is seen as a source for economic activity, more precisely, financial transactions. The new economy, however, is more about creativity and innovation, and about social and cultural qualities. Talented individuals are seeking a meaningful and inspiring life, they focus on their well-being over and above their material welfare and like to have a sense of endless opportunities. To serve the need for social and cultural qualities organisations and (local) governments have to look beyond the growth of quantities of products and services, and develop an interest in issues like the balance between life and work, lively neighbourhoods, good social infrastructure with a great variety of social networks, and a range of cultural spaces. Important themes are increasingly sustainability, circularity, social empowerment, community-based solutions, cultural qualities, creativity, innovation, co-creation, and sharing. Firms recognise the potential of the creative industries and increasingly realise the need for qualitative approaches, such as sharing knowledge and practices, and cultural entrepreneurship. Even urban developers are appropriating a different, more comprehensive way to revitalise a town. So, cities in the new economy strive for a great range of social and cultural practices that generate not only economic value (jobs and incomes) but also social and cultural values that are key for quality of life.

When we consider the importance of social and cultural qualities that a city generates with its practices, we get interested in the questions of where people meet and what kinds of practices they produce and share (Collins 2004). In this sense, as will be discussed in the next section, the social infrastructure and the social and cultural practices of a city over and beyond the economic value help us explore these questions. Here we side with various scholars who have challenged a single-minded focus on urban economies with its penchant to elevate economic and financial criteria as sole indicators of how well a city is doing (Jacobs 1964; Bell 1973; Harvey 1990; Pratt 2009; Florida 2017; Chetty et al. 2018; Klinenberg 2018).

An important argument pertaining to this discussion is prefaced on the idea that social and cultural qualities cannot be obtained simply by an influx of the creative class. More precisely, urban creativity is not something that an influx of highly skilled people can generate by itself. Csikszentmihalyi and others have stressed the importance of the right environmental qualities and of ecosystem for innovative activities (Csikszentmihalyi 1991; Moretti 2012). Attractive cultural spaces are only part of that. The right educational institutions can be important, too, as well as the entrepreneurial climate as depicted by Currid-Halkett for New York in *The Warhol Economy* (2008). Following this, an important question that cities have to engage with in addition to making sense of the importance of urban qualities concerns a different approach that takes into account social and cultural dimensions of city life. Those engaged in the shared practices will be more attentive to human interactions and contributions, and to the meanings and reflections that people share.

We, therefore, are in need of a different perspective that does justice to these complicated developments in cities. It must be an institutional approach that serves not only city officials but also people who are trying to figure out which cities suit them best to make a life and a living. That framework is, so we suggest, the one provided by the value-based approach (Klamer 2016).

11.2 A NEW INSTITUTIONAL APPROACH

11.2.1 *Changing the Perspective with the Value-Based Approach*

Let us begin with an example to understand the differences of Value-Based Approach (VBA) from the standard economic approach. We take a revitalisation project in the city of Hilversum of The Netherlands as an example (as one of the authors was involved in the process as political governor of the town). Hilversum is a provincial town in a green area close to Amsterdam. Its main claim to fame is the presence of the media sector with most of the radio and television studios that broadcast in The Netherlands. At the centre of the town is a market square with a farmer's market on each Wednesday and Saturday. On the other days, the square was empty and quite desolate until 2017 when a food hall opened in an old, then abandoned, building on the west side of the square. The building had housed a movie cinema until 2014. City planners and their advisors had proposed to take the building down in order to create more space and open the arteries that the city planner a century ago had designed for the town. There was some opposition to this plan. Older inhabitants had nostalgic associations with the building. The city government discussed what to do. It was pointed out that the building had historic significance for Hilversum as it was built as a factory of transistors in the 1920s, that factory had been the reason the first radio operators chose Hilversum as their residence. The television studios followed after the Second World War. The building signified the historical start of the media sector in Hilversum. Before the building became a cinema, it was also used by a car dealer. All that was not sufficient to convince the city government, but when it was discovered that the building had a facade with some sculptures and a curved cement roof that was unique in The Netherlands, the governors decided to save the building and to organise a competition for the best plan. A local entrepreneur won with his concept for a food hall. He named it Mout.

In 2017 Mout opened and ever since the centre of Hilversum has been transformed, attracting even people from Amsterdam to visit. Mout has become a bustling centre where people meet, work and relax, with regular events taking place. Even though it appears to be a commercial initiative that has turned out quite well for the entrepreneur, it adds a great deal more to the town. It has become a shared space for the inhabitants of Hilversum, a place where people meet business contacts, socialise and work. It has given a boost to the social and cultural qualities of the town. Social qualities have increased because of what people perceive as the "coziness" of Mout (coziness or "gezelligheid" is a key Dutch value). Cultural qualities have been enriched as well: the place is a source of inspiration of the creatives in town. Hilversum, as a media town, attracts all kinds of creatives who now have a place to meet, a place that reminds them of the vibrance of the city of Amsterdam. In this way, Mout has become a locally shared space over and above the commercial venue it is.

The VBA invites us to look beyond the economics of a place like Mout, and also beyond its physical (architectonic) and functional aspects that the city planners stressed. The VBA considers the values at stake, the social and cultural qualities that are affected. When we look at cities through the lenses that the VBA provides, we want to know what values are important for those who inhabit, govern, visit and work in a city, that is, what are their values. When we try to assess spaces like Mout, we are not only interested in the financial and infrastructural conditions but also in the way it enables inhabitants, businesses, workers, visitors and governors to realise their values. In terms of the VBA we would say that people are realising values by way of Mout, and that Mout has contributed to social and cultural qualities. Call this the shared goods that Mout generates.

11.2.2 *Shared Goods and Willingness to Contribute*

Shared goods are goods that are "shared by a few people, or a group of people, without a clear legal definition of ownership" (Klamer 2016: 80), and are usually practices, implying a sense of "us" exclusively. We thus use the terms shared goods and shared practices interchangeably. Shared goods include one or another kind of relationship based on co-creation/co-working, such as a social network, companionship, a neighbourhood or friendship. Shared goods mostly serve social and cultural values and require mutual contributions and participation in order to produce and consume the goods (Klamer 2016). A neighbourhood is a good because it requires efforts to acquire, and it gives all kinds of benefits, just as private and public goods. The difference is that you can acquire a private good by paying for it, or enjoy a collective good just by being part of a collective. A neighbourhood is shared by people who live and work there. When someone claims to have a great neighbourhood he or she shares that good with the neighbours. What is at stake here is that the meaning of the neighbourhood refers to something beyond the legal and spatial definition, and also includes what people do and what values people realise in the neighbourhood, such as localities, community activities and local ambience.

To acquire a shared good, to call the neighbourhood yours, you need to contribute somehow. A friendship, the typical example of a shared good, comes about when both friends contribute to it. A contribution like volunteering to do something valuable is a contribution when it is not rewarded with something equivalent in return. Willingness to contribute, thus, is the key (Table 11.1).

TABLE 11.1. *A new type of goods in the new economy*

Key terms	Description
Willingness to contribute (WTC)	• We need to focus on qualities instead of quantities • Values are qualities, price is a quantity and is therefore not a value
Shared goods	• Shared goods exist usually as a form of "practices" • Shared goods have shared ownership • Others are excluded from ownership and there is rivalry • People acquire ownership by contributing to it, using it, and participating in it • Shared goods cannot be bought and sold; they do not have a price • Examples are: practices that people share, knowledge, conversations, neighbourhood, community activities, art, music, society, outcomes of cultural economics

Source: Elaborated by authors.

Willingness to contribute promotes the production of shared goods. Shared goods are ongoing and are visible in the interactions, the conversations, the co-creations that take place. For instance, practices, which are a sort of shared goods, generate and stimulate a commons when the practices become a source for others to join. Thus, shared goods are distinguished from the commons; however, not all shared practices contribute to a commons. Friendships and families, for example, will be too exclusive to constitute a commons. Shared practices may be more exclusive than the commons. You may, for whatever reason, not be able to join a particular group of creatives. But the activities of a group of creatives who undertake diverse activities and contribute a great deal to the liveliness and creative atmosphere of an urban space will undoubtedly contribute to and add value to a particular commons, for instance, a specific knowledge commons in town.

11.2.3 *The Commons within Contemporary Cities*

The notion of the commons has been conceptualised since the 1960s: Hardin and Nobel Laureate Elinor Ostrom opened up a rich discussion, and many other scholars developed the discussion in a vast array of sectors (Hardin 1968; Ostrom 1990; Hess 2008; Harvey 2012; Frischmann, Madison and Strandburg 2014; Borch and Kornberger 2015). Among others, this study focuses on the two points: a community-based framework that Ostrom demonstrated by reviewing empirical studies and characteristics of the commons within contemporary cities. She showed that communities are able to self-regulate their commons without resorting to governmental controls or privatisation.

Following Ostrom's contribution, some city officials have become aware of the potential of the commons in understanding the new economy. To what extent Ostrom's notion of the commons is practical and useful in an urban setting is questionable, though. The main reason is that the character of urban commons is different from what Ostrom had in mind. Ostrom's notion of the commons applies especially to natural resources, common pool resources as she calls them, whereas the commons in cities are mostly about creative and knowledge activities. The latter work differently. In the case of natural resources, the main problem is excessive usage and depletion. In the case of creative and knowledge commons usage is needed for the maintenance of its values. Where people use and consume natural resources in order to benefit from them, people need to participate and contribute to creative and knowledge commons in order to benefit. Consequently, the free rider problem does not apply (Borch and Kornberger 2015; Foster and Iaione 2016; Klamer 2019; Won 2020).

The commons, as we use the concept, is therefore different from the commons as usually understood. In contemporary cities the commons are about practices rather than about natural resources and physical development. Practices are characterised mostly by qualities: some creative practices may be more creative, more engaging, more open, more intense than others (Won 2020). The commons in contemporary cities are about how involved people are, how accessible they are to newcomers, how rich they are. The reason that creatives choose Amsterdam over Hilversum, or Rotterdam for that matter, is because they appreciate the qualities of the commons of Amsterdam above those of Hilversum and Rotterdam.

We define the commons as a "source, like an ongoing conversation out there. People can participate in it, draw benefits from it, but how and to what extent depends on the conditions of participation (or of membership)" (Klamer 2016: 81). In this context, we observe commons of all sorts and see cities differently. We would argue that Mout is a place to create shared goods, such as co-creation activities. A commons as the one boosted by Mout turns out to cater especially to the creatives who are drawn to the type of food culture of Mout (like poke bowls and street food), and to the chance to run into others like themselves. This is in line with another insight of the VBA, which is that people not only work to earn an income but seek to share practices and knowledge, and to contribute to them. Much of creative activity takes place in informal settings, with fortuitous meetings and casual conversations. We therefore see in cities that are known to be creative the emergence of all kinds of spaces like Mout, where people gather to drink a cappuccino together, to have some food and to talk. This realisation calls for a new perspective that enables cities to clarify functions of buildings in a market square, or, to take another example, social infrastructures, such as public libraries.

If libraries were thought of as places where people went to borrow books, we think of them now as spaces that provide manifold shared practices in which people can participate, like storytelling for children, reading clubs, meetings of retirees or networking for moms. Public libraries become increasingly spaces not only for knowledge accumulation but also for social and cultural practices with an aim at developing the commons. So even though most of these shared goods do not generate much, if any, financial returns, they are significant for a civilised society, and for a creative economy. The point is that the qualities are characteristics of the commons that mostly are in the form of ongoing practices, knowledge, conversations in many cases, or activities of all sorts. But how can we recognise these characteristics? The big research challenge is to figure out how to "assess" the social and cultural qualities of a commons. How can we determine that, say, the commons in one city is different from or superior to the commons in another city?

In the search for answers, the GKC framework accommodates a way through which to facilitate the flow of the knowledge commons and shared goods. We argue that the knowledge commons comes about by promoting shared goods to which knowledge workers contribute, usually in informal settings, such as networking, socialisation and talking with others. Accordingly, the social sphere counts.

11.2.4 *Knowledge Commons and Shared Goods*

Let us recall the basics of this volume that Dekker and Kuchař introduced: markets are cultural and coincide with a form of culture that relies on shared goods.

The emphasis on the relationship between shared goods and the commons is because of our interest in the new market interactions that reside, above all, in the dynamics of new economic activities. The presumption is that such commons only thrive in a certain urban environment that encourages creativity and an active community (Dietz, Ostrom and Stern 2003). Important here is a supportive environment that is not merely about the great number of jobs or the increase in tax revenues, but about the presence of creative vibes based on local participation. Good educational institutions such as universities, art academies and libraries, a great variety of cafes and restaurants, museums, bookstores, cinemas, theatres and incubators constitute sources for people living in the city as well as for commercial parties in need of creative inputs. When the qualities of certain commons are considered low, people can join efforts to generate, organise and appropriate the commons by virtue of developing shared practices in order to boost such qualities.

More to the point, we argue, following Ostrom and Jacobs, that the knowledge commons, as one of the commons, requires strong social participation that enables cities to engender, organise, and govern the knowledge commons within cities, in the sense that shared goods are produced and reproduced by active contributions and sharing (Jacobs 1986; Hess and Ostrom 2007; Klamer 2016). It is, above all, the local people who enrich shared goods in neighbourhoods/ communities/ cities. Despite this, the debate on what contributes to urban qualities often misses this key point; the fallacy of the Floridian approach is the case. Albeit the commons in contemporary cities rely on social and cultural practices, the debate on the commons often misses this key point.

Consider, in this respect, the knowledge commons. The qualities of the knowledge commons that Amsterdam creates are different from those in Rotterdam, since the characteristics of shared goods that the two cities produce are different. Ostrom also points out that a revised approach to the knowledge commons is required due to the complexity and interdisciplinary nature of the knowledge commons. For example, the knowledge commons does not rely on physical resources, but focuses on the community (Levin 2007);[1] shared knowledge is engendered by participation and contribution (Klamer 2016; Won 2020). The more people who share and contribute to it, the richer the knowledge commons becomes. A high degree of social and cultural qualities is more important than a strong government intervention for the community-based governance; more and more, social interactions become important (Frischmann, Madison and Strandburg 2014). In this vein, we want to connect the GKC Framework and the VBA to identify the nature of the knowledge commons in the new economy context, and to what extent they spill over in other social and market activities.

[1] See Levine (2007).

The GKC framework describes how the knowledge commons are generated, used and governed. There have to be certain resources, a relevant community, rules or norms that participants heed, the participants, or actors as they are called in the framework: first, resource characteristics could be articulated by the economic, social and cultural dynamics; second, sense-making activities[2] and willingness to contribute characterise attributes of the community and rules-in-use; third, social and cultural practices articulate action situations, and thus, understanding the characteristics of shared goods can be said to effectively benefit the action arena of this framework; fourth, important values that people in the community strive for would help cities to understand patterns of interactions. In this sense, the VBA is useful in articulating the process of how shared goods endorse the knowledge commons.

It is worth addressing a better strategy for community self-governance of knowledge commons through this framework; yet, the focus of this chapter is more on an understanding of why shared goods are important to engender the knowledge commons. The VBA takes the questioning towards those who participate and contribute to a commons in contemporary cities. The question to ask is what are the important values and purposes that they are valorising by partaking in shared practices. Why is this question important? Consider, for instance, when people in a certain place appreciate knowing more about modern art, and value being up-to-date, they stand to benefit from the presence of a modern art museum and a series of serious art galleries as well as regular meetings, seminars and symposia about the arts. Then it is to be expected that the quality of the knowledge commons of the place is closely associated with modern art. However, the presence of those related physical infrastructures per se does not guarantee creation of the relevant knowledge commons. Therefore, we are in need of identifying what kind of social and cultural practices exist in a certain place. By doing so, we can characterise a particular social and cultural practice that enhances a certain quality of the commons at either the neighbourhood or the city level. What qualities of the knowledge commons do people produce, reproduce and appropriate for the new economy? How do we characterise different qualities of the knowledge commons?

Following the discussion, Table 11.2 illustrates the basics of the combined framework driven by the VBA. It extends the market-driven understanding and considers qualities of the commons.

We do not claim that the characteristics of shared goods denote qualities of the commons, but say that they will be of value in making sense of the relevant qualities that the given community/ group/ neighbourhood/ city produce. Based on these remarks, what matters in the following part is to pay close attention to characterising shared goods with an empirical analysis.

[2] See Klamer (2019).

TABLE 11.2. *Differences between the previous standpoint and a new perspective.*

Object/unit	Previous understanding	New understanding
Cities	Characterised by the market dynamics	Characterised by the economic, social and cultural dynamics
A commons and cities	Cities are considered as shared resources, such as CPRs in the spatial/physical sense	Cities in themselves are not considered as a commons and instead cities are considered as a place full of different qualities of the commons
Framework for understanding a commons	CPRs Framework	GKC Framework
Goods in cities	Private/Public goods	Shared goods
Major drivers that generate the goods	Preference/Surplus The amount of production and consumption	Willingness to contribute Shared practices Sense-making activities[a]
Determinant	Transactions/Pricing (Cost–benefit analysis)	Value proposition (Value-oriented production and consumption)
Spheres	Market and Governance (Market-driven approach)	Cultural, Social, Market, Governance, and Oikos Spheres (Value-based approach)

[a] See Klamer (2019).
Source: Won 2020.

11.3 METHODS FOR MEASURING THE QUALITIES OF URBAN COMMONS

For the empirical analysis, let us start with a key proposition of this volume that the knowledge as a shared good constitutes our civilised society, supporting markets. And some part of knowledge exists as a commons. This section situates this idea into the contemporary urban context by raising the questions: How do we notice that some neighbourhoods/ cities provide a more supportive environment for engendering shared goods than others? What qualities contribute to civilisation of contemporary cities?

The willingness to contribute is the input of actors. But it is not possible to measure it because of a lack of data and difficulties in identifying the magnitudes or activities that we would need to record. We therefore attempt to measure these contributions in an indirect way, through what people say. A particular topic of conversation between people implies a marked knowledge creation of that domain and it supports the relevant businesses – regardless of whether the knowledge is entirely shared by the entrepreneurs or not. This study makes use of big data, mostly from social media, and analyses the patterns of what people talk about.

With an emphasis on the interpretive analysis, the data analysis attempts to interpret communications in social media channels and search engines. The attempt here is to detect patterns in a massive amount of data by means of web scraping of conversations between people by counting word frequencies. This is a popular way to analyse social media data (Schroeder 2014). This study uses open access data: NAVER (provides search engines and social media channels in South Korea) and Twitter for the case of Seoul, and Twitter for the case of Amsterdam. Due to the limitation in accessing personal information for sorting out specific population, this study sets geographical and periodic scopes: Jung-Gu in Seoul between 2013 and 2015, and Westergasfabriek (West Gas Factory) in Amsterdam between 2015 and 2016 (Won 2020). We do so because both districts have been hailed as creative neighbourhoods in their respective cities.

The idea is that these patterns reflect characteristics of shared goods, such as sense-making activities (Klamer 2019), of the two neighbourhoods and indicate certain qualities of a commons. These different qualities contribute to understanding the action arena of the GKC framework. What do people write about, what concerns do they share and what issues do they address? Do people mainly communicate about process issues, or do they also talk about the content of what they are doing? Do social themes dominate the chattering or is the creative process the big topic? The outcome matters, for example, for people considering moving to a city. In order to discern significant differences between two different neighbourhoods we attempt to characterise shared goods that both neighbourhoods produce with the empirical analysis.

11.4 EMPIRICAL METHODS FOR CHARACTERISING THE QUALITIES OF THE COMMONS

11.4.1 *Attributes of Jung-Gu, Seoul*

Seoul, the capital city of South Korea, has served an important role economically, socially and culturally. The city has been the centre of South Korean society and economy. The intervention of the Seoul Metropolitan Government has all but dominated South Korean society. However, since 1991, the central government has encouraged the local government to develop local economic, social and cultural sources independently. The city of Seoul also became one of the local governments, instead of functioning as part of the central government. Even so, it continues to be influential statewide as it governs the centre of business activity.

Jung-Gu is the smallest district of Seoul. It has served as a centre of media, business and administrative functions of the city. A major challenge that the municipality has faced is to achieve transition from manufacturing to the creative industries. For the sake of the transition, as is customary in South Korea, governmental interventions have strongly promoted creative workers, appealing to the creative economy since 2013 (Won 2020). For the transition towards the new economy, the district focused on economic prosperity by first developing tourism businesses, as did many other cities. At the same time, the municipality improved the living conditions for inhabitants, though it is unclear whether the approach contributed to creative transition via social and cultural practices.

11.4.2 *Characteristics of Shared Goods in Jung-Gu*

The interactions between people have certain qualities and so does the sense-making that the mutual conversations brings about (Klamer 2019). At this point our main objective is to identify in the districts of our research what people talk about, what is on their minds, since creating a commons requires social participation. If we find distinctive patterns we have an idea of what characterises the commons in the districts, what the central themes are. By comparing with other districts we get a first indication of the respective qualities.

Based on the methodological framework of Table 11.3, Figure 11.1 presents the conversation related to the cultural sphere. In this figure, the place and the size of the words are significant. The further removed from the centre the less relevant to the mainstream topic of the cultural sphere is the discussion. The size of a word is determined by frequency. The greater the size, the more popular is the topic. The placing implies connections between topics. The data analysis of 2013, for instance, shows that the topics related to political issues and travel were the most popular; however, the topics related to the local creative sectors, such as IT or scientific issues, were rare.

In 2015, we discovered changes in the patterns: topics related to social and cultural activities emerged significantly and climbed to the top of the rankings. It does seem that people pay close attention to socialising: the words Friends and Family emerged in 2015 as one of the top three words in the centre. This implied that interest in relationships had increased. And the term Volunteer Work emerged in 2015, which implied that the social engagement in societal value creation had increased. More precisely, what people talk about has been specified in the topic related to travel: the words of Region, Local area, Town and Village were accentuated in 2015, indicating certain cultural streets, such as Hongdae, and neighbourhoods. In addition, the topic of music education appeared.

Discussions of issues and themes related or referring to a strong governmental intervention are clear in the Jung-Gu district. However, the cultural content clearly increased from 2013 to 2015. Talk related to the cultural sphere has been more culturally focused. The primary conversation is more about social and cultural activities, travel, volunteer work and relationships without any interruption by words related to governmental initiatives. This suggests that the characteristics of shared goods in this district changed. So did the qualities of the commons.

TABLE 11.3. *Summary of methodological framework*

Purpose	Data collection: SEL	Data collection: AMS	Approach	Analysis	Research question
Characterising social and cultural practices	Social media data collected from Naver, Twitter	Social media data collected from Twitter	Hermeneutic approach	Big Data Analysis with Software R, Python	How cities get to know different social and cultural qualities? Do cities provide a supportive environment to generate the commons related to the certain creative industries? Do social and cultural practices respond to creative activities?

Source: Won 2020.

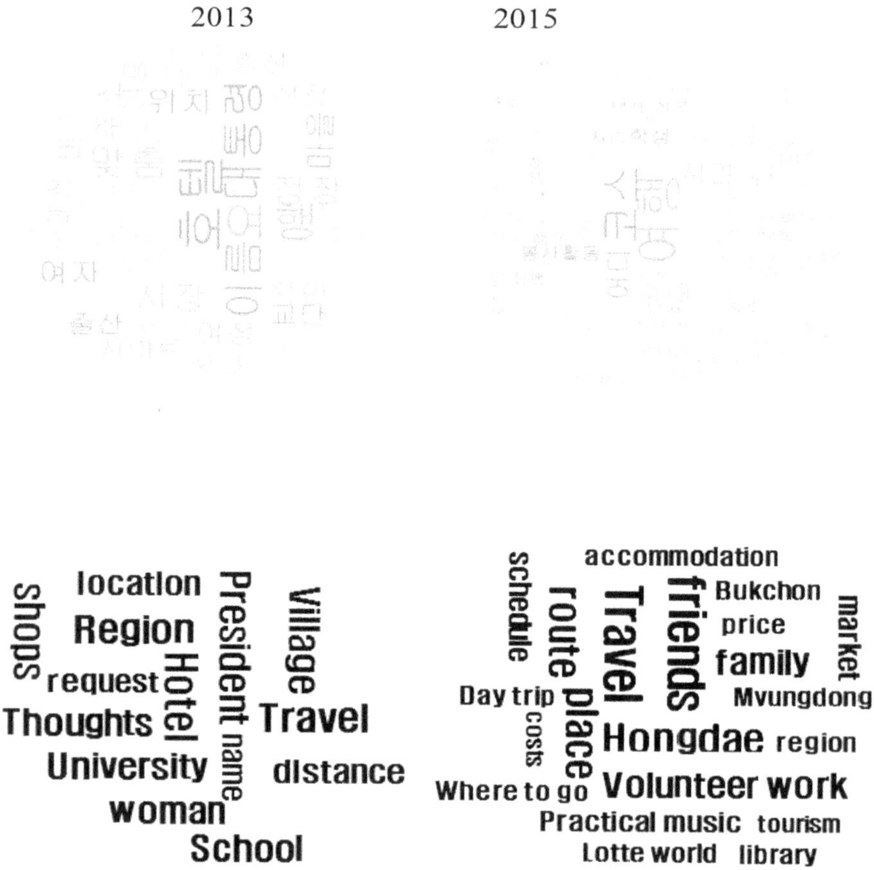

FIGURE 11.1. Conversations on culture in Jung-Gu in 2013 and 2015
Source: Won 2020

Moreover, what people talk about is irrelevant to the knowledge input of dominant creative industries of this district, such as the IT and Communication industry. Despite the remarkable commercial character of the area – its market share is about 17 per cent of the total for Seoul – with lots of IT people active and others focusing on technical processes, people talk more about political issues, travel, leisure and building relationships rather than about activities or reflections related to IT industries, innovative procedures, or the creative industries. We, thus, see that the presence of creatives itself hardly guarantees a change of local practices. More to the point, even though the public investment in the creative industry could bring about a particular knowledge and labour power, creation of shared goods and the knowledge commons related to it requires social engagement. This is the very point that Florida missed in his argument on the creative class, and that Jacobs emphasised.

In light of these remarks, the most important part of this interpretation is to identify predictable and potential avenues for the different qualities of knowledge commons. That is to say, when it comes to Figure 11.1, the action arena in this district is most likely characterised by activities related to travel and socialising rather than creative industries per se. Resource characteristics, for instance, the knowledge input, could be determined by the great influx of people employed in creative industries, such as IT and Communication industry and market activities; however, it does not mean that the qualities of the knowledge commons follow the input.

The intended contribution of this method that enables cities to make sense of what the different qualities of the commons look like in practice via describing data. We now turn to the case of Amsterdam in order to see whether we can discern significant differences and similarities.

11.4.3 *Attributes of Westergasfabriek, Amsterdam*

Like other advanced cities, the Amsterdam city government identified "creativity" as the essential engine to make the city flourish for the new economy. It endeavoured to realise and implement urban creativity through policy measures intended to focus on creative processes, creative industries, social entrepreneurialism and incubators rather than tried to become an overall business-friendly city (Bontje and Lawton 2013; Savini and Dembski 2016). A well-known Amsterdam creative policy dates back to 1999 and consists of the initiation and stimulation of incubators (broedplaatsen), intended to bring together creative start-ups and starting artists and thus to stimulate co-creative processes and strengthen the commons related to creative activities (Peck 2012). The municipality initiated projects away from the historical centre where the main cultural institutions attract overwhelming crowds of tourists, and targeted specific neighbourhoods with abandoned industrial spaces, such as Westergasfabriek (the West Gas Factory), currently named Westergas.

The "Westergasfabriek" was a large factory that produced coal-based gas in the nineteenth century; however, the site closed and left industrial facilities including a huge round gas container when coals became politically unacceptable and commercially unprofitable (Mommaas 2004). In the 1960s, the local administration embarked on a programme to redevelop the site. It took several decades before the plans materialised. It was not until 2003 when Westergas reopened the gate to the public. The one challenge was to constitute a governance that brings about a productive and pragmatic collaboration between the (commercial) owner of the site, the local government, the neighbourhood and the cultural sector. The risk was that commercial interests would take over as bills for the clean-up and the renovation of old buildings including the container had to be paid. Cultural activities usually cost money so who would pay the bills? The huge project has multiple stakeholders, such as citizens, designers, civil servants, cultural companies and organisations, and the commercial owner of the site cooperated for the project.

It really was a public–private co-creation. There was political recognition of the importance of the social context

Eventually it was conducive to the realisation of a social and cultural commons within Westergas. The government has acted in an entrepreneurial sense by giving space to the manifold creative groups to participate in the project and thus to stimulate civic engagement. Fostering creative vibes and developing creative activities are left to the social initiatives. Westergas now provides an important space for all kinds of creative events to take place in the gas container (such as opera performances, automobile show), and in a cinema. In addition, it houses several restaurants and cafes that the locals also attend, as well as shared work spaces. All these activities have given the Westergas a name, an identity that people in and around Amsterdam recognise.

11.4.4 *Characteristics of Shared Goods in Westergasfabriek*

What people talk about in Westergas was mainly focused on cultural and creative activities that this neighbourhood provides. That much becomes clear from Twitter. As Figure 11.2 shows, the shared goods that Westergas produces are closely associated with Dutch fashion industries, music festivals, creative business events and family activities. For instance, we notice lots of activity generated by the so-called TNW conference, a technology festival that the world's top technical firms attend, and that start-ups promote by sharing relevant knowledge and practices. We also note lots of

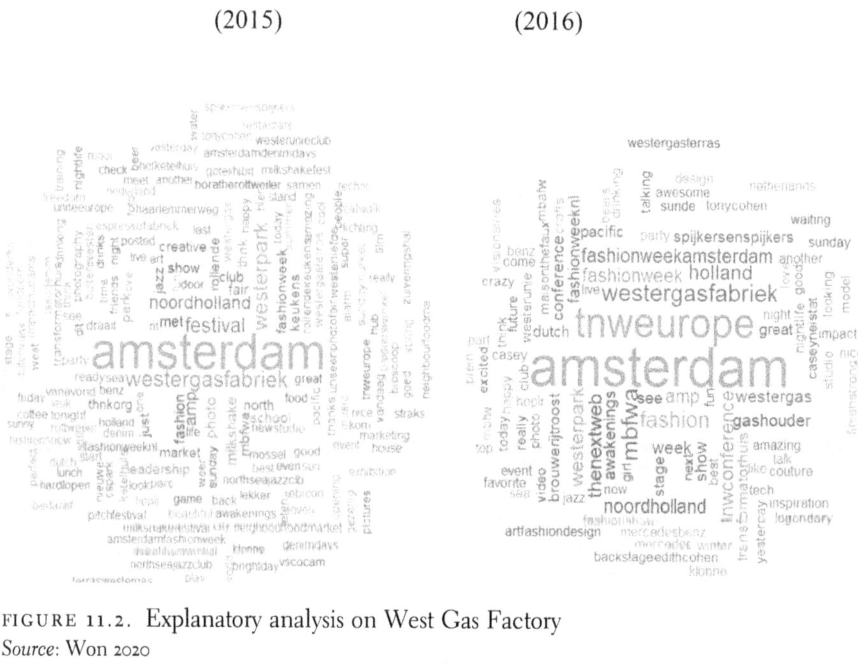

FIGURE 11.2. Explanatory analysis on West Gas Factory
Source: Won 2020

talk about a local brewery on the premise, a creativity club, music, family activities, and the park on the site.

Political conversations are all but absent. We also observe a great deal of talk about local matters and local spaces, as there are many references to the streets in the neighbourhood, such as Westerpark, Haarlemmerplein, Nassaukade and Westergasterrein. It implies that this neighbourhood provides a supportive environment for ongoing creative activities for people who work, but also for people who live a in a spatial sense. We discern appreciation through use of typically Dutch expressions such as "gezellig (cozy)" and "aardig (lovely)". In this case, the action arena is characterised by different qualities of the commons, such as design, festivals related to creative industries, and local cultural activities. The knowledge commons that this district engenders, thus, appears to influence and to be influenced by practices that people share via social and market activities.

11.5 CONCLUSION

With the notion of the commons Elinor Ostrom revived an important concept. It has a serious impact on the way we perceive contemporary cities. It allows us to look beyond the usual economic and financial criteria and, as city planners will consider, more than merely the functions of infrastructural projects. This study attempted to make sense of the notion of the commons in the contemporary urban context beyond Ostrom's sense of the commons. To this end, this study set up a theoretical framework by bringing two novel notions of shared goods/ practices, and a willingness to contribute with a value-based perspective and connecting them to the GKC framework. What is ultimately at stake, when trying to establish this idea within the new economy, is to understand that the commons in cities are social and cultural practices and the commons are qualitatively different in nature between cities.

To characterise different qualities of the commons, and to assess those qualities, we are in need of a research method for different kinds of data analysis in a more systematic way. For the empirical analysis, we set up a different methodological approach to analyse the different qualities of shared goods via interpretation of big data from social media networks and search engines, with explorations of the cases of Seoul in South Korea and Amsterdam in The Netherlands. For the sake of a comparative analysis, we narrowed the spatial scope by selecting a neighbourhood from each city designated as a creative space – Jung-Gu in Seoul and Westergas in Amsterdam – and we demonstrated our methodology to detect whether creative activities of the neighbourhoods contribute to creating the relevant commons within the given regions. It is worth noting that the primary aim of this approach is not to claim causality, but to characterise patterns of practices that people share.[3] The challenge is thus to characterise qualities of the commons within cities/ neighbourhoods in such a way that

[3] See Chetty et al. (2018).

patterns become clear and comparisons become possible, and to anticipate what qualities of knowledge commons are related to those jurisdictions.

Both cases demonstrate why shared goods and practices are important to making sense of the qualities of the commons via interpretive data analysis. Two points are of special note here: first, shared goods are hardly formed by the governmental initiatives, as the empirical studies delineate. Even though there was a strong governmental intervention to promote certain creative industries, such as high-skilled industries, without social participation, relevant shared goods are hardly produced. This indicates one of the key discourses of cultural economics: crowding out. Strong governmental involvement crowds out cultural and social activity (Frey 1997, 2000). When shared goods become too dependent on governmental support or are too strongly controlled by the government, participants defer to the government rather than take initiatives themselves and focus on what their (creative) work is all about. Second, we noticed that there was a discontinuity between characteristics of shared goods and the knowledge commons that local creative industries contribute, unless relevant local practices were developed. It became clear when we compared the local practices of Jung-Gu and Westergas: the characteristics of shared goods in Jung-gu are mostly specific to the IT sector; yet, the qualities of the knowledge commons to which local people contribute tend to be related to other industries, such as tourism and travel.

There are two limitations of this research. First, we have not specifically explored the shadowed sides of urban regeneration by means of creative policies; however, we observe the importance of a constructive practice in the case of Westergas. More to the point, it is the locals who, in turn, develop, characterise and embrace practices that engender the knowledge commons within a neighbourhood. This study, following the community-based approach to the commons by Ostrom, highlights the importance of understanding why local practices need to be involved in producing shared goods and the commons within contemporary cities. To this end, we proposed a systematic way to identify different qualities of the commons of neighbourhoods or cities. Second, we see cities as a place full of different qualities of shared goods and the commons, and do not consider those in themselves as a commons. Thus, the trajectory of this research did not deal with shared places themselves or their governance system, but focused on characterising the different qualitative nature of the commons in different places. In this vein, it was hard to confine access limitation or clear boundaries and define monitoring or sanctions processes. As this study earlier mentioned, the commons in the new economy is something beyond natural resources, more subject to social and cultural practices, and organised by contribution of participants. So the further researches should deal with the question of how shared goods are governed by communities and how practically contributions are fostered.

In conclusion, the intended contribution of this chapter is to make sense of why the commons in the new urban economy are different from those in the previous economies and how cities can extend their perspective to identify the differences. Our methodology is still limited in the sense that we have difficulty in getting data on the scale of neighbourhood/ blocks/ cities. Big data have also serious limitations (Twitter is not a representative sample of the ongoing conversations). We would like more data and more inputs to get an even richer picture of the social and cultural qualities of knowledge commons and to explore their relationship to economic practices and financial outcomes. Our contribution has been to initiate a connection of exploration of city life with the re-invigorated notion of the commons, and to show how the value-based approach can enrich the perspective on the urban commons.

REFERENCES

Bell, Daniel. 1973. *The Coming of Post-Industrial Society: A Venture in Social Forecasting*. New York: Basic Books.

Bontje, Marco and Philip Lawton. 2013. "Mobile Policies and Shifting Contexts: City-Regional Competitiveness Strategies in Amsterdam and Dublin". *Tijdschrift Voor Economische En Sociale Geografie* 104: 397–409.

Borch, Christian and Martin Kornberger. 2015. *Urban Commons: Rethinking the City (Space, Materiality and the Normative)*. Oxon: Routledge.

Chetty, Raj, John N. Friedman, Nathaniel Hendren, Maggie R. Jones and Sonya R. Porter. 2018. *The Opportunity Atlas: Mapping the Childhood Roots of Social Mobility*. NBER Working Paper Series, no. 25147.

Collins, Randall. 2004. *Interaction Ritual Chains*. Princeton, NJ: Princeton University Press.

Csikszentmihalyi, Mihaly. 1991. *Flow: The Psychology of Optimal Experience*. New York: Harper Perennial.

Currid-Halkett, Elizabeth. 2008. *The Warhol Economy*. Princeton, NJ: Princeton University Press.

Dietz, Thomas, Elinor Ostrom and Paul C. Stern. 2003. "The Struggle to Govern the Commons". *Science* 302: 1907–1912.

Florida, Richard. 2002. *The Rise of the Creative Class*. New York: Basic Books.

2017. *The New Urban Crisis: How Our Cities Are Increasing Inequality, Deepening Segregation, and Failing the Middle Class and What We Can Do about It*. New York: Basic Books.

Foster, Sheila R. and Christian Iaione. 2016. "The City as a Commons". *Yale Law & Policy Review* 34(2): 281–349.

Frey, Bruno S. 1997. *Not Just for the Money*. Cheltenham: Edward Elgar.

2000. *Art and Economics*. Heidelberg: Springer-Verlag.

Frischmann, Brett M., Michael J. Madison and Katherine Strandburg. 2014. *Governing Knowledge Commons*. Oxford: Oxford University Press.

Hardin, Garrett. 1968. "The Tragedy of the Commons". *Science* 162: 1243–1248.

Harvey, David. 1990. "Flexible Accumulation through Urbanization: Reflections on 'Post-Modernism' in the American City". *Perspecta* 26: 251–251.

2012. *Rebel Cities: From the Right to the City to the Urban Revolution*. London: Verso.

Hess, Charlotte. 2008. Mapping the New Commons. SSRN *Electronic Journal*. https://doi.org/10.2139/ssrn.1356835

Hess, Charlotte and Elinor Ostrom. 2007. *Understanding Knowledge as a Commons: From Theory to Practice*. Cambridge, MA: MIT Press.

Jacobs, Jane. 1964. *The Death and Life of Great American Cities*. Harmondsworth: Penguin Books.

1986. *Cities and the Wealth of Nations*. Harmondsworth: Penguin.

Klamer, Arjo. 2016. *Doing the Right Thing: A Value Based Economy*. London: Ubiquity Press.

2019. "Economy and Culture: The Importance of Sense-Making". In *The Oxford Handbook of Ethics and Economics*, edited by Mark D. White. Oxford: Oxford University Press. DOI: 10.1093/oxfordhb/9780198793991.013.17.

Klinenberg, Eric. 2018. *Palaces for the People: How Social Infrastructure Can Help Fight Inequality, Polarization, and the Decline of Civic Life*. New York: Crown.

Levine, Peter. 2007. "Collective Action, Civic Engagement, and the Knowledge Commons". In *Understanding Knowledge as a Commons: From Theory to Practice*, edited by Charlotte Hess and Elinor Ostrom, 247–276. Cambridge, MA: MIT Press.

Mommaas, Hans. 2004. "Cultural Clusters and the Post-Industrial City: Towards the Remapping of Urban Cultural Policy". *Urban Studies* 41: 507–532.

Moretti, Enrico. 2012. *The New Geography of Jobs*. Boston: Houghton Mifflin Harcourt.

Ostrom, Elinor. 1990. *Governing the Commons*. Cambridge, MA: Cambridge University Press.

Peck, Jamie. 2012. "Recreative City: Amsterdam, Vehicular Ideas and the Adaptive Spaces of Creativity Policy". *International Journal of Urban and Regional Research* 36: 462–485.

Pratt, Andy. 2009. "The Creative and Cultural Economy and the Recession". *Geoforum* 40: 495–496.

Savini, Federico, and Sebastian Dembski. 2016. "Manufacturing the Creative City: Symbols and Politics of Amsterdam North". *Cities* 55: 139–147.

Schroeder, Ralph. 2014. "Big Data and the Brave New World of Social Media Research". *Big Data and Society*. DOI: https://doi.org/10.1177/2053951714563194

Won, Youn Sun. 2020. *Assessing Urban Qualities within the New Economy: A Value Based Approach to Cities*. PhD Thesis, Erasmus University Rotterdam.

For EU product safety concerns, contact us at Calle de José Abascal, 56–1°,
28003 Madrid, Spain or eugpsr@cambridge.org.

www.ingramcontent.com/pod-product-compliance
Lightning Source LLC
LaVergne TN
LVHW011524200926
848484LV00001B/145

9781108483599